A Requirements Pattern

Addison-Wesley Information Technology Series
Capers Jones and David S. Linthicum, Consulting Editors

The information technology (IT) industry is in the public eye now more than ever before because of a number of major issues in which software technology and national policies are closely related. As the use of software expands, there is a continuing need for business and software professionals to stay current with the state of the art in software methodologies and technologies. The goal of the Addison-Wesley Information Technology Series is to cover any and all topics that affect the IT community: These books illustrate and explore how information technology can be aligned with business practices to achieve business goals and support business imperatives. Addison-Wesley has created this innovative series to empower you with the benefits of the industry experts' experience.

For more information point your browser to http://www.awl.com/cseng/series/it/

Sid Adelman, Larissa Terpeluk Moss, *Data Warehouse Project Management*. ISBN: 0-201-61635-1

Wayne Applehans, Alden Globe, and Greg Laugero, *Managing Knowledge: A Practical Web-Based Approach*. ISBN: 0-201-43315-X

Michael H. Brackett, *Data Resource Quality: Turning Bad Habits into Good Practices*. ISBN: 0-201-71306-3

Frank Coyle, *Wireless Web: A Manager's Guide*. ISBN: 0-201-72217-8

James Craig and Dawn Jutla, *e-Business Readiness: A Customer-Focused Framework*.ISBN: 0-201-71006-4

Gregory C. Dennis and James R. Rubin, *Mission-Critical Java™ Project Management: Business Strategies, Applications, and Development*. ISBN: 0-201-32573-X

Kevin Dick, *XML: A Manager's Guide*. ISBN: 0-201-43335-4

Jill Dyché, *e-Data: Turning Data into Information with Data Warehousing*. ISBN: 0-201-65780-5

Jill Dyché, *The CRM Handbook: A Business Guide to Customer Relationship Management*. ISBN: 0-201-73062-6

Patricia L. Ferdinandi, *A Requirements Pattern: Succeeding in the Internet Economy*. ISBN: 0-201-73826-0

Dr. Nick V. Flor, *Web Business Engineering: Using Offline Activites to Drive Internet Strategies*. ISBN: 0-201-60468-X

David Garmus and David Herron, *Function Point Analysis: Measurement Practices for Successful Software Projects*. ISBN: 0-201-69944-3

John Harney, *Application Service Providers (ASPs): A Manager's Guide*. ISBN: 0-201-72659-9

Capers Jones, *Software Assessments, Benchmarks, and Best Practices*. ISBN: 0-201-48542-7

Capers Jones, *The Year 2000 Software Problem: Quantifying the Costs and Assessing the Consequences*. ISBN: 0-201-30964-5

Ravi Kalakota and Marcia Robinson, *e-Business 2.0: Roadmap for Success*. ISBN: 0-201-72165-1

David S. Linthicum, *B2B Application Integration: e-Business-Enable Your Enterprise*. ISBN: 0-201-70936-8

Sergio Lozinsky, *Enterprise-Wide Software Solutions: Integration Strategies and Practices*. ISBN: 0-201-30971-8

Joanne Neidorf and Robin Neidorf, *e-Merchant: Retail Strategies for e-Commerce*. ISBN: 0-201-72169-4

Patrick O'Beirne, *Managing the Euro in Information Systems: Strategies for Successful Changeover*. ISBN: 0-201-60482-5

Bud Porter-Roth, *Request for Proposal: A Guide to Effective RFP Development*, ISBN: 0-201-77575-1

Mai-lan Tomsen, *Killer Content: Strategies for Web Content and E-Commerce*. ISBN: 0-201-65786-4

Karl E. Wiegers, *Peer Reviews in Software: A Practical Guide*. ISBN: 0-201-73485-0

Bill Wiley, *Essential System Requirements: A Practical Guide to Event-Driven Methods*. ISBN: 0-201-61606-8

Ralph R. Young, *Effective Requirements Practices*. ISBN: 0-201-70912-0

Bill Zoellick, *CyberRegs: A Business Guide to Web Property, Privacy, and Patents*. ISBN: 0-201-72230-5

Bill Zoellick, *Web Engagement: Connecting to Customers in e-Business*. ISBN: 0-201-65766-X

A Requirements Pattern:

*Succeeding in the
Internet Economy*

Patricia L. Ferdinandi

✦ Addison-Wesley

Boston • San Francisco • New York • Toronto • Montreal
London • Munich • Paris • Madrid • Capetown
Sydney • Tokyo • Singapore • Mexico City

Many of the designations used by manufacturers and sellers to distinguish their products are claimed as trademarks. Where those designations appear in this book, and Addison-Wesley was aware of a trademark claim, the designations have been printed with initial capital letters or in all capitals.

The author and publisher have taken care in the preparation of this book, but make no expressed or implied warranty of any kind and assume no responsibility for errors or omissions. No liability is assumed for incidental or consequential damages in connection with or arising out of the use of the information or programs contained herein.

The publisher offers discounts on this book when ordered in quantity for special sales. For more information, please contact:

Pearson Education Corporate Sales Division
201 W. 103rd Street
Indianapolis, IN 46290
(800) 428-5331
corpsales@pearsoned.com

Visit AW on the Web: www.aw.com/cseng/

Library of Congress Cataloging-in-Publication Data
Ferdinandi, Patricia L.
    A requirements pattern: succeeding in the Internet ecomony / Patricia L. Ferdinandi
        p. cm.—(Addison-Wesley information technology series)
    Included bibliographical references and index.
    ISBN 0-201-73826-0 (alk. paper)
    1. Computer software—Development. 2. Internet. 3. Electronic commerce
  4. Information technology—Standards. I. Title. II Series.
    QA76.76.D47 F49 2002
    005.1'068—dc21

                      2001045801

Pearson Education, Inc.
Rights and Contracts Department
75 Arlington Street, Suite 300
Boston, MA 02116
Fax: (617) 848-7047

ISBN 0-201-73826-0
Text printed on recycled paper
1 2 3 4 5 6 7 8 9 10—MA—0504030201
First printing, November 2001

To my husband, Giuseppe,
for his continual loving support,
and to Scarlet,
for keeping me amused
throughout the writing effort.

Contents

Preface

Corporations today allocate billions of dollars to information technology (IT), not only to stay afloat but also to expand market share in the fast-paced global marketplace. The combination of hardware, software, and networks provides valuable information and performs critical functions for a corporation, its stockholders, and clients. Indeed, information technology has become the backbone of the modern corporation. Without successful and high-quality IT solutions, the success of a corporation can be compromised. Defects in IT products can result in missed market opportunities, ineffective strategic decisions, and lost market share.

The first step toward developing, enhancing, or maintaining IT solutions is to understand the needs and wants of the business. This is the most challenging part of the entire effort. As you will discover in this book, if you get the requirements wrong, the final product will not satisfy the needs of the business. In fact, this wasted effort will cost the company greatly.

The Standish Group has been following failed IT projects since 1995. Across the board, the researchers have found poor requirements, in one form or another, to be one of the top causes of costly project failures. "Poor requirements" refers to a failure to capture the needs that must be satisifed by the solution. Typically, failures in IT projects are not the fault of an individual or even a department. Nor are these failures the fault of a specific technique or tool used to gather the requirements of a project. The problem, more often, lies in misunderstanding the definition, process, practices, and management of requirements. In the end, requirements have a major impact on a project's success. The project may be done on time and within budget, but unless the requirements are complete and accurate, the project *will* be a failure.

Requirement is an ambiguous term. Different people will provide valid but different points of view, with perhaps some overlap. There lies the problem! Our individual views of requirements have been narrow, allowing for gaps that lead to defects in the final product. The final set of requirements may turn out to be full of intangible, moving targets that are inherently inconsistent. This leads to a poor-quality product, which in turn diminishes the return on investment for the corporation.

Why This Book?

The purpose of this book is to clarify this ambiguity. The book focuses on several perspectives designed to create a common understanding of requirements, from concept through implementation. The evolution, classification, and management of requirements are placed in easy-to-understand terms, so that everyone can share a common level of understanding. A framework is provided that categorizes and organizes the different types of requirements, forming a requirements set. The requirements pattern, based on the requirements set framework, is provided to assist in capturing and evolving the individual requirements. Information on the best requirement-related practices is provided to ensure the quality and integrity of the individual requirements and the requirements set.

The ideas in *A Requirements Pattern* can be applied to any product (including non-IT-oriented ones). The Internet is used here primarily for illustrative purposes. This volatile environment provides many examples that clearly explain the four key topics of this book:

1. The breadth of requirements that comprise the requirements set
2. The evolutionary process of a requirement from the conceptual idea to the implemented feature
3. The need to initiate parallel *and* coordinated requirement development efforts
4. The impact of change (including scope creep) on Internet products

By understanding the concepts presented, you will be able to see the gaps created with current methodologies, methods, and techniques. It is important to be able to see that requirements are not just documentation but rather a full understanding of the problem, the environment in which requirements are developed, and the delivered features of the solution.

The generic role responsible for requirement-related activities is the *requirements engineer,* the primary audience for this book. Requirements engineers must have a detailed understanding of the requirements process and the valuable role requirements engineers play in maximizing the product's return on investment. The more they understand, the better equipped they will be to tackle the nuances of the Internet.

Technical analysts and *architects* many times must gather specific types of requirements and therefore will also benefit from reading this book. Each may have a different focus during the development process. It is important to realize the impact their requirements have on other areas of the project. Even if the analysts and architects are not involved in eliciting the business requirements, they will have an impact on those requirements. These personnel need to have an understanding of the evolution of the requirements from inception until they are allocated for development.

The quality of requirements has a direct impact on the cost of the final product. It is the job of the *quality control analyst* to assist with validating the specified requirements for possible defects, a topic addressed in *A Requirements Pattern.* By understanding how to identify the quality of a requirement, quality control analysts can actively participate in validation. They contribute to the requirements process by identifying inconsistencies long before code testing.

Many books already exist on the requirements process, techniques, and methods. Other books address what good requirements are as well as various elicitation, analysis, verification, and management techniques. Examples of such books are provided in the Additional Resources section at the back of the book. This helpful compilation provides suggestions for a continual path of education in the field of requirements engineering. The Internet requirements pattern presented in this book complements all of the recommendations by introducing readers to the basics of requirements, requirements engineering, and requirements management.

Requirements engineering is an integral part of developing software. It is time consuming and at times a tedious activity. The size and type of a project seem to have little effect on the complexity of this process. The incorporation of the Internet requirements pattern (and anti-patterns) and activities described in this book will enhance the requirements engineer's efforts. With the fuller understanding of requirements, readers can make positive impacts when developing quality solutions for their companies.

Pat Ferdinandi
June 2001

Acknowledgments

Although this is not my first writing project, I am still humbled by the experience. Writing of any type is never a solo experience. It takes years of experience and relationships to build a knowledge base strong enough to substantiate an entire book. This book may have only the author's name on its cover, but in reality it takes a team to write and publish a book.

I could never have accomplished this milestone without the support of my family, friends, and colleagues, not all of whom have expertise in requirements engineering. However, their support and encouragement were just as important. The following people deserve special mention:

- My husband, Giuseppe, for his constant encouragement, attention to detail, and his specific knowledge on network engineering
- My mother, Louise Smith, who checked that I wrote at least one page every day (yes, kids still don't always obey their mothers)
- My nieces, Ellen D'Onofrio and Tracy Glock, for checking on me with continual encouragement between checking on their kids: David, Stephen, Jaclyn, and Delanie Rose
- My closest and dearest friend, Susan E. Pirog, for her constant enthusiasm and shopping trips to keep me sane
- My aunt, Edna Leather, who has always told me since I was a little girl, "If you get just one recipe from a book, the book is worth it"

- Rebecca Moeller, Robert Moore, and the boys for the gentle nudging to make sure I was continuing on this project through all the many bumps in the road
- Maureen Sullivan for her continual moral support and for adjusting my expectation level to reduce the stress of writing such a book
- Thomas O'Hara for his continual support and understanding and for allowing me the time to write the book during a crucial phase of a mission-critical project
- Kassy Cassidy, Michael Conroy, and Joanne O'Neill for reviewing specific chapters that were in very rough form
- Susan Farenci, Irene Voce, Robert Appelbaum, and Brian Tan for being sounding boards on technical information
- My requirements engineering compadres—Tom Cagley, Merlin Dorfman, William Frank, Don Gause, Ellen Gottesdiener, Rob Sabourin, Chuck Tryon, and Karl Wiegers—for their thought-provoking conversations
- T. Capers Jones, who reminded me that requirement basics (scope creep, metrics, and so on) need to be discussed in every book on requirements
- The employees of Telelogic, especially Nancy Rundlet, for their professionalism and expertise
- Charles Austin for losing a bet and, in good humor, reading the manuscript and providing great feedback
- Tony Vlamis, who insisted that I have more than one book in my brain (and soul)
- Debbie Lafferty for rekindling my faith in the publishing process
- All those unknown reviewers for their great feedback and patience with the "brain-dump" version of the book
- Erika Heilman, who made this manuscript readable
- My agent, Dianne Littman, who helped me out of a jam
- Diane Freed and Chrysta Meadowbrooke, who stood by me when I reached a panic level completing this book, with special thanks to Chrysta, whose copyediting helped make this book readable
- Kim Arney Mulcahy, whose typesetting skills have transformed my words into a presentation masterpiece

Finally, I wrote this book in memory of my writing mentor, Michael Rothstein, who opened my mind to the possibility of writing books.

CHAPTER ONE

Requirements Engineering for Internet Products: An Introduction

---

Chapter Key Topics

- **What is the Internet?**
- **What is requirements engineering?**
- **How do the Internet and requirements engineering interact with one another?**
- **Requirements engineering and Internet terminology**

The Internet Impact

The Internet has enabled people around the world to access all types of information—when they want it and from wherever they want it. It has blurred corporate boundaries so that responsibilities have been realigned to those best suited to satisfy the business task (for example, Amazon.com serving as the virtual storefront for ToysRUs.com). Having a successful presence on the Internet demands skills beyond the typical requirements of information technology (IT), such as marketing, legal, and network. Rather, it takes a person skilled in requirements engineering to know how to capture, specify, organize, validate, and manage this information in order for products and services to be represented well on the Web.

What a difference a year makes! When I began writing this book, Internet start-up companies such as Amazon.com, eBay.com, eCost.com, Pets.com, and eToys.com had stock values in the hundreds of dollars. They were taking business away from the traditional brick-and-mortar companies. When the manuscript was completed, however, the stock values of these online giants had plummeted, leaving many with double- and even single-digit stock prices—that is, for those start-up companies still in business. The "time to market" driver that had prevailed in the early days of the Internet economy had taken a back seat as many stockholders and consumers wanted to see profits and quality products above all else.

Though this is a turbulent time, the Internet is here to stay. The customer base for Internet usage continues to grow each year. For as many companies that have fallen by the wayside, there are others that continue to jump onto the Internet during these ever-changing financial times. Futhermore, these start-ups have forced many brick-and-mortar companies (for example, Sears, Ford Motor Company, Crate and Barrel) to expand their use of electronic media in order to reach consumers directly throughout the global market.

The Internet[1] has no doubt changed the way business is conducted. It has emerged as a powerful economic driver, forcing small and large companies alike to have a presence on the Web or lose their market share. Advances in technology have made the Internet a viable means for supplying goods and services. The same technology has also dramatically increased the speed at which business is conducted, making it necessary for current business processes to be redefined to keep pace. But it wasn't always this way. Let's go back to the beginning.

It was a day like any other day. A bill was presented to then President George Bush, Sr., that would open the Internet for public use. Before that time, the Internet, then called the "Arpanet," consisted of less than 100 nodes between government and academic facilities. In those days, the Internet was used as a vehicle to transfer information or process queries between research facilities. By signing the bill, President Bush opened the world of the Internet to a mass-market community, which dramatically changed the way business was conducted.

Let's take a look at some specific situations brought about by the explosion of the Internet economy that have an impact on the requirements engineering process. Opening the Internet for commercial use would not have been as suc-

---

1. For the purposes of this book, the term *Internet* will be used to represent all Internet-based applications: e-business (business-to-business or B2B), application-to-application (A2A), application-to-staff (A2S), e-commerce (business-to-consumer B2C), and Internet-to-wireless (B2W), except when explaining a specific type of Internet-based application.

cessful had it not been for other key advancements in technology. Such advancements include (but are certainly not limited to) the following:

- The personal computer
- Browsers
- The Uniform Resource Locator system
- Graphical user interfaces
- Electronic mail
- Encryption and secure transaction technologies such as SSL

Until this point, technology was the means by which businesses were supported. However, in the Internet environment, technology became the driving force. The technology of the Internet *caused* this paradigm shift!

The Power of the Internet

The Internet has changed the way we think about the global market. To be successful, corporations have had to redefine what they mean by *customer, competitor,* and *business partner.* A single individual, thanks to Internet technology, can be any or all three and can be located anywhere in the world for a relatively small technological investment.

Though the Internet currently represents only a small fraction of the world's economic activity, the possibilities seem limitless. The business community, in turn, is demanding that new Internet applications be developed at what is being called "Internet pace."[2] For this reason, increasing pressure to meet this challenge is being felt by information technology development staff as well as by all other business departments. Customers, suppliers, business partners, and competitors (all users of the Internet) are requiring Internet solutions to be developed more quickly than other software applications. Projects are expected to turn around from concept to operational (live) status in a period of a few months . . . or even weeks! Major requirement changes occur frequently and must be much more rigorously managed to avoid costly design or product corrections. Furthermore, the software engineering processes necessary for managing project requirements must remain flexible, efficient, light, and thorough to keep up with the constant market changes.

---

2. Also known as "Internet speed" or "Internet time." Roughly, an Internet year has been equated to three months of real time!

In addition to demanding speed, users of the Internet are also demanding quality. Consumers are voting with their pocketbooks and mouse clicks. Businesses with better-quality software get and keep customers. Those companies that do not will fail. The positive aspect of this trend is that the consumer is defining the acceptable level of quality. The competition is just too great for companies to be late with projects or to deliver a substandard product; poor quality can easily steer a potential customer to a competitor. Both scenarios, being late and delivering poor-quality products, can result in reducing the company's market share, which translates into missing the opportunity to be the leader or to attain "brand acceptance."[3]

To meet the time demands and quality challenges of Internet solutions, Internet-based applications must be done quickly and done right! How does one accomplish such a feat? Through the use of an Internet requirements pattern. A *requirements pattern* is a reusable template of questions that can be used to elicit the requirements necessary for building an Internet product. An Internet requirements pattern takes the stance that in order to meet these needs, one must be able to capture *all* of the requirements of an application in a high-quality manner. This can be done only if one first understands all the different types of requirements that must be captured. Requirements that span an array of subjects—from the time it takes to bring the product to market to quality expectations for the product to budgetary concerns—must be reviewed for potential conflicts among them. Giving one priority over another will compromise the success of the others (see Figure 1.1).

Internet products will continue to change and evolve over time. Captured requirements, therefore, will be for each iteration of the Internet product. Requirements will be captured that will be constrained by previous releases of the product. This evolutionary characteristic is common among all successful Internet solutions. Internet products require continual changes in the form of new features, functions, and information. The applications must evolve with the continual feedback from users, customers and employees. This means that the requirements process must provide the ability to implement a high-quality *iteration* or *component* of the product on a continuing basis (usually every one to three months) to keep customers coming back. This can be successful only with the proper allocation of responsibilities coupled with parallel efforts across cor-

---

3. A good example of brand acceptance is Amazon.com, which defined the level of service, the consumer experience, for the Internet. As time has passed, the brand acceptance for Amazon.com has dwindled as other Internet sites, such as eBay.com, have improved with each new release.

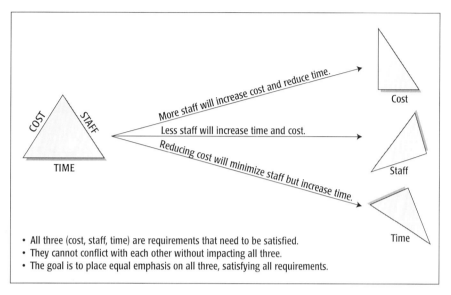

Figure 1.1   Impact of Changing Emphasis

porate boundaries. Defining responsibilities begins with the requirements phase and continues as the requirements evolve from concept to implementation. It continues through each iteration of a product as individual components are developed according to the continual changes in the market and technology.

In addition to the need for continual enhancements, Internet-based applications are expected to "get up on the Web fast." This expectation has prompted many companies to act too quickly. The first instinct is to add a Web-based front end to existing business functions and technology applications while not anticipating potential problems that may occur. Typical examples include

- Making an order-entry system available to the public without the training material to which in-house users are privy
- Using the same interdepartment interfaces to work between different corporations, creating performance problems for the end user

It is easy to rush through the requirements process to quickly put up a Web page full of grammatical errors and undeveloped features and backed by slow servers (the "World Wide Wait"). Additionally, although a pretty front end is being delivered to the consumer, the same old outdated business policies, rules, workflows, and corporate boundaries are still in existence behind the scenes. The potential result? A loss in consumer confidence, an increase in global financial exposures, and a reduction of market share—all of which will prevent a corporation from being successful using this new medium.

The Internet has enabled corporations to restrategize their businesses, building relationships with other diverse corporations. These partnerships enable each corporation to specialize in what it does best while requiring almost seamless boundaries (see Figure 1.2) to support a single end-to-end workflow. One company can support the ordering, another the inventory, and yet another the delivery, while another company processes the payments. All the companies in the partnership have direct exchanges of information via the Internet, ensuring the highest level of security, usability, and performance.

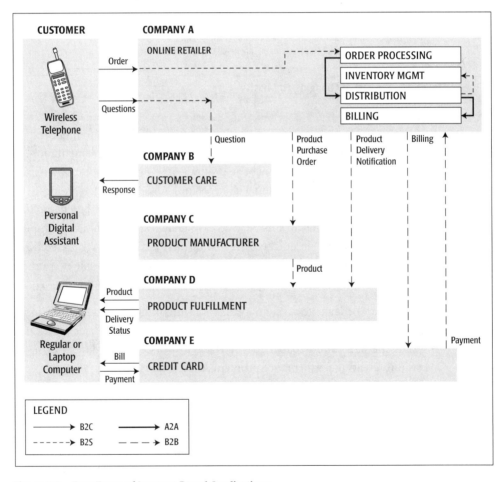

Figure 1.2   Four Types of Internet-Based Applications

The requirements process crosses not only divisional boundaries but also corporate boundaries. Because of this, it is imperative to document all the requirements that are needed for end-to-end processing. This new, complex environment will change each corporation's normal business processing, corporate policies, and scope of responsibilities. It also affects accountability if and when the "seamless" workflow does not meet the agreed-upon parameters of the business contracts.

Defining Requirements Engineering

Every product, including the Internet, should be based upon requirements. Requirements can be divided into three components: the process of capturing requirements, a standard format that further defines the requirements, and a set of responsibilities for the person in charge of enacting those requirements. These three components, when combined, constitute *requirements engineering*. Requirements engineering was originally defined as a subset of systems and software engineering. It is the discipline concerned with analyzing and documenting the needs of a business from an engineering perspective. What will be illustrated in this book is that requirements engineering is a reusable process—that it can be used not only for software solutions but also for implementing broader business goals. In fact, by limiting the definition to software requirements alone (see Figure 1.3), one will not capture important nontechnological requirements that are imperative for a business to succeed on the Internet.

In simplistic terms, *a requirement describes a need or desire to be satisfied by the product or service.* It starts out as a simple request and evolves into realms of individual requirements required to support that simple request. All of the additional requirements refine the need with important details. These too must also be satisfied. The additional requirements could describe any of the following:

- A user or system
- A piece of information
- Connectivity
- Time sensitivity
- Workflow
- Enforced policies
- Restrictions

All of these support the initial request.

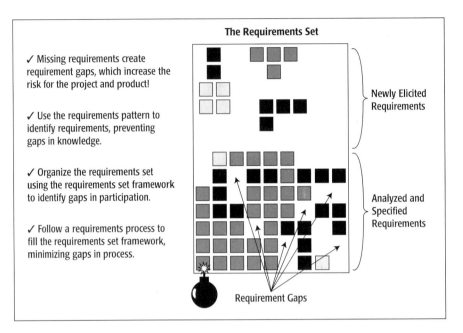

Figure 1.3   Requirement Gaps (Game first developed by Alexey Pajitnov. Currently owned by the Tetris Company. Currently licensed to Nintendo.)

Requirements Engineering and the Internet

Internet applications differ from other types of IT projects due to the complexity of the Internet as well as the need to realign business processes beyond corporate boundaries. This complicates the requirements engineering effort because the requirements that need to be captured, managed, and implemented are generally greater and more complex than those for a non-Internet-based IT project; the requirements pertain not only to software but also to business procedures.

In turn, Internet-based projects complicate the responsibilities of the requirements engineer. The person charged with this role must have an understanding of:

- The Internet (its scope and purpose)
- Corporate integration
- Requirements definition beyond software
- The limitations and potential of relevant technologies
- Communication with different groups both within and external to the corporation

The purpose of this book is to educate those persons charged with eliciting, analyzing, specifying, validating, and managing requirements for an Internet-based application. An Internet requirements pattern will be introduced that categorizes the types of requirements needed in order to build successful, high-quality Internet products. The value of the Internet requirements pattern is threefold:

1. It serves as a guide to facilitate the speed with which requirements must be satisfied.
2. The pattern is designed to include component-based development along the way, that is, those continual iterations[4] (or refinements) necessary for a product to succeed.
3. The process incorporates checkpoints along the way to continually ensure an end product of superior quality.

The State of Requirements Today

Traditionally, business has been contained within the walls of the corporation. With the dramatic growth of the Internet, however, the boundaries between businesses, and the clear definition of "the customer," have been blurred. The global market is now a reality rather than a dream. The "Net" has transformed previously expensive specialized processes to inexpensive processes for the masses.

Unfortunately, all businesses, large and small, are quickly attempting to "be on the Net." The speed at which applications have been built has exposed corporations to unforeseen risks. If a customer feels any dissatisfaction while using your Web site, he or she might quickly turn to a competitor. This occurs at a much faster pace than with any other form of media. As ToysRUs.com discovered with its first attempt to be on the Web, people will not necessarily stay with a business because of its prior reputation as a retail chain. Before joining forces with Amazon.com, the ToysRUs site was slow and hard to navigate, and it did not provide all the information a customer might want (such as out-of-stock information). Examples of what might cause a customer's departure include

- Poor response time
- Unclear instructions or processes

---

4. This requires that each component be independent and cross-compatible with other components. Old and new versions of programs must be able to coexist and interoperate. If a component fails, one needs to downgrade to a previous version without compromising the system. This describes a form of compatibility and maintainability where both need to be captured as requirements. This will be described further in Chapter Three.

- Unsecure security notification
- Too many clicks or poor navigational design
- Too much of a delay in service delivery
- Too many "I'll get back to you" messages

The Internet has opened the door to many new businesses. It has changed the demographics of the marketplace. This is a new medium, one in which small and large companies are considered equal in a consumer's mind. What becomes important to the customer is the quality of the information the company provides and the manner in which it is handled (for example, service, security, and flexibility).

Defining Technology's Involvement

We all know that the Internet cannot survive without technology, the key components of which are security, flexibility, and integration. *Security* pertains to protecting clients but also to protecting a corporation's assets. *Flexibility* means that a company must be able to quickly alter its infrastructure according to customer comments in order to compete in the global marketplace. *Integration* is the need to leverage the existing infrastructure to the new paradigm. These three components create different categories of requirements that must be given equal or higher priority relative to the functional requirements that we typically think of first.

A Paradoxical View

When a project is begun, many technical team members do not realize or accept the direct correlation between the requirements and the final product. Yet technical team members are quick to blame faulty requirements when held accountable for the final results.

Consider, for example, the way many projects are approached. Project teams are assembled with an emphasis placed upon technical knowledge. Employees and consultants for a new effort are hired primarily because of their specific technical expertise (for example, Java or BEA WebLogic). The result is that requirements are developed according to the latest technology, technique, or tool. Unfortunately, this usually produces an incomplete—and narrowly drawn—set of requirements. The final product is developed based upon the technology, first, and the business needs, second. In this manner, if the business objectives are met, it is by chance. Ask any information technologist if he really understands the business implication of his solution. Ask him to rate which of the two is more important: the technology or the requirements. Because so often businesses need to reinvent themselves, technology may be the driving force; however, it must still *facilitate* the business, not *be* the business.

Affecting the Return on Investment

As stated earlier, nothing has a more dramatic impact on a project than requirements. A review of the *Standish Group CHAOS Report*,[5] indicates that faulty requirements are unfortunately among the top five causes for failed technology projects, meaning that the technology project in one way or another did not reach the optimum return on investment as defined by the business case and as approved by executive management. This could be due to cost overruns, delayed deliverables, or failure to meet the needs of the customer or business. These are all symptoms of poor requirement elicitation, analysis, specification, validation, approval, and management. The effect on the business could be missed market opportunities, loss of consumer confidence, and/or loss of market share. Even if the software is considered worthy enough for the first release, the repairs needed for mistakes in later releases can erode the initial return on investment for the product and the business.

Requirements Engineering Skill Set

With Internet-based applications, you may not even get the chance to produce a second release of a product. By that time, consumers may have found a different source to satisfy their needs, or another company may have been accepted as the "brand leader." Because of the potential losses, it is imperative that companies improve the requirements engineering skill set by taking the following actions:

- Develop nontechnical and unbiased requirements for the business.
- Develop a complete set of clear, concise, and organized requirements.

---

5. The Standish Group has conducted surveys over the past several years and issues reports that depict the "chaos" that has been occurring in the software industry. The 1994 *Standish Group CHAOS Report* was accessed in August 2001 at www.pm2go.com/sample_research/chaos_1994_1.asp; a follow-up to the report appeared at www.pm2go.com/sample_research/unfinished_voyages_1.asp.

- Get all the business units involved as soon as possible.
- Get the right people to do the job.
- Develop the Internet solution using parallel efforts.
- Follow a standard, easy-to-follow process.
- Improve people communication.
- Keep team members involved in requirements prioritization aware of all key business drivers.
- Ensure that the process smoothly handles changing requirements.

Most of these topics are discussed in more detail in future chapters. However, it is important to introduce the ideas here to capture the concepts behind and need for requirements engineering.

Identifying Requirements for Business

Every project that a corporation undertakes requires some action from the IT organization and is impacted by the Internet.[6] The application can be the actual Internet application (online order entry) or a supporting application (click-stream data reviewing). The application could be as simple as maintaining a product table or adding an employee to a human resources system, or it could enhance future Internet releases with new product features.

All projects require the identification of requirements to reach the business objective. Each type of project (maintenance, enhancement, and new development) needs requirements to describe the business need in a way that can be analyzed, designed, coded, tested, and implemented with a technological solution. If it is a new initiative, the solution will probably require additional requirements, thus affecting other applications through enhancement or maintenance or by adding another data value (product number). It is important to note that Internet-based applications typically involve all three types of development (maintenance, enhancement, and new).

---

6. A member of a chat forum on parrots notified other members that a leading pet store was mistreating its parrots. As a result of this post, the pet store chain received a deluge of e-mails, letters, faxes, and telephone calls from the chat participants. Some individuals even visited the stores in person to express their disapproval. The company had to respond to prevent the further spread of bad Internet press and the loss of potential customers. The fact that the pet store chain did or did not have an Internet presence did not matter. The damage of consumer awareness affected the corporation's bottom line.

The Need for Clear, Concise, and Organized Requirements

The *Standish Group CHAOS Report* illustrated that the top reasons for project failure can be directly associated to the quality of requirements. It is imperative to identify ways to improve both the process and format of the requirements. Before they can be clear, concise, and organized, they must exist in writing!

The first step is to understand the different views of requirements. Requirements have a broader scope and definition than what many individuals working on a project may realize. The different views of requirements are multidimensional and have many intersecting needs. Without this understanding, requirements are either missed or misunderstood. In either case, the risk for failure increases.

If the requirements are organized in a standard, multidimensional infrastructure (*a requirements set framework*), any missing requirements will be quickly identified. Placing each requirement in the correct position will clearly identify the proper view of the requirement and its impact on other requirements.

Getting Business Units Involved

A business unit concentrating on a specific area of the business is called a *business community*. Community categories correlate to the business organization chart. Every requirements engineering effort should identify all the communities. A community may not be directly involved in defining the final product but may need to be involved in the area of support. For example, if new skills are required to build the Internet-based application, it is the responsibility of human resources to begin the search. Without the involvement of the human resources community, the product may fail due to insufficient staff.

Different organizational communities become involved in the requirement effort through the *allocation process,* which means simply that delegates are given the responsibility of defining the requirement details[7] for their particular communities. Adding an Internet facility to a brick-and-mortar company may involve making a change to a seemingly separate but existing software application (for example, product inventory). In actuality, however, what may have been needed was to add a data value to a data file maintained by the new development community (for example, a new product number). Without proper allocation, the addition of the product number may have been overlooked.

---

7. The process of allocation is described in more detail in Chapter Two.

This allocated business community may not have to react to requirements as early as those who are developing the requirements for the final product. However, it is optimal for each department to be able to plan ahead instead of reacting quickly, and possibly inaccurately, to the allocated requirement. Projects that fail due to missed deadlines are most commonly traced to the fact that allocated requirements were received late in the development process. Defects occur when employees are in reactive mode and aren't given the opportunity to be proactive.

Allocating requirements also allows for parallel efforts. As the requirements are allocated, each community can act upon them. For instance, once an Internet-based project is approved to move forward, the marketing department can act on it at the same time as human resources or the legal department. Each community's involvement is a negotiation between the *allocator* (that is, the person responsible for assuring that the requirement is delegated to the appropriate group) and the *allocatee* (that is, the chosen member from each community). The allocation process follows a thorough review of each community's area of responsibility within the organization. Once these roles have been determined, the importance of full participation becomes clear. Being understaffed is never a reason not to accept allocation.

The Right Person for the Job

Since incorrectly allocated requirements can cost a company a great deal of wasted funding, it is important to place the right people on the job. Fortunately, requirements engineering is beginning to be widely accepted due to the results of several surveys and quality initiatives.[8]

The responsibilities of the requirements engineer (or a requirements engineering organization) must be clearly defined.[9] The evolving role must be defined to work with other key quality processes. Today's requirements engineer must receive training in order to handle the influx of requests that he will receive.

---

8. For example, the Capability Maturity Model (CMM) is a framework refined by the Software Engineering Institute (SEI) of Carnegie Mellon University that demonstrates the key elements of an effective software process. The CMM describes an evolutionary improvement path for software development. Requirements management is one of the key process areas (KPAs) in the first level toward developing quality software.
9. The requirements engineering role and its place in organizations is described in more detail in Chapter Eight.

The Need for Parallel Efforts

Building an Internet product requires the efforts of many persons to develop individual work products that together form a complete Internet solution. All these individual work products (no matter whether they are within the same corporate boundaries or across boundaries because of business partnerships) need to be developed in parallel, which only complicates the coordination of requirements.

Thanks to the Internet, competition among companies has not only become more global and fast-paced but also more complicated. Corporations are merging to expand their focus and prospects in the marketplace. Other corporations are forming business partnerships and delegating (or outsourcing) part of the end-to-end process to meet the demands of the marketplace. With the faster pace of competition, it is no longer acceptable to supply the best product or service. The need is to do so before the competition! Time to market is everything.[10] This requires product development to be quick and evolutionary, producing products that are adaptable to market changes.

For example, let's take a drive. Take a look at a map. Pick a starting location and an end point. You can drive below the speed limit, at the speed limit, or above the speed limit. For the sake of this example, you are driving at the speed limit. One of your oldest competitors is driving below the speed limit. Your newest competitor is driving above the speed limit. All of you are using the same method of transportation. All of you reach the same location. The crucial point here is when you reach that destination. Remember, being first to market puts your Internet project in a dominant (branding) position. However, you can easily lose that dominant position if you deliver a poor-quality product. The trick is to find a medium for delivering a high-quality product in the shortest amount of time. To do so means initiating parallel efforts with coordination through the entire requirements process.

People tend to react to the time-crisis problem by cutting out some tasks or steps in the process. The term "good-enough software" and the "Just Do It!" management style have improved the time to market. However, the downside of working according to speed alone can be seen in the cost of rework software, loss of customer respect due to poor quality, and a demoralized employee force. In

---

10. With the turn of events regarding Internet stocks, profitability is now a much higher priority. However, a corporation's profitability is still dependent on its products entering the market as quickly as possible.

this case, the return on investment would not be as positive as it could be. By readjusting the requirements process, rather than simply eliminating tasks and steps, not only would the time-crisis issue be avoided but also the return on investment would be dramatically improved. Remember, you may reach market first and *temporarily* have brand acceptance. However, if your competitor comes up with a better-quality product shortly thereafter, your brand acceptance will be quickly lost. It is important to reduce the time to market not by cutting corners but rather by adhering to a more disciplined quality requirements process!

An Easy-to-Follow Process

To fulfill the multidimensional aspect of requirements and all the related needs, requirements engineering *must* follow a process. This is true regardless of the size of the company or project. Each stage of the process will go through several iterations on the way to producing the final product. Along the way, those persons designing the process must remain flexible as they will no doubt identify additional needs that must be satisfied.

At each level of refinement, an analytical process, or subprocess, can be followed. Using the same subprocess will ensure consistency across the different views, providing for easier validation and identification of missing requirements. The review should always assume change in market conditions and be able to react in a quick and cost-effective manner.

Improving Communication

Having this so-called easy-to-follow process—written down!—*will* facilitate good communication between the different business communities. Let's face it: you can have a defined process and an understanding of what a requirement is, but if you cannot articulate the requirement in writing, it will surely be inaccurately satisfied. Remember the "telephone game" you played as a child? Whisper your story down the line and it is always open to interpretation and miscommunication. Writing it down ensures that the team is on the same page, so to speak.

It is true that some individuals (and therefore business communities) are fully disciplined in the activities of requirements engineering. With them, all requirements for the requirements set (definition) are written down, validated, and approved. At the other end of the spectrum are those individuals who verbally communicate the need for their group, and it travels like a whisper as in the children's game of telephone. Completely altered in the translation, the business need is lost in the filtered-down version of the solution.

The bottom line is that *the requirements must be written down* in a format that is understood by the originator of the requirements and those persons who must act upon them, including the following:

- Executive committee
- Management
- Requester
- Planner
- Designer
- Builder
- Tester
- Supporter of the final product

All of these people will generate additional requirements that must be satisfied by the final product. A requirement needed by more than one department is identified and described *once*, but can be reused by any other community with the use of a "qualifier." A qualifier clarifies the reuse of the requirement to meet the needs of the other community.[11]

However, simply writing down the requirements does not mean they are correct or that they can be satisfied. They must be validated and approved by the persons allocating the requirements and by those who must act upon them.[12] They must remain adaptable. This is the mark of a good requirements management process. Those requirements that cannot currently be satisfied (for example, the handheld organizer that must fit on a wristwatch band) can be validated and approved in the short term. However, the requirements can be postponed for execution until it is feasible technologically to complete the project.

Writing out the requirements is only one way to minimize the communication barrier. Following a defined requirements engineering process will facilitate the elicitation, analysis, specification, validation, authorization/approval, prioritization, and management of the requirements set. This means completing a full review for each community, perspective, and focus, including

- The activities to be performed (the subactivities for elicitation, analysis, specification, validation, and management)
- The tasks for each of the activities and subactivities
- The deliverables

---

11. This is very important and will be discussed in detail in Chapter Three.
12. Validation of requirements is discussed in more detail in Chapter Seven.

- The roles
- The responsibilities of each role by task
- Quality checklists
- Examples of how the deliverable should look or can be illustrated
- Auditability of the process usage

Keeping the Team Apprised of All Requirements

Following the process requires team participation. Team participation requires verbal and written correspondence among other team participants. Speaking and writing skills must be enhanced to communicate with a variety of personalities and work styles. This is further complicated by the growing spectrum of requirements for the global market. As an example, a new handheld organizer may be intended for an international customer base. As a result, additional requirements are elicited that describe the needs of the international customer base. The person responsible for defining the requirements (requirement owner) may speak a different language than the requirements engineer eliciting the requirements. The requirements engineer must ask questions in a way that works with the requirement owner's communication style. In fact, it is the responsibility of the requirements engineer to communicate effectively with the requirement owner, who, as the business user, must understand, validate, and approve the requirements. Specifying the requirements only in the code will probably be inadequate for this task. The requirements engineer must present the requirements in a format that will be understood by the requirement owner and by the requirement user, who builds work products from the requirements.

A Flexible and Evolving Process

A successful Internet product is based on a high-quality requirements set. The development of this set occurs by following a defined process. This process needs to be light and effective without bureaucratic paperwork. Key process activities need to be incorporated along the way if they contribute to the following:

- The need for parallel development
- The need for high-quality products or components
- The need for coordination
- The need for continual change

This will ensure that the process is flexible enough to evolve with the Internet product.

The Internet and Requirements Engineering: Working Together

So, how do these two—the Internet and requirements engineering—come together? An Internet-based project, like all other projects, requires a whole host of requirements in order to make it successful: requirements to change the business as well as those to develop the technology solution.

First let's consider the impact on business itself. The Internet has changed the basic framework of how business is conducted by:

- Collapsing the hierarchy structure, thereby eliminating middle tiers
- Blurring corporate boundaries with additional business partnerships
- Creating new lines of business to support the Internet explosion
- Switching to a customer-centric rather than cost-cutting focus
- Changing the financial focus from profits to potential revenue

Each of these has an impact on the requirements engineering process.

The Collapsing Hierarchy Structure

With the Internet model, the business workflow is streamlined, minimizing the involvement of many departments. The Internet integrates business with business partners and business competitors, as well as with vendors and customers, resulting in closer interaction between enterprises. Middle-tier management and middlemen are being collapsed for the sake of cost and speed. The result is a change in business policies and procedures to facilitate the flatter organization. As a result, corporate middle tiers are fighting for their existence in the Internet world. Let's look at two industries that are currently wrestling with this: the automotive industry and brokerage houses.

In the automotive industry, car manufacturers wish to sell cars directly to consumers via the Internet. This medium allows consumers to pick and choose car features without going from lot to lot. The car manufacturer, since it already has the information in its database, can match the consumer's choice with the dealer who has the perfect match. Certainly, car dealers can still sell cars from the lots. Dealers live on the commissions from cars they sell. However, while doing so, the manufacturer may "pull" a car from a lot because of an Internet-based sale.

Although manufacturers can satisfy the requests of their customers in this way, they also need to develop different compensation packages that include incentives for dealers to relinquish their cars for Internet sales that they might otherwise sell for commissions. In this example, new requirements are needed to change existing business policies, procedures, and rules.

In the area of brokerage houses, consumers now often trade stocks for themselves. Major brokerages allow clients to bypass brokers in order to minimize the cost of fees for the company (as well as to eliminate commission fees for the consumer). Although this may look as if cost-cutting is the primary focus of the corporation, in truth it is illustrating a trend of the new Internet consumer. In the Internet model, the primary focus is to satisfy the wants of the consumer. Whichever product or service the customer is seeking, it must meet the specific needs of the customer. Therefore, requirements for an Internet solution must include a discussion on performance needs, ease of use, and customizable options. In the brokerage example, the consumer is satisfied with a self-service solution, selecting multiple trades in a single order that results in faster trading. The behind-the-scenes process is transparent to the consumer. Traders, as with car dealers, are affected by the loss of commission.[13]

Blurred Corporate Lines and Business Partnerships

Business adjustment is not just a flattening of the organizational chart. As with any paradigm shift, new opportunities for business alliances appear. Internet systems are complex, adaptive, expensive, and mission-sensitive. They demand a change in corporate philosophy. An organization can no longer do it all. Each must consider outsourcing anything beyond its main line of business, focusing on where it can add value and outsourcing the rest (that is, process outsourcing).

Businesses are rethinking corporate strategies and forming partnerships with different organizations. No longer must a company specializing in order-entry services be responsible for just-in-time inventory. The partnership utilizes the strengths of each corporation to best meet the needs of the customer—all of which is done seamlessly through Internet connections and Internet-based applications.

In response to these developments in business structure, service-level agreements between corporations need to be developed. Requirements for these kinds of arrangements include such nonfunctional components as security, perfor-

---

13. This points out the need for the requirements engineer to be a skilled diplomat. A supplier of requirements may be a person who may have his responsibilities reduced, his revenues reduced, or his position eliminated!

mance, and stability of the interfaces. Requirements for such agreements need to be elicited by the requirements engineer assigned to this task.

New Lines of Business

Business partnerships are also creating an opportunity for new lines of business. Nowhere is this more apparent than with the influx of electronic mail (e-mail). This simple application spurred tremendous Internet-based usage. It is used for a multitude of functions: ordering products, sending inquiries, canceling services, changing information, and contacting companies. The information contained in these e-mails is extremely valuable to corporations. However, the growth in the numbers of e-mails has reached the point beyond what many corporations can handle. As a result, new companies specializing in "customer care" or customer relationship management (CRM) are entering the Internet-based companies, taking on the responsibility of answering 80 percent of the standard e-mails within 48 hours.

Again, a new company requires new business rules and policies. These will define the soul and culture of the new company, which need to be addressed prior to launching the application. Business rules are a type of requirement that needs to be defined, as we will see later. These requirements will impact the other types of requirements needed to be satisfied by the CRM application.

Customer-Centric versus Cost-Cutting Focus

New e-businesses, like Amazon.com, must become the brand name (for online ordering) on consumer's mind at all times. As Jeff Bezos, founder of Amazon.com, stated, "Ultimately, we are an information broker."[14] The information is what to buy and how to buy it. Amazon.com has mastered the personalization concept by selecting products based on previous search criteria executed by the consumer and by comparing those selections with those of other consumers. This company serves as an example for all Internet companies. It has become the "brand" that other Internet-based applications attempt to simulate. Amazon.com focuses on customer wants (product availability) and needs (ease of use and quick response).

---

14. As quoted on "Internet Shopping in the 21st Century," hosted by Jeff Greenfield, PBS Home Video, 2000.

Being customer-centric requires capturing the usability type of requirements. In order for the application to be successful, all users must be able to easily understand and use it. This requires defining scenarios with few clicks to provide clients what they want, when they want it. In the case of the automatic electronic response, this means that the response has to be clear and concise, delivering the answer the customer needs in a timely manner—if not with the first message (the "We'll get back to you" message), then certainly by the second message shortly thereafter.

Profits versus Potential Revenue[15]

The Internet has also changed the way Wall Street evaluates some companies. The evaluation is based not on the company's profits (expense/revenue-based formula) but rather on the value of the company's revenue and potential revenue! Market capitalization of "dot-com" companies is now valued over investments in long-standing, successful, profitable companies. Amazon.com, with its customer-centric focus, has not turned a profit since its inception, yet it is the pioneer that swayed Wall Street's philosophy on evaluating a company's performance.

In response to this change, new and updated reports need to be created for executive management that illustrate the customer base. A data warehouse of the click history (click-stream data) needs to be captured. These applications support the main line of business (online retailing). These requirements need to be captured and satisfied in order for the *entire business* to be successful on the Internet.

Putting It All Together

As you embark upon the requirements process, remember that you are not alone. Mention "requirements" to any project team member and you will witness a variety of responses. All will agree that the requirements process needs improvement. Some team members can tout the most commonly spouted reasons for improvement that they heard from experts and vendors. Many will explain the need to implement the "silver bullet" of a new technique or tool as the silver-coded solution. Some will explain that it is someone else's responsibility to develop the requirements and that this task has no or minimal impact on what they are doing. The truth is, there is no simple solution. In fact, no solution

---

15. The pendulum is beginning to turn; stockholders are beginning to demand to see profit within a shorter time frame.

will be defined until we understand the business implication of our efforts. In order to do so, we first need to speak a common language.

Terminology: A Common Understanding

With a better understanding of the nature of Internet-based applications, it is time to look at the area of capturing requirements for Internet applications. We in the world of information technology are our own worst enemies. We develop acronyms and mnemonics on a daily basis, some of which are reused to mean something entirely different. The field of requirements engineering is no different. It is important to define a common level of understanding, some basic terms used throughout this book and in the field of requirements engineering. The site you are working on must be "buzzword compliant" even when the buzzwords get invented, reinvented, cycled, and recycled every day!

Information technologists are the biggest offender. Just check out the world-wide acronym server at *www.ucc.ie/info/net/acronyms/acro.html.* Technologies tend to use the same terms to mean different things, components of things, or even how to do things. New terms are developed that are basically the same as another term with a slight "marketing" enhancement. Technicians are known to rapidly invent new mnemonics or acronyms even if they are duplicates of one already being used. [16]

Requirements engineers are also found among the culprits. These individuals use the term "requirements" to define everything related to requirements: individual, specifications, process, design functions, and even constraints. It is important to be very careful of the terminology used in the area of requirements.

For the purposes of this book, let us use the following basic terms. These terms will be further described in the individual chapters to follow and are also contained in the Glossary. The objective here is to lay out a common language that will be used throughout the book.

The terms used in this book are

- Internet
- Requirement
- Internet requirement

---

16. When I first started my career at IBM, I learned the mnemonic **SDLC** to represent **S**oftware **D**evelopment **L**ife **C**ycle. As I continued my career into the world of telecommunications, I heard **SDLC** again. This time, the mnemonic stood for **S**ynchronous **D**ata **L**ink **C**ontrol. Of course, some of this reuse can be attributed to marketers and product vendors.

- Requirements set
- Pattern
- Requirements pattern
- Internet requirements pattern
- Anti-pattern
- Internet requirements anti-pattern
- Requirements specification
- Requirements engineer
- Requirements engineering
- Requirements management
- Requirements process
- Requirement versus requirements specification versus requirements set

Let's briefly take them one by one.

What Is the Internet?

Simply put, the Internet provides a method for buying and selling products and services over a network. The network can be open to the public (Internet) or between companies (Extranet). It is the online transaction between two or more parties. The exchange on the Internet is the commodity of information. This is a very important point. The final transaction in the workflow does not have to be a tangible product like a toy or car part that is physically delivered to a doorstep.

The Internet is different from other applications because of the nature of the Internet. It is a rapidly changing environment that requires whatever is implemented to be flexible and touches all business divisions and sectors. Internet solutions must react quickly to changing business initiatives while still providing an end-to-end integrated solution. The boundaries of the corporation no longer depict the boundaries of the solutions. The ends are also now within the scope of analysis.

In technical terms, the Internet can be defined as five application types:

1. Business-to-consumer applications
2. Business-to-business integration
3. Business-to-staff applications
4. Application-to-application integration
5. Business-to-wireless applications

A successful Internet solution will, in fact, incorporate all five types of applications. For the purposes of this book, the term *Internet* will be used interchangeably to represent all five types of applications.

Business-to-consumer (B2C). A business-to-consumer interface is what the consumer sees every time he or she accesses a Web-based application. This is the type of application everyone thinks of as they look for information or products for purchasing. These are most common corporate applications that interface directly with the consumer via the Internet.[17] These applications, such as electronic catalogs, must have an easy-to-use front end to entice existing and new clients to buy products after minimal browsing. Depending on whether you are a buyer or seller, the structure of the information is different. Buyers look for competitive information (mysimon.com); sellers present information to entice customers to buy (eBay.com). All such applications should be strong on presentation. They require special attention to usability-type requirements that streamline the workflow for the consumer. They require special attention to security to minimize consumer fears of privacy violation. They require special attention to capturing of consumers' usage patterns to enhance the experience. These "special attention" components are needs that must be satisfied. It is extremely important that these types of requirements be captured.

Business-to-business (B2B). A business-to-business workflow involves multiple functions. Many corporations perform the entire end-to-end process of that workflow. However, the Internet has forced companies to take another look at what their businesses really are. As a result, workflows previously supported by one organization are now being outsourced to companies whose line of business is best suited to perform that function in the workflow. Seamless integration of applications across corporate boundaries is the nature of B2B. These applications concentrate on streamlining functionality. They are designed for high-volume transactions (for example, supply chain applications).

---

17. ToysRUs, however, now uses the front-end application of a different company (Amazon.com). The scope is the same but the boundaries for ToysRUs have narrowed. This is a perfect example that Internet applications must capture requirements for the end-to-end transaction even if it does cross corporation boundaries.

EZ Pass[18] is an application that electronically captures data about cars that pass through tolls on highways, bridges, and tunnels. Each consumer's tolls are tallied and debited from his or her account. This account is continually refilled through a credit card number that is kept on file. There are as many as three separate businesses involved in the workflows across the Internet:

1. EZ Pass supports the high-volume transactions of consumers passing through tolls.
2. Credit card companies support the charging of refill amounts to consumers.
3. Banks (which may or may not be associated with the credit card companies) process the billing records to consumers and credit card companies.

The business workflow consists of four functions:

1. A consumer passes through the toll.
2. The consumer's account is debited for the toll.
3. The account is replenished if it falls below the contractual amount.
4. The consumer is invoiced for the replenishing.

EZ Pass does not need to have the responsibility for all four functions. Consumers can view the status of their accounts (a B2C application), but the continual flow of the work crosses corporate boundaries. The information can be passed to the different corporations via the Internet as a batch (a group of transactions) or as a single transaction.

The requirements, therefore, must include the description of the functions and responsibilities within the scope of each corporation. Requirements must include what information is expected by each organization for each function and when the information is needed and passed between the organizations (and how to deal with incorrect or incomplete information or transactions). Special attention on the volume of transactions must be documented in the requirements as well as the expected response time for each transaction between organizations.

Business-to-staff (B2S). These are corporate applications that interface directly with internal staff via the Internet. The most common example is internal e-mail. However, a B2S application can be any B2C application that is within

---

18. EZ Pass is located in the northeastern U.S. area that captures tolls throughout New York, New Jersey, Connecticut and extends geographically continually. Other states have developed similar applications under different names.

the boundaries of a single corporation. B2S applications can be the internal ordering system for supplies and the automatic notification system for requirements set changes. The same types of requirements need to be captured as with the B2C application.

Application-to-application (A2A).   As with B2B applications, successful Internet products require the integration of multiple corporate applications. This represents communication between existing applications within the boundaries of the corporation (for example, customer orders and inventory control). The twist with the Internet is due to the change in focus and velocity. Corporations must streamline their internal workflows to increase the capacity for transactions as well as the speed and concurrency. In other words, current stops or holding patterns in the current workflow must be eliminated wherever possible. Each policy must be reevaluated according to its need in the new Internet environment. New checks and balances may also be required.

Business-to-wireless (B2W).   Handheld devices and the telephone industry have added another advancement of Internet-based applications, satisfying the need to communicate to and from wireless devices. This fifth category is not considered a separate Internet-based category by many persons (and hence is not illustrated in Figure 1.2). This fifth type is considered by many to be simply an extension of the other types. Wireless communication can fall into multiple other Internet-based applications categories, including B2C, B2B, and B2S applications when the communication device used to transfer or access information is a wireless device. However, B2W applications have unique characteristics and complexity issues. Wireless Internet applications (m-commerce) require modification of Internet applications to send condensed information to small-screen devices. Wireless application protocols (WAPs) have added complexity to ensure the secure transfer of information.

What Is a Requirement?

A requirement? It is the first step in any project, whether or not it involves technology, yet the activity of requirements gathering is taken for granted by many project team members as a simple task. Project team members (consisting of users, analysts, designers, builders, testers, managers, and so on) view requirements as a relatively short activity in the whole process. The requirements activity, in their minds, is an informal communication between team members to formulate the basis of a solution.

Varying studies, such as the *Standish Group CHAOS Report*,[19] state that approximately 67 percent of technology projects fail. According to the *CHAOS Report*, one-third of the reasons for failure can be attributed to requirements. So, how difficult is the requirements process? The truth of the matter is that requirements are the most ambiguous part of the entire project.

In simplistic terms, *a requirement describes a need or desire to be satisfied by the product or service*. It starts out as a simple request and evolves into realms of individual requirements required to support the simple request. All of the additional requirements refine the need with important details. These too must also be satisfied. Additional requirements could describe

- A user or system
- A piece of information
- Connectivity
- Time sensitivity
- Workflow
- Enforced policies
- Restrictions

All of these exist to support the initial request. *A requirement is not a solution!*

Artifact versus requirement.   It is important to distinguish the difference between an artifact and a requirement. An *artifact* defines the business and its operations. A *requirement* is a need to be satisfied by the product or service. The requirement is dependent upon the artifacts of the business. However, not all artifacts are needed to implement the requirements set. It is important to begin with the artifacts when developing the requirements set. The artifacts must be challenged as to their continual need in their current form for the survival of the business and for the implementation of the product.

A requirement case study.   To help define the terms, consider the example of an IT product, a handheld organizer.[20] The concept of a handheld organizer describes the need but is still open to many interpretations. The requirement is still ambiguous. However, it is a start—something that can be clarified, elaborated, and refined. It describes the *primary requirement* on which all others will

---

19. The CHAOS Report published by the Standish Group can be found at
www.pm2go.com/sample_research/chaos_1994_1.dsp.
20. A personal digital assistant (PDA) is used in this example as a reminder of the potential wireless devices that will need to be understood when capturing requirements.

be based. A requirement has a beginning and evolves into more detail. This primary requirement may be very clear to the executive, customer, or marketing director. However, it may not give enough detail to actually build a solution. Additional requirements are spawned from the primary requirement to remove the ambiguity for the builders, testers, and other project workers involved in the process. The additional *derived requirements* must all support the marketing initiative of building a handheld organizer.

It is important to state over and over again that *a requirement is not a solution.* A requirement may restrict the solution, but it does not define the solution. A requirement also does not specify the approach or method used to develop the solution. A requirement only describes the need as clearly and concisely as possible.

Expanding on the original requirement leads to further requirements: *"The handheld organizer serves the use of holding addresses, expenses, and checklists and synchronizes with a personal computer at will."* Each of these requirements describes the handheld organizer in a bit more detail, however, not enough detail to build a solution.

Satisfying the requirements to hold addresses, expenses, and checklists falls under the area of software. However, hardware requirements will also be involved for creating, editing, and deleting the addresses, expenses, and checklists. Synchronization with a personal computer is another requirement.

As with any new product, other business areas need to be involved, for instance, advertising, marketing, staffing, legal, and so forth. The derived requirements are based upon the area responsible for further clarifying the requirement. The requirement is *allocated* to the area most able to satisfy (to refine and clarify) the requirement. Each business area may need to allocate the requirement further to define the requirement to the level at which it can be acted upon with a solution.

For example, the handheld organizer may first be allocated to information technology, where the system components are defined. The requirements are then allocated between hardware, software, and network (synchronize).

A requirement perspective is a stage in refining the primary requirement to describe the need in a format that is understood by the person or role responsible for satisfying the need. Each phase of the software development process has a different perspective, or a stage in the process whereby the primary requirement is defined in terms understandable to the group responsible for implementation. With each perspective comes another level of detail with additional derived requirements. Again, what is important is that the perspective of the initiators (the executives) is satisfied in the final product. For instance, going back to our example, the software department interprets the requirement "addresses" to mean creating, reading, editing, searching, and deleting an individual address. Additional requirements describe the amount and type of information an address should keep. The functions (create, read, edit, search, delete) and information (address lines, telephone numbers, number of addresses) are types of focus that may be applied to clarify the requirement.

The point at which a requirement completes the allocation process is when the requirement and the additional derived requirements are described in such a clear, concise, complete, and correct manner that a solution can be developed. At this time, the group responsible for acting on the requirement has all the information necessary to develop a solution.

For example, the "hold addresses" requirement would be allocated to the software department. The software department would then parse the requirement and allocate to coworkers in the data and process area the responsibility to refine the allocated requirement and clearly, concisely, completely, and correctly define it to include their focus or point of view. The focus areas are required since they provide different views of the requirement. Each view generates specific requirements clarifying the area of focus and concentrates on a specific area for that perspective.

Allocating the requirement to both the data and the process means simply that there are additional derived requirements to supply the data and process information. It does not imply that two *different* groups are to work on the requirement separately. Focus, rather, represents a view of the requirement. One or more individuals may be responsible for eliciting, analyzing, specifying, validating, and managing the requirements.

What Is an Internet Requirement?

As stated previously, a successful Internet solution requires the implementation of all five types of applications. All focus on different needs that must be satisfied. To understand the different kinds of needs requires a full understanding of the term *requirement*.

An Internet requirement is a specific type of requirement. e-Requirements are those requirements needed to build an Internet/commerce solution. This does not limit the discussion to IT requirements. Internet solutions require additional non-IT requirements.

What Is a Requirements Set?

The requirements set contains *all* requirements (primary and derived) that specify the need to be satisfied (see Figure 1.4). The requirements set combines all

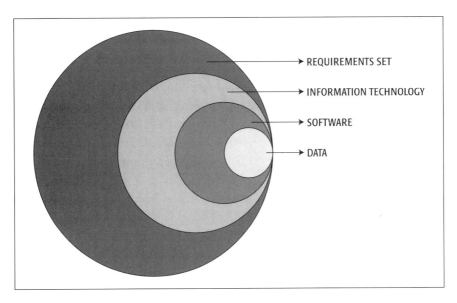

Figure 1.4   Requirements Set Consists of Many Requirements Subsets.

the different individual requirements subsets by community, by perspective, and by focus-specific requirements. This includes all the details associated with each individual requirement and any models or diagrams used to further clarify the requirement.

These too are not solutions. A design is not included, nor is the code in the requirements set. However, requirements on what the design is to include or requirements that will assist in developing the design would be part of the requirements set, as would the need for specific development environment components (such as on what hardware and software to build the product).

What Is a Pattern?

Patterns have been around for centuries. Cabinetmakers and dressmakers develop patterns that are reused to build or make a product. Information technologists use the term *pattern* to represent either a reusable architecture or a template. Patterns readily available include:

- Analysis pattern
- Data pattern
- Design pattern
- Framework

- Fundamental pattern
- Message pattern
- Transaction pattern

Until now no pattern existed specifically for requirements set. In order to build a reusable template for requirements, it must adhere to the general rules of patterns. It must also be generic to support all types of requirements. As used in this book, *a pattern is any reusable template based on experience that can be used to guide the creation of a solution to the problem or need in a specific context.* The key words are:

- Reusable
- Template
- Guide

What Is a Requirements Pattern?

A requirements pattern is a framework for requirements that supports the product needs, minimizing gaps in knowledge that may cause project failure. A requirements pattern supports multiple designs and implementations.

A requirements pattern also supports any technique for capturing and specifying requirements. It is a reusable framework based on experience that can be used to identify pieces of the need, and it provides a common framework to support all the needs that a solution must satisfy (requirements set).

What Is an Internet Requirements Pattern?[21]

An Internet requirements pattern is a reusable framework for requirements that supports the building of an *Internet-based* solution, capturing the entire Internet needs and minimizing gaps that may cause the failure of the business.

What Is an Anti-Pattern?

No process or framework is perfect. Anti-patterns are written guides to avoid commonly occurring instances in design. The same premises can be applied to avoid gaps in the requirements set that will cause either product or project risk. Anti-patterns provide a means to coach the requirements engineer around common requirement-related obstacles that could affect the quality of the project or product.

---

21. Appendix B contains the Internet requirements pattern. The appendix supports Chapter Four.

What Is an Internet Requirements Anti-Pattern?[22]

An Internet requirements anti-pattern is a warning on how to avoid common traps or mistakes in capturing Internet requirements. Such anti-patterns are written to avoid gaps in knowledge, process, and participation. Anti-patterns provide a means to coach the requirements engineer around common requirement-related obstacles for Internet programs.

What Is a Requirements Specification?

A requirements specification is a written description of the requirements set or a subset of the requirements set. The format of the requirement is important. Each subset of requirements will have its own means of describing the requirement. For example, information requirements may be depicted in an information model. What is important is that the format be easily understood by those with the previous and next perspectives within the focus areas. If the specification is the final, complete set of requirements, it must be in a format that is understood by the person or group responsible for providing a solution.

What Is a Requirements Engineer?

A requirements engineer is responsible for allocating, eliciting, analyzing, documenting, validating, and managing the requirements set. Depending upon the requirements subset, a different name may be assigned to the role. These other subset roles (such as systems analyst, business analyst, data analyst, network engineer), as part or all of their responsibilities, must define the requirements for their requirements subsets.

The term *role* does not mean *individual*. A person may have the responsibilities of performing a set of functions, one of which is requirements engineering of the customer data. However, his or her other responsibilities may include managing a group of data analysts. A person may perform many roles.

Similarly different areas do not imply different organizations, groups, or individuals. They represent a subset of the requirements.[23] The different areas must be accounted for in the final requirements set. More or fewer people (or even just one person) can be responsible for developing the requirements set and may cross different areas. The number of people depends on the size of the project and the organization.

---

22. Appendix D contains a sample of Internet requirements anti-patterns. The appendix supports discussion in Chapter Five.
23. The different requirements subsets are discussed further in Chapter Three.

A requirements engineer is a role that has the responsibility for following a defined process to clarify the derived requirements that satisfy the primary need. The role may be filled by one person with other responsibilities or by a group of individuals responsible for a specific community, perspective, and focus. Again, what is important is that all requirements are accounted for.

What Is Requirements Engineering?

Requirements engineering encompasses two groups: development and management (see Figure 1.5). The activities include

1. Allocating the responsibility of defining the requirements
2. Capturing individual requirements (eliciting, analyzing, documenting, validating)
3. Managing the requirements set

The first two have to do with capturing requirements. The third has to do with managing what was captured.

The defined process has two levels: the requirement allocation process and the individual requirement development process. The first level, the requirement allocation process, is the process that allocates the responsibility of the requirement for further clarification. The second, the individual requirement development process, is the subprocess that takes the allocated requirements, elicits

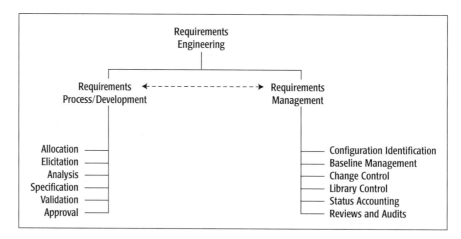

Figure 1.5 Requirements-Related Activities

derived requirements, analyzes the requirements, specifies the requirements, validates the requirements, and manages the approved requirements.

What Is Requirements Management?

Requirements management is the process of baselining approved requirements and managing any changes and their impacts on other requirements and work products. Configuration management is just as important for requirements as it is for file structures or code modules. It does not prevent changes; it manages the changes. Requirements management, a type of configuration management, defines the process, procedures, and responsibilities involved in managing changes to approved requirements. The requirements are configuration items to be managed under a defined configuration management process.

What Is a Requirements Process?

The requirements process is at two separate levels. The first, high level has the purpose of allocating the responsibility to the correct division for further detailing. The second level is what most software engineers are familiar with: elicitation, analysis, specification, validation, and management. Due to the complexity and mission-critical nature of the Internet, another activity, approval, is added after validation.

What Is the Difference between Requirement, Requirements Specification, and Requirements Set?

When a team participant states, "We need to write down the requirements," he usually means writing the requirements for a specific requirements specification (business or functional). Reviewing the preceding terminology, one can see that requirements are much more. The common understanding (functional requirements) of the requirements set is really only a subset of what needs to be captured. A *requirements set* may contain multiple *requirements specifications* (see Figure 1.4). Both requirements specifications and the requirements set contain individual requirements. A requirements set consists of all the individual requirements documented in multiple requirements specifications. All requirements are based on the original initiating requirement. The individual requirement may be tailored or may be explicit for a specific community, perspective, and/or focus. A requirements specification is explicit by community and perspective and possibly by focus.

Conclusion

A simple signature by Former President George Bush stimulated a new era for the Internet. The "dot-com" industry exploded over only a few years. As a point of reference, Amazon.com, one of the leading Internet solutions, entered the Web in 1995.

There is no doubt that the Internet has dramatically influenced the way business is conducted. Each corporation, small or large, requires a presence on the "Net" to remain competitive. However, it is a high-risk initiative with potentially high rewards if applications are built quickly and correctly. Building the solution correctly requires changes in current business processes and in the definition of such terms as *the customer* and *competitive market.*

Unlike other types of information technology applications, the Internet and Internet solutions require skilled requirements engineers to capture all the requirements in the most efficient manner. Being on the Web is not a simplistic application. The number and types of requirements that need to be captured go beyond the typical software requirements most information technology groups are used to capturing.

The purpose of this chapter was to illustrate the nature of Internet-based applications and to introduce the twists in requirements engineering to meet the challenges of the Internet pace. The Internet requirements pattern and the associated activities were developed specifically for this purpose. The rest of this book discusses the requirements, the different types, the activities, and the roles and responsibilities associated with them. Before discussing these requirement-related topics, it was important to clarify the terminology that is so loosely used in the technology industry.

The Internet requirements pattern is a tool used to assist requirements engineers in capturing all the requirements needed to build high-quality Internet-based applications. The pattern reaches further than just software requirements. This is because the first truth about requirements is that *a need must be satisfied!*

CHAPTER TWO

Requirement Evolution

> **Chapter Key Topics**
> - The evolution of requirements
> - The requirements process
> - The requirements subprocess
>
> **The Internet Impact**
> The Internet impacts existing business community structures, streamlining the many processes that exist between divisions and corporations. A simple requirement has an effect on multiple divisions and requires analysis by multiple business communities to specify the individual requirement as it pertains to each community.

Internet applications require the involvement of several departments (for example, marketing, legal, procurement) across multiple corporations (for example, one that records the sale, another that processes the sale, and another that delivers the goods). Each department must satisfy different needs (requirements) so it can build its specific work products for the end result (for example, network, B2B agreements, JavaBeans). As discussed in Chapter One, all these requirements need to be captured, analyzed, documented, validated, and approved. Each requirement *evolves* throughout the process and is viewed as a component of the overall solution. Each evolutionary step may represent the requirements in a separate and distinct work product. As a project evolves, additional requirements are identified and existing requirements may change

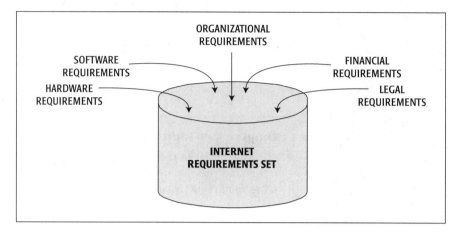

Figure 2.1   All Internet-Related Requirements Comprise a Requirements Set.

(in some cases, frequently), all of which must be coordinated as to the potential impact on other requirements (and work products). There must be continual verification that the requirements (new, existing, and changed) lead toward the business objective.[1] The compilation of all the requirements, in their different evolutionary states, is called the *requirements set* (see Figure 2.1).

Evolution of Requirements

All work products are based upon the requirements set. All work products must be built to meet the same business objectives. As such, intermediary work products lead to building the final components of the Internet product. This evolutionary process is similar to that of manufacturing any product. Manufacturing follows some sort of process that produces an intermediary or final product (or a component of the product). This repeatable process can be broken into the following phases:

• Birthing an idea
• Analyzing the feasibility

---

1. It is not uncommon for business objectives to change as the Internet product is being developed. The Internet environment is quite dynamic and will not stand still while the product is being developed. Strict change control and continual verification of the requirements against this moving target are keys to the success of the product.

- Designing the product
- Developing the product
- Assembling and testing the product
- Implementing the product
- Maintaining and enhancing the product
- Discontinuing the product

The design, development, and testing of the product may have many iterations. Each iteration, called "prototyping," refines the requirements or design of the final product. The product continues its life until it is discontinued. Until that time, however, the fixing of defects after implementation is called "maintenance." Adding new features to future models is called "enhancements."

In the world of the Internet, the product is developed and implemented in discrete stages similar to a release of any commercial off-the-shelf (COTS) software product. Simultaneous to a release, the same product has several versions in development. Each of the releases is an iteration that goes through the same process of analysis through implementation. Maintenance and enhancements from a specific release may be held until the next scheduled or future release (iteration), depending on the severity of the change needed.

Wrapped around the manufacturing process are the planning and management of the ultimate delivery of the final product. The whole approach is a repeatable process filled with quality checkpoints (gates) to ensure the best product is delivered to the customer and that the product (or component of the product) is in line with the business objectives.

The Internet Development Process

Development of an Internet-based application should be viewed no differently than the manufacturing process. The development of Internet work products follows the same repeatable process as the previously discussed manufacturing process:

- Birthing an idea
- Analyzing the feasibility
- Designing the Internet product
- Developing the Internet product
- Assembling and testing the Internet product
- Implementing the Internet product

- Maintaining and enhancing the Internet product
- Discontinuing the product

As with manufacturing, the process is a spiral of iterations of repeatable design, development, and testing. Each iteration refines the requirements or design of the Internet product. This prototyping also may be referred to as "proof of concept." The prototype validates the requirements as to their interpretation or feasibility. Wrapped around the manufacturing process (hardware, software, network, and so forth) are the product development plan and management of the ultimate delivery of the final product.

Maintenance activities fix defects after the product is implemented. Adding new features to the existing product results in enhancements, upgrades, iterations,[2] or new releases. Both maintenance and enhancement projects have requirements and follow a similar workflow. The product lives on with continual maintenance and enhancements until it becomes obsolete and is either removed from usage (for internal-use products) or removed from the shelves.[3]

The cost of maintenance of any product, including the Internet, is extremely high. Some information technology organizations tend to skip or rush through the early steps (requirements elicitation, analysis, and specification) and fail to apply quality checkpoints (validation). Others fail to follow any repeatable development process at all. Some tend to simply extend their traditional work without a disciplined software engineering approach. All of these scenarios allow for defects to be implemented and repaired (at a greater cost in time and money) during maintenance. Maintenance has a high price that erodes the potential revenue gains of a product.

Development of an Internet product should be as repeatable as the manufacturing process. A clearly defined process is full of opportunities for quality checkpoints to ensure the best product is delivered to the business community. The process should not be bureaucratic; rather, the development of the product should be streamlined. Having a well-defined process provides opportunities for parallel efforts, keeping all parties notified and involved at the right time. It also helps cut costs (when maintenance due to defects is added into the equation) and time (again, minimizing the time and resources needed to clarify and correct the defects).

---

2. Internet products can be developed and released in components that can be delivered independently (or removed due to defects, obsolescence, or upgrades).
3. Even obsolescence creates requirements. The product number may need to be removed from inventory files, the security access denied, and so on.

The Requirements Development Process

An Internet product is composed of several implemented work products as well as support work products, all of which come together to form the specified solution. Each work product has its own development process that coordinates with the manufacturing process (see Table 2.1).

Two of the stages in the manufacturing process require additional steps in the work product evolution: feasibility analysis and development of the product. Feasibility analysis requires several steps that define and clarify the relationships between parts of the work product as well as within the same work product. The steps identify the scope and responsibilities for those involved in developing the work product. Developing the product defines what is to be implemented by which portion, as well as when and how. The purpose of these expanded steps is to evolve the product (in this case, the requirements in the requirements set) in terms of detail and level of abstraction. Each evolutionary step is important to develop a high-quality end product, which ultimately comes together to create the final high-quality Internet iteration.

Requirements are intermediary work products. The requirements are specified in all the stages of development. The requirements evolve in detail and level

Table 2.1 Manufacturing and Work Product Correlation

Manufacturing Process	Internet Work Product Evolution
Birth of an idea	Birth of an idea
Analyze the feasibility	Business concept Organizational scope Divisional relationships
Design the product	Product attributes
Develop the product	Product delineation Physical design
Assemble and test the product	Abstract definition
Implement the product	Implemented product
Maintain/enhance the product	Iteration request
Discontinue the product	Replacement strategy

of abstraction as does any other Internet-related work product (see Figure 2.2). These steps and deliverables will become clearer as this book progresses. The point now is to illustrate that requirements evolve through a process that is correlated to the manufacturing of an Internet product. Both the Internet product and the requirements set are initiated with the birth of an idea.

The Birth of an Idea

The idea to build an Internet product (whether within a corporation or as a start-up company) can be sparked from different sources. Requirements come from external sources and internal sources (see Figure 2.3). The idea may come from outside the corporate boundaries as a problem or need (including compet-

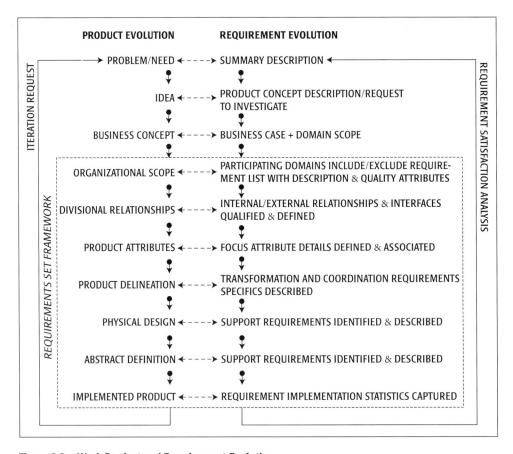

Figure 2.2   Work Product and Requirement Evolution

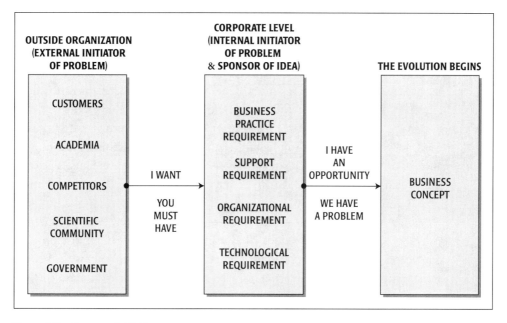

Figure 2.3   Program Initiation

itive information) and be sent to someone internally. The idea is then developed into a business concept; then it can be evaluated for feasibility. The idea can also be initiated internally, within the boundaries of the corporation. In this scenario, the idea is formed and developed into a business concept and again is evaluated for feasibility.

External Sources

In the old paradigm of doing business, *initiating requirements* (ideas) were provided externally by clients, vendors, academia, government, and competitors. This is still true in the world of the Internet. The difference is the pace at which they are received and the definition of "client."

An existing application continually receives new requirements that enhance the existing Internet product. The feedback for Internet-based applications is intense and continuous. Business conditions change frequently and influence the existing requirements set. They result in new functions and features that could cripple an existing infrastructure. In order for the Internet-based system to survive to maintain and expand market share, customer suggestions are key and must be analyzed and grouped by similarities. The sheer number of suggestions and the impact on the current infrastructure can help establish priorities for new requirements.

Competitors too are an external source of requirements. However, they are not the only external source. For example, if you read about an Internet disaster that occurred with a noncompetitor, it should become a requirement to check *your* Internet product to see if the same potential exists for your product.

More and more, hardware and software continue to improve that safeguard your Internet applications from failure. Many of these requirements fall into the category of nonfunctional or quality of service (QoS) requirements. They are independent of the line of business. They incorporate both the expectation of the user and the corporation.

Functionally (within the line of business), online shoppers expect more than just timely delivery of the product. They want services and features not found at competitor sites or ones they cannot find at their local mall. What is the benefit of shopping at your site or using your service in an Internet scenario? These questions must be definitively answered.

The most common source for ideas for an Internet work product (initial release or any iteration) is e-mail. Consumers and business partners are quick to shoot off an e-mail with an idea or complaint. Both serve as valuable input for a new Internet solution, for an extension of an existing Internet-based solution, or for an enhancement for the next iteration. In any case, all must be captured, analyzed, documented, validated, and approved for inclusion into the product.

No matter which external source the idea stems from, someone now owns the idea within the organization. This person becomes the initial requirement sponsor. This person or group is charged with the task of implementing an Internet application and gathering (or delegating the gathering of) the initial set of requirements. This person, an internal person for each corporation involved, is typically on the business side of the house. However, due to the technological nature of the Internet, some corporations have put the technologist in charge. If you see this, it is a red flag. Information technology has typically been isolated from customers and consumers by the business functions. Assigning an information technologist to lead the process is a sign that the Internet application is only to be a wrapper to the existing business processes. It shows that the business fails to realize the need for a change in the way business must be conducted to meet the time-to-market needs of the Internet. It further shows that the business fails to realize how the different business communities are affected by the Internet. As a result, only a subset of the requirements, the technological subset for one business unit, is typically captured. It is the responsibility of the requirements engineer to foster allocation to involve all business units.

Internal Sources

The idea to build an Internet solution could also be initiated from within the corporation, generally from three sources: an employee's idea (including an executive directive), competitive analysis, and technological improvements. No matter which one is the source, someone internal to all corporations involved owns the idea. As with the externally initiated effort, this point person is charged with the task of implementing an Internet solution.

Technological advancements are the reason that the Internet has become a viable business paradigm. Technology will continue to be a major initiating requirement to change or upgrade Internet applications. Technology continues to evolve that can have an impact on the "ilities"[4] of your Internet-based application. Advances in technology must be continually reviewed as to the possibility of exceeding user expectation (or simply meeting those not previously met). Some advances, such as the introduction of wireless devices, can support additional features that were previously not provided.

The Business Concept

Whether the idea for a product involves a brand-new Internet solution, an enhancement to an existing Internet solution, or the maintenance of an existing Internet application, it is important that the concept (an initiating set of requirements) be written down with enough information for executives to validate the need against the corporate objectives and business direction. The initiating requirements must be formulated into an idea and organized around the idea to define the business concept.

- PART A: Each idea must be written to include
  - A full description of the idea
  - The possible impact on the existing product or business
  - A business priority

---

4. "Ilities" refers to nonfunctional or quality of service requirements. Internet examples include reliability, security, flexibility, and so forth. This will be discussed in more detail in Chapter Three.

- PART B: Individual requirements must
  - Be labeled
  - Include a full description to convey a single meaning
  - Be assigned a priority
  - Define the source and the number of that source (clients)

- PART C: Supporting documentation must include
  - Competitive analysis
  - Market research
  - News articles and so on

The initial requirement sponsor assembles the information. A requirements engineer can assist in developing the initiating requirements set (Part B). The business concept package (Parts A, B, and C) of a competitive problem or a business opportunity is brought to executive management to determine the feasibility of the idea. Feasibility, at this stage of product development, is chiefly financial feasibility—how much the product will cost and what revenue and other intangible value it will bring to the corporation.

Building a Business Case

Before you jump from the idea to building an Internet product, the requirement sponsor needs to evaluate whether the idea is financially sound for the corporation. This is initiated by asking some basic questions. Answering these questions is the beginning of building a *business case* (investigating the feasibility of developing the product).

To begin, it is important to understand the type of business your corporation (large or small) is in. What product/service does the company offer? How does the client purchase the product or service? Is it viable to transact this type of business on the Internet? What advantages are obtained by using the Internet as a means to transact business? What are the disadvantages if you don't?

Doing business on the Internet requires an enterprise strategy. If you include the vendor–supplier chain, the strategy may require crossing divisional and enterprise boundaries. The primary business objective should not be to cut costs but rather to please customers so they will return on a continuing basis. Customer service (such as ease of use) is equally important as the product and its cost. The design of the Web business must continually enhance the entire purchasing experience for all the different customers.

All this information needs to be conveyed in the Internet business case, which should be updated with each iteration of the product. An iteration or enhancement to the product will not be as extensive as the initial Internet kick-off. The purpose at the onset is to determine the financial exposure to the corporation. Will the requirements cost more to implement than what the corporation (and partners) can see in potential revenue? This question of profitability should be asked at each stage of development. The business market changes so dramatically that a "go/no-go" decision is not uncommon. Decisions will be made to keep going with the development, to cut your losses and stop the effort, or to make changes and continue.

Scoping Requirements

From a requirements perspective, the business case needs to contain a *scope* section. This section defines the boundaries and potential features of the Internet product. Within this section, requirements should be listed under the following categories:

- *Who will be the customer base?* Include a description of the potential users or business partners who will interface with the B2B portion. If possible, estimate the number of customers and partners involved. Include a description of why they would be using or be involved with the Internet solution. Mention whether they are located in a concentrated area of the globe. For example, an Internet energy commodity market is mostly concentrated in Houston, Texas, U.S.A.
- *Who needs to be involved in the development process?* Include a description of the services they would provide to the effort and whether they are internal or external. If external, supply any costs for their involvement.
- *What information will be either captured or provided by the Internet-based application?* Itemize and describe a list of key business information, such as customer address and product offerings. Describe each of these in terms of the Internet product.
- *What do you need to move the development process to the next stage?* Include a development environment (hardware, software, space, and resources).
- *What functions will the Internet product perform?* Include a list of features that the product must have in order to be successful. Include some typical usage scenarios.

Each of the answers to the questions is a requirement. Some of the requirements relate to the product functionality, some pertain to expectations, and others relate to management of the project. The team assigned with the responsibility to develop the business case (primarily the business area championing the idea) develops the requirements. This team could include business personnel from other areas, financial personnel, and hopefully a requirements engineer. The requirements engineer will itemize the requirements as follows:

- Each requirement should be labeled with a unique identifier.
- Each requirement will have a definition to ensure a single interpretation.
- Each requirement will be defined as to a means to validate whether the requirement is satisfied.
- Each requirement will be prioritized.
- Each requirement will include any dependencies on other requirements.
- Each requirement will be identified as to any risks associated with implementing or not implementing the requirement, if known.
- Each requirement will be defined in terms of the benefits of implementation.
- Each requirement will be assigned a cost.
- Each requirement will be referenced to the initiating requirements set.
- Each requirement will be analyzed to determine the potential impacts on other applications, business policies, procedures, or the organization.
- Each requirement will be identified by its source.

Though these are high-level scoping requirements, they convey as much information as possible to the members of the executive committee so that they will be able to determine whether the Internet product is worth pursuing. Building a business plan for the Internet relies more on what it would cost the company if it does *not* go ahead with the product or even a specific requirement. It is a shift similar to the conversion of horse-drawn carriages to horseless (automobile) carriages! If your competitors are jumping to the Net, you may have to bite the bullet even with minimal (if any) returns on the investment.

The scoping requirements serve another purpose. These are the base requirements that define the scope of the product and the business community's scope. Once approved by the executive committee, these requirements will be *allocated* to the different corporate communities to evolve into their work products. All these work products have the same objective of supporting the development and implementation of a high-quality, successful Internet solution. Remember, a requirement is *a need to be satisfied*. A requirement can lead to creating nontechnological deliverables. Once approved for continual development, this small set of requirements becomes the base requirements. At this point the requirements are delegated or allocated[5] to the different divisions within each corporation involved for requirement evolution, and the formal requirements process begins.

The Requirements Process

The formal requirements process starts with the approval of the business concept and continues through the implemented solution using a standard set of repeatable activities. In the world of the Internet, the focus cannot be solely on software requirements for the business community sponsoring the idea. Software requirements impact other business communities; therefore, other considerations must be made. A void in the requirements process, whereby components are overlooked, may contribute to the documented 50 percent project failure rate of Internet solutions. To avoid falling into the failure category, it is important to follow a process that involves all business communities.

The approval of the business concept kicks off a *program*[6] *initiative.* Requirements are then allocated to different business communities, which evolve along with the project. Each business community initiates its own project and has its own project manager. All the project managers are "matrix-managed" to the program manager, who is responsible for coordinating the projects, initiating parallel efforts, and ensuring that all the projects meet the business objectives (as described in the approved business case).

A requirements engineer, who also reports to the program manager,[7] is responsible for delegating the requirements to the appropriate groups. The requirement delegation occurs multiple times until the primary group or individual has full responsibility for developing the requirement details (see Figure 2.4).

---

5. Allocation is sometimes referred to as "flowdown" in engineering circles. The term *allocation* is used to coincide with the Capability Maturity Model terminology.

6. A *program* is a major or master project that encompasses multiple projects. The Internet requires that work products be developed by multiple divisions of the company that are *not* all software related. Each of these work products is a component that is developed as its own project. All these projects must be coordinated through the master project or program.

7. The requirements engineer organization is discussed in more detail in Chapter Eight.

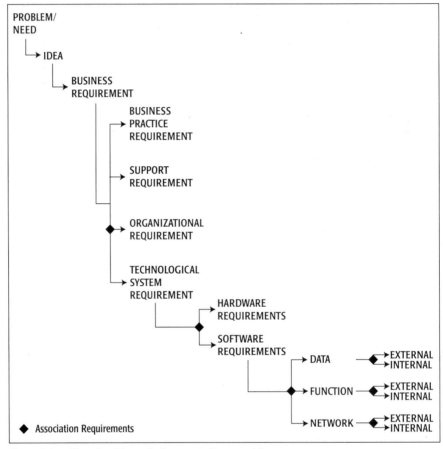

Figure 2.4   Allocation Through Corporate Communities

Allocation of Requirements

Allocation involves allocation levels: corporate, divisional, and so forth. These are common levels for any product that begins as a concept and ends as a finished product. Requirements evolve in two ways. The first is by assigning the responsibility to a requirement owner to provide the detail (allocation). The second is by providing the detail of the requirement in text and in representative models (requirement development).

There are four basic allocation levels:

1. *Corporate:* determines the level of involvement throughout the company
2. *Divisional:* determines the work products that need to be developed

3. *Architectural:* determines the pieces of the work products that need to be developed

4. *Product:* develops the pieces of the work products

Each of these levels is dependent upon the previous level to clarify the requirement as it pertains to the business community.[8] It is not until the lowest level (the product) that the details of the requirements are ultimately developed. The same initiating requirement from the base requirements set requires different business communities to develop their work products in order for the business objective to be met.

For example, a B2B initiative requires that Internet notification be picked up from a warehouse and delivered to a customer after an order is approved. Then the following corporate communities are allocated requirements, stemming from that base requirement:

- *Legal:* to develop a contract between the shipping and product companies
- *Software development:* to develop the application interface
- *Network planning:* to develop the router configuration to support the transfer of information, possibly incorporating it into the existing infrastructure
- *Billing application:* to update the application to initiate shipping after credit approval

Each of the preceding four (and many more) business communities needs to develop requirements in response to the initiating base requirement. They are notified of their responsibility through the allocation activity. The latter three are notified after the requirement is first allocated to the information technologists, who will determine the involvement of the software, hardware, and network groups as well as the different application groups. Once the requirement is allocated to IT, they rewrite the requirement to qualify the need in IT terms. Then, each of the communities (for this example, software, network planning, and billing application) refines the qualification for their specific areas of responsibility. It is important that no allocation level be missed. Skipping a level increases the risk of missed requirements, resulting in:

- Delayed projects
- Legal exposures

---

8. Size of a company is not impacted by allocation. All levels are still analyzed to determine the appropriate individual or group that will be held accountable for detailing the requirements for the work products.

- Missed business opportunities
- Parallel efforts to maintain the needed velocity of implementation

New requirements are identified as each group qualifies its requirement (see Figure 2.5). When this occurs, it is important to submit the new requirements back to the business requirement level to

- Identify the impact the requirement may have on other requirements
- Initiate the involvement of new business communities if necessary
- Determine whether the new original requirement was understood
- Determine whether the product is still financially feasible
- Prioritize the new requirement
- Reprioritize existing requirements as appropriate

Avoiding Politics

It is important that the appropriately qualified group or person develop the requirement. The group or person must have the knowledge to develop the essen-

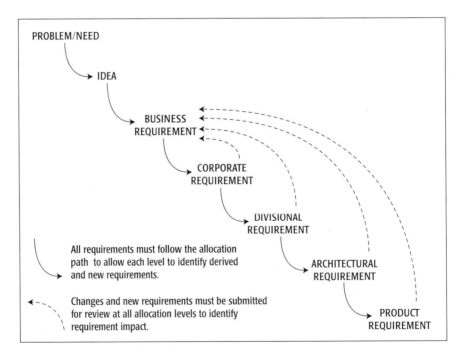

Figure 2.5   Requirement Allocation Process

tial details for the specific work product. The work products must all add value toward building a high-quality end product.

The requirements engineer is the "architect" of the requirements set. It is this person's responsibility to work with the business communities to determine the best group to evolve each specific requirement. Therefore, the requirements engineer must have a comprehensive understanding of the responsibilities of each business community. Both the business sponsor and the requirements engineer require the support of the executive sponsor to ensure that everyone understands his or her responsibilities and to resolve any conflicts between business communities.

What occurs in some organizations is *the avoidance of responsibility* or *the desire to be involved*.[9] Each of these can result in the faulty development of the requirements set. These two scenarios depict the need for an impartial requirements engineer who is supported by the executive sponsor (or executive champion) to minimize political positioning.

The less structured the organization, the greater chance the two scenarios could occur, especially if the executive sponsor takes a passive role. On the other hand, even with more bureaucratic organizations, similar scenarios can occur. The Internet requires new thinking and a change in process. A bureaucratic or extremely strict structure, simply by being too inflexible, may overlook opportunities for facilitating a speedier development process.

Determining which community should be allocated which specific requirement demands an understanding of both the requirements and the responsibilities of the business communities. This can be determined by asking questions in three categories (see Figure 2.6):

1. Reason for involvement
2. Responsibility for involvement
3. Actions for involvement

---

9. A group may be overworked on other projects and may try to avoid being pulled into a new project. If it is the best group to develop the requirement, then it should be allocated the requirement. The reverse can also occur. A group may want to be involved in the project and may make up reasons why it should be allocated the responsibility to develop specific requirements. Without the full understanding of each community's role and responsibilities, and without the support of executive management, the wrong people may develop or avoid developing key requirements.

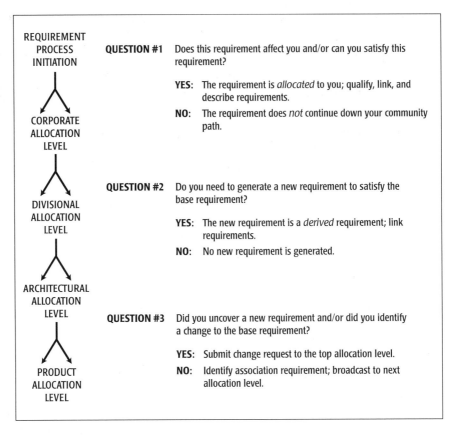

REQUIREMENT
PROCESS
INITIATION

QUESTION #1   Does this requirement affect you and/or can you satisfy this
requirement?

YES: The requirement is *allocated* to you; qualify, link, and
describe requirements.

NO: The requirement does *not* continue down your community
path.

CORPORATE
ALLOCATION
LEVEL

QUESTION #2   Do you need to generate a new requirement to satisfy the
base requirement?

YES: The new requirement is a *derived* requirement; link
requirements.

NO: No new requirement is generated.

DIVISIONAL
ALLOCATION
LEVEL

ARCHITECTURAL
ALLOCATION
LEVEL

QUESTION #3   Did you uncover a new requirement and/or did you identify
a change to the base requirement?

YES: Submit change request to the top allocation level.

NO: Identify association requirement; broadcast to next
allocation level.

PRODUCT
ALLOCATION
LEVEL

Figure 2.6   Community Involvement Determination

Reason for Involvement

The first category defines the reason for involvement. If the business community
can assist or is affected by the requirement, it is, frankly, involved. For example,
let's look at the initiating requirement that defined the concept to build an
Internet-based auction. The software development group must be involved to
develop the Internet-based solution. This group is affected by the requirement.
It is allocated the requirement to develop. Members of the legal department will
want involvement to develop the rules of the auction for participants. They
define how they can assist in reducing any legal risk to the corporation, satisfying a portion of the requirement because of the scope of their responsibility.
They too are allocated the same initiating requirement to develop their piece of
the Internet solution.

Each of the two communities, software development and legal, must evolve the requirement that has been allocated. The same requirement was allocated to each; however, they will produce different requirement details. The first step for each community is to *qualify* the requirement or, in other words, *restate* it in terms of the involvement of the specific business unit, thus creating new evolved requirements. These new requirements are linked to the originating requirement by *association requirements*, additional requirements that are identified in order to link the allocated specific requirements to the originating requirement concept and qualify their impact.

Responsibility for Involvement

The second category defines the scope of responsibility after a requirement is allocated to a community. The questions raised are to determine whether additional requirements need to be developed in order to satisfy the allocated requirement (using our example, requirements that the legal and software development groups need to develop in order to satisfy the specifics of the allocated requirement). The purpose of these *derived requirements* is to support the initiating requirement. They are linked to the qualified requirement. If the initiating requirement changes, group members will know from these linkages what else has to be considered to analyze the impact of the change.

Association requirements are further explained in the next chapter. For now, these are requirements that are needed to facilitate the work among communities. So, for the auction example, the legal group must come up with a statement that defines the terms to protect the business. This must be implemented as part of the auction site. For example, the legal group may require that before becoming an auction participant, a user must accept the legal contract.

Actions for Involvement

The third category refers to what to do if you uncover an additional requirement or if you need to change an existing requirement. When this occurs, it is important for the requirement to be reviewed from the business requirement level. The requirement will need to be approved for quality and for its impact on other requirements. If the impact is too great, the requirement may be rejected or postponed for another product release. The point is that by initiating the requirement allocation process from the business requirement level, you reduce the risk of missed requirements. By notifying those at the business level, a determination can be made as to the benefits toward the business objective. If beneficial, the requirement can be allocated to the corporate level to determine the impact at that level and so forth. Changes must be driven by business decisions and the impacts they will have on the project, product, business objectives, and business strategy.

This process can identify a great deal of requirements that need to be developed. A requirements management tool can be used to assist in linking and notifying reviewers at the different allocation levels.[10]

Why a Process?

Allocation is just one activity in the requirements process. It cannot work without the other process activities. In order for the program manager to be successful, a process needs to be defined and followed. A *process*, for the purpose of this discussion, is a *plan of action*. It states the expected deliverables, the activities, and who is involved in producing the deliverables (that is, roles, responsibilities, steps to follow). The requirements process and subprocess do not restrict how to achieve or accomplish the deliverables. The process is a means of communication among all team participants so they can plan their activities and coordinate deliverables. The process simply documents expectations by providing checklists for all the team participants to work toward.

In the heat of developing these deliverables, it is common to get caught up in the details of the day and to miss the business objective. Due to haste, checkpoints are often forgotten and mistakes are not caught before the final deliverable date. With a written process that all team participants understand and agree upon, the day-to-day activities can be aligned with the team's business expectations.

A process is not a list of how to perform the activities. A process is a contract among team participants on what will be delivered, the responsibilities of each group, and checkpoints where all can validate their filtered or narrow perceptions of the business objective.

The contents of a process are essentially the activities that are to be performed. For the requirements process, the main activity is allocation of responsibility among the different business communities and their respective subcommunities. The responsibilities should be detailed in a complete, concise, correct, and clear manner. As each responsibility is delegated to the appropriate person or group, an

---

10. Refer to Chapter Seven.

audit trail forms that includes the allocation path, the processing of requirements, and the linking of the requirements to the business objective. Through each allocation level, more requirements are captured, defined, and refined to a level of abstraction that can be implemented into the final product. Through the process and subprocess, specific deliverables are produced in a high-quality manner. Before leaving an allocation level, gates are defined in the process as to what is the expected output or deliverable. The process defines the responsibilities of those who create the deliverables as well as those who review the deliverables and those who receive the deliverables. It is a cyclical movement of responsibilities, deliverables, and processes (see Figure 2.5). If information needs to be corrected or updated during a review of the product, it is done prior to moving to the next stage.

This high-level process may remind you of a "waterfall," where one product cannot be developed until another is complete. Many deliverables are developed through this process, many at the same time. Some are passing through the quality gate to the next perspective faster than others. One deliverable does not necessarily wait for the other. However, a change in one deliverable may impact one that has already passed through the gate. In this instance, the previously approved deliverable will be updated. This is why the gate is so important: it is a means of communication between the different pieces of the Internet product that are developed simultaneously. For example, a gate to review the software requirements can be reviewed by those developing the advertising campaign. The legal department can view the designed "features"[11] of the product to see if there are any compliance issues with domestic and international law. Additionally, changes in the marketplace, which inevitably occur, can be handled before a faulty product is implemented.

---

11. As an Internet program progresses, additional features that were not part of the requirements set inevitably creep into the product. Some of these new features or enhancements to the requirements, as seen by the designer or developer of the feature, may be requirements that do add value and were not elicited earlier in the process. It is important to identify these "features" before implementation. These "features," though they may seem a good idea by the designer or developer, may actually be too costly to implement (reducing the return on investment) or may be illegal. New "features" must follow a review process, as with any requirement, as early in the process as possible. They should *never* be a surprise that has been implemented in the final solution without the approval of the validators and reviewers.

Requirements Process Scenario

Let's take a look at the requirement allocation process in greater detail. With an Internet requirements process, the requirements are allocated, analyzed, and written down. All requirements are identified to encompass a complete requirements set. The quality of each requirement is validated for correctness and completeness, ensuring no conflicts between them. The requirements are then managed through other work products by all departments involved to ensure conformity. The result is that the developer builds what the business needs. The initiative should be satisfied, producing a positive return on investment (something valuable even for not-for-profit organizations).

The downward solid arrows in Figure 2.5 document the formal process. The upward dashed arrows illustrate that if a change or new requirement is identified further into the process, the requirement is reevaluated at the business allocation level. The benefit is that every business community is informed of new requirements that could impact existing requirements or work products or necessitate the development of new requirements.

The other extreme of what typically has been occurring with Internet development is that the requirements are communicated verbally with no checks and balances in place (that is, no intermediary quality control gates). The team members want to hurry through the requirements process so that they can start designing a solution. In this scenario, if the solution is what the business needs, it is the result of sheer luck! In most cases, the initiative does not satisfy business needs and results in a negative return on investment. Iteration after iteration of producing negative returns on investment will result in the organization going out of business or being shut down by the sponsors—the "dot-com" going the way of the "dot-gone"!

In an alternate scenario, if one misses or skips allocation levels (or captures requirements only verbally) and immediately illustrates a solution in terms of design components at the architectural level, the requirements that would have been elicited from other corporate and divisional communities are missed. This bypasses the valuable validation gates that the corporate and divisional communities could have captured before design was begun. The cost of repairing a product after design is thus much more expensive than if all requirements had been sufficiently captured early in the process. [12]

---

12. Some of the repairs may be on non-software-related work products. The allocation checkpoints facilitate review for conflicts between *all* requirements.

These two scenarios are extremes. Most software development shops fall somewhere in between. Unfortunately, the pressures of being first to market have resulted in a requirements process closer to the second scenario than the first. Unfortunately, if a corporation's requirements process is closer to the second scenario, the Internet product will probably not be delivered on time, will cost much more than anticipated, and has a good chance of being cancelled before completion. If you are lucky to get the first iteration online, chances are you will have an errors and omissions requirements list for the next iteration that will keep you busy for years. Remember, Internet-based products require a minimum monthly[13] update to keep customers returning to the site. The bottom line: if the Internet requirements process is closer to the second ad hoc scenario, the business will most likely not satisfy its needs! Requirements have a better chance of being high quality if a requirements process is documented and followed by all team participants.

The Correlation between Allocation Level and Perspective

An allocation level may or may not have a work product deliverable. A perspective, on the other hand, does. Approval may not occur at every allocation level. An approval activity is essential at the end of each perspective to ensure the quality of the Internet product. Each perspective consists of a set of activities that form the requirements subprocess; the process (in terms of function) is the same for each perspective. However, the specific contents of the work products vary by perspective, business community, and requirement focus.

Requirements Evolving through Perspectives

As discussed earlier, the requirements process begins with the approval of the business case that includes the scope requirements of the business communities (that is, a list of requirements pertaining to the product to be produced).

In this chapter I took a detour from the evolving requirements to talk about allocation, or how the business communities must interpret the scope requirements. Each community must qualify the initiating requirements to determine what its involvement will be. Each business community then begins to develop

---

13. Some sites require new features to be added more frequently. Content may actually need to be updated within minutes (such as news sites, for example, www.msnbc.com and www.yahoo.com).

its own list of requirements that need to be satisfied in order to meet the business objective, the same objective that was described in the approved business case.

Here, then, lies the beginning of the requirements set as it is organized in the requirements set framework (see Figure 2.3). Once the requirements have been allocated to the correct group or person, the requirements process begins to evolve in detail and level of abstraction. More information is provided as each requirement detail is captured and formulated into a level of abstraction for the perspective of the specific audience.

This is the first perspective: the organizational or business community scope level. The legal group has its own scope requirements, as do accounting, marketing, customer service, and so forth. Each of the business communities evolves the requirements. These are high-level scoping requirements documented with a planner's perspective, a list complete with:

- An identifier
- A description
- A priority
- An owner
- A means to validate compliance when implemented
- Any association or dependency with other requirements
- Any linkage to allocation requirements of a previous perspective
- The source

The remaining perspectives are discussed in detail in the next chapter. For now, understand that each perspective has a purpose in what the requirements are to convey. Each perspective has multiple audiences to whom the information should be conveyed. One is the supplier of the requirement information; the second is the user of the requirement information. No matter what perspective, the requirements should have the information shown in the preceding list.

The Requirements Subprocess

Generally speaking, the activities for the requirements subprocess are the same for each community, perspective, and focus. The requirements subprocess (see Figures 2.7 and 2.8) occurs for each of the final allocation levels. The perspective for the allocation level refines the requirement into finer detail to be implemented in the organization, service, or product. Different people are involved

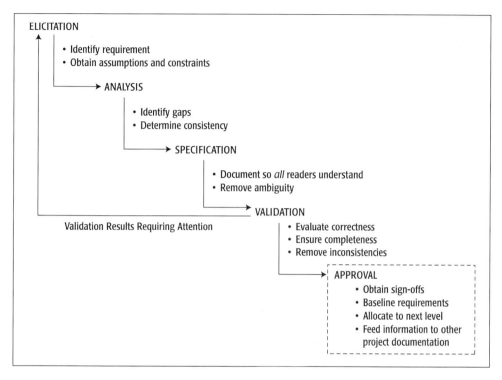

Figure 2.7   The Requirements Subprocess (*Source:* The *Capability Maturity Model* by Mark C. Paulk et al. [in "The Shuttle Project Requirement Process," Figure 6-6.])

during each activity of the requirements subprocess (see Table 2.2), each of whom has specific responsibilities.[14]

Elicitation is the process of identifying the needs of the product to be built. This process occurs at every perspective level. Each perspective level provides additional details that may also identify the need for additional requirements.

---

14. Roles and responsibilities during the requirements process are discussed in more detail in Chapter Eight. For the purpose of this discussion, the requirements engineer facilitates the capturing of requirements, the requirement supplier defines and validates the need, the requirement user takes the requirements to build his or her work products, and the executive committee approves the requirements for inclusion in the product according to the business strategy and objectives. In start-up organizations, the same person may play multiple roles. In large brick-and-mortar companies, each role may be represented by multiple individuals.

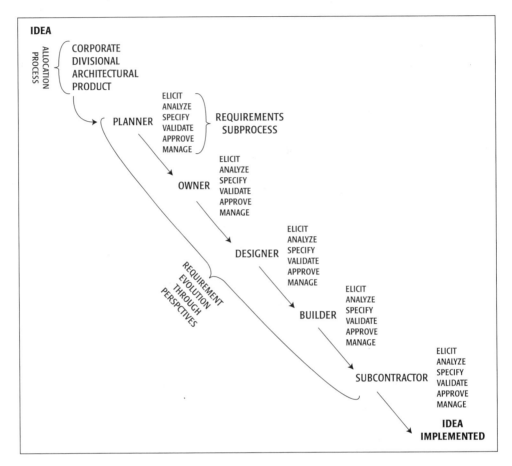

Figure 2.8   Process/Allocation/Perspective/Subprocess

If you are at the idea level, the requirement supplier needs to capture all the information that will support the idea. This can be accomplished through competitive analysis, articles, e-mails, and letters—anything that helps explain the idea. At any of the other levels, the input is approved requirements specification from the previous allocation level (that is, that you have passed the review and approval at the previous quality gate).

At the idea level, the output is the part of the business objective that describes the concepts of the Internet application. At the business requirement level, the owner of the concept develops a list of requirements that defines the scope of the effort. The output would be the business case. The requirements at this level are the initiating requirements. All other requirements will be devel-

Table 2.2   Roles and Responsibilities for the Requirements Subprocess

Activity	Description	Responsible Role
Elicitation	The tasks associated with obtaining the initial set of requirements or requirement detail	• Requirements engineer (coordinate, produce) • Requirement supplier (provides)
Analysis	The tasks associated with reviewing the requirements to uncover additional requirements or requirement gaps or inconsistencies	• Requirements engineer (produce) • Requirement supplier (assist)
Specification	The tasks associated with documenting the requirements in a standard format	• Requirements engineer (produce) • Requirement supplier (assist)
Validation	The tasks associated with the formal review of quality for each requirement	• Requirements engineer (coordinate) • Requirement supplier (review, validate) • Requirement user (review, validate) • Requirement supporter (review)
Approval	The tasks associated with approving the impact of the requirements set on the corporation	• Requirement supplier (approve) • Requirement user (approve) • Executive committee (approve)
Management	The tasks associated with placing the requirements set as a requirement package under configuration management	• Configuration management manager (promote, monitor, provide status)

oped to support the satisfaction of this initial set of requirements that have been approved by the executive committee.

At the corporate level, each community describes the scope of its involvement in the Internet product. This is the beginning of the evolution of the individual requirements. The scope requirements are the initiating requirements, the ones that all other communities must support. The idea translates to the clearly defined business objective.

Requirements can be captured from multiple sources. A sampling would include

- Existing documentation
- Individual or group interviews
- Observations of the business process

With many Internet products, the requirement supplier base is globally located. E-mail has become a popular way to capture requirements through a geographically diverse interview process. It is a means for elicitation of ideas on a global level whereby ideas can be researched inexpensively before responding to the comments. Participants, if they get pulled away, still can participate when local issues are resolved. Not all participants have to take part at the same time. They can review the requirements, questions, and such when they are available if they are using e-mail. Additionally, e-mails are a good source for ideas because they can be forwarded easily to the person or group most qualified to further research the suggestion. When responding to interviewees, requirements engineers should make e-mails brief, using good grammar and sentence structure to discuss one topic only. A maximum of five to seven[15] questions should be addressed per e-mail. Anything longer than one screen may tempt the reader to store the question(s) for review later (which may never happen).

Other more common techniques[16] for capturing requirements are

- Prototypes
- Storyboards
- Videos
- Facilitation with an experienced facilitator

These techniques help flesh out requirements. Each individual who participates provides his or her own viewpoint on the business objective. Different viewpoints add information to the requirements set and assist in developing high-quality requirements.

Requirements Analysis

The analysis of requirements is necessary for understanding what you have heard and putting it in context, for looking at your notes to obtain an understanding of how the requirements are related and how they are not. It is impor-

---

15. It has been my experience that it is better to send multiple e-mails containing a maximum of three questions to get faster results rather than longer e-mails containing five to seven questions.

16. Techniques for requirements elicitation are numerous and are not included in this book.

tant to organize and clarify the requirements to arrive at a refined definition of the requirements.

The input to this activity is the requirements that were elicited. You may have developed meeting minutes to verify that what you heard was correct. The difference is that this activity *studies* what you heard. The requirements engineer may begin to develop models from the requirements to identify any conflicts or gaps between them. These models are reviewed with the requirement suppliers and are to be documented with:

- A notation legend
- An explanation of the purpose of the model
- An explanation of how to read the model
- A description of what to look for when reviewing the model

A model is a tool that should be organized in a format that is easy for all reviewers to follow. It is not the actual specification, however. All diagrams and models should contain a textual description of the requirements, the next activity in the requirements subprocess.

Specification

So far this book has covered two important points: (1) that a requirement is a need to be satisfied and (2) that a requirement evolves from a concept or idea to an implemented work product. These two concepts require a third concept to be accepted, namely that *it is important to document every requirement*! This does not imply that requirements are documented in the source code. Rather, requirements should be documented so that multiple people (including non-technical individuals and testers) can read the requirements, understand them, validate them, and determine whether they are impacted by them.

The development of a requirements specification is for the purpose of clearly and precisely recording each of the requirements for the product. The document should consist of a standard document structure (see Appendix A). Whatever template is used, it should satisfy the following criteria:

- Contains a table of contents
- References sources of information
- Uniquely identifies the individual requirement
- Is easy for reviewers to access and review with comments captured easily

- Is easy to change
- Has a section that explains terms and acronyms
- Uses language that is simple, consistent, and concise
- Defines the validation checklists
- States the process for conflict resolution

Some of the information may be defined in the requirement validation process or through the configuration management process. Where a requirement is documented is not as important as that it *is* documented—and that the project team understands and abides by the process. What is most important is that the specification is readable by all reviewers (requirement users, executive committee, and requirement suppliers).

Validation

Elicitation, analysis, and specification activities work in a continuous cycle. The requirements engineer asks questions, listens to the answers, and records the information in some fashion. He looks at the answers and the way they have been specified and notices gaps in knowledge. He then goes back to the requirement supplier to ask more specific questions, listens to those answers, writes down the information in some fashion, and again notices gaps in knowledge. This is a continuous cycle. The objective is to know when you have enough information to proceed to a formal review of the requirements. The requirements engineer does not want to have large holes in understanding nor get caught in "analysis paralysis" (that is, never being ready for a formal review and never turning the information over to the next step).

The next chapter discusses a pattern of requirements information, the basic premise of the book. The pattern is a framework to hold all the different types of requirements that are captured at every perspective. Each perspective, as described here and in the next chapter, has an objective to meet. The level of experience that the requirements engineer has determines when validation occurs. For instance, a trainee may initiate the validation too early. A junior-level requirements engineer, feeling burned once and twice shy, may fall into the trap of waiting until the specification is perfect.

The requirements set is rarely completed to perfection. New requirements will be identified along the way that will have an impact on the work that has already been accomplished. This is why with Internet solutions one has multiple iterations. Requirements captured late in the process may be delayed until the next iteration. This is also why validation checkpoints should occur at every perspective. It enables you to change interdependent requirements or make a decision to postpone a change until another iteration. The validation process looks for large gaps in knowledge that could reduce the risk of success with the implementation of the iteration. The objective of the requirements pattern is to be able to spot these major gaps in knowledge. Although the pattern organizes the requirements, it does not validate the contents. The validation process, rather, reviews the individual requirements to see if they meet the quality characteristics. Individual requirements must be complete, correct, concise, and clear. They must not conflict with other requirements. This is such an important topic that a later chapter is dedicated to the quality of individual requirements and the quality of the requirements set.

To summarize, the validation process looks at the requirements set both as a set and as individual requirements. To accomplish this, the requirements set for the perspective must be distributed for all to review informally as well as formally. Reviewers will vary depending upon the stage of the requirement evolution. They also could vary by the specific requirement. The names of the reviewers should be established at either the beginning of the project or at the beginning of the perspective. Generically, the reviewers of the requirements are those who:[17]

- *Supplied the requirements (requirement suppliers),* to determine if what they meant to say was conveyed correctly and specified correctly.
- *Need to work from the requirements information (requirement users),* to determine if they have the same understanding as the rest of the team. They will document any concerns related to feasibility.
- *Specialize in quality control (requirement supporters),* to determine if the individual requirement satisfies the quality characteristics. They determine the quality of the requirements set to ensure it contains no gaps in knowledge or inconsistencies.
- *Specified the requirements for another perspective or business community (requirements engineers),* to uncover any potential changes to their piece of the requirements set as well as any conflicts between the requirements being reviewed against the ones they developed.

---

17. It is a good practice to allow everyone, whether or not they are part of the project or program, to view requirements. This educates people who later may become part of the team and provides a source of training for future projects.

Each allocated area (which could be down to the product level on the allocation chain) develops its work product at its own pace, some requiring outside assistance (market research) that could delay the final implementation. This should not, however, delay the progress of other work products. The requirements engineers in charge of developing requirements for other areas should be reviewers of other related requirement work products. With their involvement, they can, as stated previously, look at the requirements set for potential conflicts with their requirements subset.

The output of this stage is either approval or rejection of the requirements. Approvals are requirements that meet the quality characteristics. Conditional approvals may be defined that include a list of required changes or enhancements to specific requirements and additional information to develop requirements for specific gaps that were identified. A decision is made determining whether the entire requirements set must be revalidated after the changes and enhancements are made.

This approval, the output of the validation activity, is only the approval of the accuracy and contents of the requirements set. For every project, but especially for Internet products, it is important to have another, final approval. In this final approval activity, the executive committee determines the current condition of the project, the cost to develop the requirements, and any other potential risks or issues that may have been uncovered during the previous development stage. As the executive approval activity takes place, work can begin on the next stage of evolution, with the understanding that the executive decision can change the direction or end the program at any time.

Approval as a Separate Activity

This executive approval is the process of obtaining concordance of the requirements set and what shall be perused for the next stage. Why is this a separate activity? In one simple word—risk! The requirements set may be validated as being correct, concise, complete, and clear. However, it is important from a program standpoint to review the requirements as far as resources. This is a checkpoint to determine whether it is cost-effective to continue with the entire requirements set or to partition the requirements and implement only a portion (if at all). Approval is the executive review of the requirements set with a time and material focus.

To prepare for the final approval, the executives for each area must look at any risks associated with any of the requirements. Risks can include delayed delivery (due to a better understanding of the Internet details), too much expense to produce (network charges) given the potential revenue, and so forth. It is important for the executive sponsor of the Internet application to provide additional adjustments to the business case based on the better understanding of the requirements.

This additional activity, approval, must occur at the end of each perspective. This provides a checkpoint at the most efficient financial decision point to make changes to the program. It provides an opportunity to negotiate what will be part of which iteration (based upon each requirement's priority) given the time frame in which the next iteration is due.

Quality Gate Checkpoints[18]

To obtain a high-quality requirements set, several gates are used that provide checkpoints to verify accuracy, clarity, consistency, and completeness of the set. All work products, at each checkpoint, are compared to each other across business communities for correctness, consistency, and completeness. Each requirement must evolve through each gate to be implemented in the final business solution.

Between each gate (see Figure 2.9) is a requirements subprocess that is more commonly known and accepted in the software community. The subprocess elicits information and prepares it through the next evolutionary stage of requirements development. Each requirement developed through the requirements subprocess should encompass the individual quality characteristics to assist in improving the product's return on investment.

Managing the Requirements and the Requirements Set

Once the requirements are approved, they should be baselined (see Chapter Seven for detailed discussion). All changes to the baseline require approval and should be evaluated as to their impact on other work products, including resources and

---

18. Quality is such an important topic that it is discussed in detail in Chapter Six.

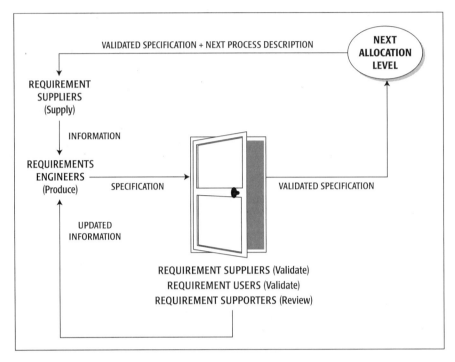

VALIDATED SPECIFICATION + NEXT PROCESS DESCRIPTION

NEXT
ALLOCATION
LEVEL

REQUIREMENT
SUPPLIERS
(Supply)

INFORMATION

REQUIREMENTS
ENGINEERS
(Produce)   SPECIFICATION

VALIDATED SPECIFICATION

UPDATED
INFORMATION

REQUIREMENT SUPPLIERS (Validate)
REQUIREMENT USERS (Validate)
REQUIREMENT SUPPORTERS (Review)

Figure 2.9   Process/Quality Gate

schedule (time and cost). Configuration management of requirements is a comprehensive topic that requires a chapter unto itself (see Chapter Seven). For the purposes of this chapter, understand that this is another activity that is part of the requirements subprocess. As with the other activities, it occurs at each perspective.

The Subprocess Is a Generic Process

The requirements subprocess of elicitation, analysis, specification, validation, approval, and management occurs at the end of the perspectives. Through the perspectives, the requirements are captured and evolved through the creation of several work products. The objective of each work product is to build a high-quality Internet solution that will provide the utmost return on investment to the business (for all corporations involved).

Throughout the preceding discussion of the requirements subprocess, no reference was made to specific technology methods such as structured diagrams, data models, object models, use cases, and so forth. This is because the requirements subprocess is generic. It describes activities that should take place to deliver a work product. It does not say how to develop the work products. Technology methods come and go. Technologists are extremely opinionated as to which method is better than the next. As far as the *process* is concerned, it doesn't matter! Use whatever approach you prefer. Just make sure that you capture *all* the requirements. Specify them in a format that is easy to read and expresses one interpretation. Ensure that the individual requirements are specified so that they satisfy all the quality characteristics. Make sure that you obtain approvals (requirement quality and business risk) at each stage of evolution of the requirements set.

Reuse of Requirements

Requirements can be reused for different iterations of the same product or for different products. To facilitate requirement reuse, follow a requirements process and subprocess of good quality. Write the requirements in a manner that meets all the quality characteristics. Keep the requirements in a requirements management tool to facilitate the multiple uses for the requirement.

Reuse evaluation occurs at every perspective. During the analysis, the requirements engineer should review existing requirements by searching a requirements management tool for similar requirements. The requirements should be reviewed with the requirement suppliers to validate that they could be reused. Some may be reused with a qualifier. Depending on the tool, the requirement may need to be rewritten as a separate requirement incorporating the qualifier. A note should be made with the requirement that it is based upon the previous requirement. This way, if a change is made to the new requirement, it can be tracked to see if the change should also occur to the original "reused" requirement. Some tools allow linkages with a space for inputting the qualifier.

Conclusion

In summary, Internet-based products require the involvement of all the business communities in a corporation—and sometimes multiple communities of different corporations. Each of the communities must understand the initial idea and the business objective. The success of Internet products depends on the requirements engineer accepting that he must capture more than just software requirements. The evolution of the requirements requires a lead requirements engineer to act as an "architect." The requirements architect allocates the responsibility to develop each requirement. The same requirement may be allocated to different groups. A requirement is allocated multiple times until it is delegated to the appropriate persons or groups within each business community responsible for developing the requirement into a specific work product required to implement the Internet solution.

Each work product is necessary to build a high-quality Internet product. All work products must be validated for accuracy, consistency conflicts, and adherence to the business objective.

CHAPTER THREE

The Requirements Set

Chapter Key Topics
- **Requirement categories**
- **Requirement organization**
- **Organization benefits**

The Internet Impact

The Internet opens doors for many new business opportunities. Each business community from one or multiple corporations is involved in producing a successful product through this medium. The implementation of an Internet solution involves capturing requirements from all the business communities. Organization of the requirements assists in identifying gaps and conflicts sooner in the process, when the cost of change is less.

This chapter introduces a *requirements set framework* that organizes individual requirements into specific categories. The purpose of this organization is to assist in the validation of requirement coverage for the problem domain, in this case, the Internet product. By arranging requirements in an organized fashion, gaps in knowledge and inconsistencies can be identified more readily and corrected earlier in the process. Organizing the requirements set according to the framework increases the speed with which products can be developed because its structure works with the evolutionary process and promotes parallelism.

While discussing the evolution of the requirements, different types of requirements emerged (see Figure 3.1). These are:

- **Initiating requirements:** requirements that clarify the concept as it pertains to the business objective. These are typically the requirements identified by the sponsor of the business idea in the business case.
- **Primary requirements:** business requirements that need to be satisfied in order to fulfill the concept. These are the requirements that each business community has identified as its scope in order to satisfy the business objective.
- **Derived requirements:** requirements that need to be satisfied in order to satisfy the primary requirements. Derived requirements come in two types:
  1. *Supporting:* requirements that have been allocated to a specific category because of their ability to supply essential details.
  2. *Association:* requirements that have been written to support other requirements in a different category of the requirements set.

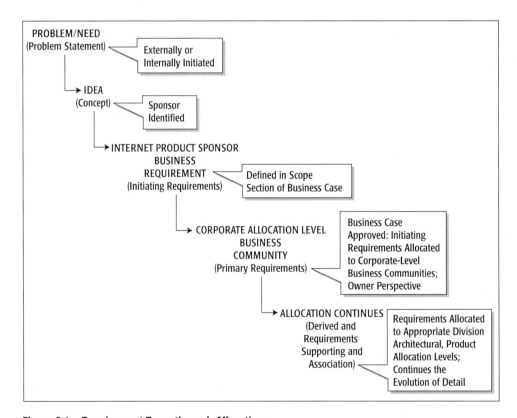

Figure 3.1   Requirement Types through Allocation

All of these types of requirements can be categorized and organized within the requirements set framework. All of them need the same components to create a high-quality requirement: identifier, description, priority, validation criteria, source, and so forth. The requirements set framework does not enforce the individual quality rules; it only categorizes the individual requirements of the requirements set into a specific organization. The category, and not the type of requirement, defines its placement in the requirements set framework.

Requirement Categories

A *requirement category* is the subject matter of the requirement. It takes three dimensions to properly categorize each individual requirement. These dimensions clarify the special interest of the subject matter and refer to the type of questions that need to be answered in order to define the specific needs for the category. These questions, when applied to the requirements set framework, create the requirements pattern.

The three dimensions are

1. *Community:* corporate function
2. *Perspective:* level of detail
3. *Focus:* specialized view

A specific requirement is categorized before placing it into the requirements set framework (see Figure 3.2). The figure identifies a fourth category, *association.* This additional category is required to meld, link, or associate the different subject matter requirements together. To avoid confusion, this fundamental discussion appears later in the chapter. For now, let's review the different dimensions in closer detail.

Requirement Community

During the requirements process, each requirement is assigned (allocated) to different organizational areas that develop the requirement in order to satisfy the business objective. These different business communities correlate to the allocation process discussed in the previous chapter. The business objective of an Internet product is to develop a B2B product that will have the scope delivered to each of the business organizations. Each organization will identify a list of primary requirements to be incorporated into its own specific deliverables.

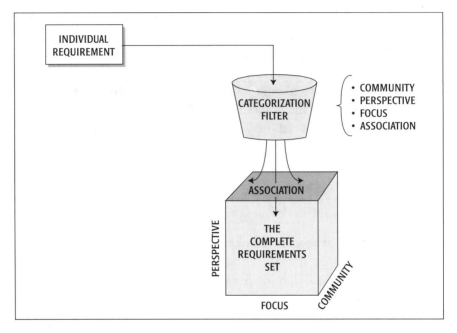

Figure 3.2   Requirement Categorization

The communities are separated into four business areas (see Figure 3.3). Each of these areas can be subdivided into finer organizational communities. The four main corporate or business community areas are:

1. *Business practice:* organizational divisions directly associated with the businesses that relate directly to the business objective. These include business areas such as product development, marketing, and customer service. For e-business, there may be multiple product objectives, one for each business in the B2B connection. In this scenario, a single goal for the product will have specific business objectives that correlate specifically to the company's purpose.

   For example (see Figure 3.4), a book retailer has a B2B link with a shipping company. Each of these companies has its own product that is distinguished from the other company's product. Each has a common product objective of streamlining the product order to the logistics of shipment. Each company has a business project with different corporate objectives but the same product objective. Each of these companies will have to develop

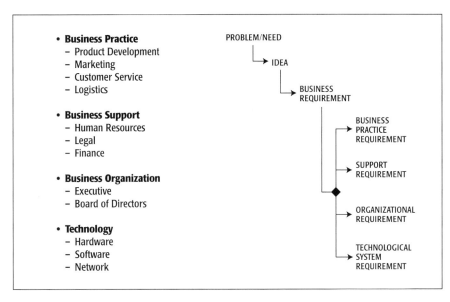

Figure 3.3   Requirement Community Category

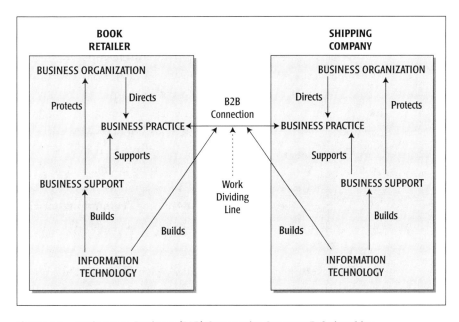

Figure 3.4   Business-to-Business (B2B) Community Category Relationships

and manage *business practice community requirements.* And, finally, each of the companies has its own requirements set. The links (association) between the requirements are additional requirements defined by both organizational communities. This will enable them to identify the impact of a change instituted by one corporation on the other.

2. *Business support:* organizational divisions that support the running of the organization. These include human resources, finance, and legal. Their objective is to support the project by identifying requirements that need satisfying to meet the Internet product objectives. In a B2B scenario, the business support areas support their own company's interest. No cross-company correlation is necessary.

3. *Business organization:* divisions that dictate direction and business objectives, including the executive committee and the board of directors. Their objective is to support the Internet project by identifying requirements that need satisfying to meet the product objectives. As with business support, in a B2B scenario, the business organization areas support their own company's interest. They are instrumental in developing the vision for forming the relationship between B2B companies. It may be necessary to correlate these requirements across corporate requirements sets if one company requirement is dependent on the other.

4. *Technology:* divisions that relate only to the technological aspects of supporting the business objective. This does not include systems that developed as products to be sold. For example, Microsoft applications are products developed under the community business practice. These are external technology products. The sales-tracking systems, however, fall under the technology community. These are internal technology products. In a B2B situation, they are not only working to connect with different systems within their corporate boundaries but also are responsible for working jointly with other companies to develop the connection to the B2B company. A requirement could be dependent upon another requirement being satisfied by another company. The technology community may also need to develop derived requirements that will support the other company's primary requirements.

Just to make things more complicated, each of the first three communities receives requests to build technology products (external or internal). In fact, so too will the technology area (for example, system software/hardware upgrades). Each request needs to satisfy the needs of one, two, three, or all four of the communities.

Here, then, lies the definition of community. *Community* segments the types of deliverables according to business organization. Each deliverable is specific to meeting the needs of the business community. The needs (that is, requirements) will continue to evolve and be allocated further into the community (corporate to division to architectural to product levels) to build the deliverable for the business community. The evolutionary state within the business community can be correlated to perspective, discussed next.

Requirement Perspective

Perspective relates to the evolution of the Internet product from idea to the implemented solution. Throughout the evolution of requirements, they will be further refined and specific details will be provided to enable the building of the solution. Through each step, a level of extraction takes place that eventually leads to the specific parts of the whole Internet product. A separate deliverable is produced for each perspective. Each deliverable takes a step toward building the product. Skipping an evolutionary step may provide a solution, but the solution will be flawed due to the missing detail or missing requirement. The solution will probably be delayed due to the need to go back and get the detail or requirement that should have been obtained earlier in the process. The final product is built but on incorrect information.

The idea phase (that is, *initiating requirement*) identifies the business community that has the primary interest in the product. The idea is then allocated to each community to develop the initial set of primary requirements (*scoping* and *business requirements*). Each community has its own perspective. Each perspective evolves the community's requirements through its specific allocation levels, developing essential details to the requirements and developing additional requirements (*derived requirements*) that are needed to support the idea. Different individuals are responsible for developing the requirements for the community and perspective. Each of these individuals has a specific point of view as to the categories of requirements that need to be captured. This specific point of view relates to the third requirements set category: requirement focus.

Requirement Focus

Focus looks at each perspective for the community from an abstract view of the product to be developed. For example, with respect to information systems, the focus would be the type of system component: interfaces, data, process, network, timing, rules, and constraints. The role of a specific community is to be responsible for creating an end deliverable. Through the evolution of requirements, the role has a specific, tailored view of the overall business idea. The person responsible for that focus develops a slice of the product that evolves through the same perspectives for the community as any other view.

For data focus,[1] the list of entities evolves into an entity relationship. This high-level data model evolves into a fully attributed business model. This model is customized for the technical architecture which, in turn, is transformed into a data language that runs in production.

Relationships between Categories

To recap, *community* refers to the business unit, *perspective* relates to the level of abstract detail for the community, and *focus* pertains to the point of view of the community and perspective. The combination of community, perspective, and focus defines the *category*. The category is represented by a *cell* in the *framework*. Following a requirements process (and subprocess) fills the framework. To assist in filling the framework, the *requirements pattern* has questions that are tailored to the subject matter for each cell or category.

Requirement Organization

The development of any Internet-based application requires the development of different work products that stem from the idea. Each of these work products is needed to build a high-quality Internet-based application. Each of these individual work products follows a process similar to a manufacturing process described in the previous chapter. Community, perspective, and focus are dimensions of the organization, which when working together will develop one or more of these work products.

This process is no different from any other manufacturing process. The perspective is the evolution of any product. The development of any product requires different roles for building each piece of the product. To explain the

---

1. This is for illustrative purposes only. The requirements set framework holds requirements. How the requirements are captured, analyzed, and specified is independent of method or technique.

finer details of the framework and the association between categories, the example of building a house is used below.[2]

A Quality Home

When a house is being built, the idea (or architectural plan) evolves through perspectives (levels of abstraction from the concept) to produce a deliverable (the home). Each different perspective refines the details until the house is built. Each perspective is paired with a specific individual (or contractor) to build a deliverable that assists in creating the final product (see Table 3.1). The deliverable is built according to the perspective of the responsible individual. Each of these phases evolves from the information gathered and analyzed from the previous phase. Each phase has the perspective of another individual role. Figure 3.5 shows those involved in developing a home. Each individual with his own focus evolves deliverables (work products) through the different perspectives.

Skipping a perspective in building the home increases the risk of building a faulty home. No one would want to live in a home they knew had skipped a

Table 3.1   Manufacturing a Home

Manufacturing Phase	Architectural Output	Perspective
The birth of an idea	A ballpark view of how big, how many rooms, etc.; documents the scope	Planner
Analyzing the feasibility	A small model depicting and confirming understanding; provides the vision and funding	Owner
Designing the product	A detailed design of what is to be built; specifies the physical design	Designer
Developing the product	The specifications of how to build it; constructs the physical product	Builder
Assembling and testing the product	The individual components; provides the components	Subcontractor
Implementing the product	The house; utilizes the end product	User

2. For the purposes of this discussion, only the phases up to the first implementation are discussed. Each iteration of an Internet-based application evolves similarly.

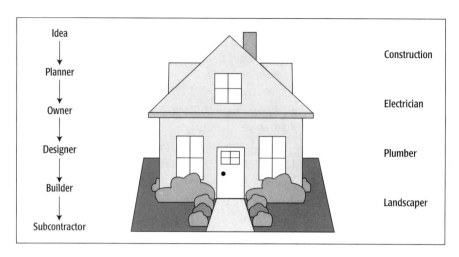

Figure 3.5   Perspectives and Focus Areas for Building a Quality Home

phase of this process. Instead, inspectors are available at each phase (perspective) to spot possible defects and correct them early in the process (quality gate). The cost of correction after implementation, if possible at all, is too risky and expensive. To further reduce the cost of building a home, specifications or any of the deliverables from each phase can be reused or expanded upon to build other homes.[3] This is only doable if the deliverable passed quality inspections for the original product.

The House That Zachman Built

In 1987 while working for IBM, John A. Zachman published a framework for discussing information systems architecture.[4] He described the analogy between the software development process and the construction and manufacturing processes. This architecture is the basis of the requirements set framework. To understand the requirements set framework, it is important to understand John Zachman's architecture.

---

3. One of the unique characteristics of Former President James Carter's Houses for Humanity program (under Habitat for Humanity) is the reuse of standard plans. Each house is built from the same plan following the same process. Each reuse of the specification reduces the cost without sacrificing the quality of each house.
4. See Zachman 1987.

Zachman illustrated how the process, deliverables, perspective, and focus are conceptually the same. The process can also conceptually be the same for different business communities (for example, legal, human resources, and shipping). For simplicity, we will focus on software products for this example. The output of software development deliverables correlates to architectural output (see Table 3.2). The table documents the evolution of the software detail and how it is a process similar to construction and manufacturing.

Different Perspectives for Either Process

The roles involved in building a home (see Table 3.3) identify the need for different perspectives. Each individual has a responsibility to concentrate on his particular perspective to ensure the building of a quality end product. As the evolution of the idea to final product occurs, different phases are followed through the different perspectives. Perspectives reflect the areas of responsibility of each role. For example, a designer's perspective is quite different from the owner's perspective;

Table 3.2 Software Development Deliverables Compared with Architectural Output

Manufacturing Phase	Architectural Output	Information Technology Output
The birth of an idea	A ballpark view of how big, how many rooms, etc.; documents the scope	The scope of the investigation for the software product
Analyzing the feasibility	A small model depicting and confirming understanding; provides the vision and funding	The vision or business view of the software product to be developed along with the appropriate funding
Designing the product	A detailed physical design of what is to be built	The detailed physical representation of the software product to be built
Developing the product	The specifications of how to build it; constructs the physical product	The detail specifications of how the software is to be built
Assembling and testing the product	Provides the individual components	The actual software code and file definitions
Implementing the product	The house; utilizes the end product	The software product

Table 3.3   Information Technology Community Perspective

Manufacturing Phase	The Architectural Perspective	The Information Technology Perspective[a]
The birth of an idea	Planner	Business executive
Analyzing the feasibility	Owner	Business representative[b]
Designing the product	Designer	Systems analyst
Developing the product	Builder	Developer/programmer
Assembling and testing the product	Subcontractor	Quality analyst
Implementing the product	User	Business end user

a. The names for these roles vary from organization to organization. For the purposes of this discussion, the most commonly used role titles are used. These roles are not all the roles that are involved in developing or managing the deliverable. Multiple roles may be performed by the same individual in small organizations.

b. This phase is accomplished with the assistance of a requirements engineer who can also assist at any of these phases.

the builder's perspective is different from a designer's.[5] What is important is that the owner's perspective is satisfied in the final product. Though each role has a different perspective, all roles work together as a team to build the quality end product.[6]

The same is true with software development (including Internet-based products). Each phase (see Table 3.3) has a different perspective. Each phase develops another level of detail to build the final quality product. What is important is that the perspective of the "owner" (business executive) is satisfied in the final product.

Different Perspectives for Requirements

Each of the Zachman framework perspectives involved defining requirements and requirement details (see Table 3.4). The first three perspectives are requirements that are more commonly referred to as "business requirements." The first perspective (planner) identifies the list of what is in and out of scope (primary

---

5. Material derived from a demonstration of Structure for Information Systems Architecture by Framework Software, Inc., www.frameworksoft.com.

6. Material derived from Bruce 1992.

Table 3.4   Perspective Requirements

Manufacturing Phase	Zachman Perspective	Information Technology Translation	Requirement Deliverable
The birth of an idea	Entity classes and scope (*planner*)	Defines the scope of the investigation	Lists descriptive needs by each business community that define the scope of the investigation; includes lists of what is to be investigated and what is not included
Analyzing the feasibility	Model of the business (*owner*)	Defines how the business communities view the scope	Takes the lists one step into descriptive detail by providing association and dependencies between requirements (relationships)
Designing the product	Model of the information system (*designer*)	Defines the essential details to run the business; still technology independent	Each requirement and its relationship with other requirements within and outside of the business community fully attributed with the details that clearly define the need
Developing the product	Technology model (*builder*)	Defines the technological solution to the logical view; technology dependent	Derived requirements associated to specific needs of the builders to help them develop the solution to the requirements
Assembling and testing the product	Technology model (*subcontractor*)	Assembly and testing	Derived requirements associated to specific needs of the testers and distributors of the solution to help them implement the solution to the requirements
Implementing the product	Functioning system (*user*)	Implementation	Continue capturing feedback for process improvement or product improvement requirements

requirements) as it relates to the initiating requirement (the product concept). The second perspective (owner) defines the requirements and their dependencies (derived requirements) on other requirements. The third perspective (designer) defines the specific details that are essential in defining the requirements and their relationship with other requirements. The details may include additional derived requirements due to the specific interaction between business communities.

The fourth perspective (builder) is the break away from the business requirements. These define specific requirements (derived requirements) that need to be satisfied in order to build the solution. These requirements may or may not be captured by the requirements engineer. In some companies, technology specialists such as a database administrator or technical architect may capture these requirements. In truth, these specialists are the suppliers of this perspective's requirements. It is the responsibility of the requirements engineer to ensure that the requirements are elicited, analyzed, specified, validated, and approved (especially high-price items or items that go against corporate standards) and to ensure they are managed.

The fifth perspective (subcontractor) begins the process for the next iteration of the product. These requirements include what metrics or information should be captured in order to judge the success of the product. For Internet applications, requirements may state the need to capture customer feedback, click history, response time, and sales figures. These are requirements geared toward understanding the success of the first iteration and providing valuable information that could foster a change in direction to retain market presence.

The sixth perspective (user) is the implemented product or iteration. Requirements relate more to the next iteration of the product, thus initiating the next cycle, which begins with the planner perspective.

Each business community has the same perspectives; each perspective for each community has a different specification. Each perspective follows the same subprocess to elicit, analyze, specify, validate, and approve the requirements for its community and perspective.

Different Views of the Same House

When building a home, each phase or perspective requires a different focus or view. These views concentrate on a specific area for that perspective. For example, the house requires an architect's view, a plumber's view, an electrician's view, a landscaper's view, and so forth (see Table 3.5). Each has similar deliverables: scope, owner's model, physical model, specifications, components, and the final product. Each deliverable at each perspective level has its own focus. Each focus (see Table 3.5) still has the same architectural perspective. Nothing can be viewed independently! All views and perspectives are important to build a high-quality house. Each focus area must narrow down a concept into finite detail to ensure compliance and quality and to ultimately meet the owner's needs.

Table 3.5   Focuses for Building a Home

The Architectural Perspective	Architect's Focus	Plumber's Focus	Electrician's Focus	Landscaper's Focus
Planner: documents scope	*Planner:* number of rooms, size of property, etc.	*Planner:* number of facilities, features, etc.	*Planner:* number of connections, etc.	*Planner:* number of shrubs, trees, sprinklers, etc.
Owner: documents view	*Owner:* look of building	*Owner:* look and location of kitchens and bathrooms	*Owner:* each room's electrical requirements	*Owner:* layout of the outside
Designer: documents design	*Designer:* physical design and material of the house	*Designer:* physical design and material for the water rooms	*Designer:* physical design and material of the electrical system	*Designer:* physical design and material of the landscape
Builder: documents specifications	*Builder:* detailed specifications on how to build the house	*Builder:* detailed specifications on how to insert the plumbing	*Builder:* detailed specifications on how to wire the house	*Builder:* detailed specifications on what and where to plant
Subcontractor: documents components	*Subcontractor:* the building	*Subcontractor:* the plumbing	*Subcontractor:* the electrical wiring	*Subcontractor:* the trees and shrubs
User: uses the final product	*User:* the home	*User:* the kitchen, laundry, and bathrooms	*User:* the electrical outlets and fixtures	*User:* the landscape

Different Focuses of the Same Software Solution

Building software solutions also requires different focuses. In his Information Systems Architecture, John Zachman identified the following areas of focus:[7]

- **Who** is involved (people/organization/systems)?
- **What** is it made of (data)?
- **Where** are things located (network)?
- **When** do things happen (business events)?
- **Why** are things done (business policy)?
- **How** does it function (process)?

---

7. "A Framework for Information Systems Architecture." John A. Zachman. IBM Systems Journal, Vol. 26, No. 3, 1987. IBM Publication G321–5298 (*www.zifa.com*).

Though we are concentrating on the business area of information technology, the same focuses apply to each of the other business communities: business practice, business organization, and business support. Each of the business communities has a deliverable that has "who, what, where, when, why, and how" requirements to capture. They all need to be elicited, analyzed, specified, validated, and approved in order to build the specific deliverable.

The purpose of drawings, models, and other documentation deliverables is to enable the reviewers and those who must act on the deliverables to relate to them and to agree or disagree with the contents. The deliverables, in respect to requirements, are specifications used to validate for quality and to build upon.

Let's walk through the focus (special interest) areas to obtain an understanding of the specifics of each one. Note that each of these focus areas captures the *functionality* the product must have. This functionality lives with the product through each iteration until either the requirement is no longer needed or the entire product is no longer needed.

The People ("Who") View

This view focuses on associations to the product. The importance is that all the people, departments, organizations, and systems that interface with the product are well documented as to their needs. They trigger action on the part of the product.

The "who" needs include supplying information, accessing information, triggering functionality, and receiving results (such as reports). For example, a customer may submit an order and receive merchandise. The Internal Revenue Service may also be involved by being the recipient of quarterly financial reports. For the book retailer example, the shipping company personnel may have access to the book retailer's system in addition to the book retailer personnel having access to portions of the shipping system. For B2B, both forms of access from opposite systems are documented. In the world of the Internet, businesses, including competitors, are users. This category of requirements may need information such as supplier data.

It is important to also note who should *not* have access to the product. This observation spawns additional security-related requirements. The most common example in traditional manufacturering is the childproof cap used on medicine bottles. For the book retailer application, requirements could call for a user-initiated security key of the user's specified functionality and information. The objective is to prevent hackers from obtaining valuable customer or company information.

"Who" refers to the product interfaces. At each perspective, the interfaces may evolve into identifying security requirements as to what information they may have access to and what functionality they may perform. At the first perspective, you have a list of who should have access. You have a second list that clearly defines who should not have access. The "should not" list evolves as you refine the requirements through each perspective for specific functionality and information.

The Information ('What") View

This view focuses on the information requirements of the product. For software, this describes all the data needed to fulfill the requirement. For the book retailer and shipping connection, examples are the pickup location (warehouse) and the delivery location (customer site).

"What" represents the data needed by the Internet-based application. Data come in different forms, thanks to multimedia. Data can be textual, video, graphical, animation, and audio, all of which can be transmitted via files or messages across the Internet on cable, telephone, or wireless connections. The information can be distributed to PCs, laptops, televisions, personal digital assistants, and cellular telephones. All of these details are captured as requirements evolve through the different perspectives.

Data or object models are the most common deliverables in defining the "what" requirements. The models are more than just diagrams. A model contains textual information about the contents of the diagram. In fact, the diagram *supports* the textual description. Data and entity classes can be classified as information models for the purpose of explaining the "what" focus area.

An information model defines the common business vocabulary. Getting concurrence on specific definitions is the challenge of all good modelers. The models and the diagram depict relationships. These relationships define many of the business rules that must be supported. For example, a person cannot place an order without supplying at least one valid credit card number and a valid address. In the United States, the credit card address may be a post office box, but a shipping address must be a street address (a common oversight made by many online shopping sites) if a non–United States Postal Service (USPS) company is used.

Technical information models organize the information for performance for a specific technology. They are a step removed from defining the business. Both the business information model (defined at early perspective levels) and the technical information model are required. The technical model is built *from* the business model and will change more frequently than the business model. These changes are typically intended to improve performance or to take advantage of new technologies. These technology-related changes rarely affect the business model. However, any changes to the business model must be reflected in the technology model. The business model defines the business; the technology model defines how the business is supported technically. The businesspeople validate the business model, whereas technicians (and requirements engineers) validate the technology model.

In many business information models, audit trails may be left to the technology models. This is not true in the Internet world. When capturing "what" requirements, it is important to include confidential information that will provide audit trails. This requires information about the data that was captured: when and by whom. It must be proven that a transaction took place (especially changes and deletions). This information must be incorporated and approved by the business community.

The Location ('Where") View

"Where," the third focus area, represents the location or networking type of requirement. The "where" requirements, as with the "who" and "what" requirements, evolve through the different perspectives. Unfortunately, many requirements engineers capture this type of information later rather than earlier in the process.

Network engineers must meet the expectations of the different users as well as maintain the network infrastructure for the organization. Their requirement needs may be captured in other focus areas, but they must still take that information and reformulate it into their own models, evolving them into router configurations and other network work products. The information they need to capture includes

- *The type of access by user, event, and function.* The type of access could be batch file, online access, wireless access, or Internet access. Knowing this information assists in determining the type of communication that is needed to meet the requirement of the user.
- *What is needed at each location.* This includes what data and how much data will be transmitted from one node to another. How often will the transactions be executed? Are there peak periods? The objective is to determine the load on the network.
- *Security requirements for each location.* This includes security at the data and function by actor ("who") *and* access type. For example, a wireless transmission to a mobile telephone may be restricted to only summary information.

The "where" view focuses on connectivity. This entails describing the desired location where the product will be used and who must have access to it. For a stock-trading system, locations may be worldwide. Wireless has added a new dimension to the Internet. Devices such as handheld organizers can connect to the Internet application from anywhere. No longer must a device be physically attached. For the "where" requirements of an Internet application, location pertains to the traffic concentration areas for the customer base and the functions and amount of data they transmit.

The Event ('When") View

This view focuses on timings that trigger action by the product. It identifies when things must or usually occur, for example, the closing of the U.S. stock market at 4 P.M. EST. Can the book retailer accept the order for a next-day delivery request with the shipping company's logistics plan? The shipping company may have rules on what they can pick up late in the day and still be able to deliver to certain locations within a 24-hour period.

There are four basic types of events:

1. Initiated by time (for example, order received past shipper's latest pickup time)
2. Initiated by action from outside the product (for example, order placed for next-day shipment)
3. Conditionally triggered (for example, back-order products arrived at warehouse)
4. Arrival of information (for example, order picked up)

There are different models that can be created to reflect "when" requirements. The first perspective includes lists of the events with a list of associated responses. The events are to be correlated (requirement relationship) with "who" requirements in the detailed perspective, along with a list of conditions and actions the event incurs. When capturing the essential requirement details, the correlations between "what," and "how," and "where" as well as other focus areas have not yet been discussed. The point is that just as with any of the other focus areas, the "when" requirements evolve in detail and level of abstraction through the different perspectives.

The Rule ("Why") View

This view focuses on business rules and policies that must be adhered to when arriving at the solution. Rules are critical to the survival of a corporation. They can *never* be violated. Rules are defined for both normal and abnormal business circumstances. For example, an automobile can be sold as "new" only once during its life. A stock trader cannot cancel a submitted stock trade (buy) if the other party has already submitted his side (sell) of the transaction. The information about a customer order cannot be displayed if it is marked as secure without a password being supplied by the user.

The Internet has changed the way business is conducted. This means that the current business rules and policies that exist may need to be changed or tweaked or perhaps totally abandoned. This is a new economy based on a new business model that is filled with a new set of business rules. *Keeping outdated business rules in place can limit business opportunities on the Net!*[8]

Rules define the policies for a particular situation. When the situation in question occurs, it is an obligation that the rule be satisfied. These rules may affect the other focus areas, and these other focus area models must include a correlation to the business rule.

Some rules are defined outside the organization, including governmental (legal, IRS) and others rules dictated by competitors or the culture of the times. For example, state laws may prohibit a car from being sold as new when the mileage exceeds a specific number, which varies from state to state. Another example is the tax applied to the purchase. Is the ship-to or the ship-from tax charged according to the product's or service's value, and is it according to the date of order or the date shipped? This also varies from state to state and from country to country.

Policies that control the processing of the organization are usually defined internally. They define the culture and style of the organization. For example, the business rule for an Internet application for purchasing merchandise may state that the item must be requested from the supplier when the inventory dips below a specific level. Each item in the inventory may have its own specific reorder business rule.

Rules can also be technical in nature. For example, when the transaction reaches a specific level on the network, additional lines, typically reserved for backup situations, will be used to handle short periods of unexpected traffic.

---

8. Automobile manufacturers keep cars at individual dealers' car lots. For Internet sales, why should a dealer offer up one of its cars at a reduced cost? Why should the manufacturer have to pay dealer commission if a deal was not involved? New business rules concerning dealer commission had to be redefined to support the new Internet medium for car sales.

There are five different types of business rules:

1. **Constraints:** *limiting instructions.* A person must respond to an end-of-auction notice within three days.
2. **Heuristics:** *characterization instructions.* A customer in good credit standing should be notified of sales of similar products that have been purchased by the customer in the past.
3. **Computations:** *calculation instructions.* Foreign currency will be calculated by using the value of the currency for the day the item was shipped multiplied by the price of the item.
4. **Inference:** *implied instructions.* A customer who charges 35 percent more than his average daily transaction level will be placed on the customer watch list.
5. **Timing:** *conditional instructions.* Once a back-ordered item is received in the warehouse, it must be shipped to the next customer in line by the end of the next business day.

Timing is a type of rule associated with or often documented as a "when" requirement. In fact, all the business rules must be associated with other focus-type requirements. They may correlate to "what, how, when, and where" requirements. They may affect community requirements other than those of information technology. It is important during validation to evaluate each business rule for its impact on other requirements.

The Process ("How") View

This view focuses on the workflow of a specific function: the procedure, step by step. For example, an invoice that is 30 days past due requires a secondary notice and placement of the client's name on the delinquent watch list. Alternatively, for the online access to your customized view, one of the process requirements could describe:

1. If an incorrect password is supplied to retrieve secure information, the user will be allowed three opportunities.
2. If after the third opportunity the correct password is not supplied, the secure data will not be displayed.
3. If the user has forgotten his password, he is allowed to select the "secret word" to remind himself of the password.

4. If the user assesses the "secret word," another opportunity to supply a correct password is made available.

5. If the password is correct, the system displays the information.

6. If the password is incorrect, the system notifies the user that he can request a new password.

In our Internet example, the key business processes for the book retailer are

- *Order entry:* includes presentation and ease of use for the client
- *Payment:* involves calculating the cost of the product plus any surcharges (taxes and delivery) in the client currency via the acceptable methods (credit card, bank note, and so on)
- *Delivery:* involves packaging the requested item (virtual or physical) and delivering the goods after the payment has been determined acceptable (but not cleared)
- *Inventory management:* involves the supply chain
- *Settlement:* involves the actual conversion for goods and services

Volumetrics

The following rules of thumb depict the average number of functional requirements. This is helpful when you are planning the requirement effort. It is also helpful when taking a first cut at validation to identify whether you have a complete set of requirements for a specific community, perspective, and focus. Again, this is just a rough estimate to raise a potential flag that something may be missing from the requirements set.

- There should be a "how" requirement associated with every "when" requirement.
- There should be five "how" transactions requirements (including object methods) that impact a business entity "what" to support: (1) a create function, (2) a read function, (3) an update function, (4) a delete function, and (5) a list (includes search) function.
- There should be at least one requirement for each cell (category described by community, perspective, and focus).
- There should be a business rule "why" for every relationship between "what" entities or entity classes.
- There should be a "who" associated with every "how," "when," and "where" requirement.

These guidelines pertain to functional requirements. As shown in the next section, functional requirements are only a portion of the requirements set.

Extensions to the Information Systems Architecture

The Zachman framework for Information Systems Architecture ties the perspective, focus, and deliverable together for developing software (see Figure 3.6). To develop a business solution using information technology requires different *integrated* views and details. The contents of each cell identify possible deliverables for a software development project. This comprises the *functional* focus. These areas describe what features the Internet product must have and perform.

Additional Focuses

Two additional focuses are required to cover the needed information to build the product, as they constrain the product development decisions. One area describes

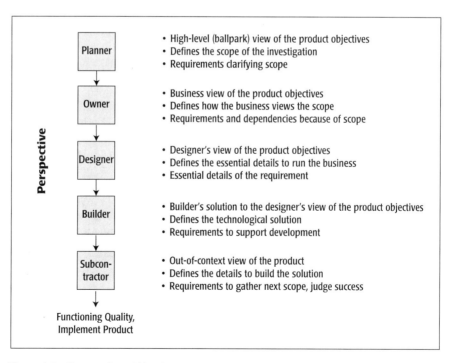

Figure 3.6   Perspectives Objectives

the constraints that must be applied to the product, and the other the constraints on running the project.[9] These are called *nonfunctional requirements.*

1. **The product constraint's view** documents any restrictions that may affect how the product will be designed. In system engineering terms, these would include the system requirements[10] pertaining to expectations as far as response time, security, and fault tolerance. Design constraints could also include restrictions as to the size of the application. Here they describe the environment and operation of the product. They may be referred to as quality of service (QoS) requirements.

2. **The project constraint's view** documents any restrictions that may affect the running of the project. This might include the number of resources and time constraints.[11] (Restrictions of tools, standards, and formats also fall under the category of project constraints.[12])

The requirements that fall into these views should be written in a format that meets the same quality characteristics as functional requirements. They

---

9. Discussions continue in the field of requirements engineering as to whether constraints are requirements. In this book I chose to separate them from functional requirements but keep them within the list of focus areas. Constraints are needed for developing the product and could impact functional requirements. They should be elicited, analyzed, specified, verified, and managed.

10. The IEEE has a System Requirements Specification Template (Std 1233) implying that the system requirements are to be defined prior to software requirements. This is true as system requirements are identified, then allocated to hardware and software. Refer to Chapter Two under the discussion of requirement allocation.

11. The IEEE Software Requirements Specification Template (Std 830) is very clear in noting that a deadline is *not* a software requirement. It is a project constraint. Care must be taken to validate an imposed deliverable schedule. The deliverable date should be based on the approved functional, support, and design requirements. Delivery date should be negotiated during the review of the requirements. *However, there is a point in the life of the product where the revenue will decrease.* For example, a product, in order to meet projected revenue, must be the first to market or close thereafter. If the product does not meet that date, it might not be worth the time and effort for the company to build the product. This is an extremely important point! In reality, a delay in product delivery could cost the company a slice of global revenues or key holiday opportunities (for example, Mother's Day). Deadlines should be established but reviewed as to the feasibility during the validation phase. Negotiations will adjust the scope of the implementation effort to meet any market demand. Deadlines are requirements, just not software requirements!

12. Different companies developed parts of the Mars satellite. A missing project constraint was that all formulas were to use the same metric form of measurement.

evolve through the same perspectives as the product's functional requirements. These additional focus areas include requirements that are crucial to the success of the Internet application.

Product Constraints

Product constraints, in the information technology world, refer to the "ilities."[13] To provide an example of different product constraints, the following six "ilities" are discussed in more detail below.

- Adaptability
- Reliability
- Scalability
- Security
- Usability
- Maintainability

The proceeding examples are crucial to the success of the Internet application.

Adaptability Requirements

One business model that is evolving is sometimes referred to as the "choice-board." This is where the consumer, through the Internet, clicks on the features and prices of what he or she wishes to purchase. The manufacturer provides an online configurator that allows the consumer to select what options he or she is willing to buy and at what price. This new business model requires additional requirements that extend beyond software. This change also affects both the sales and manufacturing processes for the company.

Hence, the Internet application involves changes in the normal business process. In order for the product to succeed, changes in other business areas, or business communities, are required. The community represents the other business units that are impacted by the Internet application.

---

13. For a more complete list of nonfunctional requirements, see the IEEE System Requirement Specification (Std 1233). Remember that nonfunctional or QoS requirements pertain to product limitations. They constrain the designing and building of the product.

These changes may not be known when the Internet-based application is being designed for its first iteration. The application must, therefore, be adaptable, meaning that the application must continually change to meet the demands of the customer and the market. It is important to document this requirement to remind the project development team during design reviews of what will occur with each iteration of the product.

Reliability Requirements

Reliability refers to the expectations of the users as to the continual availability of the Internet application (including performance and fault tolerance requirements). Users expect applications to be available on a 24-hour-per-day basis. Reliability requirements speak to the mean time between failures. The Internet application runs on equipment that the users expect to have a minimal mean time between failures. This may require backups in hardware and networks. These, combined with the location requirements, provide valuable input to the network engineers when designing the network infrastructure.

Reliability needs may vary by function and location, so it is important to build a table that correlates the reliability by either "when" or "how" requirements. Tables 3.6 and 3.7 illustrate a means by which specific reliability and performance requirements can be captured and organized. It is important to identify a pattern as to what functions really require high availability and when. With a stock-trading application, for example, the day that stock options become due, volumes are highest. If this is for a specific type of stock, say, an energy stock, the prior clientele may likely reside in Texas. To guarantee reliabil-

Table 3.6   Reliability (Mean Time Between Failures, MTBF) Requirements

	MTBF 1				MTBF 2				MTBF 3			
Function	LOC. 1	LOC. 2	LOC. 3	LOC. 4	LOC. 1	LOC. 2	LOC. 3	LOC. 4	LOC. 1	LOC. 2	LOC. 3	LOC. 4
Function One												
Function Two												
Function Three												

Table 3.7   Reliability (Performance) Requirements

Function	Performance 1				Performance 2				Performance 3			
	LOC. 1	LOC. 2	LOC. 3	LOC. 4	LOC. 1	LOC. 2	LOC. 3	LOC. 4	LOC. 1	LOC. 2	LOC. 3	LOC. 4
Function One												
Function Two												
Function Three												

ity for that location on their biggest trading day, equipment may be diverted to support the one-day peak instead of having excess capacity for the entire year. In any case, the requirements need to be explicit so those in charge of planning the capacity for hardware and networks have sufficient knowledge of the users' expectations.

Scalability Requirements

A good example of the importance of scalability was recently depicted in an advertisement in which a small group of entrepreneurially spirited individuals are standing around a personal computer. They are watching the opening of their new business venture, holding their breath as they eagerly await the first customer's order. Elated screams of success grow as the customer orders grow beyond their dreams. Then, quickly, the happiness turns to panic as the orders keep growing and growing. How are they going to satisfy what is now an unanticipated order volume?

This commercial illustrates the need for scalability on two fronts: technology and business community. Technology is the infrastructure that supports the Internet application. Business community is the business infrastructure that supports the product claims.

First, the technology. The technology must be scalable to adapt to the growth of the Internet application without the continual need to throw everything away and start over, the cost of which would deplete any revenue gain. Scalability is building an infrastructure that supports both vertical growth (increase in the number of sales for a specific product) as well as horizontal growth (increase in breadth of product).

It is important to anticipate some growth. Growth will impact the performance of the Internet application. The infrastructure must be flexible enough to support growth in network size, transaction handling, data throughput, page load timings, and security. This requires sophisticated tools that can model capacity planning on the site and network.

With regard to scalability technology requirements, it is important to document the potential growth in increments. A spreadsheet (see Table 3.8) or some CASE tools can be used to document these associative requirement details.

What is important is to determine the minimum, average, and maximum number of occurrences for each requirement. In other words, it is important to determine the anticipated volume of events (when), the number of transactions (how), and the number of users (by each type/actor). You also need to capture the timeframe for these volumes. For example, some time-initiated events may be dormant except when the time is triggered (close of the stock exchange or the end of the business day for that country). It is important for the network engineers to model the performance under the worst-case scenarios.

Growth will also impact the business infrastructure that is put in place. It is important to anticipate the risk of a supplier not being able to meet the growth of your business. Some small companies went out of business when UPS went on strike! eCost took a beating when 3Com could not get the chips for Palm Pilots. Scalability, in a business sense, requires risk analysis of all dependent business partners.

B2B supply-chain applications involve multiple vendors using multiple vendors. Scalability business requirements need to anticipate the possibility of a supplier not being able to meet the necessary volumes. In most cases, you can split the anticipated volume across multiple vendors. The business has minimal control over what vendors your vendors use. The scalability business requirements must contain scenarios of supply-chain interruption.

First, identify the possible breaks in the supply chain. Anticipate the worst scenario as well as the probable scenario. Table 3.8 can be adjusted to determine the severity of each possible outage.

At the scope level, scalability will be defined as *the need to implement a flexible infrastructure to support the projected growth*. At this point, the requirement is still ambiguous; all the volumetrics will most likely not be known. This requirement evolves as more requirements are captured. It is still important to document the scalability need at this point as a reminder that more information is required.

Table 3.8 Capacity Requirements Spreadsheet

Timeframe	Who			What			Where			When			Why			How		
	Min.	Avg.	Max.	Min.	Avg.	Max.	Min.	Avg.	Max.	Min.	Avg.	Max.	Min.	Avg.	Max.	Min.	Avg.	Max.
Day One																		
Week One																		
Month One																		
Quarter One																		
Quarter Two																		
Quarter Three																		
First Year																		
Second Year																		
Third Year																		
Fourth Year																		
Fifth Year																		

At the planner level, volumetrics begin to emerge. The business units should be able to provide projected numbers of the customers, orders, transactions, and so forth. These volumetrics should be applied to all models. Relationships among functional requirements are also being formed at the business level. As part of defining the relationships, the business unit should be able to project volumetrics about the relationships. For example:

1. Each potential client will search for five product descriptions, including price and availability, at one time.
2. One out of three searching clients will, on average, order two products with each order placed.
3. One out of five customers will bypass the search and place an order for one item.
4. The bulk of orders are placed between 10 A.M. and 1 P.M. EST on Mondays. The exception is the seven weeks before the end of the calendar year. During that time, the peak period expands to all weekdays.

Large companies that are dabbling in the Internet must not take these volume estimates lightly. There is a possibility that the Internet-based product may outperform the corporation's standard business, making the Internet the leading business unit.

Security Requirements

All of these business processes and information require some level of security processing. One type of security is required to protect the client, another to protect the corporation. The requirements engineer must spend time with all requirement suppliers on the impact of poor security. Security requirements must be captured on two fronts: (1) to protect the Internet user from intruders, and (2) to protect the corporation from theft or corruption (viruses).

It is critical to answer the simple question of what would be the impact to the corporation or the customer if data or processing were lost due to a security breach. If possible, attempt to obtain a quantifiable number at the following levels:

- Five-minute outage
- Day-long outage
- Week-long outage

Then try to determine through awareness-type questioning whether the data would actually be lost or corrupted. Sample scenarios include

- If data became corrupted
- If a competitor obtained any data
- If any file (data, voice, media) became corrupted

Clients must feel comfortable doing business with you. They must feel that you are reputable and that the payment process is a *private* transaction used for this purchase alone.

There are thieves among us. The first one who comes to mind is the predator who tries to destroy or capture corporate information.[14] The other type of thief is one who wants to steal the product or service. When a thief of this sort obtains confidential information by using stolen payment options, it can cripple a company. Security must be taken very seriously and viewed as having a potentially negative impact at any level.

The seven worst security mistakes that senior executives make[15] include four that can be documented during the requirements process:

1. Pretending the problem will go away if they ignore it
2. Relying primarily on a firewall
3. Failing to understand the relationship of information security to the business problem (understanding physical security but not seeing the consequences of poor information security)
4. Failing to realize how much money their information and organizational reputations are worth

It is up to the requirements engineer to capture security requirements and associate the need to "who," "what," "how," and "where" as well as any interactions between these functional focus areas.

Usability Requirements

The Internet has evolved current business models to a point where the consumer holds the power. This has changed—and will continue to change—the way companies relate to their customers and compete with one another. Usability is a

---

14. This is discussed in more detail in Chapter Five.
15. The SANS Institute, *Newsletter*, May 2000, p. 7 (www.sans.org).

product constraint that directly speaks to the customer's ability to use the Internet product, and it must be captured. It should include

- The maximum allowed response time
- The availability to access 24 hours a day, seven days per week
- The ability to customize views at specific points
- The ability to filter information, minimizing what the user would perceive as "clutter data"
- The availability of choices for the product

Most importantly, a consideration for usability is how many clicks it takes to retrieve information and how many clicks to complete a workflow. Response time can be eaten away with every screen of updated or new information. This translates to time that the user is not willing to give up if he perceives that the usability of the application is at fault. The requirements engineer should capture this type of need and associate the information with each "how" requirement, similar to how you related scalability requirements. This assists the designers (users of these requirements) in developing an effective product with an emphasis on usability.

Maintainability Requirements

Every one to three months (sometimes sooner), new features are offered in new product iterations. Many of these iterations are developed in parallel with each other. The work products, from the requirements to the code, must be easily maintained in order to keep to this rigorous schedule. Conforming to standards defined by the organization (and by international standards organizations) facilitates the making of products that are easily updated and maintained through each iteration. A general maintainability requirement must be defined at the owner level. As the relationships to other nonfunctional and functional focus areas are defined, the maintainability should be clarified as to its specific impact on the work products produced in those other focus areas. As the other requirements evolve, so should the maintainability requirement by describing the detail requirements as they relate to the structure and standard for the different perspectives and focus work products.

Project Constraints

Deadlines are not software requirements; they are project constraints. When attempting to be the first to market with a new concept, deadlines may be set in stone rather than simply imposed arbitrarily. Another project-type constraint is the budget or venture capital dollars available to be used toward the development of the product. The amount of staff that can be hired to work on product development is also a constraint. These three examples are project constraints that have a direct impact on how the project is planned and tracked and on what can be developed by a specific point in time. When project-type constraints emerge, a negotiation process begins for what can feasibly be delivered for any given product.

Project constraints are important requirements to capture. As with functional and product constraints, project constraints also evolve through the different perspectives. Although the Internet program has one budget for resources, dollars, and time, each community is allocated its portion of the pot.

The project constraints are also important for other phases of development aside from requirements. Different choices can be made on hardware and network configurations based on the budget, staff, and time allocated to them. The project constraints impact those decisions.

Adding Community to the Infrastructure

The Zachman Information Systems Architecture (see Figure 3.7) shows how the framework works for software deliverables. Figure 3.8 shows the framework extended to support the important nonfunctional requirements. Notice that product and project constraints fit with the same perspectives as the six functional requirement types.

Although Figure 3.8 expands the number of focus areas compared with the Zachman framework, it still omits some of the different organizations involved in developing an Internet product. For example, to actually roll out an Internet application, other business areas are involved:

- *Advertising:* to develop the media representation for the product
- *Legal:* to develop product liability, copyright, and warranty documentation
- *Customer Service:* to develop processes to train persons assisting customers with questions, complaints, and returns

Each of these additional areas has its own process to provide the details for each perspective and focus. Each may have assigned a different project identifier, but the project objectives must satisfy the initiating requirements. Each has a different deliverable for each perspective and focus cell, organized as previously discussed for the information technology cells.

	DATA *What*	FUNCTION *How*	NETWORK *Where*	PEOPLE *Who*	TIME *When*	MOTIVATION *Why*	
SCOPE (CONTEXTUAL)	List of Things Important to the Business	List of Processes the Business Performs	List of Locations in which the Business Operates	List of Organizations Important to the Business	List of Events Significant to the Business	List of Business Goals/Strat	SCOPE (CONTEXTUAL)
Planner	ENTITY = Class of Business Thing	Function = Class of Business Process	Node = Major Business Location	People = Major Organizations	Time = Major Business Event	Ends/Means=Major Bus. Goal/ Critical Success Factor	*Planner*
ENTERPRISE MODEL (CONCEPTUAL)	e.g. Semantic Model	e.g. Business Process Model	e.g. Business Logistics System	e.g. Work Flow Model	e.g. Master Schedule	e.g. Business Plan	ENTERPRISE MODEL (CONCEPTUAL)
Owner	Ent = Business Entity Reln = Business Relationship	Proc. = Business Process I/O = Business Resources	Node = Business Location Link = Business Linkage	People = Organization Unit Work = Work Product	Time = Business Event Cycle = Business Cycle	End = Business Objective Means = Business Strategy	*Owner*
SYSTEM MODEL (LOGICAL)	e.g. Logical Data Model	e.g. Application Architecture	e.g. Distributed System Architecture	e.g. Human Interface Architecture	e.g. Processing Structure	e.g. Business Rule Model	SYSTEM MODEL (LOGICAL)
Designer	Ent = Data Entity Reln = Data Relationship	Proc. = Application Function I/O = User Views	Node = I/S Function (Processor, Storage, etc) Link = Line Characteristics	People = Role Work = Deliverable	Time = System Event Cycle = Processing Cycle	End = Structural Assertion Means =Action Assertion	*Designer*
TECHNOLOGY MODEL (PHYSICAL)	e.g. Physical Data Model	e.g. System Design	e.g. Technology Architecture	e.g. Presentation Architecture	e.g. Control Structure	e.g. Rule Design	TECHNOLOGY MODEL (PHYSICAL)
Builder	Ent = Segment/Table/etc. Reln = Pointer/Key/etc.	Proc. = Computer Function I/O = Data Elements/Sets	Node = Hardware/System Software Link = Line Specifications	People = User Work = Screen Format	Time = Execute Cycle = Component Cycle	End = Condition Means = Action	*Builder*
DETAILED REPRESEN-TATIONS (OUT-OF CONTEXT)	e.g. Data Definition	e.g. Program	e.g. Network Architecture	e.g. Security Architecture	e.g. Timing Definition	e.g. Rule Specification	DETAILED REPRESEN-TATIONS (OUT-OF CONTEXT)
Sub-Contractor	Ent = Field Reln = Address	Proc. = Language Stmt I/O = Control Block	Node = Addresses Link = Protocols	People = Identity Work = Job	Time = Interrupt Cycle = Machine Cycle	End = Sub-condition Means = Step	*Sub-Contractor*
FUNCTIONING ENTERPRISE	e.g. DATA	e.g. FUNCTION	e.g. NETWORK	e.g. ORGANIZATION	e.g. SCHEDULE	e.g. STRATEGY	FUNCTIONING ENTERPRISE

Figure 3.7   John Zachman Information Systems Architecture for Software Perspectives and Focus (*Source*: John A. Zachman, Zachman International, 810-231-0531, www.zifa.com.)

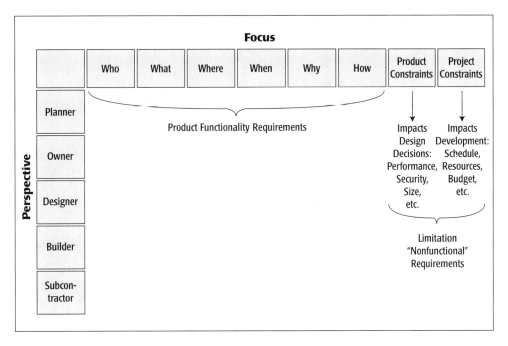

Figure 3.8   Zachman's Framework, Expanded Focus

With regards to the overall product plan, this creates a third dimension to the requirements set. This dimension, *community,* represents the different areas of business concentration. A community could be a business unit or a department of a business unit. The way in which a community is defined varies by organization and should be determined at the beginning of the program. The organization chart for your company is a good start for selecting communities. Here are some points to consider for communities:

- Product development and implementation require additional involvement by other organizations.
- Other organization areas will be dependent on perspective and focus requirements.
- Other organization areas will develop perspective and focus requirements that may impact software.
- Each organization area will have its own process that develops focus requirements through perspective levels.

Community changes the two-dimensional pattern shown in Figure 3.8 so that each requirement cell becomes multidimensional (see Figure 3.11 on page 111). As stated earlier in this chapter, we can categorize the communities into:

- Business practices (BP)
- Business support (BS)
- Business organization (BO)
- Information technology (IT)

Each of these areas can be broken into finer detail, depending on the deliverables that are required to develop a piece of the end product. For example, under business practice one may find marketing. Marketing may be further segmented into advertising and market research. Again, the breakdown will vary from organization to organization. No matter what level of breakdown, each subdivision has a separate deliverable and a different set of requirements it needs to satisfy to develop the complete end product. Each would follow the same objectives for each cell. To customize the framework for your business communities:

- Apply the organizational structure to the framework.
- Have each community represent specific areas of concentration that relate specifically to the organizational structure.
- Create Zachman's focus and perspectives for each organization or area initiating a subproject to satisfy the business objective.
- Add the two nonfunctional focus areas.
- Create embedded matrices of focus and perspective details specific to the community area.
- Create the association requirements to keep all cubes in sync in order to reach the common objectives of the product to be delivered.
- Derive all requirements from the initial business need (initiating requirement) or wants (the requirement request).

Requirement Associations

Requirements may not succeed all on their own. They need to be implemented with other requirements. For example, the process needs data to be able to perform its operations. For this reason, it is important to "link" or associate requirements that are dependent on each other. There is no need to define the data for both the "what" focus and the "how" focus. The data should be documented once and "used by" the process. To identify the process needs for the data, the data is associated to the process at the point it is needed. This builds a relationship requirement between data and process for specific purposes.

This association allows requirements to be normalized, in other words, to be stated once. One requirement may impact many requirements. For example, using the nonfunctional product constraints of reliability, a reliability requirement affects multiple "how" or "where" requirements. They need to be associated to build the quality requirement. Each association needs to be qualified in order to reflect the specific details of the reliability impact.

Just as any other requirement, association requirements must be satisfied to have a high-quality Internet product. These requirements are spawned by a specific requirement cell (perspective, focus, and community) to be satisfied by another area in order for them to work together. They are the glue that holds the different requirements together in a multidimensional model. (See Figure 3.9.)

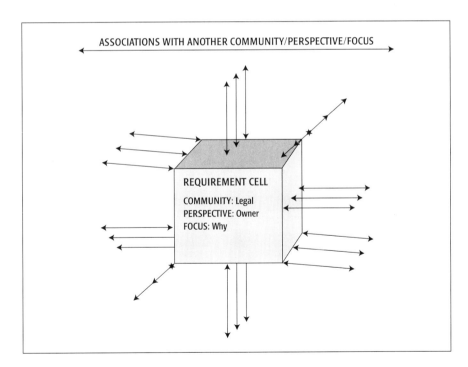

Figure 3.9 Potential Requirement Associations

Within each cell, specific needs must be addressed to refine the requirements set. For example, both the inventory subset of requirements and the billing subset of requirements can be defined separately. They may be two existing systems in larger brick-and-mortar type companies. In order to streamline the workflow between inventory management and billing, each system needs to be modified to work together. These special derived requirements are important for holding two separate requirements subsets (billing and inventory) together.

When one requirement needs to use (or reference) information captured in another cell, it is important to build a link between them. Most CASE tools do this automatically. This creates a "usage trail" so that if either requirement changes during the development process, you can easily identify the potential impact on other requirements. All affected requirements (the two independent and the one relationship) need to be implemented in order to have a successful Internet system. They can be tested and implemented independently. (See Figure 3.10.)

In Figure 3.11 the Zachman framework is extended, showing how the relationships (associations) form the mortar between the requirement cells.

Two pieces of information are required in order for the association requirement to be connected. One is the actual content; the other is the usage trail (link). The usage trail is the identifier of both requirements that are being associated.

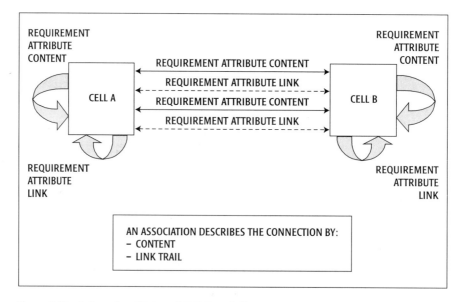

Figure 3.10   Internal and External Cell Association

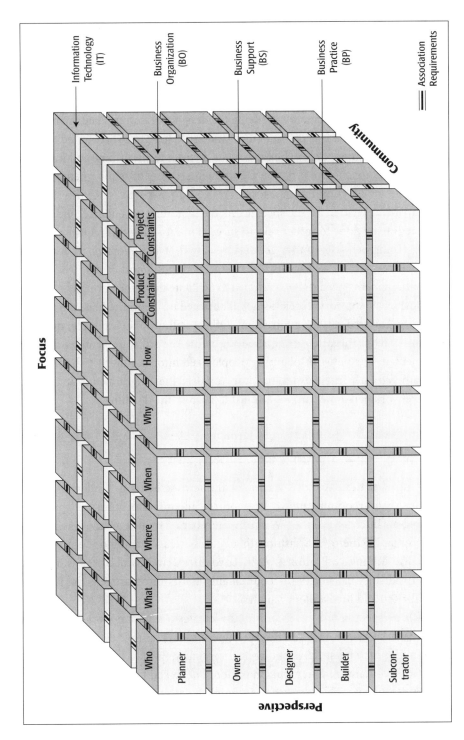

Figure 3.11 Requirements Set Framework Showing Perspective and Focus Categories

These types of requirements are often overlooked. Once a requirement is allocated to a specific community, the community may satisfy its requirements without thinking of the possible impact the requirement may have on another community. The need for these types of requirements is finally realized somewhere down the product's development path. The result is that the other areas are playing catch-up or that both areas are modifying the design to accommodate the interaction. The modification is usually not ideal and could have been accounted for earlier in the development cycle. The catch-up is costly in terms of time and money.

To account for these association requirements, the set of requirements should be available for all communities, focus areas, and perspectives. As the requirements are being written for the specific cell, the requirements engineer should ask what needs to be done for other cells to succeed in satisfying this requirement. As existing requirements for other cells are reviewed, it is important to ask those same questions. If one cell needs to be associated with another cell, what additional requirements need to be developed to facilitate the association?

Some of the support associations will be noted by the individual community as its "who" or association requirement. Others will not. For example, network planning is often forgotten until a month before the software product is to be implemented. The network-planning people need information that should have been gathered early in the program. Unfortunately, the program ends up delayed or the network personnel run ragged just to keep to the deadline.

Organization Impact

If nothing else, the expanded Zachman framework helps us understand that there are many requirements to be captured in order to build any product, including an Internet product. With this number of requirements, it is important to organize them in a fashion that makes it easy to identify any gaps in knowledge. Adding community, perspective, focus, and association as another means to identify categories of requirements assists in organizing the requirements for gap and inconsistency analysis.

Each perspective for each community creates a separate work product. A separate work product may be (but is not necessarily) further delivered for each focus and for each perspective and each community. Each of these work product deliverables contains requirements that should be linked to related requirements in other documents. This is easier to accomplish with the assistance of a requirements management tool.

Most requirements management tools can support the framework. Implementing the requirements set framework requires a requirements engineer who possesses a full understanding of the requirements set framework and the requirements process (including allocation) to define the filter process for each requirement. The benefits of implementing the framework in the requirements management tool are (1) easier validation and (2) a reporting process between perspectives and iterations of the Internet product.

CASE tools are available that capture some of the categories of requirements. None of them captures all the different types of requirements. Each of these tools can provide a documented output of the requirements for its concentrated focus and perspective. This document should be fed into the requirements management tool for gap and consistency analysis as well as for change control within the entire requirements set.

Conclusion

This chapter introduced how the different types of requirements can be organized. Categorizing the requirements makes it easier to develop the question list as well as to identify gaps in knowledge. The objective is to ensure that the product to be developed is fully understood from all angles. Adding the question list and process to the organizational structure turns the framework into a pattern (see Appendix B).

Perspectives reflect the areas of responsibility for each role. For example, a designer's perspective is quite different from the owner's perspective; the builder's perspective is different from a designer's. Each evolves the requirements by providing details needed to interpret his perspective. The owner's perspective must be satisfied in the final product. Though each role has a different perspective, all roles work together as a team to build the quality product.

When building a home, each perspective requires a different focus or view. These views concentrate on a specific area for that perspective. For example, the house requires a plumber's view, an electrician's view, a landscaper's view, and so forth. Each has similar deliverables: scope, owner's model, physical model, specifications, components, and the final product. The deliverables at each perspective level have their own focus areas.

In software engineering terms, the focus includes both functional and nonfunctional requirements. Functional requirements are the "who" (interface associations), "what" (data), "where" (networks), "when" (events), "why" (business rules), and "how" (processes). The nonfunctional requirements are the product and project constraints. Similarly, each perspective has eight different views, one for each of these eight areas.

It is important to realize that nothing can be viewed independently. All focuses and perspectives are important for building a high-quality product. Each view must drill down a concept into finite detail to ensure compliance and quality and to meet the business needs. Each focus and perspective requires different probing questions.

Linking the different focuses and perspectives requires additional association or support-type requirements that will tie all intersecting squares. For example, when building a home, electricians need to ensure they do not affect the plumber's requirements. This creates additional association requirements for the electrician and plumber. In system engineering terms, association requirements are created for hardware and software to work together. Probing questions are required to tie the focus and perspective to other focus areas and perspectives.

We need to expand our view of requirements beyond software-implemented requirements. Additional dimensions need to be included to incorporate all business areas that may be affected by the business request. This includes such business areas as legal and human resources. Each business area will react in some way to the original requirement. Each business area will have its own process for satisfying a specific need. Each business community may spawn additional IT requirements. These may initiate additional software projects that enhance existing systems (for example, change billing system) or require maintaining data contents (for example, add a new product number), or they may initiate non-IT projects (for example, modify legal contracts).

The Zachman framework can be expanded to include the additional dimension of community to support each business area. Each community has its own focus and perspective. Each multidimensional cube requires additional association requirements to support the linkage of the requirements.

The requirements that fall into each community, perspective, focus, and association create a full requirements set. A requirements set contains all the individual requirements and related information associated with a business objective. Some general guidelines follow:

- Each requirement should be stated only once.
- Requirements should not overlap, that is, they should not refer to other requirements or the capabilities of other requirements.

- Explicit relationships should be defined among individual requirements to show how the requirements are related to or dependent on each other to form a complete product.
- The requirements set should include all requirements needed by the business user as well as those needed for the definition of the product.
- The requirements set should be consistent and noncontradictory in the level of detail between formats.
- Community and perspective should be used to subdivide the requirements set. Though many different groups may develop specific focuses, this is not recommended since it increases the risk of missing association requirements or requirements that tie focus requirements with other focus areas.
- A skilled requirements engineer should be involved in implementing the framework into a requirements management tool. This includes the transition from different CASE tools and other formats into the requirements management tool.

Adding a process for filling each cell, as well as filter rules for each cell, turns the framework into a pattern. This requirements pattern is a meta pattern that can be tailored to any type of application. The next chapter does just this: it takes the requirements set framework and discusses the objectives and the types of questions that should be asked to capture the needs of the Internet product.

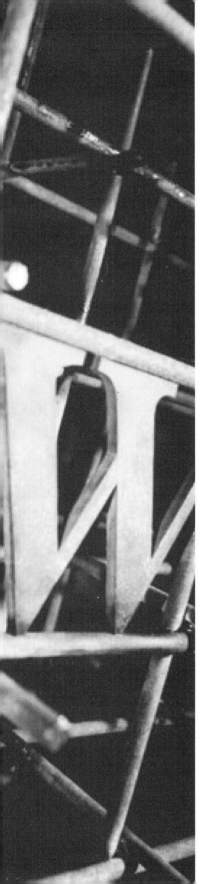

CHAPTER FOUR

The Internet Requirements Pattern

> **Chapter Key Topics**
> - **The kickoff**
> - **The pattern specifics**
> - **Gap analysis**
>
> **The Internet Impact**
> **The Internet may look simple on the surface. However, the risk to the corporation demands that requirements be captured beyond simply software. A requirements pattern can provide a framework for this process, which will minimize a gap in the type of requirements that need to be captured.**

As we discussed in Chapter Threee, the requirements set framework is a template that guides the organization of the requirements set by community, perspective, and focus. Requirements must be implemented individually but may be dependent on other requirements. These requirements are linked with association requirements, a derived type of requirement (see Figure 4.1).

The framework is filled with requirements by following a defined process and subprocess. The process allocates (at four levels: corporate, divisional, architectural, and product) the responsibility to detail each requirement through the different business communities. The subprocess (that is, elicitation, analysis, specification, validation, and approval) occurs at each perspective of the different allocation levels.

A requirements meta pattern (RMP) is dependent on the use of the requirements set framework

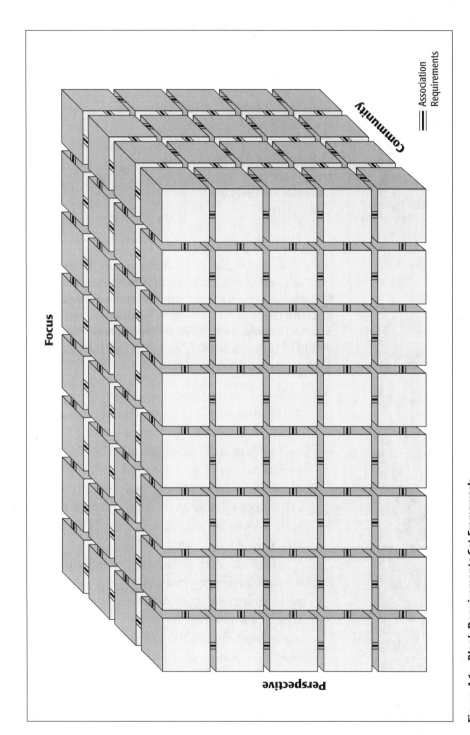

Figure 4.1   Blank Requirements Set Framework

and the requirements process, as discussed in the previous paragraphs. Questions and checklists are applied to each framework cell to guide the requirements engineer in capturing individual requirements and to develop the appropriate associations. The questions are written so that the requirement can evolve from concept through to product implementation.

Every product and program is different and has its unique set of specific questions and checklists to add to the already existing RMP cell question set. The Internet requirements pattern (IRP), although built on the requirements meta pattern, has questions and checklists (see Appendix B) that are tailored to the nuances of the specific product. The purpose of this chapter is to introduce the concept of a requirements pattern using an Internet-based product as an example.

The Kickoff

The requirements pattern is applied after two work products (the business concept and the business case) have been developed and approved. These products need to answer specific questions and address management concerns. The sooner a requirements engineer is assigned, the sooner he can assist in the development of the requirements by asking thought-provoking questions (elicitation and analysis). He can help specify the work products for executive review (validation) and approval, following the requirements subprocess.

Changing the Business Model

The process for developing Internet-based applications begins with a look at the current business model. The new business framework may be able to leverage some of the existing processes with some tweaking. It is important to look at the Internet as a whole and not a small information technology system. The Internet requires a restructuring of current business models used by new and existing companies. A new business strategy must be designed to be flexible to changing trends. You are looking at the business as a whole, developing a new business architecture that crosses all business communities, streamlining interfaces between the different internal and external communities.

Start-up companies may not have existing information processes, so they have to develop them or partner with someone who performs these functions (for example, billing). The same workflow will be defined as with brick-and-mortar companies, although the steps in the workflow will vary in number and complexity. Still, the function (workflow) must be performed nonetheless!

Understanding the Problem or Need

The evolution of the Internet solution (or any iteration) begins with an idea. The idea begins with outside information such as:

- *Competitive analysis* such as the success or failure of competitors on the Web
- *Customer or business partner feedback* such as e-mails or conversations with potential partners
- *Government regulations* such as opening the Internet for general use and acceptance of electronic signatures for legal purposes
- *Academic study* such as new and improved methods and techniques that increase the velocity of development
- *Technological advancement* such as faster communication, user-friendly associations, commercial off-the-shelf functions (easy pay, subject-oriented data marts, search engines)

All of these sources provide information that can spark an idea. It is the responsibility of the business sponsor to investigate the impact of the external (and internal) sources of information on the corporation. All the information needs to be categorized for two broad reasons (whether oriented toward customers or business partnerships) to build an Internet solution. The requirements engineer can assist by looking at the information in a "functional focus"[1] manner, asking questions that assist in identifying any constraints (product and project) in achieving the broad categories. The objective is to uncover the business drivers for developing the Internet product. These business drivers will require continual monitoring while the program is under development since changes in the market will not stop while you are developing the product. Continual monitoring will enable the business to initiate changes in the requirements set based upon changes in the business.

Customer-Oriented Ideas

The following questions should be considered when evaluating customer-oriented ideas:

1. How will it make it easier to use the product?
2. What will make the customer continually return to the site?
3. Why would the customer use this means of access over another?

---

1. Who, what, where, when, why, and how.

4. How does this improve the service to the customer?
5. Will this provide a new, expanded customer base?

An important point to remember is that it is just as important for a customer to visit the site as it is to purchase the product or service. An Internet-based application can capture the reason why a customer does or does not buy a product. For example, is it an issue of cost, ease of use, or lack of desired features? When a customer visits the site, information can be captured that provides a detailed profile of the customer: his needs, the way he searches, the way he peruses the site.

Business Partnership–Oriented
Consider the following questions for business partnership–oriented ideas:

1. How will this improve the end-to-end workflow for the customer?
2. What costs and benefits of the alliance would affect the other business partner (define the win–win scenario)?
3. What new opportunities would be generated with the alliance for all business partners?
4. What manual processes would be eliminated?
5. What new processes would have to be created?

For the business partnership, it is important to identify a win–win situation. All partnerships must see a cost reduction in supplying the service, a time reduction in delivering the service, and increased business. Without seeing a means of satisfying *all* criteria, sufficient revenue will not be made by both parties involved in the partnership. The relationship (and your Internet solution) will have a premature death!

These broad customer and business partnership areas initiate a change in focus for the corporation. The Internet is customer driven from two sides of the workflow (see Figure 4.2). The two types of "customers" are (1) those who purchase the product or service and (2) the business partners. Both need to see benefits to them. The objective is to ease the customer's experience in hopes of his return, over and over.

Preparing for Allocation

The idea can be formalized and presented with the supporting research references to management. The objective is to define the concept correctly, clearly, concisely, and as completely as possible so management can decide whether to

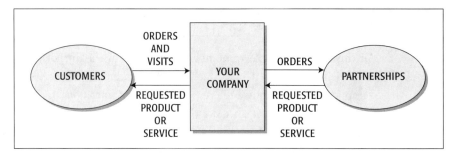

Figure 4.2   **Business-to-Customer and Business-to-Business**

grant the time to investigate further. With the idea approved, the formalized idea has to be expanded into a formal business case that itemizes the costs, the potential revenue, and the exposure (financial, legal, and so forth) to the corporation. Management will be looking for specific information to determine whether they should embark with the Internet concept. Therefore, the business case needs to address specific questions (Table 4.1).

The business case is the starting point for the planner perspective for the business community spearheading the effort (the product business sponsor). The business community defines the scope of the Internet product and develops the initiating requirements, which are allocated to the corporate communities flowing down to the appropriate group that can develop the detailed requirements. These initiating requirements spark the initiation of several projects. Each project has a project manager who has the responsibility to build the quality work products. These project managers coordinate their efforts with a program manager who is accountable for delivering a high-quality Internet product.[2]

The business case needs to show a positive return on investment within some prescribed period of time, as deemed acceptable by the executive management. The return should be calculated in two ways: (1) for implementing the Internet solution and (2) for not implementing an Internet solution (that is, opportunity costs). It must be understood that not being on the Web can have a negative effect on the corporate bottom line. In many scenarios, a corporation must be on the Web simply to survive. To do so, it must change its business culture to be more customer-focused.

---

2. Roles and responsibilities of persons involved in developing the Internet product are discussed in more detail in Chapter Eight.

Table 4.1 Business Case Questions

Customer/ partnership functionality orientation	*Who*	• Who will use the product/service? • Who will benefit from using the product/service? • Who should be prevented from using the product/ service?
	What	• What information will be supplied by the product/service and to whom? • What information will be needed, and from whom? • What information needs to be protected from which users? • What are the business drivers to initiate this effort?
	Where	• Where will users be primarily and secondarily located? • What type of access will be used by whom and when? • Which transactions require what security? • When will the transaction volume be heaviest? • When will information be transferred to/from each source?

	When	• When will the customers be accessing the product/service
		  and for what purpose?
		• When should someone be prevented from using the
		  product/service?

	Why	• Why should customers use this mechanism? • Are changes in business policy required and what are they?
	How	• How will the users use the product/service? • How will the new end-to-end workflow work? • How and when will customers be using the features? • How will internal applications be affected?
Customer/ partnership expectations	*Product constraints*	• What are the work flow needs (changes to current processing)? • What are the customer expectations (security, performance, usability)?
	Project constraints	• What are the reasons for deliverable time frames (market conditions, competitive analysis, customer loyalty)?
Risk orientation	*Benefits (include potential revenue)*	• Tangible/intangible benefits to the customer • Tangible/intangible benefits to the partnership • Tangible/intangible benefits to the corporation
	Costs	• Potential cost to develop the Internet-based product • Potential cost to develop supporting products (marketing, legal) • Cost of maintaining the work products

Table continued on next page.

Table 4.1   Business Case Questions (*continued*)

Risk orientation (*continued*)	*Exposures with Internet product*	• Security issues • Delayed positive return on investment • Added costs
	Risks without Internet product	• Lack of presence on the Web • Increased end-to-end time and cost • Missed customer contact
Next steps	*Management deliverables*	• Approval process • Level of corporate involvement • Priority setting • Intermediary funding • Resources (people, work space, equipment) • Program manager and executive sponsor nomination
	Organizational changes	• Program office • Reallocation of resources • Status reporting
	Program deliverables	• Planner perspective requirements • Owner perspective costs • Feasibility analysis

The Pattern Specifics

The requirements set framework and requirements pattern can be applied to all types of product development. Internet-based applications are currently in such high demand that it is important to develop a customized requirements set framework and requirements pattern to support this new business media. The requirements process introduced in the previous chapters laid the groundwork for discussing the specifics as it relates to Internet products. The purpose of this section is not to review the contents of each cell but rather to discuss specific points that need addressing during the requirements engineering process for an Internet solution. The specifics will be categorized in the following areas:

- *Important communities:* the four high-level allocation groups and the specific subgroups identified as key Internet business units involved in the requirements effort

- *Perspective specifics:* the different perspectives identifying the objective with respect to the Internet
- *Focus details:* the eight focus areas in terms of the central work product, the Internet-based application, of the Internet solution
- *Cell association checklist:* how the different cells, in an e-requirements pattern, must correlate in order to build a high-quality Internet product

Community Allocation

With an approved business case and funding to complete the cost of the Internet solution, it is time to begin the allocation process. The executive committee generally includes all the corporate communities' executives. An executive representative from each community (marketing, customer service, legal, human resources, finance, and so forth) will have reviewed and approved the business case. They will be quick to offer an explanation of their involvement and who should be contacted.

Start-up companies may delegate the development of these work products to outside organizations. For example, a three-person company may have a lawyer on retainer who can review all contracts with potential business partners. They may discuss a shipping discount plan with a major shipping company to pick up all orders from an alternate inventory location. The same three people may hire a consulting company to build the actual Web site. The need for the partnerships is identified in the business case. Each of the partnered businesses (lawyer, shippers, Web builders) is delegated (allocated) a portion of the initiating requirements, which they need to understand to complete a high-quality work product (or arrangement). The three-person company has the responsibility to watch over these business arrangements and coordinate the efforts.

In both scenarios, whether for large companies or start-ups, all business partners will want to view the business case to determine the risk they may incur. A business case is a valuable tool to organize what you want the product to do and the financial risks associated with this venture. An experienced requirements engineer is valuable for eliciting requirements that define the functionality, expectations, and organizational needs to build a high-quality Internet solution.

Important Community Specifics

As stated in previous chapters, each community (internal or external) initiates and/or is allocated requirements that evolve throughout the process. The communities are defined by the organizational structure of the corporation, which varies widely. Here, structures are grouped into four categories:

1. Organizational
2. Business practice
3. Corporate support
4. Information technology

Each of these groups participates in the development of the Internet solution. Start-ups have these same categories of communities since the business function must be performed either inside or outside of the company.

Organizational

The business communities that fall within the organizational category are those that dictate the direction of the corporation. Small companies may not have all of these communities, but the responsibilities still need to be accounted for. Specifically, these include

- *Executive management:* heads of all the business units (finance, marketing, information technology, and so on) that set the direction of the company
- *Board of directors:* individuals from other companies that advise and approve executive direction
- *Stockholders:* those who have a financial interest in the company's success (could include venture capital firms)

Any changes to requirements must be captured by the requirements engineer and validated by the executive management, the board of directors, or the stockholders. These reviewers must validate that the changes are in line with the Internet solution and the business strategy. An example would be the requirement to outsource one of the business functions, creating an end-to-end workflow that crosses corporate boundaries.

Business Practice

The business communities that fall within this category are the primary suppliers of requirements. Any department that contributes to the development and sale of the product or service should be included in this community.

For the end-to-end process of product development and delivery, the following business communities are involved:

- *Marketing:* to develop the work products to promote the product
- *Product development:* to develop the work products to be sold

- *Inventory management:* to manage the supply of the product
- *Logistics (or supply-chain management):* to distribute the product
- *Billing:* to charge the customers for the product
- *Customer service (or customer relationship management, CRM):* to manage customer use of the product

Many Internet products have failed because only one of these business areas controlled the requirements set, resulting in an Internet-based product that supplied a product without the infrastructure to support it. In most cases, marketing drives the requirements set. The result is a wonderful front-end ordering. This narrow set of requirements, however, misses key requirements that would have been identified if a full end-to-end workflow had been developed as part of the "how" requirements. A product must look enticing to buy, but the product must also:

- Be made as it was promoted to be (that is, product development)
- Be available in inventory (that is, inventory management)
- Be charged correctly and at the time of delivery, not while the product is backordered (that is, billing)
- Have a support team to help with usage of the product (that is, customer service)

With start-up companies, requirements need to be captured to build these important infrastructure components. With existing companies that are adding the Internet product as another means to offer their products or services, each of these workflow steps may already be in place. Each of them will require some changes to meet the new business strategy (customer focus). Again, all the changes and the impact of the changes need to be captured by the requirements engineer and approved by the executive committee.

Corporate Support

This community protects the interests of the corporation. The business units within this area include

- *Human resources:* to staff the project and product and define new policies and procedures
- *Legal:* to define the legal contracts between business partners as well as the corporate-to-client relationship
- *Finance:* to protect the financial interests of the company

Human resources. The primary role of human resources is to be the user of requirements. This group takes the program requirements and finds the staff required to build and support the product (warehouse staff, help desk support, and so forth).

The other responsibilities for this area include assisting in the development or alteration of business policies and procedures. These are work products developed from the business rules that are allocated to them. Human resources can help change the corporate image from being focused on the corporation to the new customer-centric philosophy.

Legal. Legal too plays an important role (see Figure 4.3) since this group is responsible for developing key Internet-related work products:

- Business partnership agreements
- Intellectual property protection
- Support information

A business-to-business relationship is a direct connection between corporations to complete end-to-end workflow. This requires negotiations as to the roles and responsibilities of each business, including a description of the level of service that is expected of each corporation (for example, response time for e-mail

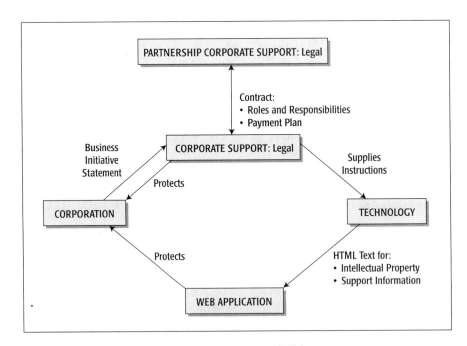

Figure 4.3   Legal Community Allocation and Responsibilities

questions). Price and performance variables are negotiated and included in the contract. Examples of other service contract items include

- Payment parameters (when payment is due and how it is determined)
- Issue resolution procedures (whom to contact when the terms of the contract are not met; what to do when something is not working as planned)
- Product service definitions (how many guaranteed packages are required to deliver a specific discount; how long products will be kept in the warehouse; what temperature the product must be kept)

The results of the negotiation will have an impact on what text is placed in portions of the Internet-based product. Descriptions of the level of service to the customer must be taken into account in the agreement with other businesses to fulfill the end-to-end workflow. For example:

1. Can a toy retailer with a Web site (such as ToysRUs.com, eToys.com, or Amazon.com) agree to have a toy delivered in time for the holidays if the service agreement with the shipping company does not have a maximum time to deliver a package?
2. Should a company offer overnight service in time for the holidays if the service agreement does not include overnight service guarantees?

These questions reflect the textual content of the Internet-based application. During review sessions, legal reviewers need to ensure that conflicts do not exist between what is being marketed and what can be achieved given legal agreements with business partners.

Further, when it comes to legal responsibilities, a controversial debate exists today in the United States concerning intellectual property, which includes what falls within the realm of copyright laws, patents, and the First Amendment (freedom of speech). Issues of intellectual property currently under discussion include the text, pictures, and movies on Web sites (protected speech); the "look and feel" of Web-based applications; the "click" process; and database contents (with regards to selling customer e-mail addresses). With traditional legal concepts being challenged, patents are being developed for a new category of intellectual property that has surfaced in the Internet economy. This expands the traditional concerns about copying or displaying of text to the mere use of the contents and process of an Internet product. It takes a lawyer who specializes in intellectual property law to decipher the laws governing content and actions for Internet-based products. He or she must be a reviewer of all requirements to prepare the necessary legal documents to protect the corporation.

Creating Internet-based products requires lawyers with other specializations as well. For example, international tax laws for Internet transactions are an important consideration, requiring a specialized tax attorney to supply calculation requirements.

In addition, support information (such as disclaimers and assurances) is supplied to the consumer to build confidence in the product. This information states the legal responsibility of the company providing the product or service to the client. For instance, security for electronic payments has advanced, and a legal notice ("the small print") needs to be provided to protect both the corporation as well as the client. These legal notices must be part of the site in a place that consumers can easily access. Again, this protects both the corporation and the consumer on a *global* level.

A requirements engineer must be sure to notify the legal department of requirements to review. The requirements engineer must allocate the responsibility to develop the different forms of legal work products (for example, business partnership agreements, intellectual property documents, tax laws, support information). The lawyers need to be aware of the business requirements (scope through essential details) as they develop these work products.

Finance. Members of the finance group supply and track the funds for doing business. They can provide valuable details as to the cost of each phase of the workflow. They can define boundaries on minimum purchases or free shipping and the effects on the corporate bottom line. In addition, they can define the scope of what can be financially supported for a particular sale.

For example, *www.Pets.com* has become a casualty of the Internet. Pets.com[3] had an excellent marketing and sales strategy, with its trademark sock puppet, which is still being requested for purchase on auction sites like eBay.com. One of the reasons for the company's failure was the lack of finance involvement in the planning process. Finance can *and should* determine the cost of doing business for the *entire* workflow. The cost of logistics (warehousing and delivery) can add tremendous cost to a product. For instance, delivering 100 fifty-pound bags of dog food to a store is much cheaper than delivering one pound to individual homes (to potentially 100 geographically disbursed addresses).

---

3. This company sold pet-related products for any type of pet. Its mascot was a sock puppet that looked like a Dalmation with an attitude. His collar was a wristwatch. Commercials showed him holding a microphone and interviewing different types of animals as he delivered different pet products.

Finance can also supply product constraints that impact the development of the Internet-based product—not the information technology requirements, per se, but the business requirements that change or define the marketing strategy. These requirements affect the Internet-based product by supplying rules that need to be implemented through either data or process.

Furthermore, finance dictates the financial portion of the project requirements (the make-or-break requirements). This group defines the limits of what can be spent on hardware, software, network, personnel, and other important aspects while building the product.

The requirements engineer must be aware of the roles, responsibilities, and impact that finance can have to support the successful implementation of the Internet product. Understanding the purpose of finance reminds requirements engineers to ensure that they have allocated responsibilities to develop financial requirements as well as to review the financial feasibility of other communities' requirements. If people from finance are not involved from the beginning, it is the requirements engineer's responsibility to get them involved!

Information Technology

Information technology (IT) is the primary tangible piece of the Internet solution. It represents the Internet product and its key deliverable. The individual work products of each business community must reflect

- The management of the technology projects (for example, finance, human resources)
- The contents of the technology product (for example, business practice, legal)
- The reaction to the usage of the technology product (for example, billing, inventory management, business partnerships such as outsourced auto-reply, shipping, or credit authorization)

In larger companies, the Internet-based product initiates changes in existing applications (such as sales databases, billing, and shipping). The requirements engineer and the business product sponsor are responsible for ensuring

- That all groups drive toward the same business objective
- That all requirements are properly allocated to the appropriate community
- That all requirements are captured
- That no conflicts exist between requirements

The rest of this chapter focuses on the IT community.

The IT community needs to address specific topics that are directly affected by the Internet. Each of these adds to the customer's experience of using the Internet product. Each of these items adds a different question set across many requirement cells. This sample of special topics transforms a requirements meta pattern into an Internet-specific pattern:

- *Application and technological architecture:* Will it support quick growth and continual enhancements?
- *Network:* Will it support the performance, reliability, different types of access, and security requirements that customers demand?
- *Security:* Will it prevent hackers from getting important corporate or customer information? Will consumer privacy be preserved?
- *Human factors engineering:* How many clicks does it take to place an order? Is there proper language for a global audience? This addresses adapting to the special needs of the target market and its associated locales.
- *Clickstream data:* What needs to be captured about the way people use the site and what should be done with that information?
- *Auto-response messaging:* What types of auto-response will be acceptable to the customer?

Let's consider each in detail.

Application and technological architecture. The technical architecture defines the hardware, software, and network that support the Internet-based application and the interface to other back-office applications. Application architecture defines what business processes will be handled on which hardware components. Discussion of these architectures usually begins to surface during the design perspective. The actual design of the technological application occurs during the builder perspective.

The first question when developing the architectures is: What will be kept and what will be changed? Integration (between business partners and internal applications) is key for handling the flexibility of and need for incremental releases (iterations) of the Internet application. It is important to accept that changes will always involve incorporating old processing, data, network, rules, and so forth. The need to blend the old environment with the new can be tricky at times.

The architecture must meet customer demands in the areas of speed, convenience, personalization, and price.[4] Customers want the cheapest, the most

---

4. See Kalakota and Robinson 1999.

familiar, or the best product or service from your Web site, all of which are based on the entire customer experience.[5]

The technological architecture consists of work products based on the requirements. The needs of the work products must be incorporated into the question matrix. For example, wireless access must be part of the Internet solution. This will also include the format of the communication (voice, data, or video). It is important for the requirements engineer to elicit specific types of information, processing, events, and business rules as well as who will access them. Nonfunctional (product constraints) requirements that pertain to performance and security need to be captured with wireless access in mind.

Network. One cannot discuss architectures (application and technology) without discussing the network. The Internet is the largest network model, comprised of multiple network subsets, some of which are within the control of the Internet application.

The network, as with the application and technical architecture, does require additional information (requirements) to fulfill the network-related work products. Network is different and therefore separate from technical architecture because only the network can be directly correlated to one of the points of view (focus areas) that requirements engineers capture from the beginning. This is particularly true for the "where" requirements. Location is one of the major pieces of information that drives the development of the network—who needs to access or receive what information, and when, as well as what actions each will perform, are all factors driven by the location. The network is essentially a system of pipes that allows communication between multiple points. As the network evolves, additional information is gathered and associated with the two ends of the communication pipeline.

Having a poorly designed network can create bottlenecks that cause poor response time and could allow access to valuable corporate information by non-authorized individuals. Both of these issues are crucial to the effectiveness and success of the Internet application. For Internet applications, it is imperative that the network engineers be alerted of the requirements and involved from the beginning. Waiting until the application and technical architecture are complete

---

5. I found one book supplier that offered the best price, but the book I wanted was back-ordered. When I found the book available from another source, I discovered that the first supplier could not easily cancel the previous book order due to their system. That was the last time I ever used that book supplier.

before involving the network engineers guarantees a late delivery date and prob-ably forces network engineers to pull something together with existing hardware (routers, lines, hubs) that will not optimize performance and security.

Security. The general public is still afraid of the Internet. They fear their iden-tity will be lost, sold, or worse yet, stolen. In order for an Internet application to be successful, it must be secure! Security is one of the critical product constraints that needs to be captured, and it does not come without cost. It is expensive to implement because it can be affected by a variety of sources and methods. Iden-tifying security as a nonfunctional requirement is the first important step. Secu-rity then needs to be viewed as it associates with all other functional focus areas. The level of security must be determined for each requirement within those focus areas.

To determine the level of security, each requirement must be reviewed as to the potential risk to the corporation if security is breached. Costs must be associ-ated with each security requirement; this determines whether the added security is worth the cost for the potential risk.

Risk should always be identified in financial terms. For example, if the cus-tomer does not feel safe submitting a credit card online, will you lose the cus-tomer? How many customers may feel wary of online transactions? What other methods can you provide to assist in increasing the comfort level of users? All of these security questions, and others that surface along the way, must be addressed.

Human factors engineering. It is important that the customer's experience be a pleasant one. This separates the product from the service. Both are important, taking equal priority. Graphic designers streamline the workflow for the custom-ers and suppliers in an easy-to-use (and perhaps entertaining) way.

Language is another issue that sends a message to the customer. "Are you want to confirm?" was an error message seen on a Fortune 500 company's sys-tem. This error provided an image of sloppy work to the customer, giving pause as to whether he should purchase something from the company. English is not an easy language, yet it has become a standard for Internet communication. It can be globally understood when the rules are followed. This includes

- Correct spelling.
- Minimized use of acronyms and mnemonics.
- Expressive formatting.

- Clear, concise style, and correct grammar.[6]
- Well-understood terminology based on the target audience (for example, if a typical user is expected to have a ninth-grade education, avoid terminology and vocabulary more typical of a post-graduate level).

The Internet, as part of a globalization business strategy, requires cultural awareness and the ability to adapt to different locales, all of which have different:

- Languages
- Data coding mechanisms
- Collating sequences
- Cultural metaphors
- Laws
- Tax systems
- Currencies
- Date and time formats
- Searching and sorting mechanisms

If you decide to sell internationally (assuming that your clients pay shipping and duties), avoid using metaphors that are locally specific (for example, baseball metaphors; boundaries on maps, on which not all folks agree; names of countries). The bottom line is to know your target customer completely!

Clickstream data. Managing Web traffic is one of the more important aspects of the Internet. It is important to anticipate the traffic for performance enhancements but also to anticipate the next incremental requirements. Once you have an idea of the kinds of visitors coming to your site, you can often find new products and services to offer them.

The data captured on all visitors is called "clickstream data." Every visitor who clicks on the Internet provides valuable information to marketing, such as:

- What products do people inquire about the most?
- How many clients purchase the product after the inquiry?
- Is the Frequently Asked Questions section used? Or are the same questions continually asked via separate e-mails?

---

6. Being an author does not mean that I am good at grammar. In fact, I'm terrible. I give special thanks to my grammar experts (my mother, sister, niece, and editors), all of whom are much better than I . . . or should I say "me"?

- How much time is saved by having clients access their own bank account information online versus telephone calls or teller visits?
- What type of computer and which version and configuration of Web browser does the consumer use?

Amazon.com is the king of clickstream data, using the information for very specialized target marketing. The company uses clever algorithms, mining through each client's click history and providing "suggestions and recommendations" on the customer's next visit to the site.

Auto-response messaging. A current *conservative* estimate is that 3 percent of all site hits trigger requests requiring some type of response.[7] For a small company with 30 hits a week, this may require that only one response be written. If the company estimates 10,000 hits per day, the number of potential responses may be 300 per day. Custom responses take, on average, three to five minutes for a person to interpret the incoming message, compose the response , and send it.

As you can see, there is a fine line between when to use auto-response (canned response based on keywords or actions) and when to supply a customized, *personal* e-mail response. Examples for each type are shown below:

- eBay.com sent auto-response confirmation messages when a bid was received, cancelled, out-bid, or successful.
- Sweetsinbloom.com sent auto-response delivery messages when an order had been shipped.
- eCost.com did not issue enough responses when it was caught for months in a backlog of order requests for Palm V handheld organizers!
- Pets.com (before it went out of business) sent a single customized response based upon several messages received from the same individual.
- Disney.com responded by telephone, instead of sending an e-mail, to a question that the representative felt would prevent a customer from visiting Disney World.
- Palmgear.com auto-replied to a service question with a message that the customer should hear back within the next 48 hours.
- Sheraton.com provided a customized, apologetic response that a particular hotel did not have ground transportation from the airport or train station.

---

7. This very rough number is used by auto-response companies during presentations and sales estimations. The percentage can vary due to promotions, poorly designed sites, how extensive the Frequently Asked Questions section is, or not providing contact information.

What all these Internet scenarios indicate is that a company must develop business rules as to how to handle the onslaught of e-mails that are inherent with the Internet. All three types of responses (automatic, customized, and telephone) cost the company in time and money and must be weighed against the need for proper customer service and satisfaction.

Perspective Questions

Reviewing by perspective identifies different types of questions that the requirements engineer should ask (see Figure 4.4). A quality gate (formal inspections) exists at the end of *each* perspective to review the contents and quality of the work products. Additional questions are asked to validate the requirement coverage for each cell. A wide range of perspectives, ranging from the planner to the subcontractor, must be considered, as addressed on the following pages.

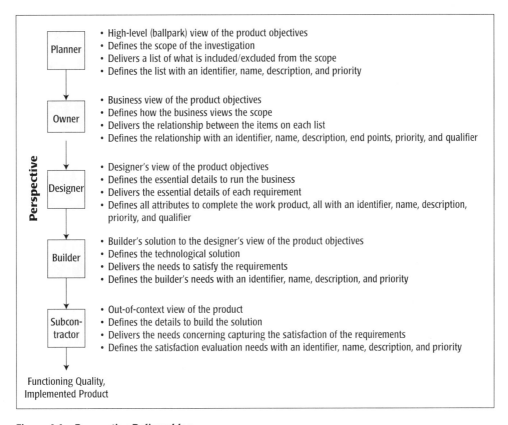

Figure 4.4 Perspective Deliverables

Planner. The objective of the planner perspective is to provide a ballpark view of the product. The planner perspective defines the scope or boundary of the investigation. Questions that typically arise surround the initiating requirements set for this business community. Within each focus area is a list of what is in and out of scope. Each entry is defined with a label, name, and description that clarifies it. Volumetric information (for example, estimated number of customers, products, deliveries, number of hits) should be available even at this early stage. Remember that each requirement must have a priority that is approved by the executive committee!

At this perspective, the requirements engineer should concentrate on capturing descriptive lists. The relationships and details of each requirement will be elicited during later perspectives.

Owner. The objective of the owner perspective is to provide information on how the business views the scope, in other words, what the business sees and operates within the boundaries set in the previous planner perspective. Within each focus area there is a list of requirements that defines the relationship between requirements as well as between other focus areas. Every relationship (association requirement) must be defined with an identifier (for traceability), such as name, description, the scope items to which it relates, and any other qualifiers as necessary.

A good place to start is to identify how things are currently done (either manually or automatically) at the corporation. For example, the current workflow (order fulfillment) should be studied to see if specific activities can be streamlined, what business rules must be updated, and what new data should be captured.

Designer. The objective of the designer perspective is not to define the product design (which comes later in product development) but rather to define the details of how the business operates within the boundaries defined in the planner perspective. The requirements are then detailed with the needed information that fully describes the items initially documented at the planner level and the relationships between the items. New requirements are developed that describe the essential details. Every new requirement must be defined in detail along with the relationship to the original requirement it is describing.

Builder. The objective of the builder perspective is to define the scope of the product, not the business. This will indicate what the Internet product will satisfy and what will need to be defined as manual intervention. At this level the roles and responsibilities are adjusted within and between corporations. Additionally, the requirements are transformed into work products that build the end product. In technological terms, this is the physical design of the Internet site. It is the infrastructure that runs the Internet business.

At this point in the process, alternate solutions can be investigated. Parts or all of the Internet-based solutions may be satisfied with commercial off-the-shelf (COTS) products. This is especially true with, but not limited to, "dot-com" start-ups (for example, shopping cart, credit card approval, user authentication). Buy, build, and outsource decisions are based on the requirements captured before this perspective. These decisions initiate the builder question set.

With detailed requirements, it is easier to determine which products are available to provide the solution for the documented needs. The purchased solution must satisfy the documented constraints, including cost, performance, and implemented time frames, to name a few. When evaluating these products, determine the level of customization that is possible and needed in order to support the entire requirements set. A requirements engineer should be part of the team that evaluates the COTS products. They have the best understanding of the full set of requirements and will ask the appropriate questions as they relate to the requirements set.

If COTS products are not an option for part or all of the Internet-based solution, requirements still need to be captured at this perspective. At this point, all requirements are support-type requirements. These requirements are needed to assist the team participants in building the product. An environment needs to be developed to build the Internet service. These are needs that must be elicited, analyzed, specified, validated, and approved. Nontraditional requirements engineers (for example, system architects and project managers) may capture these requirements, but in so doing they will be wearing the requirements engineer hat. The builder requirements need to be associated to the designer-level business requirements.

This stage represents the transformation of the business architecture to physical architectures. The requirements engineer's objective changes from the needs *of* the product to the needs for *building* the product. Requirements captured at this point all relate to the physical Internet parts (for example, software components, advertising campaigns, and so forth).

Subcontractor. The objective of the subcontractor perspective is to build work products that are capable of being implemented. These are the programs, the object definitions, the legal statements, and so forth. They are the building components that *become* the Internet solution.

For the original requirements engineer, it is important to be a reviewer at the gate to ensure that the requirements have been satisfied in the implemented version of the Internet product. Requirements engineers, along with quality engineers, can participate in validating the requirements, making sure they are met in the final product. After all, who else is better qualified to understand the requirements?

As an elicitor of requirements, the requirements engineer once again focuses on change. Requirements captured from this perspective pertain to three subjects:

1. Running the product (building the physical production environment)
2. Monitoring the success of the product and program
3. Facilitating the capturing of requirements for future iterations

Once the technical design is complete, new requirements will be defined to build the technical architecture (such as how many PCs are needed to support staff, what network equipment is required, what run-time software should be used). The architects in charge of designing the solution may define these, but these are still requirements that need to be defined in a high-quality manner— requirements that pertain to running the product.

At this perspective the requirements engineer works with all communities that need statistics for monitoring the success of the product. Some of these statistics are captured earlier as the communities define their "reporting" needs.

Using an Internet product tends to add twists for which no plans were made. Having a means for capturing information, both expected (reporting) and not expected (ad hoc analysis information), provides valuable knowledge for future iterations of the product. The requirements engineer assists by capturing requirements, at the subcontractor perspective, on how to analyze and react to the new information captured with the implemented product for use in the next iteration of the Internet product.

Focus Details

As we now know, each of the communities evolves through the perspectives. Each of the perspectives has eight views. This is the third dimension of the requirements set framework. Each view has a specific focus for identifying and evolving the different requirements:

A. Functional requirements
1. Who
2. What

3. Where

4. When

5. Why

6. How

B. Nonfunctional requirements

    7. Product constraints or quality of service

    8. Project constraints

Each of the focus areas may have a work product that depicts the point of view. They may evolve at different paces. What is important is that each work product be reviewed, validated, and approved to move to the next perspective. Members of the program team who represent different communities and perspectives should be part of the review so they can react to any change that may be required to their respective work products (approved or not). The sooner they are notified, the less the impact will have on the overall cost of the product and the time to market.

Who

"Who" requirements (see Figure 4.5) capture the people, organizations, and systems that should and should not have access to the product. For Internet applications, the following should be considered for inclusion at the scope level:

- *Customers:* anyone who should use the Internet product
- *Systems:* both internal and external to the corporation that will be part of the end-to-end workflow, including those that will react to triggers such as automatic-reply systems, billing, shipping, and parts ordering
- *Business units:* units that will interact with the Internet product, whether to react to triggers (personal answer to questions, pick up and ship packages) or to monitor activity (sales, inventory, marketing, executive management)
- *Outside organizations:* groups that will require information for example, the IRS
- *Hackers:* anyone (person or system) that should not have access to the application, including a targeted group (for example, under age) that could possibly try to use the Internet product

Each of these should be described as to their roles. Depending on the method used to develop systems, they may be defined as terminators, external entities,

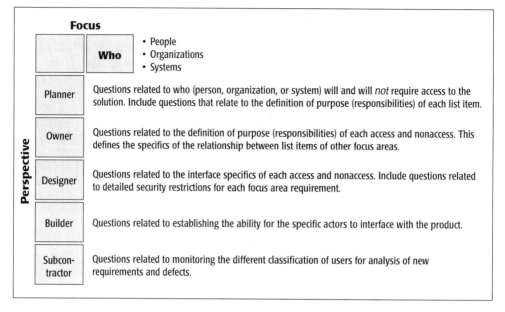

Figure 4.5 "Who" Requirement Objectives

source/recipients, or actors.[8] The point is that all those who will need to or should not be allowed to interact with the Internet application are identified.

At the *planner* level, the list of potential users is described by

- Identifier
- Name
- Description of purpose (as it relates to the Internet product)
- Priority

At the *owner* level, relationships begin to be defined. For the "who" requirements, relationships take the form of relationships between other focus-level requirements. In other words, what data, what functions, and so forth will the particular actor be using?

At the *designer* level, details about the relationships are defined, describing any detail about the specific usage of the other focus area list items. Details of security access and usage are included at this perspective.

---

8. These terms are methodology dependent. *Actors* refer to UML; *terminators* and *external entities* are terms from structured analysis.

At the *builder* level, details pertain to establishing the different users. What does the builder need to set up the different user bases? What does the quality engineer need to build specific, detailed test cases?

The actors are depicted on many other focus area deliverables throughout the perspectives. It is good to document the users' usage of other requirements in matrices (see Table 4.2). This provides a summary that will be useful for determining any impacts a change in user responsibilities will have on the entire Internet requirements set.

What

This focus area elicits requirements about use of information by the product (see Figure 4.6). The resulting work product is a model of the enterprise that defines the strategy and culture of the corporation. If the Internet directive is to change existing strategy to be more customer-centric, it is the responsibility of the requirements engineer to document the changes these new requirements have on the corporation and to obtain concurrence from the executive committee. If this is a new start-up, the Internet model will be the beginning of the enterprise model that defines its strategic direction.

The evolution of data requirements begins *(planner)* with a list of things that are important to the business. The requirements evolve into an entity or class relationship diagram *(owner)* with each entity relationship fully defined. Relationship also refers to the relationship to requirements outside the "what" focus. This is especially true for security. It is important to document the level of security access for specific pieces of business information and who has access to read, create, update, delete, and list.

Table 4.2   Sample Matrix of Roles and Requirements

	Requirement A	Requirement B	Requirement C	Requirement D
Customer	X	X		
Marketing		X	X	
Business supplier				X
Executive committee	X	X	X	X

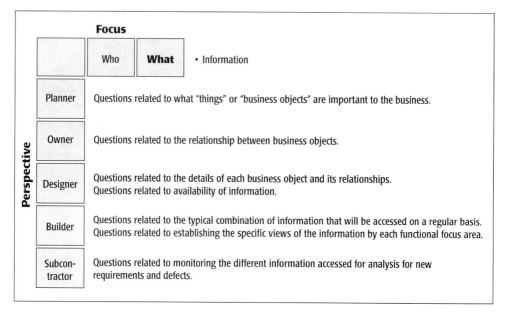

Figure 4.6   "What" Requirement Objectives

At the *designer* level, entity attributes are fully defined along with any clarification of volumetrics[9] that can be determined. Remember, the design level contains all the information to begin the transformation for the application and technological architecture. Also at the design level may be a definition of what entities (or portions of the entities) will be implemented during which product iteration. Not all entities may be fully implemented in the first release. At this level the specifics of the priority definitions emerge.[10]

The *builder* level takes the business or logical data/class model and turns it into the physical architecture. If the resulting technical environment requires a combination of relational and object-building pieces, the information model may need to be transformed into a logical data model first. This depends on the meth-

---

9. The first cut of volumetric information should be captured during the scope perspective. These values will fluctuate as more information analysis takes place during the development of the requirements.

10. Priority in this sense should not be confused with priority that is identified at the planner perspective. Priority at the designer level can segment the data contents. For example, the data entity product will support only two products. The data class delivery location may be only on the east coast. Priority at the planner perspective defines the priority for the entire entity class.

odology and technical products used to develop the "what" requirements. The *subcontractor* level produces the data definition language (object definition language) specifics. The requirements engineer is primarily interested in capturing requirements related to the monitoring of defects and clickstream data results.

Though it may be handled as a separate project within the Internet program, a data warehouse/mart may be needed to truly evaluate the usage of the Internet product. These data warehouse requirements need to be captured and evolved as with the Internet "what" requirements. Additional questions will be asked as to the availability of the information to be cleansed, populated, and used by those who will use the data warehouse. Though this project may be handled separately from the online transaction processing of the Internet application, requirements engineers responsible for the data warehouse must be part of the review process to be able to react to any impact of change. Users of the data warehouse will expect the data warehouse to be available as soon as the Internet application is live!

Where

Network requirements evolve (see Figure 4.7) as any other focus area from a list of potential locations *(planner)* to a detailed router configuration *(subcontractor)*. No other focus area requires as much information from other focus areas. In order

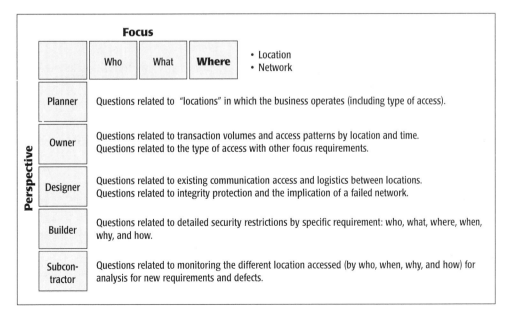

Figure 4.7   "Where" Requirement Objectives

to build a quality network, the location requirements need to be matrixed (in multiple matrices) to display:

- Who accesses what from which location?
- Who performs what from each location?
- What level of security access is required for each user, for what information, and for what type of activity?
- When does each user type access the information and perform what activity from each location?
- What conditions must be met before a user can have network access?
- What is the priority level for each of the preceding?
- What performance expectations are required?
- What type of access (for example, wireless) is needed from each location and for each type of user?
- What is the data volume and transaction volume from each location at what point in the day (or peak season)?

This is the basic information captured throughout the evolution of the "where" requirements. It is the responsibility of the requirements engineer to capture and correlate the information to the different locations. At the *builder* level, the requirements engineer captures the needs of the network engineer (including additional resources to help build and support the network).

When

Events trigger action from the product. Questions for this focus area evolve the requirements and define timing-related "when" requirements (see Figure 4.8). Depending on the methodology used, this information may be documented in event descriptions, use cases, sequence diagrams, or event correspondence diagrams. The chosen method must supply the information described in Table 4.3.

Why

Business rules define the culture and strategy of the corporation. "Why" requirements must be evaluated in minute detail (see Figure 4.9). Any changes in corporate philosophy are identified and noted, and the corporation documents its changes to a customer-centric philosophy.

Business rules should be documented individually in text as with any other focus area requirement. The illustration of requirements appears primarily in either the data ("what") or process ("how") requirements. Notes on the impact of changes in business policies (or new policies for dot-com start-ups) also need

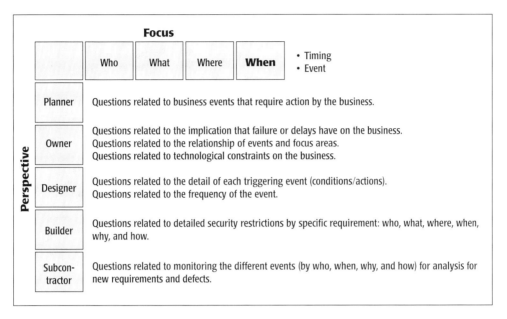

Figure 4.8 **"When" Requirement Objectives**

to illustrate the impact on other focus areas ("who, where, when"). Business rules, the "why" requirements, go through the same evolution before transforming into new business policies and procedures. For example:

- *Who:* roles and responsibility-type business rules
- *Where:* security clearance
- *When:* how long to respond to a complaint

Table 4.3 Event Details

Perspective	Requirement deliverable
Planner	Event identifier, name, priority, and brief description
Owner	Description of relationships between events (order, dependencies, correspondence), users, data, locations, processes, business rules, and business risk
Designer	Event details: conditions, actions, invariants, and volumetrics
Builder	Implementation of events
Subcontractor	Monitoring of needs to identify new requirements and defects

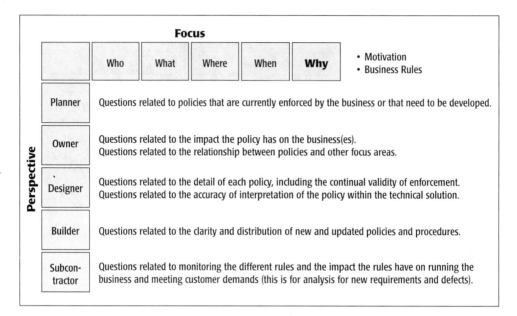

Figure 4.9   "Why" Requirement Objectives

In a B2B situation, it is important to note any potential conflicts between business rules of the different business partners. A difference in philosophy can create a risk of lost orders, missed deadlines, and such that will have a negative impact on both companies.

Throughout the evolution of the business rules, it is important to continually validate whether the "why" requirement overly constrains or opens the corporation to unneeded risk. Too vague or too restrictive rules can expose the corporation to:

- Risk of lost consumer base
- Loss of flexibility to meet customer demands
- Misinterpretation and misguided efforts of employees

How

The workflow of the Internet product is defined in this focus area. The step-by-step functions are elaborated as these requirements evolve (see Figure 4.10). Depending on the methodology used to develop the software, the diagrams and models used to reflect the requirements will differ. The same details need to be defined and captured. Most CASE tools support the data ("what") and process-

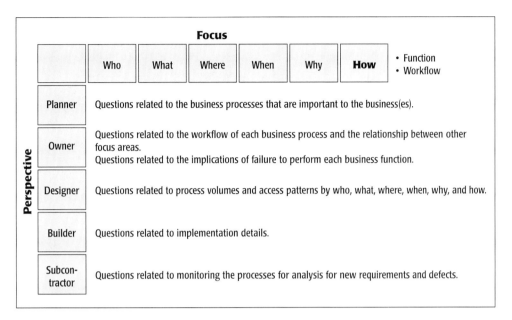

Figure 4.10   "How" Requirement Objectives

ing ("how") requirements and the relationship between the "who, what, and how." The timings and business rule requirements may be "implied" in the details. Any implied requirements can be easily missed or forgotten in the requirement evolution. With the previously described focus areas, it is apparent that additional relationships need to be defined during the owner level to fully populate the requirements set framework, all of which should be described in text that can accompany the process/object models.

Product Constraints

Any product-type restrictions that will impact design decisions are specified in this focus column of the requirements set framework (see Figure 4.11). The most common quality of service requirements[11] for Internet products relate to:

- Accessibility
- Compatibility to existing systems (interoperability)
- Conversion

---

11. This partial list is written in more detail in IEEE Standard 1233: Developing System Requirements Specifications.

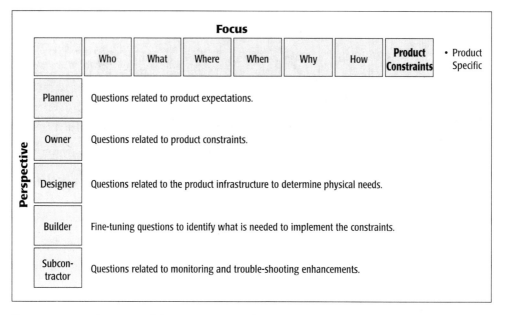

Figure 4.11   Product-Constraining Requirement Objectives

- Documentation
- Ergonomics (usability)
- Growth capacity (scalability)
- Maintainability
- Performance
- Reliability
- Security[12]
- Training

Each of these needs to clarify the capabilities and conditions in which they need to be met. They will, as with the functional focus area requirements, evolve in detail. Unlike functional focus area requirements, volumes will not be captured. Instead, each of these must define the impact on other requirements with qualifications documented clearly and concisely.

For example, performance requirements may vary by function. Querying a product's availability may have an acceptable performance of a 3-second response time. Credit card approval may allow for a 4-second response time. The association/

---

12. When thinking about security-related requirements, keep in mind privacy issues. This includes privacy of the customers, the business partnerships, and the corporation.

relationship between performance and these two functions would be qualified with the exact acceptable performance.

Project Constraints

Project constraints are *not* functional requirements. They do not live with the product throughout the product's life. They evolve (see Figure 4.12) and live with each iteration and each community (and possibly focus) that support the evolution of all requirements through the perspectives. For each iteration, all project constraints need to be coordinated to ensure that all work products have the same business objective. Project constraint requirements are reflected in common work products such as project plans, project charters, and, of course, project schedules.

As with product constraints, volumes are not captured. Instead, each of the project-related requirements affects all other types of requirements. Each of the project constraints is applied to the other requirements, at which time the other requirements negotiate to be in the iteration. A sample of project constraints includes:

- Budget
- Resources
- Time-to-market pressures (in other words, target delivery date)

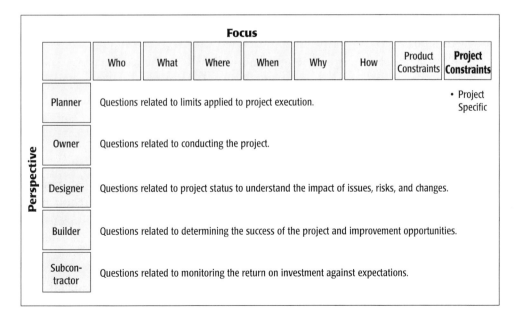

Figure 4.12 Project-Constraining Requirement Objectives

This is the one type of requirements that is often overlooked. How much can you afford to do in the first release? The other side of the equation is also forgotten—how much can be done within the budget and time frame with only these resources? Both sides of the equation have a dramatic effect on Internet success. This information forms the basis of negotiation (time-boxing) of what gets implemented (and what does not).

Cell Association Checklist

According to guidelines for writing good requirements, requirements should be specified in a manner that can be implemented independently of any other requirement. This is true . . . to a degree. Any successful system requires more than one requirement to be implemented in order for it to be successful. Processing needs information. Internet needs a network to move the information. Legal needs to approve the direction and text to protect the corporation. The requirement dependency can go on through each community, perspective, and focus. In other words, requirements will be developed that associate one requirement to another one located in a different requirements set framework cell.

Bottom line, a requirement should be specified so that everyone understands what must be implemented in order to satisfy the specific requirement. The requirement should also be specified so it can be tested on its own merits. This does not mean that a specific requirement does not need information from other cells in order to define the need. It just needs to be specified to fully explain its needs.

Check for association requirements while writing the requirements. Analyze each requirement for what it needs (from other cells) and which cell requirements it might impact. It is important to check all potential linkages during review. This includes inside and outside the community, perspective, and focus area. Basically, the five key questions to ask yourself are:

1. Does another requirement cell need my requirement to clarify itself?
2. Do I need another requirement cell's requirement in order to satisfy mine?
3. Do I need to develop another requirement in order for another requirement (inside or outside my requirements set framework cell) to be satisfied?
4. How do I qualify my requirement to work with another?
5. How does the other requirement qualify to work with mine?

Answering these five questions helps identify missing requirements that provide the mortar for the requirements set framework.

Gap Analysis

In many instances, the view of the requirements is tied to the CASE modeling tool(s) or to specific techniques (data, event, process, or object). The resulting requirements set produces a narrow, incomplete set of requirements. Common scenarios in the requirements specifications are that the initial requirements set is missing important functional components (network, for example) or it misses key impacted business units (legal, human resources, or billing, for example). Missing nonfunctional requirements (product constraints) cause the product to fall prey to the technical person's desire to use the latest technologies, leading to incorrect priorities and cost overruns. Product constraints are not known or are linked to other requirements that limit the design or functionality included in a specific iteration.

Whether or not a requirements set was captured and organized as described in the requirements pattern presented in this book, the requirements can be re-organized to fit the requirements set framework. The objective is to identify any gaps in knowledge (cells or associations with minimal or absent requirements) before the evolution of the requirement (or even the transition to the imple-mentable product).

The requirements process creates a pattern similar to the game Tetris (see Figure 4.13). With each missing or misplaced requirement (or square), the pile of mistakes grows until the game ends with a failed product. Each gap increases the risk of product failure by adding another defect. Quality engineers, as well as other reviewers/validators of the requirements set, should review the require-ments set to see whether each focus area has at least one requirement.

Every Internet product contains one or more requirements that can be cate-gorized into one of the cells (community, perspective, and focus). No one method or technique captures all requirements. The requirements process tied to the requirements pattern opens the communication to capture the specific cell contents.

Using the requirements set framework can assist reviewers in identifying missing requirements. The objective is to spot the gaps in the requirements set as soon as possible. Thus, the pattern provides value to the Internet bottom line by minimizing costly product failures due to an incomplete requirements set. This is an effective way to find defects early.

Even if the requirements set is not organized in the requirements set frame-work, reviewers can ask questions during formal inspections by category while

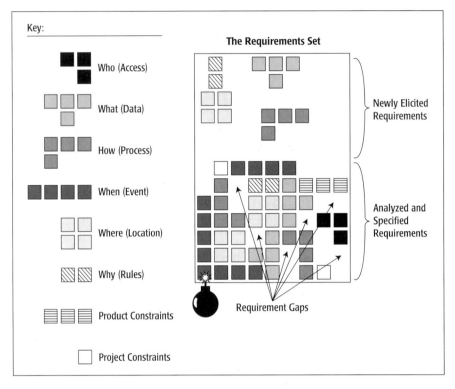

Figure 4.13   Requirement Gap Analysis (Game first developed by Alexey Pajitnov. Currently owned by the Tetris Company. Currently licensed to Nintendo.)

reading the requirements specification. Reviewers could identify gaps and notify the team before the design effort begins. Identifying these gaps helps prevent faulty design or the need for redesign.

Conclusion

A requirements meta pattern is a framework for requirements that includes guidelines on how it should be filled. The Internet requirements pattern (see Appendix B) goes one step further by adding specific Internet related questions for each of the requirement category cells. Since one of the primary deliverables for the Internet-based application is software, those Internet cells were described with objectives and questions in this chapter (see Table 4.4).

Table 4.4 Information Systems Architecture with Expanded Focus

	Focus							
Perspective	Who: People Organizations Systems	What: Data	Where: Network	When: Timing Event	Why: Motivational Business Rules	How: Functional	Product Constraints: Product Specific	Project Constraints: Project Specific
Objectives/ Scope (Ballpark View) Defines the scope of the investigation	The objective is to understand the scope of the external interfaces.	The objective is to understand the scope of the information to investigate.	The objective is to understand the scope of the connectivity requirements. This includes Web access.	The objective is to understand the scope of the transaction volume that must be supported.	The objective is to understand the scope of the business rules and policies that are to be analyzed.	The objective is to understand the scope of the functionality to investigate and business events that trigger action.	The objective is to understand the perceived expectations of system capabilities.	The objective is to understand the restrictions associated with running the program/ project.
Model of the Business (Owner's Logical/Business View) Defines how the business views the scope	The objective is to understand the responsibilities of each access, including the reasons.	The objective is to understand the cardinality between the business objects.	The objective is to determine the impact on the existing network. This may put constraints on possible solutions.	The objective is to understand the impact on the who, what, where, when, and how.	The objective is to understand and to analyze the impact on who, what, where, when, and how.	The objective is to understand the business and to uncover what is essential to the business, eliminating imposed constraints.	The objective is to determine if they can work with what you have or if you will require upgrades or new hardware and software. This may put constraints on possible solutions.	The objective is to define the project organization and managerial process.

Table continued on next page.

Table 4.4 Information Systems Architecture with Expanded Focus (*continued*)

	Focus							
Perspective	**Who:** *People Organizations Systems*	**What:** *Data*	**Where:** *Network*	**When:** *Timing Event*	**Why:** *Motivational Business Rules*	**How:** *Functional*	**Product Constraints:** *Product Specific*	**Project Constraints:** *Project Specific*
Model of the Information System (*Designer's View*) Defines the essential details to run the business; technology independent	The *objective* is to understand the specific needs related to information, function, and means of access to the solution.	The *objective* is to fine-tune the information to be accessed in the most efficient manner.	The *objective* is to determine if they will have enough network bandwidth to support your new system.	The *objective* is to understand what triggers each event and the responses that are required.	The *objective* is to understand and remove outdated business rules and policies or adjust them to reflect the current business environment.	The *objective* is to clearly define the specifications of the system for a specific technological platform.	The *objective* is to determine if they will have enough hardware to support the solution.	The *objective* is to understand the impact of issues, risks, and changes to the plan.
Technology Model (Builder's View) Defines the technological solution to the logical view; technology dependent	The *objective* is to understand the detailed security restrictions.	The *objective* is to plan for the capacity.	The *objective* is to verify performance characteristics.	The *objective* is to understand the performance tuning requirements constrained by the technology.	The *objective* is to understand the exact wording required for the updated and new policies and procedures.	The *objective* is to verify performance characteristics. Help information will also be the center of concern.	The *objective* is to understand the performance and space restrictions for application and data deployment strategy.	The *objective* is to understand the impact of issues, risks, and changes to the plan.

Table 4.4 Information Systems Architecture with Expanded Focus (*continued*)

Perspective		Who: People Organizations Systems	What: Data	Where: Network	When: Timing Event	Why: Motivational Business Rules	How: Functional	Product Constraints: Product Specific	Project Constraints: Project Specific
	Focus								
Detailed Representations (Out-of-Context View) Defines the details to build the technological solution; language specific		The *objective* is to understand the detailed security restrictions.	The *objective* is to customize user views of the information that will maintain security access privileges.	The *objective* is to understand the implication of a failed network.	The *objective* is to understand the implication of a failed system.	The *objective* is to understand the accuracy of newly written or updated policies and procedures.	The *objective* is to write the programs for your software system. This will include functionality and security.	The *objective* is to understand the capacity limits and performance fine-tuning requirements.	The *objective* is to identify improvements to the process for the next project or implementation of the solution.
Functioning System (House) The software system solution		User-friendly access.	Data available.	Communication access.	Transactions triggered.	Published policy and procedures.	Functioning software system.	System software and hardware available.	Project (phase) implemented. Monitoring phase initiated.

CHAPTER FIVE

Internet Requirements Anti-Patterns

> **Chapter Key Topics**
> - **Knowledge gap anti-patterns**
> - **Participation anti-patterns**
> - **Process-oriented anti-patterns**
> - **Creating additional anti-patterns**
>
> **The Internet Impact**
> The Internet exposes companies to risk on a global level. The speed at which the business must operate and the increased volume of traffic can bring out numerous bumps and trips while building the Internet product. Anti-patterns need to be developed and followed to help requirements engineers avoid common mistakes that could cripple the product and program.

The requirements meta pattern is not a silver bullet. It is a template that can be applied to assist in identifying as many requirements as possible. An Internet requirements pattern is simply a tailored version of a pattern for Internet-based applications; it does not guard against common requirement-related pitfalls. *Anti-patterns*, therefore, are descriptive guides that serve this purpose. They describe a solution for a commonly occurring problem that generates decidedly negative consequences. A *requirements anti-pattern* addresses a defective requirements set.

Anti-patterns began to appear in the world of design due to the work of Christopher Alexander.[1] The need for anti-patterns grew out of planning

---

1. See Alexander, 1977.

towns and constructing buildings within towns. Alexander designed a method whereby checks and balances were devised to ward off any potential problems. Around 1986, Ward Cunningham and Kent Beck[2] applied Alexander's approach to developing user interfaces in Smalltalk programming language. It wasn't until 1994, when Jim Coplien[3] submitted a paper to the first Pattern Languages of Program Design industry conference, that anti-patterns were launched into the mainstream.

The basic premise of anti-patterns is that developmental processes can be variable; however, there is always a single common, invariant, underlying process. This underlying process is the common framework in which all programs, objects, towns, buildings, requirements sets, and so forth can be built. All anti-patterns:[4]

- Are a method for efficiently mapping a general situation to a specific class of solutions
- Provide real-world experience in recognizing recurring problems in the software industry and provide a detailed remedy for the most common predicaments
- Provide a common vocabulary for identifying problems and discussing solutions
- Support the holistic resolution of conflicts, utilizing organizational resources at several levels where possible
- Provide stress release in the form of shared misery for the most common pitfalls in the software industry

The requirements anti-patterns use the same preceding premise and apply it to the development of the requirements set (see Figure 5.1). They are written to avoid commonly occurring gaps in the requirements set that will cause either product or project risk. *Product risk* causes defects in the functionality of the Internet product (lacking features or not working as desired). *Project risk* affects the project's return on investment due to cost overruns, delayed implementation (especially if it results in missed market opportunities or allows another dot-com to obtain brand acceptance), or resource conflicts (for example, lack of staff, insufficient skills). Anti-patterns provide a means for coaching the require-

---

2. See Cunningham and Beck, 1986.
3. See Coplien and Schmidt, 1995.
4. See Brown et al., 1998.

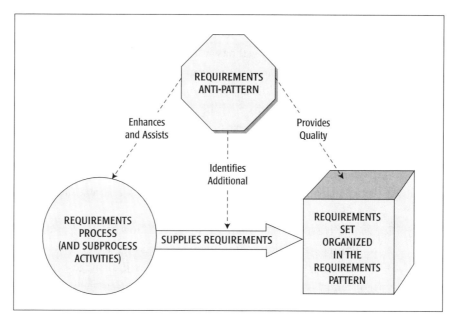

Figure 5.1   Anti-Pattern Purpose

ments engineer around common obstacles that could lead to either type of risk. These obstacles can be grouped into three gap groups:

1. *Gaps in knowledge:* problems caused by missing key requirements
2. *Gaps in participation:* problems caused by groups that should not be involved and accepted groups that aren't involved at the right time
3. *Gaps in process:* problems caused by omitting stages of the requirements evolution

The following sections in this chapter review each of these different gap groups. Sample Internet-based requirements set anti-patterns are provided for each group. The text form for each is available in Appendix D. These forms are provided as a starting point and can be customized to meet the specific needs of your organization.

Gaps in Knowledge

The most common type of anti-pattern for any requirement effort addresses gaps in knowledge. The requirements pattern, with the cell formation (community, perspective, focus, and association), identifies the different types of requirements, and it is quite noticeable if no requirements have been captured for a particular cell or association. If every cell has at least one requirement, it may not be as easy to identify whether a cell is missing one or more requirements. Even with answers to all the questions (including questions added by your project) in the requirements pattern (see Appendix B), gaps in knowledge may still result.

Three different anti-patterns are discussed here to illustrate the breadth of anti-patterns that fall in this gap in knowledge group:

1. *Predators (hacker intervention and other security issues):* to suggest how an anti-pattern can be used to handle negative scenarios, such as using child-proof caps on pill bottles to prevent harm
2. *Quality of service (QoS) impact:* to suggest how an anti-pattern can be used to capture association requirements for product constraints
3. *Create, read, update, delete, and list (CRUDL):* to suggest how an anti-pattern can be used to verify the contents of a different cell

Predators: Hacker Intervention and Other Security Issues

With any Internet application, the requirements engineer is the first line of defense. With each new idea, the requirements engineer must elicit, analyze, specify, and validate requirements that include the possibility of a hacker. It is a "must" for all new development, enhancements, or even maintenance to add requirements targeted toward preventing predator attacks on any corporate assets. To accomplish this, one must understand two concepts:

1. What is a hacker?
2. What are corporate assets?

What Is a "Hacker"?

A hacker is a predator that infiltrates an organization's information resources via the Internet. A predator can be any person, organization, or system that should not have access to any part of the corporate technological infrastructure. The hacker can attach itself to anything and disguise itself as anything.

As the recent outbreak of computer viruses has illustrated, it is impossible to ward off all attacks. Even handheld devices and mobile telephones have been attacked through wireless e-mail facilities. By simply acknowledging their existence, some planning efforts and additional security requirements can be built into existing and new applications.

What Are Corporate Assets?

Hacker infiltration can cost corporations billions of dollars each year. Important data can be lost or, worse yet, corrupted (with or without knowledge) to a point that it often goes undetected by the organization. Data that can be attacked include customer database information, new product requirements, corporate (or personal) financial data, workers' address books, signatures,[5] and so forth.

Corporate assets are composed of not only data. Corporate assets can also take the form of programs and networks that control the movement of information. If program structures are corrupted, business rules and policies can be lost or manipulated to reduce corporate revenues.

What Can Be Done?

Requirements engineers can take steps to minimize hacker infiltrations. This activity is similar to the childproof cap scenario for medicine and toxins.[6] To minimize predator infiltration, enforce the following four precautions:

1. *Predator requirement:* Add an actor or user called "predator" to your list of "who" requirements.
2. *Scenario development:* Add a scenario for every use case or workflow where other users are listed.
3. *Predator association and priority matrices:* Develop an association between the predator and each class/subclass (entity/subtype), network node, event, business policy/rule, and function.
4. *Preparation for the inevitable:* Document a process and procedure to use if a predator slips through the cracks and infiltrates the system.

Predator requirement. "Who" types of requirements define the roles, people, organizations, and systems that require access to the solution. They are the potential users and external interfaces. By documenting the predator as a potential user or actor, the requirements engineer can begin to elicit any security requirements. The objective is to identify who *should not* have access to the sys-

---

5. Written signatures are an extra means of security to validate a given transaction. Electronic signatures are not considered legal. To protect the organization and client, when developing predator scenarios consider the implication if a hacker obtains customer signatures.

6. To learn more about the childproof cap scenario and requirements, see Gause and Weinberg, 1990.

tem. After labeling the actor, describe the predator. Document any previous infiltration known to the business. Document the possible forms it may take to enter the corporate resources. Most importantly, add to the description that the predator desires access to corporate data. By writing this down, this fact is available for all reviewers (such as network engineers) to see. Once seen, it will spark additional thought and additional requirements to prevent infiltration.

Table 5.1 illustrates an actor definition for a predator. Notice that the type of actor can be a user, file, or computer program. The purpose is to prepare for any type of infiltration, including an attachment to any e-mail[7] (for example, the Happy99 or ILOVEYOU viruses).[8] Although the Happy99 virus did not destroy any files, it used an unsuspecting e-mail user's address book to infect the systems of others. This virus was a wake-up call for other more damaging viruses. Unfortunately, the ILOVEYOU virus had a much more devastating effect on unsuspecting e-mail users.

Many people are involved in providing a piece of the solution: data security, network engineers, business users, and so on. When the requirements engineer lists the predator as a possible user of the system, everyone on the team is alerted to prevent such infiltration.

Table 5.1   Predator Description

Label	Predator
Type of actor	User (single and organization), file, or program
Type of access[a]	Internet, wireless, direct
Description	Any uninvited access to corporate assets
Responsibilities	1. To minimize any access at all entry points 2. To provide additional checks after entry to minimize the impact of infiltration to sensitive data and processing

a. "One of the most widely used—and overlooked—points of entry into a company's network is dialing in through an analog modem. Hackers call a company's phones, one after another, or use 'war dialer' to sweep the company's extensions, hoping to stumble on an open modem to answer the call." (Hulme, 2000)

---

7. Another type of intrusion is a Trojan horse. Often viruses are used to provide back doors that hackers use to break into corporate and personal computers.

8. To learn more about viruses, refer to Norton Utilities (www.norton.com).

Scenario development. Scenarios should be developed for hackers as for any other actor. In fact, hackers need to be part of all scenarios developed for other type of actors. Remember, a hacker can take many forms, including that of a potentially valid user during other scenarios. Hackers can become invisible by attaching themselves to other means of access. Document any precautions that need to be in place at each point of possible entry for every scenario developed. Keep in mind that a hacker can be internal. A disgruntled employee can erase valuable material from a department LAN drive and e-mail the information to a competitor. Additional requirements may be identified to validate that the user is not a predator in this specific instance.

Table 5.2 shows an example of how one can add security precautions against predators. This very high level scenario is an example from an online trading application between corporate entities.

This example shows security being placed at both the broker organization level and the individual broker level. This high-level (planner perspective) event

Table 5.2 Predator Scenarios

Label	Submitting multiple broker trades
Actors	Approved broker, predator
Description	Submission of multiple trades from one specific broker
Conditions	Broker is approved (valid broker identifier with approved status)
Actions	1. Validate all trades for content and form. 2. Apply trades to the account. 3. Notify broker of account status.
Predator precautions	1. A copy of the previous broker account is taken. 2. All trades must be within the acceptable boundary for the broker. 3. The summation of the trades must be within the bounds of what the broker is allowed to execute. 4. The pattern of trades submitted must be within the varying limits that are characteristic for this broker. 5. If any of the preceding failed, notification is sent to the broker as well as to the risk manager responsible for the broker.
Volumetrics	Each broker typically submits: • min. 10 transactions per hour • avg. 25 transactions per hour • max. 100 transactions per hour

anticipates the predator by instituting acceptable dollar ranges for each broker and broker organization. These ranges were developed as part of contractual negotiations. A risk manager is assigned to each broker with daily and ad hoc reports of broker transactional analysis. The volumetrics provide an additional check for any unusual change in the volume of transactions.

The point of this anti-pattern is to plan ahead. If requirements engineers don't mention *predator precautions*, busy executives may not take the time to anticipate the possible infiltration.

Predator association and priority matrices. Security comes at a price. It is important to identify what level of security each type of corporate asset needs. This can be accomplished by developing a simple matrix and associating the hacker to each corporate asset. Document the priority of the association (low security, medium security, high security, critical). This association prioritizes the security restriction of what the predator *cannot* have access to *at any cost*. Make sure the people who approve the requirements also review these associations and priorities.

The association can be done by using many CASE tools, requirements management tools, or simply a spreadsheet. In an Excel spreadsheet, for instance, create a "book" called "predator." Each "sheet" should be for each kind of corporate asset or, at this level, each type of requirement (perspective/focus). The sheets relate the predator to:

- Data classes, attributes, and relationships
- Locations, nodes, and data available at these nodes
- Events, scenarios, and each activity
- Business rules
- Business functions

With the understanding that the predator can emulate any actor, the rows list each actor. The columns are for each of the other functional focus areas. Each matrix identifies the level of security (see Table 5.3). The security priority is to prevent predator access.

Due to the cost issues, the business community states the level of security. The level of security for each event and each actor is a separate and individual requirement. Check for consistency between the cells. (For example, at what condition does one actor have a higher security than another? Why does one event have higher security clearance than another?)

Preparation for the inevitable. Unfortunately, not all hackers or other types of predators may be prevented from infiltrating a system. It is important to docu-

Table 5.3   Predator Security Priority Matrix

Actor	Event			
	Submit Trade	**Change Trade**	**Delete Trade**	**Inquiry Trade**
Broker	H	H	H	M
Risk manager	N/A	H	H	M
Administrator	M	H	L	M

ment a process and procedure for action in case a predator cracks the system. For Internet applications, quality assurance or software process improvement specialists should be notified of possible infiltration risks so they can coordinate policies and countermeasures based on the kind of access and the security priorities.

Creating Your Own Protection Program against Predators

To customize the hacker anti-pattern, begin with the predator anti-pattern shown in Appendix D. Initiate a meeting between key security representatives for all corporate assets, especially from business, finance, legal, and information technology. If possible, include representatives from vendors that supply wireless/mobile devices. Then, ask each representative the following questions:

- What corporate assets do you represent?
- What do you need to know to grant the different security levels?
- Who typically grants access and at what level?
- What is the risk to the corporation if a predator obtains access?
- What different countermeasures can be put in place to avoid the risk?
- What is the relative cost of each type of countermeasure?

With this type of information, develop a specific question list that will help elicit the security needs from the requirement supplier.

The Objective of the Predator Anti-Pattern

The objective of the previous steps is to plan ahead. By documenting the potential predator, everyone thinks about it. Without documenting the possibility, important security requirements may be overlooked and omitted. The hacker anti-pattern is a form of protection against predators.

Thanks to the Internet, everyone is vulnerable to attacks from predators that mean harm. Corporate assets (for example, users, data, networks, processes, policies, and procedures) are at risk. Though it is impossible to ward against all attacks, it is possible to plan ahead for the inevitable. With any information technology project, the first step is to define the scope of the effort. Requirements engineers can help protect against predators by adding them as potential users whose infiltration must be guarded against.

Quality of Service Impact

Many requirements engineers base the requirements set on what is captured by the CASE tool they are using. They assume that the CASE tool captures all types of requirements. Sad to say, this is not true. Most CASE tools capture only functional requirements and, in fact, only a subset of functional requirements. For instance, network requirements are notoriously forgotten!

Furthermore, many requirements engineers base the requirements set on a specific technique or method of developing software. Again, they assume that the technique (such as use cases) or method (for example, event-driven) captures all types of requirements. These techniques and methods were never intended to be the only means of capturing the requirements. They were developed only to satisfy a specific subset of requirements.

Both of the preceding scenarios have in common the lack of coverage for nonfunctional requirements. As discussed in previous chapters, it is important to capture the nonfunctional requirements to determine the impact they will have on the functional requirements (see Figure 5.2). Missing either type of requirements increases the risk of failure for the project (or iteration) and the Internet product.

This anti-pattern concentrates on the subset of product constraints that pertain to QoS requirements, a type of nonfunctional requirement. A similar anti-pattern can be tailored to support other product and project constraints. The reason for segregating the QoS requirements from the other types of constraints is because of the direct impact they have on the Internet product.

Specifically, this anti-pattern covers the following three constraints:

1. *Performance:* The Internet product must perform within the time frame specified for each functional requirement.[9]
2. *Usability:* The Internet product must be easy to use as specified by each functional requirement. Associating this requirement to functional requirements supplies a way to quantify the ease of use.

---

9. Reliability should be considered a separate type of product constraint requirement from performance.

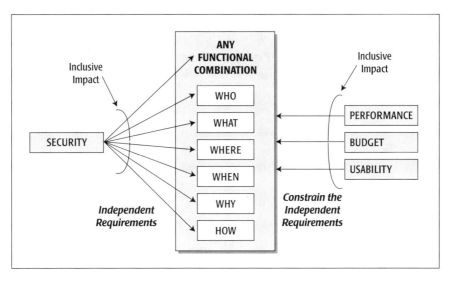

Figure 5.2   Constraints Have Multiple Impacts.

3. *Privacy:* The Internet product must protect the identities of customers and business partners from all potential viewers, internal and external to the corporation. Customer information (for example, e-mail addresses) cannot be sold to any individual or organization without permission. They must not be spammed with a flood of e-mails, newsletters, or announcements.

The preceding three QoS requirements were selected as examples because they often take high priority when defining a customer-centric approach to the Internet. They all affect users (customers and business partners) of the Internet product. The same technique described in the anti-pattern should be used for all the QoS indicators.

These sample QoS requirements are specified in an ambiguous manner because the value (the means of identifying that the requirement is satisfied) will vary by the relation to functional requirements.

What Can Be Done?

First, the requirements engineer must identify the list of QoS topics (subject areas) that need to be considered. A partial but thoughtful list (which includes the three used here as examples) exists in the IEEE System Requirement Specification Standard (Std 1233: SyRS). The list identifies an assortment of nonfunctional product constraint requirements.

The second step is to describe what is meant by each of the QoS topics. For example, what do usability, performance, and privacy mean in general? *All reviewers must agree on the definitions during the planner perspective.* It is important to identify the need for such QoS requirements and to create definitions that are clear, concise, and correct. The QoS requirements will be further defined when associated to specific individual requirements.

The owner perspective is the key to understanding the impact that each of the QoS requirements has on the Internet product. Each functional requirement must be identified and the impact quantified, meaning that there is an understanding of the expectation the requirement supplier has with respect to usability, performance, and privacy. A table similar to Table 5.4 can be created, or a separate list of functional requirements can be prepared that lays out expectations for specific QoS requirements.

The correlations between the individual functional requirement and the QoS requirements are to be considered separate derived requirements. They associate the general QoS requirement with the functional cells.

In addition, each of these specific QoS requirements should be written to meet the quality standards of individual requirements (see Chapter Six) and categorized under the product constraints category. Under the association section of the requirements specification (see Appendix A) should be a list of cross-cell association identifiers and names with any qualification instructions.

Gap Analysis

Listing all the QoS requirements in the product constraint cell illustrates that product expectations were elicited from the requirement supplier. They can be reviewed individually for feasibility (by technology as well as by cost) during the review sessions.

Table 5.4   Matrix for Clarifying Quality of Service Impacts or Expectations

Individual Requirement	Quality of Service		
	Usability[a]	Performance	Privacy
Requirement name	Qualifier description[b]	Qualifier description	Qualifier description

a. In a completed matrix, a general definition of each quality of service topic would be included with each heading in this row.

b. The text in each qualifier cell describes how the functional requirement listed in the row relates to the nonfunctional requirement listed in the column.

The requirement reviewers also need to review the association section under the product constraints and the functional (who, what, where, when, why, and how) requirement cells. For each functional requirement cell, the QoS expectation for the individual requirement should be clear. This will also illustrate whether there are multiple QoS effects on individual requirements, enabling reviewers to see any conflicts that exist between the different QoS effects and the requirements. Under the QoS association section, the requirement users can see how a single expectation affects multiple individual functional requirements. A pattern can be seen that will facilitate the selection of technical options.[10]

The Objective of the QoS Anti-Pattern

The QoS anti-pattern is designed to ensure that the requirement supplier's expectations are understood. Expectations are requirements that constrain the designer's choices for the Internet technical solution. Defining a list of QoS requirements without an association with the functional requirements does not specifically identify the impact of the requirement. Without the association, the expectations will be vague and probably not satisfied.

Create, Read, Update, Delete, and List

There are basically five things that can be done to any individual piece of data: it can be created, read/inquired,[11] updated, deleted, or listed. Events must exist to manipulate the data in those five ways. For example, here is a scenario in which one of the five events on data was overlooked. One of the leading Internet book retailers had the best price on technical books. The site was easy to use. A customer could order a book and continually inquire about the status of the order. However, if he wished to cancel the book order, no automated facility existed.[12]

---

10. This is an important point. A single QoS expectation can be applied to multiple functional requirements. At the same time, a single functional requirement may be affected by several QoS expectations. It is important to review both sides of the impact for correctness and feasibility. It may be important to relax some of the QoS expectations that are not high priority in order to satisfy others that are. A compromise enables the designers of the technical solution to physically design the best solution that is scalable, flexible, and supportive of the business objectives.

11. This includes searching for the item.

12. This scenario occurred during an early release of the product. The problem was corrected in a future iteration.

Every piece of data should have events that can create, read, update, *and delete* (even if you want to only logically delete) the item!

It is always important to plan for all possible scenarios. If one customer does not have the facility to cancel an order easily, he will hesitate to order from you again. This is what may occur if you do not use the anti-pattern to identify and develop all the CRUDL events needed to build a high-quality system.

The CRUDL anti-pattern assists the requirements engineer in identifying all the possible events that need to be triggered. It ensures that all the requirements have been identified that relate to manipulating data in these five basic areas (that is, all functions that control the data). It confirms that all data is

- Captured properly
- Deleted when necessary
- Updated properly
- Inquired upon
- Provided as a list selection

Events must exist to trigger *each* of the five types of data manipulation for *each* entity class.[13] The same event may trigger multiple entity class manipulations, but each entity class must be triggered by at least one event for each manipulation type (create, read, update, delete, and list).

What Is an Event?

In order to begin to build the correlation between events and data, it is important to review what an event is. An event represents the *timing* functional focus ("when") in the requirements meta pattern. An event is a stimulus that causes processing to take place within the scope of analysis—in other words, a trigger.

The four types of events (standard, ad hoc, time-initiated, and conditional)[14] do not apply just to business events. Even physical events—such as using a pull-down menu, pushing a button, selecting an option—are events that trigger processing. Typically, a single selection or a combination of selections initiates processing that represents a standard kind of event. No matter which kind of event, it triggers processing that manipulates data. Each piece of data needs to be created,

---

13. For the purposes of this discussion only, entity class is used to describe both the object and the entity (including subtypes). At this point in the discussion, it does not matter if you are modeling in data modeling or object-oriented notation.

14. Events are described in more detail in Chapter Three.

read, updated, deleted, and listed by an event. For the Internet, the primary types of events fall into the standard and conditional categories.

Data-event correlation. Each one of these kinds of events manipulates data by creating, reading, updating, or deleting (either physically or virtually). It is important to look at all the data requirements and note how each event manipulates the data. This can be accomplished by using many CASE tools, a requirements management tool, or a simple spreadsheet. A CRUDL "when" matrix lists the entity class as rows and the events as column headers. Each cell indicates the type of manipulation, for example, create (C), read (R), and so on (see Table 5.5).

The key to the CRUDL "when" matrix is that every entity class has a life: each has a birth (create), lives (read and update), and dies (delete), and each is listed during those four states. Since data are inanimate objects, events must be triggered to manipulate them. So, for each entity class, make sure that events manipulate the data in the five ways.

When describing your entities, make notes as to which events create, read, update, delete, and list them. This simple association is the beginning of the CRUDL "when" matrix. As the requirements evolve, the matrix should also evolve to include all the attributes of the entity classes.

Data-processing correlation. Just as you can correlate the data to the events, you also can correlate the data with processing. After all, the events trigger processing. By correlating the data directly to the processing, you can quickly identify when in the process of reacting to an event the manipulation takes place. This matrix is the CRUDL "how" matrix.

Table 5.5   Entity Class Correlation Matrix

	Event				
Class	**Become a Member**	**Submit Trade**	**Supply Margin**	**Trade Summary**	**Broker Defaults**
Broker membership	C	R	R	R	D
Stock position	C	C	R	R	U
Margin account	C	U	U	R	U

In this case, a spreadsheet may become cumbersome as the requirements evolve into programs and data attributes. This information is extremely valuable to anyone who must debug a system. It may be easier to use a formal CASE tool that allows simple associations between these meta objects. All CASE tools have some reporting mechanism that allows you to print the association.

The Objective of the CRUDL Matrix Anti-Pattern

The CRUDL anti-pattern is the application of a matrix technique. Its objective is to double-check that all the events and entity classes have been identified. Events are the initiating trigger of all processing. As exemplified in the book-ordering system, miss one event and you may lose the customer. Oversights as blatant as not allowing customers to delete orders do not portray professionalism. Entity classes form the information that supports the business. By creating a simple two-dimensional matrix, you can cross-check to find any missing gaps in maintaining that information.

Gaps in Participation

The success of an Internet product requires that many different types of requirements be supplied by different individuals. If even one business community is missing, the resulting gap in knowledge can potentially destroy any chance of succeeding with the product. Since this discussion deals with Internet products, gaps in participation apply to all parties involved, including those that cross corporate boundaries.

To illustrate the breadth of anti-patterns for this gap group, three different ones are discussed here:

1. *Network engineers:* to suggest how an anti-pattern can be used to include internal business communities
2. *Business model tolerance indicators:* to suggest how an anti-pattern can be used to include external business communities
3. *Click-stream data:* to suggest how an anti-pattern can be used when interests vary among business communities

Involvement of Network Engineers

The Internet has expanded the idea of distribution to include not only distributed data but also distributed applications. The result is the distribution of fully functional, file-sharing applications online from one to an infinite number of computers. This creates, via the Internet, a virtual supercomputer by linking the many parts into a whole. This also creates a networking nightmare. Security and performance must be analyzed and controlled. (Security was discussed previously under the predator anti-pattern. The performance aspect is partially handled by the QoS anti-pattern.) The purpose of this additional anti-pattern is to involve the network people before the physical design is established. This group serves a critical purpose and could make or break the chance of success for the Internet product. The needs that affect the network engineers are captured as a separate functional focus ("where").

Network engineers tend to need information as soon as possible. In general, they are overworked[15] and have to worry about the impact the application may have on the corporate infrastructure. Networks are also costly and take time to install or upgrade. It is important to provide network engineers with the information they need as the requirements evolve.

The Network Problem

The most notorious problem with Internet-based application development is that network engineers are brought in too late. They must work with existing equipment, creating ways to solve such problems as slow response time and, worse yet, network down time. Network engineers need to understand the requirements in two areas:

1. Fault tolerance and recovery
2. Communication

Both of these can be derived from the different focus areas (functional and nonfunctional).

What Can Be Done?

As with many groups that work on producing Internet products, network engineers are notoriously swamped as they try to meet their deadlines. They must

---

15. This is not to imply that the rest of the project team is not overworked. Network engineers are often left for last and are thus a good example for this gap in participation anti-pattern. This same anti-pattern can be adjusted to facilitate the involvement of whatever group is often overlooked or brought into the process late.

support not only the Internet-based application but also the network that allows the program team and the rest of the organization to work together. They will probably be too busy to participate in any requirement elicitation.

One way to encourage their involvement is to include them in the review process. They should review all requirements that affect them. They will not appreciate having to review the entire requirements specification for any of the perspectives. They will appreciate seeing the requirements specification organized in a format (see Appendix A) that enables them to concentrate on the requirements that impact them. Showing this level of respect for their time encourages them to read through most (do not expect all) of the specifications.

If you are new to networking, ask network engineers for their assistance to specify the requirements with supporting diagrams. The engineers will be able to either translate what the current network is or provide ideas on how to illustrate the requirements to facilitate their evolution into the physical network design.

Requirement Conflicts

Project constraints impact the network architecture. Even if the network requirement calls for full fault tolerance and a ten-minute recovery period, if the budget cannot withstand the dollars needed to purchase the equipment required, the network requirements or the project requirements need to be reevaluated. This is one of the requirement conflicts typically seen when reviewing the requirements set.

The Network Involvement Anti-Pattern

The key to involving network engineers in the requirements process is to illustrate that you respect their time. The information they need to do their physical work must be captured by the requirements engineer. The questions include

- What has to be transferred across the network?
- From what point to what point does it need to be transferred?
- How much has to be transferred?
- When does it need to be transferred?
- By whom does it need to be transferred?

Network engineers need to know data from all the other focus areas and how the information intersects with the different locations that are within and outside the scope. Developing a matrix (see Table 5.6) to illustrate the associa-

Table 5.6   Network Location Impact Matrix

Individual Requirement	Network Locations		
	From Location A to Location B	From Location A to Location C	From Location B to Location C
Requirement name[a]	Qualifier description	Qualifier description	Qualifier description

a. In a completed matrix, rows would be included for the "who," "what," "when," "why," and "how" functional requirements as well as the product and project constraints.

tions by location and other requirements facilitates the involvement of network engineers.

Business Model Tolerance Indicators

The business model defines the strategy for the corporation. The business models for many corporations must change to be successful in the Internet environment. They must switch to be more customer-centric while keeping costs low. As Amazon.com has shown, profits do not need to be seen in the first year (or years). This not-so-new paradigm allows for the high cost of implementation to exceed revenue with the prospect of high return on the investment . . . eventually.[16]

A business model is a deliverable that is imperative for the success of the Internet product. It is a work product that cannot be omitted or developed once without continual revisiting. eToys.com was a good example of this.[17] People in the company understood the customer's needs and built an extremely efficient

16. This was true when the writing for this book began. By the time the final manuscript was handed to the publisher, the stock market had plunged, illustrating that the tolerance of "no profits" had been reached!

17. EToys.com was a good example on usability, a good illustration of capturing all the front-end software requirements. The company was more customer-centric than its competitor ToysRUs.com. Although ToysRUs.com already had the bricks-and-mortar infrastructure to support the back-end processing and intercompany transfer of information, the company did not capture all the front-end requirements. ToysRUs.com corrected its mistake by joining forces with the already brand accepted Amazon.com.

and useful site that met the expectations of its users. However, the rest of the model was flawed. They underestimated a number of things:

- *The number of holiday sales:* They expected many more Internet users during this critical time for retail.
- *Their brick-and-mortar competition:* They underestimated the larger toy companies that came to the Internet as an alternate means of reaching customers.
- *Order fulfillment:* They underestimated the extent and cost of services associated with delivering products to customers. They eventually contemplated ending partnerships and bringing distribution in-house—not the best move, given the already high-cost/low-revenue scenario.

An anti-pattern can be created to prevent or monitor each situation that affects the business model by capturing specific tolerance parameters. Here lies the first business model anti-pattern: to capture tolerance requirements.

What Can Be Done?

The business model tolerance indicators anti-pattern assists the requirements engineer in identifying all the conditional events that need to be triggered. The condition in this case is that a tolerance has been reached that indicates a need for a reaction from management. In order for managers to interpret the effects of reaching or exceeding tolerance, they require information. Based on this information, executive management makes key decisions that may affect the business model and/or affect the life of the corporation or business relationships.

Preconditions

In order for the business model tolerance indicator to work, you must have a business model. It is not the responsibility of the requirements engineer to develop the business model, but he or she does assist by asking business strategy questions.[18]

The business model is generally part of the business case. It defines the customers, business relationships, revenue, expense flows, and so forth. For Internet products, the business model will project costs and profits in time slots of first year (by quarters) up to five to ten years.[19]

---

18. Senior requirements engineers understand business models and can ask questions to help ensure that the model makes sense.

19. Larger corporations have plans that project ten, fifteen, even twenty-five years out. The Internet is changing so rapidly that even larger companies have to pay special attention within the first five years. Smaller companies may project out to only three years.

Kinds of Questions

Many business models identify specific tolerance points. It is usually the newer dot-com companies that fail to develop a complete business model and thus omit this information. Whatever the case, questions should be asked (or reasked) to ensure that the tolerance-related requirements are captured. Whether the requirements engineer is involved during the writing of the business model or is involved later in the product development cycle, these kinds of questions should be asked of executive management.[20] Executive management is allocated the business idea and scope (also defined in the business case and the basis for the business model) to identify when they want to be notified and what they want to know.

The purpose of this questioning is to monitor the success of the Internet product and the effect it has on the business. Even larger companies, for whom the Internet product is only a portion of their business, can sustain the growth of this Internet business with other business units for only so long. Each business community needs to know how it is contributing to the success of the product. The questions that the requirements engineer needs to elicit include those listed below.

- *What must be monitored to determine the success of the Internet product?* This identifies what conditions must be monitored. Make sure that information about monitoring business partner relationships is included.
- *What is the tolerance point?* This identifies the trigger of the condition.[21] The information may vary by business community. For example, the sales department may have a lower tolerance point for a potential problem than does executive management. This serves as a yellow flag to alert the sales department to correct something before management notices the problem.
- *What information needs to be captured when the trigger is initiated?* This determines the action to take place. Data to capture include actual information related to sales, cost (development of the product and running the business),

---

20. Other subgroups (business practice, organizational support, and information technology) will want similar tolerance information. These requirements should also be captured and be based on the executive tolerance requirements (they will probably be the same requirements associated with different qualifiers).

21. This information will probably vary from month to month (or even week to week) until the Internet product settles into a pattern. The requirement that may be captured at this point might be the need for a data attribute for the specific tolerance value that executive management can alter at will.

analysis of customer feedback, service-level agreements with business partners, and so forth.

- *When and how should the information be captured?* This determines that the activity may be continual with a trigger to stop capturing the information and report on it. The information to be captured may be from external sources (for example, sales data of competitors).

Requirement Impact

It is important to remember that the Internet is a program, a program with many projects. The projects need to work in parallel but be coordinated throughout the life of the Internet product. The need for parallel efforts is necessary to shorten the time between concept and implementation of the iteration.

The tolerance indicators form an executive-level report on (1) what has taken place, (2) a comparison of that with the business projections, and (3) an adjustment of the projections against the actuals. This can be handled as a separate project from the development of the B2C and/or B2B portion.

Executive reporting must be part of the first iteration. The Internet is such a risky and ever-changing environment that all executives need to have information as soon as possible to correct a potentially negative situation quickly.

The Objective of the Business Model Tolerance Indicator Anti-Pattern

The objective of this anti-pattern is to spark discussion on how to monitor the success of the Internet product. Each business community has a monitoring need. Each business community is allocated the responsibility to clarify business risks and countermeasures for them. In addition, each business community has input on what it wants to see happen. All of these actions are dependent on what executive management wants to monitor. The goal is to illustrate not only the differences between but also the similarities with executive management's requirements.

Multiple tolerance indicators will be identified for each risk countermeasure. Each of the tolerance indicators will require different information to be captured, processed, and output in a specific format. The value of each tolerance indicator will probably change as business conditions change. Table 5.7 can be used to depict the needs for each tolerance event to be satisfied. The matrix shown in Table 5.8 illustrates the association requirements that also need to be defined and associated to the tolerance requirement.

Table 5.7   Allocation/Requirement Tolerance Value Matrix

Individual Scope Requirement	Allocation Level (Communities)																			
	Business Practice				Executive				Organizational				Information Technology							
	BU 1	BU 2	BU 3	BU 4	BU 5	BU 6	BU 7	BU 8	BU 9	BU 10	BU 11	BU 12	F 1	F 2	F 3	F 4	F 5	F 6	F 7	F 8
Tolerance requirement name		#[a]		#		#			#					#				#		

a. The "#" can be the tolerance value or it can be the specific qualifier that documents the specifics for the community.

Click-Stream Data

Every action an actor takes can be captured and kept as click-stream data. This information can be extremely voluminous and unwieldy. It is separated from the transaction processing of the system for performance reasons. The data are cleansed, organized, and placed into a data warehouse for analytical processing.

What can be done with the data may not be understood at the time the Internet project is initiated. The information may provide value to both the consumer and the corporation. Amazon.com provides to returning customers a list of new products that are similar to the products they have already purchased.

Table 5.8   Allocation/Focus Matrix

Individual Requirement	Information Technology Allocation for Focus							
	Functional						Nonfunctional	
	Who	What	Where	When	Why	How	Product Constraints	Project Constraints
Tolerance Requirement Name	X	X		X		X	X	

The company views each customer as one who buys for business reasons as well as for personal use.[22]

Data Warehousing and the Internet

Data warehousing is part of the Internet solution in two ways. One is internal (for example, for sales, marketing, and executive management) to analyze and "mine" the information to determine product usage and to spot coming trends. Click-stream data provide a great deal of "noise" that can hide important trend signals from internal staff. The data-mining activity cuts down the noise and gaps in knowledge to help analysts interpret trends more effectively.

Analytical processing of click-stream data can also provide analytical features to customers that allow them to search in diverse ways to find information. Search engines are built with ferrets and spiders to search the Web for information that customers want. These engines are built very differently than those needed for capture and act on information. These databases are designed for analytical processing versus the transactional (order-focused) processing engines used by customers.

The complexity of the Internet is due to the need for both analytical and transactional processing. A single database cannot usually be organized to support both types of processing efficiently. The kind of Internet application dictates which takes priority over the other. Regardless, the databases need to be synchronized to support both kinds of processing.[23]

Identifying Click-Stream Requirements

Many of the requirements to support click-stream analysis are contained in the information captured to run the site, including:

---

22. I have purchased many books in preparation of writing this book. I also have hobbies that are quite different from the reference books. Each time I enter the site I am notified of new products in both professional and personal subject areas. It is amazing how accurate the offered selections are!

23. For example, if the company offers a wide range of products and customers need to perform a wide search for "like" items, a separate database may be provided to support the search. When the customer places the order, the order may go against a different database that is optimized for transaction processing (high-volume performance). The two databases must be synchronized. As illustrated during the 1999 holiday season, finding the product and not knowing until after the order was placed whether the product was in stock eroded the customer experience.

- The kind of data captured
- The kind of values captured
- The pattern of the user tool to receive and provide information

This information may be merged with external reservoirs of information such as marketing data, competitor data, and demographic data.

The Objective of the Click-Stream Anti-Pattern

To meet the demanding implementation deadline, an Internet-based product solution needs to be separated into separate projects (see Table 5.9), all of which have the same business objective defined for the program. The danger of separating these into discrete projects is the potential for a lack of communication, coordination, and sharing of requirements. The allocation process delegates the requirements. The requirements, as they evolve, may take different directions. Each requirement could be reused by multiple projects.

The click-stream anti-pattern is just one example of how many projects use similar requirements. The objective of this anti-pattern is to provide a guide to ensure that the people who use the click-stream information are kept in the loop of capturing all the requirements and are involved in the requirement effort from the beginning so that:

- All Internet projects use the same requirements set.
- Click-stream information users' needs are captured at the same time as all the other requirements.
- Analytical needs are coordinated with the project needs.

Table 5.9   Requirement/Project Impact Matrix

Individual Requirement	Individual Projects		
	Click-Stream (OLAP)	Order Fulfillment (OLTP)	Auto-Response (OLTP)
Requirement name	Qualifier description	Qualifier description	Qualifier description

Abbreviations: OLAP, online analytical processing; OLTP, online transaction processing.

Gaps in Process

The two gap groups previously discussed primarily affect the functionality of the Internet product. Inevitably, they also affect the return on investment for the product at a project level. Project risk applies to the resources (staff, budget, time) for each iteration of the project. Underestimating or overestimating what the business can tolerate will also affect the success of the Internet product. The best control over the project risk is through the requirements process. The third group of anti-patterns addresses gaps in process.

Two different anti-patterns are discussed here to illustrate the breadth of anti-patterns that fall in this gap group:

1. *Scope creep:* to suggest how an anti-pattern can react to changes in the requirements set
2. *Technology for the sake of technology:* to suggest how an anti-pattern can be used to ensure that the requirements are satisfied
3. *Imposed deadlines:* to suggest how an anti-pattern can help with deadline issues

Scope Creep

Scope creep occurs when additional requirements are inserted late in the project without any alteration in budget, resources, and schedule. Scope creep increases the chance of a project's failure by delaying the implementation, depleting the return on investment, and possibly adding stress to the product's infrastructure.

Every project, whether Internet-based or not, encounters scope creep; it is inevitable. New marketing ideas and competitor information spark changes or new requirements throughout the development process. The problem is not that scope creep exists but how it is managed.

The trick for handling this problem is to initiate a process that minimizes the impact of change. The scope creep anti-pattern helps to anticipate change in the requirements set and handle that change when it occurs.

The scope creep anti-pattern covers the following areas to prevent a dramatic impact on the requirements set:

- Stability component for the individual requirement quality characteristics
- Requirements set gap analysis at each perspective for each community
- Change notification to all project members even remotely affected by the change to the requirements set

- Impact analysis to determine the cost and delivery of the product *before approval*
- Insistence on approval of all changes and the impact to the requirements set

What Can Be Done?

The first step in managing scope creep is to define the dependencies between requirements. This may imply that the requirements pattern goes against one of the golden rules of individual requirement quality: that each individual requirement must be able to be implemented and verified independently of other requirements. The dependency between requirements illustrates the cascading effect a change could have. If a change is made to the definition of an actor's responsibilities, the potential impact of the change on "what, where, when, why, and how" can be determined. The dependency, if the requirements pattern is populated correctly, is partially illustrated through the association requirements. A change to an approved requirement lowers the stability of all the affected requirements.

The degree of dependency is also a factor. If a change is made to a high-priority requirement, or if any of the association requirements have a high priority, the change will be more costly. The cost will also increase if the physical design is based on any of the high-priority requirements impacted by the scope creep.

An impact analysis matrix (see Table 5.10) illustrates the cascading effect of the change. Only those requirements that are affected by the change should be included. Each requirement is cross-checked against the other requirements. The priority of the impact is determined by the highest priority of the intersecting requirements.

The purpose of this correlation is to identify any change that may impact the infrastructure of other work products (for example, a design based on the priority of specific requirements). The matrix identifies where to begin looking for

Table 5.10   Requirement Correlation and Priority Matrix

	Requirement A	Requirement B	Requirement C	Requirement D
Requirement A	N/A	H	H	M
Requirement B	L	N/A	H	M
Requirement C	M	H	N/A	M
Requirement D	H	L	M	N/A

the level of impact. Begin by looking at each correlation with high priority. Then begin to identify the level of impact by creating another matrix.

The impact of next change matrix (see Table 5.11) takes the requirement correlation with the highest priority and determines the level of the impact. The rows identify all the requirements that may potentially change if the change is approved. The level of change as it affects the individual requirement is identified in parentheses. The columns identify all the requirements with their individual requirement priorities. They are ordered by the requirement correlation priority determined in the previous matrix. The cross cell identifies the impact the requested change has on the requirement.

Looking at the results, one could determine that a low-priority change that has a high impact on any high-level requirement may not be worth implementing in the current iteration, if at all. In this scenario, the best answer is to *just say no*! At least you have the supporting information to back up your decision.

A high-priority change that has a minimal or low impact on high-priority requirements could probably be implemented in the current release of a product. The cost and impact to the schedule would most likely be minimal.

A high-priority change that has a high impact on high-priority requirements is where the negotiations begin. Inevitably, the change will increase the risk of failure for the product and program. Quantifying the impact by cost, schedule, and other factors provides enough information to determine whether the change should be implemented in this iteration. The schedule will change and must be accepted by the requirement suppliers, including the executive sponsor, before proceeding.

No new requirement or change to an existing one should be accepted without the understanding and accepting its impact. To blindly accept any change or

Table 5.11   Requirement Correlation and Impact Matrix

	Requirement A (High)	Requirement B (High)	Requirement C (Medium)	Requirement D (Low)
Requirement A (L)	N/A	H	H	M
Requirement B (L)	L	N/A	M	L
Requirement C (H)	L	L	N/A	L
Requirement D (M)	M	H	H	N/A

new requirement after the requirements set has been approved is to give the product a death sentence.

Requirement Change Process

One of the keys to success with Internet development is to manage change well. With the Internet evolving daily, expect significant changes to requirements in the middle of the development cycle. Each requirement (and its change) must be reprioritized. Some requirements will be dropped (with approval), in favor of new requirements. Reprioritization of requirements is a business process that has a strong impact on all players involved in the development process. Measuring things like requirement turbulence is critical. It is important to ensure that everyone reviews any changing requirements for the Internet product. The notification process can be made easier with an automated requirements management tool (see Chapter Seven for more details).

The Objective of the Scope Creep Anti-Pattern

The objective of this anti-pattern is to capture enough information to make a determination as to whether a change should be made now, during a future iteration, or never. Everyone needs to understand the impacts that the change will have on both the product infrastructure and the product schedule. Both kinds of risk could have major impacts on the cost of the iteration as well.

Technology for the Sake of Technology

The growth of the Internet and the potential for high rewards have caused technology to evolve at a rapid pace. In order for technologists to remain competitive and command their ever-rising rates, technicians need to get their hands dirty using the new technology. Every technician wants to use the latest and greatest technology to create even the smallest project.

Is the use of this technology really needed to satisfy the requirements? Is it cost-effective to use the technology? Designers need to have their expectations controlled. This is the reason why requirements for purchasing software defined during the building perspective must be correlated to project budgetary requirements defined in earlier perspectives. The review of requirements must be monitored to ensure that the requirements set is not modified to fit the technician's desire to use new technology.

This is a difficult trade-off. In the world of the Internet, technology rules, and being "buzz word compliant" actually has a business impact! For example, flash technology is quite dominant, and users often expect it. Therefore, project members who oppose the use of the technology must consider and describe the market need for technological innovation. Part of the cost of doing business on the Internet must address the need for some members of the technical community to be involved with and experiment with new technologies. This should be accompanied with a contingency plan in case the dreaded risk of pursuing new technologies occurs (that is, they don't perform as expected). An example of this type of contingency plan would be to fall back to using JavaScript if a different technology does not do what the designer proposed.

Controlled Selection

Use the requirements you have to select the right technology. Include not only the functional but also the nonfunctional focus requirements. Product constraints include performance, security, and scalability needs. The project constraints are also extremely important. You need to spread the budget to cover all aspects of building the product, including marketing and legal expenses as well as technology expenses. Network engineers and application engineers wanting to use the latest and greatest tools will all be vying for their piece of the budget.

The Too-Much-Technology Anti-Pattern

This anti-pattern for too much technology is applied in three ways:

1. Ensuring design-independent requirements are written
2. Ensuring that reviews do not convert requirements to be design dependent
3. Interfacing project budgetary requirements to all requirements

All three ways are monitored during the review process. The first item is one of the guidelines of good requirement writing. Each requirement should specify a need and not a solution. The second item refers to designers participating as reviewers of the requirements during all the perspectives. Their suggestions for improving requirements cannot imply a design. The third items concerns the review of conflicts for all perspectives, especially of the requirements elicited during the builder perspective. The choice of products needs to fit within the budgetary restrictions (project constraint requirements) approved during earlier perspectives.

Imposed Deadlines

In order to meet the demands of the business, many professionals cut corners to meet hard-and-fast deadlines. Activities are minimized and tasks omitted, all in the pursuit of meeting deadlines, often sacrificing the quality of the end product and increasing the product and project risk. Deadlines are important and have a ripple effect on all work products. They are requirements and should be documented as such. They should also follow the evolutionary process that includes passing through the quality gates. These reviews validate that the deadline requirements are described in the proper format; the purpose for the deadline must be defined along with a priority of need.

Deadlines should not be ignored. They also should not be universally accepted without an explanation of the reason for the deadline. During the review, deadlines must be examined for feasibility. Negotiations with regard to deadlines begin to determine what can be done by when. Inevitably, priorities will change for some of the requirements.

The imposed deadline anti-pattern ensures that a deadline is *not* automatically accepted as valid *without* having supporting information. If the deadline is validated, the anti-pattern also checks that the other requirements are validated or adjusted to work with the deadline requirement.

What Can Be Done?

Validate, incorporate, and adjust. These are the three activities used to effectively handle deadlines. To prepare for this process, the deadline must be fully documented and approved as a quality requirement. This means that the deadline must be specified to meet the quality characteristics of a good requirement (see Chapter Six). All parts of the requirement must be defined, including a description of why and how the date was chosen. The contents of all of the requirements must be validated.

As previously stated, the deadline requirement must be incorporated into the requirements set and validated against other requirements as to feasibility. This requires that all other requirements have defined priorities. All dependencies between requirements must also be clearly documented. A report should be created that illustrates

- The individual requirements, ordered by priority
- Their dependencies, in order of priority

This document should be the basis of discussion about what can feasibly be accomplished by the deadline. The requirements should be included only if they have been fully documented and approved.

The purpose of the requirement dependencies is to begin to determine which requirements must be implemented together. Adjustments are made to the requirements set, possibly to the deadline requirement as well as other requirements. Changing the priority of a requirement or eliminating it from an iteration of a product has a ripple effect. The change must be reviewed as to its impact.

The Objective of the Imposed Deadline Anti-Pattern

The objective of this anti-pattern is to ensure that the deadline is valid and achievable and that the impacts of the requirement are reflected in the other requirements of the set. It must be understood what can be accomplished during the time frame set for the program or iteration. Executives need to make tough decisions and segment the requirements set into iterations that can be implemented successfully.

Creating Additional Anti-Patterns

This chapter has discussed only a sampling of anti-patterns that are common to the information technology community for Internet-based programs. Each program, even an Internet program, is a little bit different. Each program:

- Has its own staff with different skill sets
- Has a different business goal in mind
- Uses different technology
- Uses different methods, techniques, and tools to build the site

Each project team encounters horror stories of bumps that occurred with previous projects that could easily occur again. These experiences should be noted somewhere in the development process to avoid the risk of reoccurrence. Creating an anti-pattern is one way to accomplish this.

Decide whether the risk in question could occur with this program (or iteration). If it could, begin by looking at the Internet requirements pattern (see Appendix B). Determine whether the scenario could be avoided if the pattern is followed. If not, create an anti-pattern to ensure that a negative scenario is avoided (see Figure 5.3).

Looking at the experiences of now-defunct dot-coms provides a host of scenarios that need to be avoided. EToys.com, a B2C product so loved by consumers, did not reach its sales expectations for the 2000 holiday season. Costs exceeded revenue and forced the company to join the "dot-gone" ranks by the end of Feb-

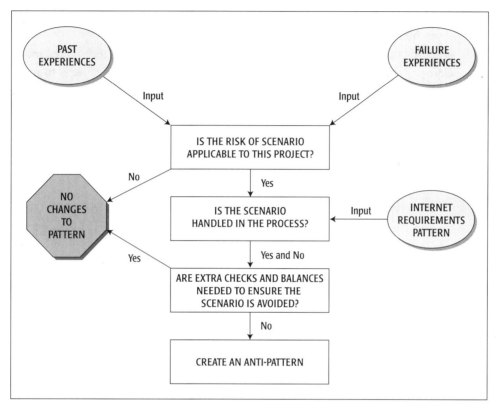

Figure 5.3   Are Anti-Patterns Needed?

ruary 2001. To help avoid this fate, eToys.com could have created an anti-pattern to address

- Tolerance factors to consider if sales fall below expectations
- Triggers to evaluate the protected sales
- Risks incurred and countermeasures to take when the tolerance factors are reached

These kinds of input illustrate sources for determining whether anti-patterns are needed. When anti-patterns are required, the first step is to write the summary lead using the anti-pattern language. Since these anti-patterns are requirements related, the requirements engineer is usually the person responsible for creating the summary lead and any details to further explain the risk. In large organizations, the anti-pattern may be developed by requirement supporters, such as quality assurance, but should never be done without the assistance of the requirements engineer.

Requirements engineers have their preferences for certain techniques, methods, or tools. These should remain as *preferences only*. The objective is to minimize requirement gaps. Therefore, a requirements anti-pattern should not be written to impose a specific technique, method, or tool, but rather to provide a general guide. The ultimate choice of technique, method, or tool should be left to the user. The requirements patterns and anti-patterns are designed to be tools, not standards.

Basic Information to Include in an Anti-Pattern

Each anti-pattern must contain the following information and be in proper format (see Appendix D).[24]

- Identifier
- Name
- Also known as
- Based upon
- Cell applicability
- Problem
- Refactored solution type
- Context
- Forces
- Solution
- Resulting context
- Rationale
- Syntax
- Suggested requirements patterns
- Suggested anti-patterns

Identifier

As with all requirements, anti-patterns require an *identifier*, or a way to trace the usage and associate this to specific cells of the Internet requirements pat-

---

24. This format is similar to the full anti-pattern template described in Brown et al. (1998). Adjustments to the template were made to reflect the requirements set framework portrayed in this book.

tern. The identifier should be unique for each pattern and anti-pattern for any project.[25]

Name

The *name* of the anti-pattern should be concise, clear, and unique. The name should indicate the topic of the anti-pattern. If the anti-pattern is basically the same as another anti-pattern but with minor adjustments (such as a kind of attribute), then the name for each anti-pattern should be generic with a qualifier in parentheses. For example, several performance anti-patterns may be created. They all have similar problems and similar solutions. They differ only in a narrow sense. The difference can probably be defined as a qualifier. In this scenario, a generic anti-pattern should be created; the specific anti-pattern to support each performance-related issue should be documented as a qualifier. Using performance as an example, a general anti-pattern could be named "Identifying All Critical Performance Points." Additional anti-patterns could be created based on this generically named anti-pattern:

- Identifying All Critical (Network) Performance Points
- Identifying All Critical (Cache) Performance Points
- Identifying All Critical (Record-Locking) Performance Points

Each sub-anti-pattern notes the specifics (qualifier) of each issue that must be addressed to avoid product risk.

Also Known As

With the global nature of software development (and the Internet), many names can be used to represent the same piece of information. *Also known as* (aka) identifies any additional popular or descriptive names or phrases for the anti-pattern and takes into account a name that could be tailored to a specific geographic region.

Based Upon

All requirement-related anti-patterns should be *based upon* the requirements meta pattern. The objective of the meta pattern is to assist in identifying all requirement types (community, perspective, focus, and associations). Each requirement-related

---

25. No matter how specific a scenario is to the project under development, the same scenario may occur with other projects. An anti-pattern may be reusable with minor qualifiers identified.

anti-pattern should strive to do the same but in a smaller context. The "based upon" clause should *always* be the "Identifying All Types" pattern. If the anti-pattern can only apply to Internet-based development or only describe the means to assist the specifics of the Internet, then the "based upon" clause can identify the subpattern (the Internet). "The Internet" would be set in parentheses to qualify the specific usage of the requirements meta pattern. This information is specific to requirements patterns and is not seen in design patterns.

Cell Applicability

Since the requirements anti-patterns are based upon a requirements pattern, they can probably apply to specific requirement cells or a group of them (community, perspective, focus, association). Use *cell applicability* to indicate the range of cells the anti-pattern addresses. The format should be in the order of community, perspective, focus, and association, with a slash "/" to separate them. Use a short dash ("–") to represent a range for a specific community, perspective, or focus, or use commas for a list of specifics. For example:

- *IT/planner/who, what, where:* states that the anti-pattern supports only three specific focus areas for the IT community and the planner perspective
- *IT/planner–builder/product constraints:* states that the anti-pattern captures only requirements for the product constraint focus area but for the first three perspectives (owner, designer, and builder)

When multiple or groups of cells are listed, the association between the cells should be included as part of the description (for example, "what–when" includes the association between data and events). If the cell is intended to discuss the relationship between requirements within the cell (for example, one event occurs before another), then this must be discussed explicitly in the anti-pattern description.

Problem

The *problem* is simply what the anti-pattern is meant to address. It describes the recurrent problem that causes negative consequences. For requirements,[26] they come in three flavors: gaps in knowledge, gaps in participation, and gaps in process. All three prevent the identification of all requirements that complete

---

26. These are different from design anti-patterns that pertain to software, technology, process, or role.

the Internet requirements set. The problem should not contain a solution. It is a brief description (one to three sentences) of how to identify whether the problem is occurring on the project. It should clearly define the risk in terms of root cause.

Refactored Solution Type

The refactored solution type identifies what kind of problem the anti-pattern addresses: a gap in knowledge, a gap in participation, or a gap in process. This information should be included in every anti-pattern, as shown in Appendix D.

Context

Context describes the scenario in which the risk could occur. It is similar to the preconditions of the use case. The purpose is to extend the problem description by stating the specifics of how the problem could occur. It provides the warning sign that the problem will probably occur.

Forces

Why the problem must be avoided is described in the *forces* section so that other requirements engineers, requirement suppliers, requirement users, and requirement supporters understand the risks involved if the anti-pattern is not implemented and followed. The problem describes the issues the requirements anti-pattern needs to address. These issues, itemized and explained in the forces section, affect either the product or project risks described previously.

Solution

The *solution* describes the countermeasure to the risk. It is the "activity" description of a use case. The description of the solution should be clear. It can be in narrative or bulleted form. Be careful in the description that the solution does not create additional risks to the requirements set, involvement, or process. A specific anti-pattern should never create a need for additional specific anti-patterns to counteract the solution.

Resulting Context

The *resulting context* is the postcondition if the solution is followed. It describes how to determine whether the solution avoided the risk. It is a means of validating the success of the anti-pattern.

Rationale

The *rationale* section of the anti-pattern describes the requirements engineer's reasoning why this anti-pattern should be incorporated into the process. The description must be objective and brief.

Syntax

The anti-pattern must be written in the same manner as the pattern on which it is based. The *syntax* section of the Internet anti-pattern must adhere to the syntax rules of the requirements meta pattern (identify *all* types). Additionally, the identity of all Internet types must be specific to Internet applications with a high priority applied to performance, security, usability, and business risk.

Suggested Requirements Patterns and Anti-Patterns

The *Suggested Requirements Patterns* and *Suggested Anti-Patterns* sections provide an opportunity for identifying additional patterns and anti-patterns that could be developed given the knowledge of this anti-pattern. This section is primarily for generic patterns/anti-patterns such as the performance example described earlier. These two sections are optional. Their use depends on whether the writer of the summary, or the reviewers, see specific reasons for use. Each of the instances would inherit all the restrictions and traits described in the higher generic patterns and anti-patterns.

Additional sections to the requirements anti-pattern could include:

- *Probability of risk:* to define the chances of occurrence
- *Reference to past examples:* to provide reviewers and users of the anti-pattern additional examples of the risk or how the solution avoided the risk
- *Referenced projects:* to identify specific projects that are currently using the anti-pattern

Review and Use of Created Anti-Patterns

All Internet anti-patterns should be reviewed before being used. The review team should include all categories of requirement participants (requirement suppliers, requirement users, requirements engineers, and requirement supporters). The responsibilities of the reviewers are to review each section for:

- Clarity of understanding
- Conflicts with other patterns (generic or specific)

- Conflicts with other anti-patterns (generic or specific)
- Completeness (in sections and section detail)
- Accuracy of the potential risk (problem, context, and forces)
- Accuracy of the countermeasure (solution, resulting context, and rationale)

Anti-patterns are work products. They are configuration items to be managed and controlled similar to individual requirements. An audit trail should be included that defines any changes.

The anti-pattern should be used at two points in the project schedule: the elicitation subactivity and the validation subactivity. During the subactivity, the anti-pattern should be incorporated as questions to be asked to ensure that:

- The right questions are asked to elicit the potentially missing requirements.
- The right people are involved in supplying the requirements.
- The process is working as it should be to capture, evaluate, and evolve the requirements.

The anti-pattern should be documented as a checklist item for all reviews. The reviewers should have on their lists the name of the anti-pattern with the problem description so they can review the requirements set with eyes open. The anti-pattern should be included for all reviews even if the requirements engineer thinks that the risk does not pertain to the specific review. Reviewers' input is colored by their past experiences, and no single requirements engineer can capture all requirements. The review process provides the opportunity to capture additional requirements.

Anti-patterns also provide a process-improvement opportunity. If, after following the anti-pattern, the risk was avoided, the requirements pattern should be reviewed to see if the scenario can be incorporated through cell-specific questions or clarification of cell contents. The goal of the process-improvement specialist is to eliminate the need for any anti-patterns to live forever.

Conclusion

This chapter proposed ways to minimize gaps in the requirements set. All the anti-patterns mentioned are common scenarios of requirement gaps that can cause an Internet program to fail. Administering the use of these anti-patterns with the Internet requirements pattern minimizes the risk of product or program failure that can be directly attributed to requirements.

The requirements pattern and its supporting anti-patterns are not standards; they are tools. These patterns should be defined with a minimal life expectancy. They are intended either to support the specific iteration or to be implemented into the pattern or requirements process for continual use for all programs.

CHAPTER SIX

Requirement Quality

Chapter Key Topics
- Quality of the individual requirements
- Quality of the requirements specification
- Quality of the requirements set
- Quality-checking techniques

The Internet Impact
Development on the Internet is fast paced, with demands for continual product enhancements. Defects in products are exposed on a global level, with the ultimate risk being loss of market share. It is important to develop requirements that are clear, concise, complete, and correct the first time around to use time wisely for enhancing product features rather than correcting defects.

A familiar phrase to those who work in the Internet environment is, "Write once, debug everywhere." This could very well be true beginning in the initial stages of determining the requirements. As the old information technology adage goes, "Garbage in, garbage out." The Internet requirements pattern is a tool. It does not prevent the insertion of poor-quality requirements.

The Internet is a risky endeavor, as illustrated by the failures of what used to be considered stable sites (such as eToys.com). The potential for risk starts at the beginning of the development process. Risks can be introduced from the initial idea and carried through to the implemented product. The objective is to catch the risk as soon as possible because the earlier in the life cycle that potential risks are identified, the earlier they can be managed or eliminated. To eliminate the risk caused by poor requirements, it is important to understand what a good requirement is.

However, good individual requirements do not guarantee a high-quality product. It is also important to review requirements for consistency among all the individual requirements contained in the requirements set. Given the potential volume of requirements, reviews must occur in manageable subsections of the requirements set. The recommended subsections are by perspective and community. Due to the complexity of software components, a specification may be developed for each focus area for intermediate reviews.

This chapter reviews the definition of a good requirement in terms of content and structure. The chapter then addresses different review processes that assist in identifying defects in the individual requirements, the perspective specification, and the requirements set.

Quality of the Individual Requirements

Each requirement is a statement of what the requirement supplier wants. Defining each requirement in a format that describes the need well is an important step *before* attempting to create the solution. The requirements must be written down so they can be validated.

Requirements help clarify the stated problem to be solved in a well-defined manner. They describe what needs to be implemented to satisfy the business objective. In order to accomplish this, each requirements engineer must understand

- The parts of the requirement
- The quality characteristics each requirement must meet
- Any additional information the requirements pattern enforces to add to the quality of the individual requirement

This list applies to any type of product, including Internet products. Each item has an impact on the quality of the requirements set and contributes to the success or failure of the Internet product.

Quality Characteristics

The IEEE standard 830 for software requirements identifies eight characteristics that have become the initial checklist for evaluating individual requirements (see Table 6.1).

Table 6.1   Requirement Evaluation Checklist

Characteristic	Brief Description	Internet Impact
1. Correct	Each requirement should be correct in its statement of purpose.	All reviewers must agree to the statement. For example, all reviewers must have the same definition of "customer."
2. Unambiguous	Only one interpretation can be inferred from the requirement statement. No "to be determined" is allowed. Be wary of the use of words such as *large, rapid,* and *many.* If using words such as *error, fault,* and *failure,* use the standard definition defined in the IEEE glossary (Std 610).	All ease-of-use comments must be explicit with details as well as verifying information.
3. Complete	All significant information about the requirement must be included, for example, data, process, performance, responses, desired format.	All parts of the requirement must be included (identifier, name, description, priority, etc.). All cells and associations between cells must contain requirements or a validated waiver to acknowledge an absence of requirements.
4. Consistent	All requirements should look the same and not conflict with each other.	The satisfaction of this requirement should not prevent another requirement from being fulfilled. All mathematical functions should use the same measurement. All interest formulas should be identical.
5a. Ranked for importance	A priority indicator, such as essential, conditional, or optional (or high, medium, or low) should be included.	This is imperative for determining the schedule of requirement implementation across different iterations. Importance can be determined in two ways: (1) the priority of the need perceived by the requirement supplier and (2) the effect (risk) on the product if the requirement is not satisfied. The effect (penalty) on the product can pertain to the product success or the success of implementing (supporting)[a] another requirement.

Table continued on next page.

a. Each requirement should be able to be implemented separately. One requirement may facilitate the implementation of another. For example, an event may not be triggered without specific information being passed along. A specific summary cannot be displayed unless the process calculates the information.

Table 6.1   Requirement Evaluation Checklist (*continued*)

Characteristic	Brief Description	Internet Impact
5b. Ranked for stability	The requirement can be ranked in terms of whether changes are expected.	This is sometimes documented in a percent confidence ratio or also as a high, medium, or low ranking. The IEEE standard states you can use either 5a or 5b. This book recommends capturing both. A requirement can be a high-priority item but can have a 50 percent chance of changing before implementation. Both 5a and 5b are useful for determining which iteration of the requirement should be implemented and for prioritizing the resolution of stability with executive management.
6. Verifiable	There must be a way to test that the requirement has been satisfied.	This information provides the editing rules and is the basis for test cases. The information supplied for this requirement attribute must be testable.
7. Modifiable	It must be easy to modify the format of the requirement when changes do occur. Requirements should be listed individually to meet this criteria.	This includes the document and the requirement. Using both a CASE tool as well as a requirements management tool assists with this characteristic.
8. Traceable	Each requirement must contain an identifier that can be traced through the development process. Thus all changes to the requirement can also be traced to the original requirement.	Tracing is also a means of linking or associating: • The evolution of the requirement • The dependency of the requirement • The supporter of the requirement • The association of requirements for iteration

All of the requirement attributes (quality characteristics) can be applied to every requirement at every perspective, and for every focus area and business community. They guide the writer and reviewer toward writing a clear and concise statement of needs that can be traced, modified, and verified. Writing requirements with these quality characteristics assists in building a successful Internet product and increases the return on investment. Compromising any of these quality characteristics increases the product's risk related to either functionality or project resources (cost, time, and staff).

Studies have shown that when natural language is used to describe the requirements (as is most often the case), the failures that cause significant risk to the success of the product fall within three categories: ambiguity, inaccuracy, and inconsistency.[1] This can be attributed to weak sentence structure as well as the fact that many English words and phrases have several connotations.

An additional quality characteristic to be included on the list is *feasibility*. Reviewers must verify that each requirement can be fulfilled given other requirements (requirement conflicts) and technology availability. A requirement is not feasible if it conflicts with another requirement, particularly if the requirement cannot be satisfied given the limitations set for cost, time frame, and staff. An Internet system cannot be built with a budget of $10. An Internet product probably will not be built in less than five days. If the limits (validation criterion of the individual requirement) of a requirement prevent the satisfaction of another requirement, one of the requirements is considered to be unfeasible.

The other feasibility test is technology. The requirement may be feasible but just not with the current technologies. For example, it is not technically possible to have 24-hour, seven-days-a-week availability all the time. There needs to be some time set aside for system maintenance. Network outages, system failures, and batch windows also prevent 100 percent availability. However, at the rate technology is improving, this requirement may be feasible some day soon.

Guidelines for Better Requirement Writing

The components of a requirement are important and should be supplied during the planner perspective through to the subcontractor level. As details are captured, they too should be considered as separate requirements, containing the components described previously. For example, a precondition of the event description is an attribute of the event but also a requirement unto itself. This way the precondition can be applied to multiple events. The specific statement of when the precondition attribute can be applied to the event is the qualifier. For example, a precondition for calculating total payment includes applying a discount if the entire order is at least $100. Total payment is an attribute that can be used in multiple cases and, therefore, it should be defined as an individual requirement. The

---

1. See Stokes 1991.

"total payment" requirement would be associated to the "apply discount" requirement. The association would include the qualifier definition "≥$100."

A Requirement Should Be a Statement of a Single Need

The use of *and, or, with,* and *also* should be investigated to determine whether the requirement can be split into separate requirements. These "joining" words can cause difficulty if conflicts between the joining parts arise. They should be used only to clarify the limits of the requirement (for example, that the month must be recorded between one *and* twelve inclusive).

Clear and Concise Statements Avoid Confusion

If requirements are not clear or are long-winded, they are prone to errors. Keeping them short and specific makes them easier to review and validate. At all costs, avoid using the following:

- Long, rambling sentences to explain the requirement
- Speculatory language, such as *usually, generally, often, normally,* and *typically*
- Ambiguous language, such as *user-friendly* (the most common phrase for Internet-based products)

    Make sure you say what you mean by:

- Specifying explicit requirements and not possibilities with words like *should, could,* and *probably*
- Not asking for what is not possible within the budget, for example, 100 percent network availability

A Requirement Is a Need and Not a Design

Write all requirements in terms of a wish list that does not imply a specific design. This is critical for describing product constraints. Names of specific hardware and software products should be stated only if a corporate or divisional standard is imposed. Otherwise, leave open to the designer the possibilities of designing a solution with as few constraints as possible. Do not tie the requirement user's hands unless it is absolutely necessary.

A common mistake with requirement writing is to combine requirements to create an escape clause. An "if-then-except" statement should be split into two separate requirements that both need to be satisfied if a condition occurs. For example, "A bid will always be accepted unless the user's credit card has expired" should be rewritten as follows:

1. A bidder must have a valid credit card on file.
2. A bidder's credit card will be validated at sign-on.
3. A bidder will be notified of an expired credit card.

Tool Implications

CASE tools do exist that capture some of the requirement categories. For the requirement categories they support, most of the quality characteristics can be enforced and most, if not all, of the requirement components can be captured. It depends on the individual CASE tool. When evaluating the use of specific CASE tools, a requirements engineer should investigate whether the tool supports the components and quality characteristics.

For quality characteristics, the unambiguity, correctness, and consistency must be determined during the review.[2] All CASE tools ensure that the same name is not used for more than one requirement. Many CASE tools provide a mechanism for supplying information to indicate priority, stability, verifiability, and traceability. The CASE tool cannot determine whether the values (contents) are what the requirement supplier conveyed. The requirement reviewers (and approvers[3]) must validate this information, as with the other quality characteristics.

For the requirement components that need to be specified, what can be supplied depends on the CASE tool as well as the focus area. For example, a unique identifier may not be assigned to each relationship defined in the data or entity class. Many CASE tools omit the need for validation criteria. However, they may provide a comment field that can be used for this purpose.[4]

Many CASE tools have some form of exchange with a requirements management tool. The leading requirements management tools on the market today provide the ability to add columns to each requirement. These additional columns

---

2. Formal inspections are the best way to review requirements specifications. The interaction of a diverse audience places each requirement under scrutiny.
3. Approvers are separated here to remind readers that reviewers can review contents and confirm that the contents are as conveyed. Specifically for priority, executive approvals are needed to confirm they should be included for continuance in the development process.
4. Use this field *if and only if* a report can be generated that displays this information in an appropriate place (with the individual requirement and not at the end of a report). Do not expect a requirement supplier to understand the CASE tool and be able to navigate each comment field.

can be used to supply any missing quality characteristics or requirement components the CASE tools do not support.[5]

As far as requirement language, CASE tools and requirements management tools do provide minimum syntax. In fact, very minimum! Grammar is seldom verified; spelling may be. A requirement probably will not be a complete sentence. However, all requirements should have in the text such terms as *shall be, will have,* and *must be.*[6] Though the priority status may be used for this purpose, it is still preferable to make absolutely clear the intention of the requirement satisfaction. Some CASE tools provide a report generator where text templates and filters can be applied. Within those text templates, requirements can be segmented by priority status. A text line can be added to specify the *shall be, will have,* and *must be* verb phrases.

A report generator is a very powerful representation tool for requirements. The template and filter can be applied to the requirements set to document

- The requirement audit trail
- Requirement associations (for example, the data used by the process and who can initiate the event)
- Skeleton test cases

Unfortunately, report generator features are renowned for being the worst part of any CASE or requirements management tool. That does not negate the need to review the features and any extensions that can be applied. A requirements engineer on the project must be assigned the responsibility for creating the report templates that produce reports for reviewers. Some of the generated reports from CASE tools can be directly imported to the requirements management tool if a direct tool interface does not exist.

Quality of the Requirements Specification

Requirements are represented in different work products. For ease of review, one requirements specification should be created for each perspective. The work

---

5. Keep in mind that this will create more manual effort to keep the two requirements (one in the requirements management tool and one in the CASE tool) in sync. A process will need to be defined to ensure the integrity of the requirement as it is developed in both tools.
6. The use of *must* and *will* indicates mandatory compliance of the requirement. The use of *shall, should,* or *may* implies optional priority status for the requirement. For this reason, words should be carefully chosen when defining the requirement statement.

products can be segmented by focus area. Each subsection should be reviewed for quality characteristics (completion) that are general to all requirements as well as for focus-specific characteristics.

When individual focus-specific sections are produced, it is important to produce cross-check documents to illustrate the associations between requirement cells. For each association, the qualifications for the association must be clear.

Since requirements evolve, each perspective-level requirements specification must be reviewed for three additional quality checks that relate to individual quality characteristics (for example, traceability and completeness):

1. The requirements must be traceable (linked or associated) to the previous perspective's requirements.
2. The requirements from the previous perspective must be contained in the perspective under review.
3. The requirements details must not alter the requirements from the previous perspectives.

Quality of the Requirements Set

The review of the requirements set identifies gaps in knowledge and conflicts between requirements specifications and across business communities. It validates that all work products are complete and accurate and, more importantly, are built upon the same business objectives. The same quality characteristics described for individual requirement quality (along with the quality characteristics that apply to the requirements specification) apply to the entire requirements set. They are simply categorized differently.

As described in Chapter Two, the development of an Internet product can be correlated with the manufacture of any product. The work products (and the separation of work products and software components) correlate with the elements of a house and its architectural evolution. To describe the quality aspects of the requirements set, a good analogy is the evolution and valuing of a diamond—from its rough form to a beautiful gemstone to be set or stored.

Gemstones have intrigued humanity for centuries. Most people do not realize that there are over 130 kinds of gems. The worth of one kind over another is based on rarity and desire—supply and demand. Judging the quality of one gemstone over another within the same kind is based on the four Cs: color, clarity, cut, and carat (volume/size).

The requirements set, as with diamonds, can be evaluated (see Table 6.2) in four quality areas (also known as the four Cs). Each activity shown contributes to the quality of the end product. This is true of a finely cut diamond and a finely defined requirements set. The difference between the two processes is that the diamond process is well established. Grids have been developed that dramatically adjust costs if one of the activities is not performed to perfection.

Requirements would benefit from having the same standards as diamonds. Depending on the focus of the requirements, a requirement template (see Appendix A) should be followed to supply the information.

The next step in evaluating the quality of the requirements set is to determine the impact on the project. Gemstones are described by price per carat. Many individuals judge the value of a gemstone solely by the size. The truth is that price per carat is a better measurement for comparison. A five-carat, low-quality diamond could cost around $1,300 per carat or $6,500. On the other hand, a one-carat, extra-fine-quality diamond can cost around $14,000.[7]

Reviewers of the requirements set may make similar mistakes. Reviewers are typically delivered a huge binder called "Requirements Specifications." Due to the size of the binder, program participants assume the requirements *must* be complete.

In the absence of written requirements, project participants may equate size to the amount of time. In this scenario, the participants perceive they spent enough time on requirements, so they are assumed complete.

Both of these requirement scenarios use participants' perceptions to define "complete." In reality, the requirements set is complete only when the following two criteria are satisfied.

1. Each requirement must contain all the information needed to interpret its purpose. The requirements set must contain all focus areas for all communities as they relate to the purpose of the requirements.
2. No matter how time consuming the reading of each requirement may be, each should be read and discussed during the validation phase. Any changes to the requirements must be reviewed for impact before implementation.

---

7. Prices from *The Guide*, Gemworld International, Inc., January/February 2001 issue.

Table 6.2   The Four Cs for Evaluation of Diamonds and Requirements

The Four Cs	Brief Gemstone Interpretation	Brief Requirement Interpretation	Additional Checks
Color/ Correctness	Every gemstone is first evaluated by color. For example, a "D" color diamond is worth more than a "J." Standards are set by gem organizations to define the "correct" color for each kind of gem. The color is created by the amount of each mineral contained in the gem.	Each requirement should be correct in its statement of purpose. Correctness includes other individual quality characteristics such as traceability, completeness, and consistency. At the set level, correctness is the avoidance of conflicts between the business communities.	Each requirement must be verifiable in order to be considered correct. This is the way to verify that the requirement was met.
Clarity/Clarity	This describes the degree of flaws for the gemstone type. For example, diamonds should have no inclusions, feathers, fractures, etc. The closer to flawless, the higher the value of the diamond.	Only one interpretation can be inferred from the requirement statement. No "to be determined" is allowed. It is clear that the requirement is needed to meet the business objective.	Requirement users will know exactly what is needed when and where and what probable functions will be performed on what when. Requirements in one cell agree in business objective with those in all other cells.
Cut/ Consistency	The cutting and polishing of the diamond match the mathematical dimensions.	All requirements look the same and do not conflict with each other.	Every person supplying requirements uses the same format for describing each requirement. The format must allow for modifications in requirements. A requirement does not prevent another requirement from being satisfied. The requirements set must contain requirements that do not conflict with any other requirement within and outside the business community.

Table continued on next page.

Table 6.2   The Four Cs for Evaluation of Diamonds and Requirements (*continued*)

The Four Cs	Brief Gemstone Interpretation	Brief Requirement Interpretation	Additional Checks
Carat (Size)/ Completeness	After consideration of the other three characteristics, a larger stone will command a higher price.	All significant information about the requirement must be included to cover all focus areas, for example, data, process, performance, responses, and desired format.	All parts of the requirement must be supplied, including ranks for importance (essential, conditional, or optional), stability (changes expected), and traceability (identifier). Each cell and associations between cells must include at least one requirement.

Implementing Quality Procedures

It is hard for many people to understand the importance of requirement quality. Diamonds have grids that define the product value based on quality characteristics. Currently, however, no such grids exist for either individual requirements or for the requirements set. To begin to build such a grid would involve associating the final product to the original approved requirements. Added to this would be the evaluation of the individual requirements and requirements set quality characteristics.

If you do not have any written requirements, ask the users to review what they have against what is wanted. Also review the maintenance log for new requests. Are the requests corrections or new enhancements? Associate a cost to the amount of time it will take to implement the changes. Subtract that cost from the revenue side of the return on investment (ROI). That will provide a quick look at the impact of poor-quality requirements on the ROI.

There is a flip side to the situation. You must evaluate how much longer it would have taken to obtain a higher level of quality for the requirements. This needs to be compared to the amount of revenue received from the supposedly premature implementation of the product. "Analysis paralysis" or a prolonged requirements process can also chip away at the ROI.

A one-carat gemstone with ideal color but poor cut will not have the same value as an identically colored gemstone with an accurate cut. If any of the quality characteristics are sacrificed, the true value of the gemstone will never be realized. Requirement quality has a direct impact on the future stages of the development process. Each requirement quality characteristic (at either the individual or set level) has an impact on the ROI.

Requirements seem to be so far removed from the final product delivery. It is hard to associate the impact of poor-quality requirements with the product. Instead, the reason for negative impact on the ROI is usually attributed to normal operating procedures and not the poorly captured requirements. Changes and corrections are applied during the maintenance phase of the product, further lowering the ROI percentage.

A chart can be created for each type of product (Internet-based) and each size of the product [small (B2C), medium (B2C plus B2B), and large (B2C, B2B, plus existing application integration)]. The chart (see Table 6.3) could be arranged by correctness (rows) and clarity (columns) to document a quality percentage. For correctness, ask whether all the cells and associations are populated with requirements; how many gaps actually exist? For clarity, rate on a scale of 1 to 9 how clear the requirements are. In building such a matrix, the results of requirement reviews need to be documented and the impact on the final product (or iteration) must be captured.

Table 6.3 Quality Percentage Matrix

	Flawless	1	2	3	4	5	6	7	8	9
No Gaps	0%									
1–5										
6–10										
11–15										
16–20										
21–25										
26–30										
31–35										
36–40										100%

This does not preclude the need to check the quality of the individual requirements, the requirements specification, and the requirements set. Review techniques should be used to minimize the insertion of a requirement defect.

Quality-Checking Techniques

Several methods are available to check quality at both the individual level and at the set level. Some of the systems are automated and some are manual. Multiple techniques should be used since none of them are perfect.

Quality Checkpoints

Quality checkpoints come in the form of deliverables. The deliverables are usually in the form of documentation (models, diagrams, matrices, and/or text). The information contained within each document is then built upon or evolves into another level of detail (perspective).

Software projects can overlap in functionality or information needs. These deliverables, when contained in a central repository tool, can be reused and built upon when building similar software projects. This reusability expedites future projects that leverage the use of documentation, resulting in higher-quality products.

These deliverables serve as a means for validation. Writing down the requirements for every focus, perspective, and community provides a common understanding that can be reviewed and validated by the program team members. When the deliverables are unambiguous—a quality characteristic of a good requirements specification—only one meaning or interpretation can be derived from the deliverable.

Individual Gaps

Individual requirements must contain all the parts described in this chapter. As the requirement evolves through the perspectives, additional (separate but dependent) information about the requirement should be captured.

Specification Gaps

Each specification must contain the individual requirements for the perspective, focus, and community. Each specification should include all the association-type requirements that tie the different cells together. Additional information should also be included that describes the basics of the document and program (see

Appendix A). Even if a specification is created for each focus area for a specific perspective and domain, it should contain this information.

Table of contents. Every specification should include a table of contents since it adds to the readability of the document (so reviewers can find information quickly). Sufficient levels should be included to allow reviewers to find individual entity classes, specific business rules, or other specific requirements. It is acceptable, as an alternative, to have a less detailed table of contents at the beginning of the document as long as each section (usually divided by focus area) has a more detailed table of contents.

Introduction. People beyond the program team reviewers will read a requirements specification. In fact, readers who have nothing to do with the product will review the document. In light of this, the requirements engineer needs to produce the best specifications possible to set an example for those who follow.

For this reason, team members must never assume that readers understand the purpose of the program or the common vocabulary used throughout the specification. Each requirements specification should have as part of its introduction:

- A brief explanation of the purpose and scope of the document
- Definitions of terms
- A list of references that was used (and to which readers can refer later) to develop the material contained in the specification

It is acceptable, as an alternative, to have a full glossary of terms in an appendix. What is important is for the information to be accessible to readers.

Approval tracking. Many documents are issued throughout the process of developing requirements. Some of these documents are different versions of the same specification. Approval tracking is a way to identify the state (or draft) of the document. A document without approvals could be a document for a cancelled project or for a project awaiting validation.

Documentation change history. Throughout the development and validation of the requirements, it is necessary to make changes to the specification. The use of a requirements management tool assists in capturing the questions, concerns, and approved changes to individual requirements. Some CASE tools do the same for specific focus areas. It must be remembered that the individual specification is probably what is being reviewed and baselined as a "reviewed copy." It is still important to keep a change history of the specification itself.

Keeping track of changes in the document provides a checklist for the reviewers. It reminds them of what has been changed so they can look directly for the change (and any potentially impacted areas). Though it is valuable to read the entire document through several times, it is not always feasible for the reviewer (or necessary, for that matter, when the changes are minimal).

It is important to be clear about what has changed. Stating "Made the changes per Edwin Smith's requests" does not provide enough detail for other reviewers; it must be clear exactly what was changed and why.

Pattern Gap Analysis

Each cell in the Internet requirements pattern should have at least one requirement. If a cell does not, further investigation should take place to determine the legitimacy of the absence of a requirement. As common sense indicates, analytical systems still require processing [data driven (analytical processing) versus process driven (online transaction processing)]. Furthermore, that transaction processing still requires data to be searched and mined.

Not all individual requirements associate to other requirements (meaning that data requirements do not always have a process requirement that uses the data for this iteration). As with an absent cell, further investigation should occur to understand why there are no associations for that requirement, since usually requirements have associations.

- Processing (how) usually needs data (what) to perform.
- Data (what) has to be created at some point (how, when).
- Events (when) need to abide by performance restrictions (product constraints).
- Events (when) are triggered through a network (where).
- Policies (why) are enforced somehow through the product (who, what, where, when, how).

If the requirements specification for the perspective is organized as proposed with the Internet requirements pattern, then within each cell at least one requirement should associate to at least another requirement in another cell.

Unit Tests

It should be the responsibility of the requirements engineer to "unit test" his requirements. The review session of requirements should be left to identify conflicts within requirements subsets. It is the responsibility of the requirement authors to review the following questions.

- Is the requirement written in a grammatically correct manner?
- Are all the parts of the requirement supplied?
- Have any special terms been added to the glossary?
- Do the definitions conflict with any standard definitions?[8]
- Does each requirement satisfy the eight quality characteristics?
- Are all the cells accounted for?
- Are all the associations accounted for?

According to the McCall Quality Model,[9] each individual requirement must contain the following attributes to be correct: traceability, completeness, and consistency. Each individual requirement must undergo review for these attributes along with verification that the contents of the requirement describe the need as specified by the requirement supplier. In addition, while determining the maintainability of the individual requirement (modifiability), the following requirement attributes must be met: testability and stability. This is another reason why both priority and stability (items 5a and 5b of the quality characteristics listed in Table 6.1) must be supplied.

As an added benefit, the "desk test" is a valuable tool for analysis. The same questions can be asked just prior to going back to the requirement supplier to identify any additional questions.

Walkthroughs

Formal review sessions are key to the success of the Internet product. They must be well organized and held regularly. To accommodate scheduling demands, the requirements set review should be held at different levels of development and by different organizational levels.

The first walkthrough must occur with the requirement supplier to ensure that what has been specified is what the requirement supplier intended. This can

---

8. Every requirements engineer should have multiple glossaries. At minimum, the following three should be on every desk: (1) a standard glossary such as that by IEEE for software engineering terms, (2) one for the line of business (for example, banking, brokerage, insurance, medical) and (3) a company standard (usually owned by the data analyst group).
9. See Kitchenham and Pfleeger 1996.

be on a one-to-one basis between the requirements engineer and the requirement supplier. If multiple requirements engineers are working on the project, these reviews can occur simultaneously.

The second walkthrough should occur with requirement suppliers within the same community. The purpose is to get all the requirement suppliers to agree that the requirements adhere to the common understanding of the needs for their portion of the business. This walkthrough can take place any time after the previous individual walkthroughs have occurred and the appropriate changes have been made.

The third walkthrough is conducted between business communities. At this stage conflicts are identified and priorities given to different requirements are negotiated. For example, it may be the first time that the legal department sees what marketing wants to do and alerts them to the fact that international laws might be broken.[10]

Interim walkthroughs can occur within the requirements engineering team; these are good training exercises for junior-level requirements engineers. These interim walkthroughs are also valid for identifying potential conflicts that can be resolved with a smaller group (usually one or two requirement suppliers) before a larger walkthrough is arranged.[11] These reviews should occur periodically on small subsets of requirements as they evolve from perspective to perspective.

After the different requirement suppliers, requirement users, and requirement supporters approve all the requirements, a final walkthrough is initiated with the executive steering committee. The previous rounds of review validated the correctness, clarity, consistency, and completeness of the requirements set. The executive committee then approves the requirements to be implemented. The committee members look at each requirement, by priority, and the potential return on investment. This review is not as detailed as the previous walkthroughs but it must be executed before the next phase of the program begins.

Each of these levels of formal walkthrough should occur for every perspective and for each work product. Comparisons between all work products should then be done. The objective is to minimize the risk of Internet failure by identi-

---

10. Remember, walkthroughs are executed at each perspective. Legal will have caught a potentially law-breaking requirement at the scope-level review.

11. Business representatives' time is very valuable. In an Internet situation, time is just as critical to them as it is to the software developers. Using smaller interim reviews takes up less time by breaking up the review across a longer timeline. When this approach is taken, the average review time for participants is shorter than if one long review is held.

fying defects and by incorporating any necessary changes in the business environment *before* related changes are implemented in the product.

Requirement Measurement

The Goddard Space Flight Center's Software Assurance Technology Center has developed an automated tool that reviews documents (Microsoft Word being one type) for specific natural language that may indicate a potential defect in a requirement. This product shows great promise for helping to determine the quality value of a requirements set.

The automated requirements measurement (ARM) software scans the requirements specification for the number of occurrences (defects) in nine categories. There are five categories for individual statements:

1. Imperatives (*shall, must/must not, is required to, applicable, responsible for,* and so on).
2. Continuances (*as follows, listed, below, support,* and so on)
3. Directives (*figure, table, for example,* and so on)
4. Options (*can, may, optionality,* and so on)
5. Weak phrases (*timely, effective, if practical, easy,* and so on)

There are four specification levels:

1. Size (by the previous five categories and lines of text/paragraphs)
2. Text structure (number of identifiers at each hierarchical level)
3. Specification depth (number of imperatives at each hierarchical level)
4. Readability (reading level)[12]

The ARM Quality Indicator/Quality Attribute Correlation illustrates the relationship that underlies the tool (see Figure 6.1).[13] This is important because the next step is to interpret the potential risk the requirement quality has on the Internet product.

The objective is to provide a tool for program and project managers to assess the quality of the requirements specification. Although most of the quality attributes are subjective, the tool looks for key aspects that can be measured and are indicators of the quality of the requirements specification.

---

12. Requirements should be written for a seventh- to eighth-grade reading level. Special medical, scientific, and engineering terms should be included in the glossary to assist readers and keep the document at the proposed reading level.
13. Obtained from http://satc.gsfc.nasa.gov/support/pnsqc_oct(^/pmq.html. pp. 9.

	COMPLETE	CONSISTENT	CORRECT	MODIFIABLE	RANKED	TESTABLE	TRACEABLE	UNAMBIGUOUS	UNDERSTANDABLE	VALIDATABLE	VERIFIABLE
IMPERATIVES	X			X			X	X	X	X	X
CONTINUANCES	X			X	X	X	X	X	X	X	X
DIRECTIVES	X		X			X		X	X	X	X
OPTIONS	X					X		X	X	X	
WEAK PHRASES	X		X			X		X	X	X	X
SIZE	X				X	X		X	X	X	X
TEXT STRUCTURE	X	X		X			X		X		X
SPECIFICATION DEPTH	X	X		X			X		X		X
READABILITY				X		X	X	X	X	X	X

Figure 6.1   ARM Quality Indicator/Quality Attribute Correlation (from http://satc.gsfc.nasa.gov/support/PNSQC_OCT96/pnq.PDF)

The purpose of using a tool like ARM is to minimize risk to the Internet product. Remember, poor-quality requirements (and requirements set) increase the risk to the success (and return on investment) of the Internet product. The ARM Quality Attribute/Risk Type Correlation[14] (see Figure 6.2) breaks risk into the following categories:

1. *Product risks:* A defect can be implemented into the design product. These risks include six subcategories:
   a. *Acceptable risk:* that the product will not meet user's expectations
   b. *Performance risk:* that the final product will not perform as requested

---

14. http://satc.gsfc.nasa.gov/support/pnsqc_oct(^/pmq.html. pp. 11.

	COMPLETE	CONSISTENT	CORRECT	MODIFIABLE	RANKED	TESTABLE	TRACEABLE	UNAMBIGUOUS	UNDERSTANDABLE	VALIDATABLE	VERIFIABLE
PRODUCT ACCEPTABILITY	X	X	X	X	X	X	X	X	X	X	X
PRODUCT AVAILABILITY	X		X	X	X	X					
PRODUCT PERFORMANCE	X	X	X	X	X			X	X		
PRODUCT RELIABILITY	X	X	X	X	X	X	X	X	X	X	X
PRODUCT REPRODUCTIVITY	X	X	X	X	X	X	X	X	X	X	X
PRODUCT SUPPORTABILITY	X	X	X	X	X	X	X	X	X	X	X
PRODUCT UTILITY	X		X	X	X			X	X		X
RESOURCE COST	X		X	X	X	X		X	X		
RESOURCE SCHEDULE	X		X	X	X	X	X	X	X	X	X

Figure 6.2   ARM Quality Attribute/Risk Type Correlation (from http://satc.gsfc.nasa.gov/support/ PNSQC_OCT96/pnq.PDF)

    c. *Reliability risk:* that the product will fail in the operation environment

    d. *Reproducibility risk:* that the product cannot be duplicated for distribution

    e. *Supportability risk:* that the product cannot be adequately maintained.

    f. *Utility risk:* that the product will be less useful than requested by the requirement suppliers

2. *Resource risks:* The product may exceed allocated resources. Note that these risks are extremely important in determining the success of the product. These risks include two subcategories:

    a. *Cost:* that the product will exceed allocated funding (which includes development and support)

    b. *Schedule:* that the product will not be delivered as scheduled

The ARM tool is valuable for "unit testing" the requirements subset or set. It should be used prior to any walkthroughs. Any report outputs from the CASE and requirements management tools can be fed through the ARM tool. The tool is most valuable for convincing management of the need to spend time on the requirement effort (risk analysis).

Prototyping the Requirements

At the end of each quality check, it is important to identify the risky sections. Risky sections are those in which the requirements may or may not be feasible given the technology, resources, costs, or schedule requirements. These sections are prime candidates for prototyping with simulations (physical or virtual) of a portion of the requirements. It is a common practice for a subset of the high-priority requirements to be implemented into a first-cut product to act as a marketing test case, narrowing the audience that can use the product. In this scenario, the site is discarded after a short life span (one to three months). The information gathered from the test site is then fed into the requirements process to build a new and fuller product. Prototyping can occur at any perspective. In fact, it is strongly recommended that you prototype at several levels. The Internet is new to many businesses. It must be acknowledged that most new ideas fail, and prototyping is a valuable protective measure.

Scope-Level Prototypes

A program is initiated with an idea. The idea could consist of one sentence or it could be a full business proposal. In either case, it is the initial requirement, the requirement that all detailed information must support. The purpose of the scope is to define the basic boundaries of the area under discussion. This can be accomplished with a bulleted list for each focus area. Each list should be defined with an explanation as to what is meant by the bulleted item. The list can then be validated as to its need and priority with the different reviewers. Screen mockups can be created to prototype the "real estate" of what would be within scope and how it would look together. The mockup is just that: a display with no functionality executed.

Business-Level Prototypes

The purpose of the business view is to begin to develop a model of the business as it relates to the idea. This perspective illustrates how the business views the idea. Each item in the list is refined with detail as to the relationships among all items in the list. Prototypes of the software requirements at this level are usually virtual. They are walkthroughs, using Collaboration/Response Cards (CRC) or storyboards.

Designer-Level Prototypes

The purpose of the designer view is to define the boundaries of the community under investigation. For IT technology, this is the boundary of what the Internet-based application will be. The business view is segmented to illustrate what will be done manually and what will be done automatically; this then becomes the designer view. With Internet applications, particularly B2B-type Internet applications, the boundary for the information system (and probably the business unit) expands beyond the traditional corporate boundary.

Many applications have been built merging the business view and the designer view. It is important to keep the business view and the designer view separate. By merging the two perspectives, you may miss important procedures that have to be defined for the business personnel. Again, with B2B applications, many old and/or conflicting business policies need to be adjusted to work with other organizations.

Builder-Level Prototypes

In IT terms, this is the perspective where the technological architecture is applied. In other communities, this is also where the tangible solution begins to appear. In this physical model the technology is imposed onto the designer view.

Requirements for the builder view are technology oriented. The technical architecture for the corporation may require additional test equipment or software licenses to prototype the implemented solution.

Subcontractor-Level Prototypes

These requirements are the specifics for actually building the solution. In other words, they lay out the specific needs for the people who will build the Internet solution or supply work products that support the Internet solution (such as marketing flyers). Again, with the use of prototyping, a section of the site may be opened to a selected group of actors to test a new marketing promotion or a new feature of the Internet-based application. The results will again be fed into the requirements process to be implemented into a new product iteration.

Conclusion

Requirements have impacts on all stages of the design, development, implementation, and maintenance of different work products. Having a positive impact on the remainder of the software cycle requires having high-quality requirements. Improve the quality of the requirement and you improve the opportunity for an increased return on investment. Furthermore, improve the quality of the requirement and you reduce the risk of software failure.

Quality can be sacrificed at any point during the development of requirements. As with the development of an extra-fine gemstone, a poor-quality job at one perspective affects the rest of the product evolution. It is important, therefore, to look at quality from three levels: individual, specification, and set. Much is written on the review of individual requirements; many people have familiarity with reviewing specifications (at a focus level and possibly at the perspective level). However, many people forget about the impact one business community can have on other communities' work products. For this level of review, this chapter introduced the Four Cs of a high-quality requirements set.

The future of requirement quality is the responsibility of every team member. Additional tools and techniques need to be instituted to develop a means for determining the impact of poor requirements on return on investment. With this information, more time will be allocated to the requirements process, and additional training will be required in the requirements engineering disciplines.

To date, no quality matrix exists for requirements; however, the ARM product is a good beginning. Once actuals are captured, a product like ARM could be enhanced to produce quality ratings similar to those used for diamond grading. After all, requirements are the Internet product in the rough!

CHAPTER SEVEN

Managing the Requirements Set

Chapter Key Topics

- Requirements management/configuration management
- Configuration management for requirements
- How to implement configuration management for internet-type application requirements

The Internet Impact

The Internet involves multiple business communities developing and generating their own subsets of requirements. One simple requirement change could dramatically impact another community's requirements subset, other work products, and the quality of the iteration. To ensure the integrity of the requirements set, all the Internet requirements need to be managed using a built-in notification and approval mechanism that keeps all affected personnel both informed and focused. Enforcing configuration management for requirements is essential in maintaining the integrity of those requirements.

Each of the different communities, perspectives, and focuses of the Internet requirements set discussed throughout this book is developed at its own pace. The Internet also requires that new iterations be implemented every one to three months with new information and features to keep customers coming back and continuing to use the product. This creates many individual requirements that are linked to other requirements and work products. So, in addition to keeping track of all the requirements supporting all the communities, perspectives, and focus areas, it is crucial to capture all the *links* between those requirements and other work products from one iteration to another (including within an iteration).

By writing down the requirements, gaps and inconsistencies appear. Both gaps and inconsistencies could occur in the form of missing requirements, lost associations, or links with other work products. It takes multiple reviewers to uncover these gaps and inconsistencies. Each reviewer uses his own filter of knowledge when reviewing the requirements. Different reviewers identify different gaps and inconsistencies, suggesting revisions that emerge from diverse perspectives. This information adds tremendous value to the quality of the requirements set and should be encouraged during the review process.

The impact of just one simple change to any requirement, requirement link, or work product could create a domino effect that could seriously delay the implementation schedule or affect the quality of the end product. Reviewers need to know not only what to review but also whether this is the first round of review or a subsequent pass. A different community (thus a different set of reviewers) may need to adjust its requirement in response to changes. The requirements management workflow should be well defined and automated as much as possible.

Let's look at an example of how a change might have a ripple effect on other requirements. A user wants to add to the next iteration of the Internet product a feature to search by (1) product name, (2) product number, and (3) "sounds like" criteria (supporting partial names, numbers, and misspelling). The requirement evolves through the allocation levels to ensure that all communities understand the new requirement. The requirement is defined in a high-quality manner and is approved by the appropriate reviewers. The search function is an important new feature that impacts other work products (specifically, marketing material). The business community responsible for developing all marketing material (for example, television ads, mass mailings) is notified through the proper allocation of requirements to make changes to the work products already under development. Any marketing material already sent to the printers needs to be updated to note this new feature. So, as the site developers convert the requirement to a new feature through design, the marketing individuals may need to change their requirement details for promotional material. The impact on the marketing department's requirements subset needs to be determined and evaluated. The executive committee (which finally approves all requirements) can decide (1) to not include this new feature, (2) to include the feature but not include it on marketing material (thus approving the IT requirement and rejecting or delaying the requirement as it pertains to marketing material), or (3) to include the feature and to stop the presses on the marketing material to add text about the new feature.

The ripple effect, therefore, of a change to a requirement usually affects multiple communities (IT and business). This new requirement for the search feature may require a change to an existing database structure. This same database structure may be part of an existing billing system that could already show performance problems. The point here is that what may be a simple request for one community may have a dramatic and undesirable impact on another group. The new requirement could be too costly in terms of time and money to implement.

What is described here is a need to review requirements for quality as well as for potential impacts. Adjustments may need to be made to already defined, validated, and approved requirements across all communities. Requirements could be delayed or postponed. Both conditions impact the Internet application. The Internet requirements set must be managed to maintain the integrity of the work under development as well as future releases of the application. Each reviewer's input needs to be captured and collectively assessed before any action is determined or taken.

The only way the integrity of the Internet requirements set and the associated work products can be controlled is through the establishment of the following:

- An effective requirements traceability mechanism
- A rigorous review process
- The controlled migration of requirements

In order to support these three functions, two key processes need to be defined, developed, enforced, and managed: *requirements management* and *configuration management*. This chapter provides an overview of these two areas and suggestions for implementation.

The Objectives of Requirements Management and Configuration Management

The objective of requirements management is to establish a common understanding between the supplier and owner of the requirements and the people who have to realize the requirements. This is accomplished through a continual review process and concurrent management of the requirements through each iteration. After the reviews, all associated and linked requirements (such as the project plan, approved changes, design models, marketing plans, and test plans) need to be changed. This results in the Internet application, along with all its supporting documentation and deliverables, accurately reflecting the approved set of requirements. It is important to validate the common understanding between the requirements owner and the people responsible for realizing and satisfying the requirements.

On the other hand, the process of configuration management maintains the integrity of requirements as they evolve through each review and approval stage. Configuration management anticipates, accommodates, and manages the changes to work products through notifications and approvals. It is the process by which the quality and completeness of each work product are maintained by identifying each configuration item (in this instance, requirements) and by systematically controlling each approved change to the requirements set.

The Capability Maturity Model of the Software Engineering Institute

Requirements management and configuration management came into sharp focus as pivotal processes thanks to the introduction of the Capability Maturity Model (CMM).[1] The Software Engineering Institute (SEI) of Carnegie Mellon University constructed the CMM over several years as a means of determining the capability and maturity of organizations developing software or software-intensive systems. The CMM is a framework that describes the key elements of an effective software process (see Table 7.1). It draws an evolutionary path for improvement that organizations may use to continuously improve the quality of software. It also provides a good way to introduce requirements management and configuration management for building high-quality Internet-based products.

In the early days of the Internet, the objective was to "get it up fast" and "be first to market." These driving forces had most software development shops working with an ad hoc process: minimal requirements written down, costs and schedules rarely tracked, and changes often unmanaged. With the current generation of Internet applications, quality is in the eye of the customer, whether the application is a B2B, or B2C, or other type of Internet application. It is imperative that a company offer continual high-quality iterations of its Internet application. Each release creates the need to manage changes from the beginning stages of requirements. Requirements management and configuration manage-

---

1. See Paulk et al. 1995.

Table 7.1   The Five Levels of the Capability Maturity Model

Level 1, Initial	No standard process, if any exists is followed. The chances of program success are dependent on the individuals involved and their past experience. Documentation is not produced to provide knowledge for future efforts.
Level 2, Repeatable	Basic processes (for example, project management and tracking, configuration management, and management of the contract between what is desired and what is to be built) are written down, providing an opportunity to reuse them from project to project.
Level 3, Defined	Processes are integrated into the organization-wide software process as a foundation for controlling the progress of all projects for any style project.
Level 4, Managed	For product quality, detailed measurements are collected on the software process for each project and kept in a repository to identify improvement opportunities in the process.
Level 5, Optimizing	Major quality and productivity improvements are continually achieved through continual review and revision of existing processes based on the metrics results.

ment are both part of CMM Level 2 (see Table 7.1), which helps control costs, schedule, and functionality of the software.

This is not a bureaucratic way to slow the Internet delivery schedule. Improving software processes has tangible results. SEI issued a technical report[2] describing the initial results of a study on the effects of implementing a software process improvement initiative. The report showed a median return on investment of 5.0 on business value. This included such benefits as:

- A median of 35 percent gain in productivity per year
- A median of 15 percent yearly reduction in time to market for software
- A median of 59 percent yearly reduction in post-release defects

Such positive impacts on business performance are essential for Internet applications. Each iteration of the product must be of the highest quality. For example, online shoppers expect more than timely delivery; they also want quality. If high quality is not provided by your site (B2C) or interface (B2B), your competitors may gain your business. With the growing demand for Internet-based applications, the business community is initiating software process improvements

---

2. See Herbsleb et al. 1994.

to support the development of different software iterations and carrying over the effort to support all related work products (for example, marketing material, legal documents). With the Internet, there are few second chances and no room for poor quality. In order to begin to build high-quality Internet iterations, the Internet process must enforce activities that meet the qualifications of CMM Level 2.

The activities and steps described in the CMM are geared toward large organizations. However, the activities can be tailored to meet the objectives of any size organization. The model describes

- Each development process
- The actions the organization must take to ensure the endurance of the process
- The preconditions that must exist in order to have a successful phase
- The activities to be performed
- How to measure and analyze success
- How to verify the implementation of the process

Key Process Areas for CMM Level 2

Requirements management and configuration management are two of the six *key process areas* (KPAs) of the second level. KPAs are focused areas, each of which concentrates on a specific area of software development activities. The other four areas describe

1. *Project management:* the activities and tasks essential for effective project management
2. *Project tracking and oversight:* the activities and tasks essential for overseeing, updating, and readjusting the plan for risk mitigation
3. *Software quality assurance:* the activities and tasks essential for audits and reviews
4. *Software acquisition:* the activities and tasks essential for oversight and management of subcontracted sections of software to be built

All six of the KPAs are vital for building successful software products. Addressing these areas assists in the systematic maturing of the software development process, and adopting each of the six KPAs (see Figure 7.1) for Level 2 has a positive impact on the quality of requirements.

This chapter concentrates on only two of the KPAs: configuration management and requirements management. These two KPAs are primarily responsible

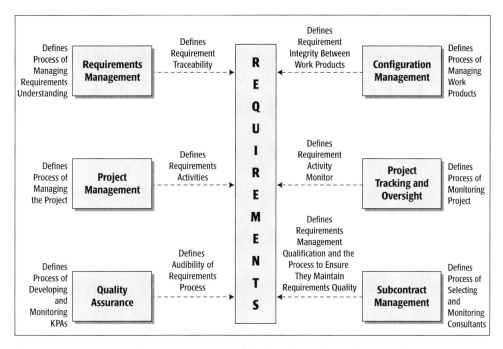

Figure 7.1   SEI/CMM Level 2 Key Process Areas (KPAs) and How They Affect Requirements

for maintaining the integrity of approved requirements through all iterations of the Internet application.

Interpreting the Capability Maturity Model

The CMM describes goals, objectives, and activities that need to be interpreted and adopted in order to enhance existing processes.[3] The CMM criteria for configuration management and requirements management have goals that are specific to each of them (see Table 7.2).

These goals should apply to any work product produced in the development of the Internet product. Examples of work products include advertisements, marketing plans, training materials, and project plans. These should be based on

---

3. It is important to note that complying with the CMM key processes does not guarantee a quality application. Poorly written requirements can be managed just as well as high-quality requirements. By not complying with these KPAs, the risk of not having the requirements and their changes managed increases, creating a negative impact on the final product iteration.

Table 7.2   Configuration and Requirements Management CMM Goals

Goals	Configuration Management	Requirements Management
Goal 1	The configuration management activities are planned.	Requirements are controlled to establish a baseline for use.
Goal 2	All work products to be managed have been identified, controlled, and are available.	All other products and activities are kept consistent with the requirements.
Goal 3	The configuration management process controls the changes to any and all of the work products.	
Goal 4	All participants are informed of the status and content of the work products.	

approved quality requirements. The central point here is that the work products produced throughout the Internet application life cycle are identified, managed, controlled, and available for the project team and reflect the needs of the business. Changes to the requirements are kept consistent with all allied work products. It would be very difficult for an individual to develop an accurate advertisement if he is basing his information on an outdated product feature list.

In order for configuration management activities to succeed, requirements must be identified, classified, linked, and associated with a list of reviewers. To understand why, here is a crash course in configuration management.

What Is Configuration Management?

As with many engineering disciplines, configuration management got its start in the defense industry. It was developed as a technique to identify and resolve problems that were producing cost overruns, including poor-quality items, wrong parts, and ill-fitting components. Hardware companies began to initiate change-control procedures in order to prevent similar situations. Both government and civil industries understood the need to identify and control the design of complex equipment and to communicate that information to all team members.

Configuration management refers to the *identification* and *control* of a corporate asset. Embedded in these activities is status accounting, which essentially is the need to know what exactly is owned and its condition. This is similar to having an up-to-date bank statement that documents all assets and transactions. The corporate asset is, in this case, a requirement work product. The requirement work product is anything that represents the requirements. This can be an individual requirement, the relationship between requirements, a model depicting the requirements, or the entire requirements set.

The following definitions help clarify configuration management.

- *Identification* means being able to identify a specific corporate asset as well as any changes that may affect the asset. Each individual requirement needs a means by which it can be identified; its relationships to other requirements as well as to other work products must also be identified. This identifier must be unique across all projects.
- *Control* involves the access and security related to the use of the corporate asset, in this case, all requirements-related configuration items. The movement and change of each identified and approved requirement, association, and link need to be captured. Procedures need to be documented in a simple, clear manner so that the activities can be followed and repeated. A single group, the change control board (also known as the configuration control board), should be responsible for this activity.
- *Status accounting* refers to the condition and state of the corporate asset. Each requirement evolves through a series of levels leading to approval and inclusion. The individual or group responsible for maintaining the repository of requirement information must manage each state change.

Software configuration management is frequently the first KPA targeted in software process improvement activities. Whether they adopt the CMM or not, most organizations have at least some form of change-control procedures. At minimum, they have some configuration management process that supports software code and files.

Tools for Managing Requirements

Tools exist to manage requirements. They fall into three categories:

1. Requirements specification tools
2. Requirements management tools
3. Configuration management tools

Before selecting any tool, it is important to identify the requirements for the tool. The evaluation of the tools should include

- The requirement functions the tool will support (specification, traceability, notification, change management, version control, Web publishing, and so on)
- The cost per seat
- The maximum number of users
- The ease of use
- The platforms they support
- Any tool interfaces

Most organizations use at least one tool containing some of the requirements. However, proper management of requirements involves using at least one tool from each category. The matter is further complicated since most of the tools do not have a direct interface. Therefore, a manual procedure needs to be established to handle the interface. The manual procedure must be clearly defined and easy to follow.

Requirements Specification Tools

The first kind of requirements record is kept in a requirements specification tool, which includes any tool used to specify requirements. Requirements specification tools are sometimes referred to as "analysis tools" and include CASE tools, word processors, and spreadsheets. Some of these tools have their own version control. Somewhere on the document, in electronic form, the date and names of the persons who approved the requirements should be noted. The file that contains the approved requirements should then be baselined. Any approved changes to the file should be versioned.

Requirements specification tools create individual work products. One tool rarely can document all requirements. As a result, many tools may be used to record the focus, perspective, and community. Each tool will satisfy one or more work product. The limitation of using only a requirements specification tool is the inability to trace the requirements to other work products.

Modeling Tools

Modeling tools, more commonly known as CASE (computer-aided software engineering) tools, maintain the smallest configuration item (such as data attribute) and its inclusion into larger configuration items (such as information model). Unfortunately, if multiple CASE tools are used on the same project (for example, one for data, one for process, and one for network), it is difficult to keep the various versions synchronized. Traceability (a key function in requirements management) could be lost if requirements are spread across different tools.

Office Tools

Smaller organizations or small projects use office-type tools such as word processors, spreadsheets, and project-planning tools. Each of these tools has version control, change-tracking, and baseline facilities. As with the CASE tools, if multiple tools are used, manual synchronization could become laborious.

Requirements Management Tools

Requirements management tools allow you to trace individual requirements to additional work products and other requirements. The state of the requirement is kept with the enforcement of a full approval effort.

Requirements management tools are growing in popularity and sophistication. They provide traceability between textual requirements, have an automated approval process, and can produce reports. These reports can be customized to use the requirements specification template described in Appendix A. Only a few of these tools interface and coordinate with the modeling tool versions. If an approved change is not retroacted in the CASE model, the physical design (based on the business architecture model of the requirements) may develop from an inaccurate set of requirements.

Configuration Management Tools

A configuration management tool can manage any electronic file you want to place under its control. A file can be a document, code, data structure, object model, and so forth. This file is considered a *configuration item*.

The configuration management tool manages the integrity of the contents by controlling who has access to the tool and by assigning read-write capability. An audit trail of all user operational activities is kept automatically.

Configuration management tools used to manage requirements have their limitations. For instance, they currently do not link directly with any of the tools used to specify software requirements. Manual procedures need to be put in place to control versions of output from the different tools. The configuration control board assists with the manual effort.

All approved work products, including changes, are sent to the team configuration manager to be placed under configuration control. This can be handled with the internal e-mail facility used in Lotus Notes, for example.

Integrating Tools for Configuration Management

As stated previously, all three categories of tools are required to fully support configuration management for requirements. To accomplish this, a manual procedure is required.

Use a requirements specification tool to record the requirements. Use the individual tool to create baselines and versions. Make sure that a requirements set identifier is included somewhere in the project file. Create an electronic document output of the contents to be used as a configuration item.

Then use the requirements management tool to manage the approval process as well as the traceability of one requirements set to another. Use the tool to create identifier baselines and versions. Record somewhere in the requirements set the source of any of the requirements specification tool information. As with the requirements specification tool, make sure that a requirements set identifier is included somewhere in the project file. For example, make a note of the tool where the data model is maintained. Include with the information the baseline date and version number that should be associated with the requirements set. Create an electronic document of the contents to be used as a configuration item.

Finally, use the configuration management tool to manage the check-in and check-out procedures of approved requirements. Use the tool as the central source for all project team members.

The Configuration Management Process

The configuration management process supports each type of work product. This process must be seamlessly integrated with other processes that create the work products. It is important to take the process to a finer level of detail in order to define the interrelationship between the processes that create the work product and the configuration management process.

Watts Humphrey[4] identified seven key meta-information elements/attributes (information about the information) to be kept about each work product placed under configuration management control:

---

4. See Humphrey 1989.

1. Configuration control
2. Change management
3. Revisions
4. Versions
5. Derivations
6. Deltas[5]
7. Conditional code

Configuration control permits access to only one copy of the requirement, including any revised and approved copies. Only one version is available for everyone to use. For example, a single requirement affects two functional areas: product order entry and inventory management. If a designer for the order entry function changes a requirement that triggers the inventory control function, the designer of the inventory control function will not be able to modify the requirement until the changes to the order entry function are completed. Though the inventory control designer can view the older approved version, he can see that the requirement is currently being altered. The key to configuration control is that the shopping cart designer and the inventory management designer cannot both modify the requirement simultaneously. The first person who captures the requirement for alteration has write access. The second person can read the requirement along with the status indicating a potential change.

These kinds of changes (see Figure 7.2) are considered *revisions*. Each module has its own revision history. The *version* change is the sum total of a particular set of revisions.

Keeping separate revisions enables you to revert back to a previously approved requirement if needed. It also provides a historic view of the changes for pattern recognition of improvement opportunities. For example, the same requirement affecting both order entry and inventory management was changed by the order entry designer. As the requirement went through the different configuration states, someone discovered that the change was not approved. Keeping revisions allows for the ability to go back through many iterations of the requirement.

Requirements may have multiple approved versions to support multiple releases. For example, for the first release of the software solution, the requirement is to support an eastern geographical region. In the second release of the software solution, the requirement is to support the western region as well. Each

---

5. Since 1989, configuration management has evolved to the point that deltas are incorporated under the topic of version control. Deltas are not discussed separately here.

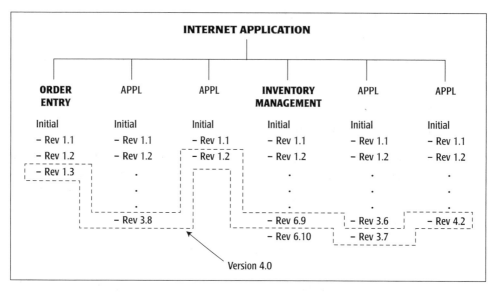

Figure 7.2   Revisions and Version

of these localized requirements sets triggers the release of a different version containing the localized, approved requirements set.

Derivation is another, more common name for the history report. All version control tools have this function. This is the ability to identify what has changed from one version to another. Reports should be periodically reviewed to identify what has changed, not necessarily just between two consecutive versions. A requirement that has undergone many revisions could have a derivation report issued that compares the initial posting of the requirement and the last approved, revised requirement. Keeping a record that compares revisions may illustrate the possible circles that develop around a single requirement. The record may also show how one requirement is the most volatile—always forced to change to support changes in other requirements. Volatility is an indication that the requirement may be either too ambiguous or unfeasible. In either case, the requirement needs to be reevaluated as to its quality characteristics and priority.

The *conditional code* defines the condition of the configuration item, in this case the requirement. For the purposes of this book, the conditional code refers to the state of the requirement (see the following).

All change must follow a defined process to ensure the integrity of the Internet application. In other words, a change must follow a defined maintenance process. Requirements are captured throughout the life cycle (see Figure 7.3).

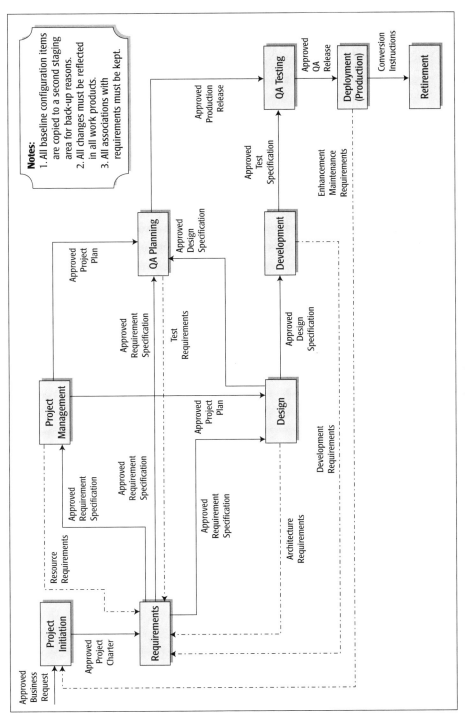

Figure 7.3 Requirements Identified Throughout the Product Life Cycle

Configuration management is not affected by *when* the requirements are captured, but once they are captured, they are managed through their evolutionary stages from being approved to being implemented.

Configuration Management States for Requirements

The maintenance process for requirements introduces the concept of *states*. These are points at which the requirement rests until another action takes place. Developed requirements, once under configuration control, evolve through four to nine configuration management states through a process called *promotion*, or the transition through a developmental state (see Figure 7.4).

A *configuration state* is a status point of reference to know and inquire upon. For example, do you need to know in what state a requirement is before approval? Do you need to know its state after the requirement has been changed, other than that it has been changed and the change has been approved?

During the early stages of development, a requirement has minimal visibility and requires frequent changes. As the requirement becomes stable, visibility increases and changes decrease. A value can be calculated over specific periods of time that indicates the stability of the requirement (see Figure 7.5). Ideally, you want to see a requirement become more stable as time progresses (moving closer to the value "1"). If there is a sudden reversal, it is time to investigate!

The different requirement configuration states (see Table 7.3) need to assist in monitoring the quality of the Internet-based product and not impede the development process. To be able to do this, each state must satisfy at least one of the following four particularities:

1. Maintain pace of development (*velocity*) by providing information to all affected individuals as soon as possible.
2. Provide the ability of *concurrent* development of different iterations.
3. Maintain the *integrity* of each incremental release.
4. Maintain the *quality* of the requirements set.

Baselines and Libraries

As a requirement leaves a state, a baseline is taken. A baseline is a snapshot—a point-in-time picture of the requirements in a given state. A baseline is taken at an individual requirement level, a requirements subset level, a group level (iteration), and a requirements set level, each being a requirement work product (RWP). Baselines provide an audit trail. Baselines are as important during the development of the product as they are after deployment.

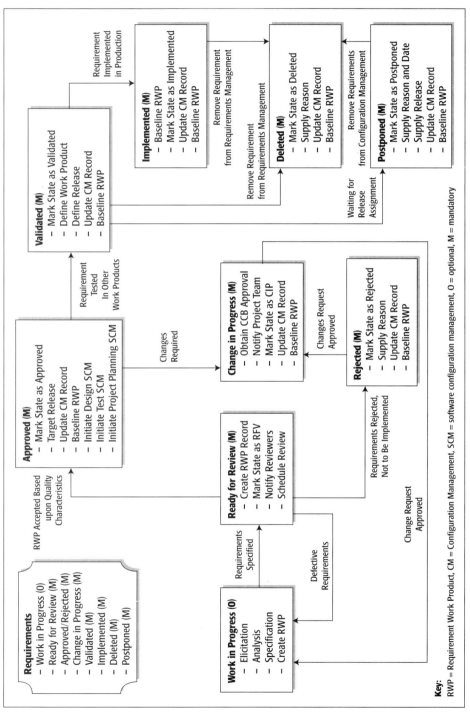

Figure 7.4 Life of a Requirement—Configuration State Transition

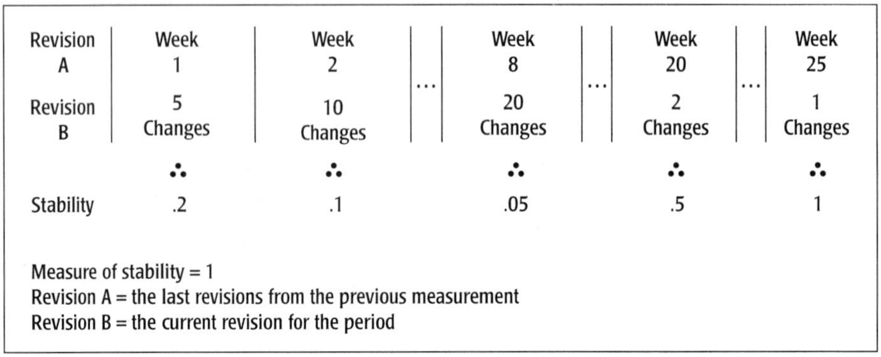

Revision A	Week 1	Week 2		Week 8		Week 20		Week 25
Revision B	5 Changes	10 Changes	...	20 Changes	...	2 Changes	...	1 Changes
	∴	∴		∴		∴		∴
Stability	.2	.1		.05		.5		1

Measure of stability = 1
Revision A = the last revisions from the previous measurement
Revision B = the current revision for the period

Figure 7.5   Stability Measurement

Table 7.3   The Different Requirement Configuration States for Internet Requirements

State	Optionality	Description	Benefit to Internet Development
Work in progress	Optional	Used to place requirements under configuration management as they are being elicited, analyzed, and specified. These requirements are for notification to other project participants *only* and are not to be acted upon until approved.	*Integrity:* Provides the ability to segregate requirements by incremental release; allowing concurrent development.
Ready for review	Mandatory	Used to notify project team members that the requirement is ready for their review. If not approved, the status is moved back to work in progress.	*Velocity:* Allows for individual requirement review as soon as possible; results in early corrections and suggestions.
Approved	Mandatory	Used to notify design team members that the requirement is approved and can be acted upon. Approved requirements initiate a notification to other development activities.	*Concurrency:* Provides open communication between different communities on what requirements are approved and ready to be implemented.

Table 7.3 The Different Requirement Configuration States for Internet Requirements (*continued*)

State	Optionality	Description	Benefit to Internet Development
Rejected	Mandatory	Used to notify that a requirement or change to a requirement was rejected.	*Integrity, velocity:* With an iteration release every one to three months, it is quite easy to reintroduce a requirement that had to be rejected for valid business reasons. Keeping a list of rejections provides a way to prevent reintroduction. If for valid reasons the requirement should be reintroduced, much of the work has already been done, requiring only minor modification.
Validated	Mandatory	Used to document that the requirement passed all quality checks but has not been approved for implementation. This does not imply that the requirement was continually carried over through the future work products. There needs to be a conscious effort to validate whether an approved requirement actually was adhered to in future work products. This status documents that a requirement has been tested in other work products. Some of these work products are design documents, codes, user manuals, and so forth.	*Quality:* Shows that a requirement is actually implementable.
Implemented	Mandatory	Used to document that the requirement has been incorporated into the product or service.	*Quality, integrity:* Shows which requirement is implemented and needs to be added to regression tests for future iterations.

Table continued on next page.

Table 7.3   The Different Requirement Configuration States for Internet Requirements (*continued*)

State	Optionality	Description	Benefit to Internet Development
Deleted	Mandatory	Used to document that either the requirement has been removed from the product or service or it has been determined not to implement it at all.	*Quality, velocity:* This is a very important state for Internet applications. A feature that seemed like a good idea at the time may be an annoyance to the customer or business. This may be discovered after it was implemented or during focus group discussions. Keeping the requirements set concise with only pertinent information saves time in the maintenance of the set.
Postponed	Mandatory	Used to document that the requirement has been postponed to a different release. It is important to document the reason for the delay for quality assurance purposes.	*Quality, Integrity:* A requirement may not get implemented for multiple reasons, for example, for business reasons or because of time and effort to implement, which may not be known until the testing phase. Should the requirement be postponed, the reason must be captured. A continual review of reasons may identify improvements that will streamline further iterations of the Internet product. The requirement may be put on hold until further market research demonstrates that the requirement is worth the cost of development, implementation, and support.
Change in progress	Mandatory	Used to notify project team members that the requirement is under consideration for change. The change is a notification and should not be acted upon. A notification of a possible change is sent to people involved in other configuration management activities (project management, test planning, design, and development). A change must be reviewed under validation and then approved before it can be acted upon.	*Velocity, concurrency:* Through the approval process, ideas or other requirements may affect another requirement, requiring that it be updated. It is important for reviewers not to waste their time reviewing a requirement that is targeted for change.

Baselines should be kept in different libraries. These libraries are staging areas that describe the condition of the requirement (see Table 7.4). Note that the deleted state is not contained in any library. Rejected and postponed requirements are not contained in the static library because these requirements are possibly more volatile and may change. The static library should contain only requirements that are to be implemented.

Authorizing Changes to Requirements

To move from one library to another requires approval and promotion. Each level may require different approval levels and personnel. For example, a businessperson would not approve a requirement for a specific Web-based testing tool used by developers of the Internet application. However, he or she would be on the review list for any requirement that may impact the business process. To clarify, a legal restriction that must be enforced may alter the business-to-business flow of information. Both legal and business personnel must approve that requirement.

The group of individuals who perform reviews is known as a *configuration control board* (CCB), which is often referred to as a *change control board*. The responsibilities of the board are to review and approve or disapprove the proposed changes and to determine the direction (the next state) the reviewed requirements set should take.

Members of the CCB can vary by work product, level of impact, and stage of product development. For example, if the change is technical in nature, a business representative may not be part of the board. However, if the change will affect the delivery date, budget, or resource allocation, an executive may be required as a

Table 7.4 Configuration Libraries and States

Library	Purpose	Internet Configuration State
Dynamic	To provide developers a place for the work-in-progress staging library	• Work in progress • Change in progress
Controlled	To control requirements that are stable but not approved as they move through the approval process	• Ready for review • Rejected • Postponed
Static	To be implemented and available for general use by others	• Approved • Validated • Implemented

member of the board. The individual or group submitting the change request usually assigns the initial classification of the change (see Table 7.5). The classification could change as the nature, scope, and impact of the change emerges through analysis.

The CCB members and their levels of approval authority (for example, a member may be able to recommend alterations but may not be allowed to approve or reject a requirement from a specific business unit) are established at the start of a project in what is called a *configuration plan*. A divisional or organizational process group may have defined recommendations. The configuration plan defines the roles, responsibilities, and rules of engagement of the CCB for the specific work product. The members vary by the kind or configuration state of work product. For requirements, the members may still vary by the community, focus, and perspective of the requirement.

As discussed earlier, tools do exist for configuration management. However, configuration management will always involve some manual intervention by reviewers and those in charge of maintaining the libraries. To ensure the integrity of the data kept about each requirement in relation to its state, approvals, and promotions, the following two questions need to be answered by the configuration management group (CMG):

1. How will the CMG ensure that the correct people have approved the requirement and any changes?
2. What conditions allow for an emergency or fast-track process on approvals and promotions?

Table 7.5   Change Category

Category of Change	Change Description	Approvals Required
Category A	Affects project constraints for the program	• Program manager • Executive committee
Category B	Cross-community impact	• Representatives of affected business communities
Category C	Cross-focus and/or perspective impact	• Application architect • Technical architect • Focus specialists
Category D	Contained within requirement cell	• Requirements engineer • Requirement supplier

Table 7.6 documents key roles that should constitute the CCB. The table specifies the perspective since a requirements specification is usually produced for a specific audience[6] correlated to that perspective. The audience will probably have different authority levels. The roles are generic to support all Internet communities. Each role is assigned one of three authorization levels:

1. Approver
2. Reviewer
3. Audience

Approver

The *approver* represents those who have the ability to change the state of the requirement as well as add comments and suggestions. Quality assurance control representatives are at each perspective level. They have the authority to reject any requirement if the requirement does not meet defined quality characteristics.

Reviewer

A *reviewer* represents those who have the ability to submit comments and suggestions concerning the requirement but who may not change the state. This usually includes the representative who is responsible for developing the work product for the next perspective. Reviewers can make comments about the financial or time impacts of satisfying the requirement. They provide information that will help the approvers in their determination.

Audience

The *audience* represents those who are interested in viewing the requirements but have no direct impact on the resulting state. They may view the requirements for information purposes only. If the review is held in a formal meeting, only those people listed in the column would attend. If the review is through notification by the requirements or configuration management tool, anyone can read the information.

The CCB must have a representative from each project area participating in the Internet application. For example, risk management should review a new requirement or change to an existing requirement that may expose the corporation to some financial risk.

---

6. Audience, in this context, refers to people who can be invited to review sessions. In general, all requirements should be available in a read-only library for anyone to access.

Table 7.6   Internet Configuration Control Board

Perspective	Approver	Reviewer	Audience
Planner	• Businessperson initiating effort • Executive sponsor • Internet program board • Quality assurance	• Business support areas (e.g., human resources, legal) • Business process areas (e.g., inventory control, billing) • Risk management • Requirements engineers	• Configuration manager • Designers • Quality assurance (process developers)
Owner	• Business process areas • Business support areas • Quality assurance • Executive sponsor (based on added cost or time to market)	• Designers • Architects • Requirements engineers • Risk management	• Configuration manager • Builders • Quality assurance • Technical writer • Usability engineer
Designer	• Business process areas • Business support areas • Quality assurance • Executive sponsor (based on added cost or time to market)	• Builders • Architects • Technical writer • Usability engineer	• Configuration manager • Quality assurance
Builder	• Quality assurance • Executive sponsor (based on added cost or time to market)	• Programmers • Technical writer • Usability engineer	• Configuration manager • Quality assurance
Subcontractor	• Quality assurance • Project manager • Executive sponsor (based on added cost or time to market)	• Requirements engineers • Technical writer • Usability engineer	• Designers of work products for future iterations • Future builders • Quality assurance • Configuration manager

For example, an online toy company issued an offer to pay $100 to anyone who did not receive his or her toy in time for the 1999 winter holidays. The risk management department probably issued a risk analysis to anticipate the chance that the product maker could not deliver the product to the toy company warehouse or that the shipping company would not be able to deliver the product to the final destination in time for the holidays. To review this new requirement "special holiday offer," a risk management representative was part of the configuration control board to provide risk analysis as additional information. Risk management could not approve or reject the "special holiday offer" requirement. That decision was left to the executive sponsor. If a state law would be broken by the offer, the legal representative had the authority to reject the "special holiday offer" requirement. However, no laws were broken; there was simply financial exposure that could have cost the toy company millions of dollars.

Selecting what should be a configuration item is the responsibility of the CCB. If the answer to any question in Table 7.7[7] is "yes," then the element should be a configuration item. Although the table discusses software characteristics, the concept can be applied to any part of a work product produced by any community (for example, marketing plans, advertisements, and role descriptions).

All requirements, no matter which community, focus, or perspective, should be considered configuration items. They are configuration items no matter what form they are represented in (for example, text with or without supporting models, matrices, or graphics).

The Components of Configuration Management

Since configuration management is the key to controlling the integrity of the requirements set, it is important to understand the responsibilities of configuration management. There are basically ten activities that must be performed by the configuration management group:

1. Baseline management
2. Change control
3. Configuration identification
4. Configuration control
5. Configuration status accounting
6. Configuration audit
7. Interface control
8. Library control
9. Release management
10. Contractor control

These activities are described briefly on the following pages.

---

7. The questions in Table 7.7 are based on Berlack 1992.

Table 7.7   Software Configuration Item Characteristics

Multiple use	Will the item/element be used in several equal or higher-level elements?
Criticality	Is the element critical, high risk, and/or a safety item? Would the failure of this assembly adversely affect security or safety? Would it have a significant financial impact?
Presence of existing or modified design elements	Have software elements been reused or borrowed? (This is especially important if an element has already been designated a configuration item in the current or past environment.)
Interface	Is the element a collection of highly data- or control-independent functions or separate functions that exhibit highly disparate input and output data rates? Does the element interface with other configuration items whose configuration is controlled by another organization?
Maintenance	Will the element be maintained by diverse groups at many different locations?
Function	Is the element one of a kind in that its application is different from that of the primary elements of test software and training/simulation?
Use of commercial off-the-shelf products or subcontractor	Can the element be procured off the shelf or must it be developed by a subcontractor?
Generality	Does the element have a general-purpose use for many other people/functions (such as mathematical tools)?
Schedule/delivery	Can several copies be delivered at different times (for example, one copy with each equipment unit delivered)?
Relationship	Is the element related to existing configuration items?
New technologies	Does the element incorporate new technologies not found in existing configuration items or candidates for configuration items?

Baseline Management

Baseline management relates to the management of the different snapshots. Baselines occur as an individual requirement or requirements set is approved. Each baseline must be managed through the different defined states and promoted through the different libraries previously described.

Change Control

Change control is what everyone thinks about when they first hear about configuration management. Change control refers to the management of the requirements as they move from one state to another. It describes the management of the change process.

Configuration Identification

Configuration identification relates to the identification of the work product or the work product component. As with any identifier (for example, a requirement identifier), there is no implicit meaning in the configuration identification; it is just a unique way to identify a work product or work product component from all others. The work product or work product component is called a configuration item (see Table 7.7).

Configuration Control

Configuration control refers to the management of the different configuration items. This includes protecting of corporate assets as well as ensuring that the latest approved version of the configuration item is presented for viewing, updating, and using by approved members.

Configuration Status Accounting

Configuration status accounting refers to the management of the status of each specific configuration item and the history of changes as the status is captured, kept, and reported. This includes those configuration items placed under configuration management as well as those with proposed changes.

Configuration Audit

Configuration audit refers to the verification that the configuration items and the program are adhering to the approved configuration management process and procedures. The audit also verifies that all proposed changes are subject to and have followed the defined change process.

Interface Control

Interface control refers to the impact the configuration item has on another configuration item. Therefore, a change to an order entry requirement that has already been validated in the design, test, and software module for compliance requires a revalidation of those work products.

Library Control

Library control involves moving designated configuration items from one library to the next as the evolution process is followed. This always requires CCB approval.

Release Management

Release management in larger organizations may be performed by a group unto itself. The activity involves providing a version description document, verifying that everything in the release has undergone the defined cycle, and verifying that only those items in the final library (production) are built for release.

Contractor Control

Contractor control refers to ensuring that vendors and contractors adhere to a defined configuration management process.

The Benefits of Configuration Management

It is imperative that configuration management be employed for Internet development. Configuration management supports a high-quality Internet system in four ways:

1. *Protection of intellectual property:* Awareness of the need to protect intellectual property is increasing. The laws protecting software and Web information are not as clear as the copyright laws that protect publications. Configuration management can provide illustrative documentation, spanning the entire development work from concept to release.

2. *Common point of integration:* The configuration management process defines a common point of integration for all planning, oversight, and implementation activities for the product. The person responsible for this activity acts as the coordinator of the work products used by multiple organizations.

3. *Product quality:* Configuration management is a critical support activity that enhances the effectiveness of product and program management.

4. *Concurrent development:* Configuration management facilitates the parallel activities often required to deliver a product to customers in a timely manner.

Configuration Management for Requirements

Both requirements management and software configuration management need to be in place in the organization if the Internet product is to maintain its continual evolution (an iteration every one to three months). Because Internet applications require frequent incremental implementations, it is vital to control the requirements set.

- A misplaced requirement could result in a failure to distinguish your site from a competitor's.
- Changing a requirement without investigating the impact on other requirements could cause significant delays in implementation as other groups attempt to react to the change.
- Failure to validate a requirement that might be contained in future work products could result in a design infrastructure that cannot support or reflect a later release.

All of the preceding scenarios may negatively impact the entire Internet product's infrastructure, minimizing its flexibility, usability, or other quality aspects. Any of the preceding could mark the difference between a successful Internet iteration and a failed attempt to "be on the Web." For this reason, requirements management and configuration management need to work together and support each other.

Requirements, for the purpose of the configuration management process, are approved, allocated requirements to be satisfied with a software technology solution. They are more commonly referred to as "software requirements." However, this process can be expanded to support all types of requirements (such as organizational, project, legal notices, marketing material, hardware, design, and so forth).

Figure 7.6 illustrates how requirements management (RM) and configuration management (CM) work together. RM establishes the agreement between the supplier and implementers of the approved requirements. Configuration management controls the integrity.

The reviewers of the requirements are responsible for signing off on the requirements set or subset,[8] acknowledging that the requirements satisfy the quality characteristics to their satisfaction.[9] The requirements set must describe

---

8. The requirements set contains all requirements. A subset represents a specific community and specific perspective. A separate specification may be developed for each focus area as well. For clarity and ease of maintenance, it is best not to mix different communities and different perspectives in a specification. A reviewer will read at least one specification if not all the specifications for an entire requirements set.

9. A good requirement is: correct, complete, clear, consistent, verifiable, traceable, feasible, modular, and design independent.

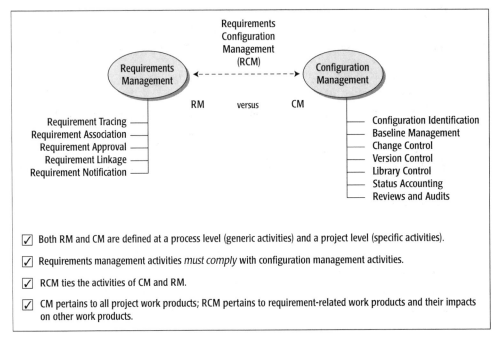

Figure 7.6   Requirements Management versus Configuration Management

the "who, what, where, when, how, and why" of the overall business objective. This set must also include expectation-type requirements such as performance, security, and constraints (product and project). In other words, all the requirements by community, perspective, and focus must be placed under the control of configuration management. The requirements are contained in different specifications and therefore must be tracked individually.

It is important to note that approving requirements does not impede the processing of changes. Configuration management supports and tracks changes as they occur. Configuration management notes the reason for the change as well as its impact on other artifacts or work products.[10]

Once a requirement has been approved, it is mandatory to place it under configuration management control. Prior to approval, it should be in the devel-

---

10. It is important to capture the impact the change has on other work products since this information may influence the decision to accept, reject, or postpone the implementation of a requirement.

opment library. All changes to requirements that occur after approval should be tracked with a configuration management tool.

Implementing Configuration Management for Requirements for Internet-Type Applications

It is important to recognize requirements as corporate assets. They are the basis for the Internet application. For this reason, they must be managed to protect the integrity of the application.

Configuration management serves as the communication vehicle for all program activities by providing technical information about each work product. This includes the audit trail of information such as date and time placed under configuration management control and who created, read, deleted, and updated the work product. Configuration management keeps the work products secure by allowing only authorized persons to make changes or read the work product. Configuration management notifies the owners of work products of any changes that may affect their work products. Information is provided about the change and is transmitted to the owners of other work products. Additionally, status and change history are available on work products.

What Needs to Be Managed?

In order for requirement configuration management to be of use to any organization and project, it must not impede development or be cumbersome to use. Furthermore, it should be accessible to all program team members.

Many tools can be used to develop requirements. Each tool can produce multiple work products, including an export file. For requirements, both a textual document specifying all requirements and an export file from the requirement representation tool should be placed under a configuration management tool as separate configuration items. Which tools to use to specify requirements should be determined by the project manager and specified in the project management plan. Most of the tools have baselining and auditing functionality; therefore, a pivotal task is to determine what would be best placed under control of the configuration management tool.

The selection of configuration items is the most important decision in configuration management. A configuration item is a stand-alone, test-alone, use-alone element (see Figure 7.7). This may seem somewhat convoluted since a

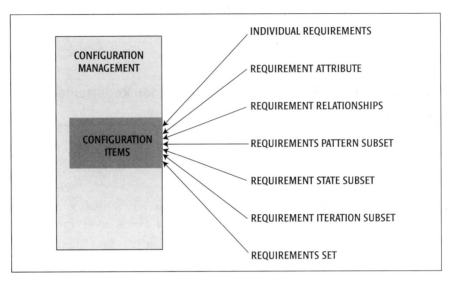

Figure 7.7   Requirements Configuration Items

configuration item can stand alone but can also be part of another product. Think about a car. A car has many parts (body, engine, wheels, and so on). Some parts (for example, the engine) are made up of many other parts. To clarify, a configuration item is the lowest level of requirement detail.

For example, in a data model, you describe an entity, a relationship, and the entity attributes of the entity or entity class. Each entity attribute, in turn, has attributes that assist in defining the requirement. The entity is a requirement; the relationship is a requirement; and each entity attribute is a requirement. The diagram representing the data model illustrates the relationships between the requirements; each relationship in turn is another requirement. Individually, these requirements may change and have little or no impact on the others. However, the importance of them being implemented together creates a need to manage the correlation between multiple requirements.

In configuration management, individual requirements must be managed as well as their associations with other requirements. This creates a baseline within a baseline. The higher (requirement relationship) configuration items can be approved only when all other associated individual requirements are approved.

The simplest way to manage a requirements set is by each specification. If you change a small piece of the requirements specification, or a product of a product, you will be reapproving the entire requirements specification at a rapid and increasing rate. If you manage the smallest product, you will have a lot of configuration items for the smallest piece as well as for its relationship to other products (for example, the engine parts are managed as well as their relationships to the functions they perform in the engine).

In software terms, let's take another look at the product within the product by looking through the data focus. If you change a data item kept in a data entity, the entire specification (which could just be the data focus data model[11] or could be the business model that may contain all focus areas) must be reapproved and rebaselined. If you manage each data item separately, then only the data item needs to be reapproved and rebaselined. This illustrates two extremes.

This points out that each specification is only a subset of the Internet requirements set. Additional information exists that traces requirements between the different perspectives and interfaces between communities. This additional detail must also be considered requirement information and must be placed under configuration management as well.

Structure for Traceability

Once you know the level of detail, the requirements set must be placed under configuration management. It is important to trace each of the individual configuration items through other work products. Therefore, it is important to set up a tracing structure that is easily maintained and simple to follow. This feature is inherent in many requirements management tools. It is often called the "bullet-proofing" where all requirements get tested.

If you are using one of the approved tools, all attributes that assist in clearly defining the requirement in a concise and unambiguous way must be supplied as part of the requirement. In addition, some organizations specify corporate or divisional recommendations.

---

11. A *data model* is an illustration depicting the relationship of things of importance to the corporation. For example, a data model illustrating a customer may have multiple forms of contact; the two entities would be *customer* and *forms of contact*. The data items *customer first name*, and *customer last name* would be attributes of the entity *customer*. For reasons of configuration management, the data items would be configuration items as would the entities *customer* and *forms of contact*. The relationship of the data items *customer first name* and *customer last name* would be kept as a configuration item, as would the relationship to the entity *customer*. The illustration of the data model would also be a configuration item. This is an example of a product consisting of other products.

As a minimum, all requirements must be listed in a requirements specification in textual form. The requirements specification may contain diagrams, often in the form of models, produced by one of the approved tools. The diagrams must contain a legend to assist in the interpretation of the requirements. A separate specification should exist for each community and perspective. The primary reason is that each community specification and each perspective is intended for a different audience. Each requirement must be traced through the different specifications. Only with this tracing will requirement gaps be avoided.

Identities and Traceability

Traceability of a requirement means that each requirement work product (RWP) must contain a distinct identifier (RWP ID). This identifier must be related to the requirements set in order to tie together all related RWPs. Each requirements set must also have a separate and distinct identifier (RS ID). The identifier should be unique across all programs in an enterprise; down the line, two projects may be merged, and if this happens (and it often does), you do not want to have to reallocate any requirement numbers!

Because a requirement may spawn several projects, it is important to tie requirements to projects. Each community involved in developing the Internet business will initiate its own project. However, a requirement must not be limited to only one project. Configuration management tools do not allow for a many-to-many relationship. Configuration management tools should allow a list of project identifiers (PROJ IDs) to be associated with the RWP for information reasons only.

Minimum Level of Requirement Documentation

Requirements can be represented in many formats. A single requirement may be represented in multiple models, each illustrating a different focus (data, process, and so forth) and perspective (high-level, design, and so forth). How are you going to correlate the different requirements in a configuration management tool? Do you want to keep other perspective requirements or only the business requirements allocated to software? These questions need to be addressed.

Requirements Contents

To review, a requirement can be represented by focus (functional and nonfunctional requirements), perspective (planner, owner, designer, builder, and subcontractor), and community (organizational, technical, support, and business).

The representation of the requirements can be documented in different formats: text or model. The formats may be based on the development technique and the notation specific to that technique. In most cases, a requirements set will probably contain multiple formats in order to depict the functional and nonfunctional requirements. Therefore, the requirements set will have multiple diagrams and models as well as textual information.

Requirements Package

As we have established, all types of requirements, original and derived, must be managed under configuration management. The compilation of the requirements creates a requirements set. The compilation of the different formats creates a requirements package.

A requirements package contains all the configuration items (formats) that will be placed under configuration management. They should be associated and traceable to each other through the use of the RS ID. This RS ID should be defined at the point of initialization.

Work Product Information

For clarity, each RWP should have all the information that fully describes the configuration item (see Table 7.8). The attributes form a complex model of information. The model must depict the rules and policies that support the requirements management and configuration management processes. Most requirements management tools have this ability.

The project sponsor owns the requirements set. The sponsor is responsible for resolving any conflicts that arise between requirements. The configuration management group owns the requirements package. The group is responsible for maintaining the integrity of the requirements set.

It is important to *not* build intelligence into a naming convention. All identifiers should be the next sequential number. The identifier should *not* imply any definition as to project, model, and so on. Adding intelligence to an identifier will

- Be obvious only to some.
- Potentially change the meaning or become outdated as similar items are added. For example, if *A* were used to represent *America*, the identifier scheme wouldn't work as intended once the product went international and other countries like *Argentina* were added to the mix.
- Make it hard to maintain as the list of possibilities grows.
- Make it hard to query against, therefore compromising its value.

Table 7.8   Attributes Required for Requirements Configuration Management. (RWP, requirement work product)

Attribute	Description
RWP name	The name of the RWP
RWP version	A version number of the RWP
RWP revision number	A revision number of the RWP
RWP format type	Information to help identify the type of output and the tool used to create the RWP
Check-in identifier	The identifier of the person who checked in the RWP
Check-in date and time	The date and time of check-in
Approval identifier	The identifier of the person who approved the requirement for the next state
Approval date and time	The date and time of approval
State identifier	The current state of the RWP in the requirements management/configuration management process
State authorization identifier	The person(s) who approved the change in state
State supporting documentation/reason	Comments on the reason for the specific state
Requirement identifier	The identifier of the individual requirement
Requirements set identifier	Information to help associate all requirements to a business objective
Requirements set name	The name of the requirements set
Requirements package ID	The identifier of the individual work product
Community identifier	The identifier of the community that the requirement was allocated to
Perspective identifier	The identifier of the perspective that the requirement has evolved to
Focus identifier	The focus area the requirement supports (who, what, where, when, why, how, product constraints, project constraints)
Interface identifier	The identifier of another cell that the RWP supports

Proper Staffing for Maintaining the Integrity of the Requirements

Effective configuration management takes time. Who will be responsible for maintaining the software product, user access and security, backups, and products stored under the product control? For a large company, this may involve a group of individuals responsible for configuration management activities for a project. For small start-ups, this may be the same individual who maintains the LAN, documents requirements, or has other similar responsibilities. The point is that these activities must be performed to maintain the integrity of the requirements set. Initially, it is a lot of work, but as the process matures it becomes much smoother.

Another staffing issue revolves around the library, which needs to be managed. It takes separate individuals or groups to administer the tools and manage the libraries that control the promotion of requirements. Additionally, someone needs to develop the process and procedures for configuration management for the requirements.

The configuration management group (or person) who is responsible for managing the integrity of the Internet requirements set will need training on the processes as well as the tools. It is recommended that the training take place prior to the pilot project. First, train the individuals participating in the pilot. The pilot staff can then educate new users on both the configuration management process and the configuration management tool set. The size of the group involved depends on the size of the program and the organization (see Table 7.9).

Table 7.9 Roles and Responsibilities for Requirements Configuration Management (RCM)

Role Name	Responsibility
Requirements engineer	• Elicit business requirements (assist)
	• Analyze business requirements (produce)
	• Specify business requirements (produce)
	• Validate business requirements (coordinate)
	• Approve business requirements (assist)
	• Baseline business requirements (create files)
	• Update business requirements to reflect change (assist)
	• Validate nonbusiness requirements (review)
	• Approve nonbusiness requirements (approve)

Table continued on next page.

Table 7.9   Roles and Responsibilities for Requirements Configuration Management (RCM), *continued*

Role Name	Responsibility
Business user or requirement supplier	• Elicit business requirements (supply, become requirement owner) • Analyze business requirements (assist) • Validate requirements (review) • Approve requirements (approve) • Issue change requests (produce) • Validate change requests (review) • Approve changes[a] (approve)
Configuration manager	• Update configuration management tool software (produce) • Make weekly backups (produce) • Maintain staging areas (produce)
Configuration control board (selected project team members)	• Validate requirements (review) • Approve requirements (approve) • Validate change requests (review) • Approve changes (approve)
Designers and architects for IT as well as other communities	• Elicit design requirements (produce) • Analyze design requirements (produce) • Specify design requirements (produce) • Trace design requirements to associated requirements (produce) • Validate design requirements (coordinate) • Approve design requirements (assist) • Baseline design requirements (create files) • Validate nondesign requirements (review) • Approve nondesign requirements (approve)
Project manager	• Validate requirements (review) • Approve requirements (approve) • Validate change requests (review) • Approve changes (approve)
Project sponsor	• Define project scope (produce) • Validate requirements (review) • Approve requirements (approve) • Validate change requests (review) • Approve changes (approve)
Programmers and developers	• Validate requirements (coordinate) • Approve requirements (assist) • Validate change requests (review)

Table 7.9   Roles and Responsibilities for Requirements Configuration Management (RCM), *continued*

Role Name	Responsibility
Programmers and developers	• Approve changes (approve) • Trace code modules and data structures to satisfied requirements (produce)
Release manager	• Baseline requirements (place under configuration management tool) • Produce weekly status reports (produce)
Quality assurance	• Define RCM process (coordinate) • Mentor on RCM process usage (produce)
Quality control	• Approve nontechnical testing requirements (approve) • Validate nontechnical testing requirements (review) • Specify technical testing requirements (produce) • Validate technical testing requirements (coordinate) • Approve technical testing requirements (assist) • Baseline technical testing requirements (create files) • Trace technical testing requirements to associated requirements (produce) • Update technical testing requirements to reflect changes (produce) • Validate change requests (review) • Approve changes (approve)
Process manager	• Develop RCM process (assist) • Monitor RCM process usage (produce)

a. Approval of a sponsored change should not be allowed unless the person is approving a specification that someone else wrote.

Preparing for Implementation

The following activities are required in order to implement a configuration management process for requirements.

1. Obtain budget and approval for both configuration management and requirements management processes from management.[12]
2. Obtain approval for configuration management tool (which may need IT support to install and maintain).
3. Define requirements configuration management (RCM) customized forms.

---

12. This is a project-type requirement if these tools are not already available.

4. Define processes and procedures in a format that is easy to read, follow, and understand.
5. Distribute a plan for the RCM process to project team members and elicit feedback.
6. Develop RCM reports for management.
7. Institute the RCM process with a trial project.
8. Review on an ongoing basis the results of the RCM trial project with all affected groups.
9. Modify the RCM process based on trial results.
10. Define accountability measures for RCM usage.
11. Implement the RCM process for all projects.
12. Implement mechanics that will support ongoing process improvement, based on feedback, of the RCM process.

The Implementation Process

Implementing a key process such as configuration management must be carefully planned and monitored to ensure that the process works within your organization. The basic philosophy of any project should follow the Shewart Cycle popularized by Dr. Edwards Deming in his book *Out of the Crisis.*

1. *Plan* what you want to implement.
2. *Do* the pilot implementation.
3. *Check* the results of the pilot.
4. *Act* on the results by tweaking the process before the next project.

Plan

Planning involves preparing for the rollout of a configuration management process to support requirements. This includes planning in six areas:

1. The development of the process
2. The development of the procedures
3. The development of the organization's roles and responsibilities
4. The tool evaluation
5. The rollout that includes selecting the right pilot
6. The assessment of the configuration management process

First, develop the configuration management plan. (One may already have been developed for supporting software modules or data files. Review that plan and identify any possible changes that may be required to support requirements management.)

Once the project has been selected, you can start following the plan. The preceding six areas can be worked on concurrently. What is important to remember is to *follow the plan!* So often project managers spend hours and even days creating the perfect plan and then fail to follow it. Planning is not just for the purpose of identifying a deliverable date. A plan is meant to be followed; it is a guide throughout the process. It is a living document that can be tweaked when necessary. It is far better to tweak a plan than to not follow a plan at all.

Do

Carry out the configuration management plan identified in the previous step. Put in place the organization that will support configuration management for requirements. Obtain input from the people who develop requirements on how the process should work. Identify what you want from the available tools and begin vendor tool evaluations (in fact, you should make a requirement list for the tool first). Select a pilot project that is important but not mission-critical. Remember, implementing a new process will not cause confusion or delays if the implementation is well planned and introduced in small increments. However, a mission-critical project is already important enough and does not need to be exposed to new pressures.

When documenting a process, obtain input from people who are involved with requirements. Ask them for their ideas on how to enhance requirement traceability. Study how they handle changes and incorporate your findings into the process you are defining. If you do not request or solicit input from personnel in the trenches, they will not follow your process.

Check

Evaluating the results of the pilot is essential to identifying areas for improvement. Remember, it is never the fault of an individual or group that a project has failed. Instead, the failure illustrates a weakness in the process.

Evaluate the configuration management process for requirements at the end of each activity. This means evaluating not only each step of the configuration management process as it pertains to the requirements but also how the requirements set is traced through all other work products that are placed under change control.

Review the process for ease of use, the impressions of the project team, and the time and cost of following the process. Look for both the strong and weak areas, keeping the positives and studying further the negatives to identify opportunities to improve without sacrificing the objectives of configuration management. Review weaknesses carefully. New processes and procedures that are poorly implemented could cause some confusion and time delays.

Pay special attention to how changes are implemented in the work product. If the change process is too cumbersome, future changes will be implemented without change management.

Act

A process is a living organism. Each software project team member who follows your defined process should be encouraged to provide input that will further enhance the process. Always obtain feedback from the project team and act upon the input. Continually review your configuration management objectives to make sure they are reasonable and obtainable. Adjust the process to enhance your ability to meet the objectives. Always assign credit to the program team members for their participation to ensure their continued support.

Conclusion

Requirements are volatile. A simple change in an approved requirement may have a cascading effect on other requirements and work products. This is complicated further by the fact that a requirement can be captured at any point in the development cycle.

Internet solutions may involve team members and customers, located globally, who are forcing the use of global requirement elicitation.[13] This adds another layer of complexity to requirements engineering. Reviewers can be located anywhere in the world, working in different time zones. For these reasons, it is imperative for a program to institute configuration management as described in this chapter to manage and control the approved requirements and the changes that will almost certainly occur.

Of all the work products created during the life of a product, requirements are the most volatile. Maintaining the integrity of work products involves apply-

---

13. Requirements can be captured from globally dispersed business communities through the use of e-mail, teleconferencing, and videoconferencing. The complexity for configuration management is providing access to all participants at the same time, given differences in time zone.

ing controls, for example, by managing the process of work product creation, controlling changes, and tracking changes and their potential effects on other work products. The objective here is communication. Any change to any product could affect other work products. What may seem to be a simple request to change one item may impact another area so drastically that the final deliverable may not be achievable on schedule or within budget. Configuration management, as described in this chapter, imposes such controls to ensure the success of Internet products.

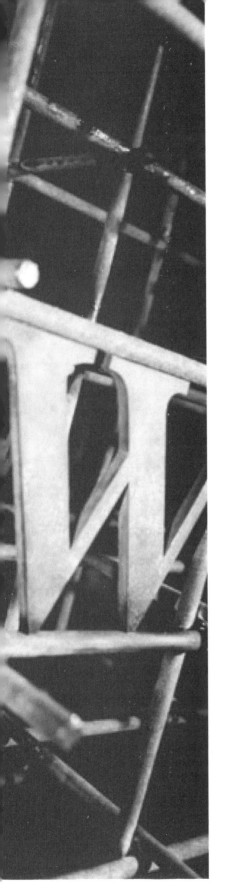

CHAPTER EIGHT

Roles and Responsibilities

Chapter Key Topics
- **Requirements-related roles**
- **Requirements engineering organizations**
- **Internet organizations**

The Internet Impact

The Internet has demanded the best from employees striving to meet the pressures associated with launching an e-business. With the fast pace of doing business on the Internet, it is critical that each team member have roles and responsibilities that are clearly defined and closely followed. Otherwise, organizational chaos results, compromising the success of the Internet project.

The success of an Internet product is never due to a single individual's effort but to a team of individuals. Earlier I introduced the concept of a "program" in which the business sponsor, the primary lead, orchestrates the different projects that make up the Internet business objectives. Each of the different projects has supporting leaders responsible for their piece of the Internet deliverable(s).

Though individuals may come and go throughout the life of the Internet product, the need to fill the roles described in this chapter is continuous. A single individual may be responsible for tasks associated with multiple roles. The reverse is also true: one role may require multiple individuals to accomplish all the role-related tasks. The business sponsor is accountable for ensuring that all the roles are filled at all times and for all projects.

It is not possible to define the exact number of individuals required to fulfill each responsibility. This requires an understanding of other factors for each project, such as the scope, return-on-investment objectives, time-to-market pressures, and so forth. However, this chapter identifies the different roles and their responsibilities that are required for all projects in general. These roles fall into the following four groups:

1. *Requirement suppliers:* those individuals who define the requirements
2. *Requirement users:* those individuals who must work from the requirements
3. *Requirement supporters:* those who help facilitate the requirements process
4. *Requirement producers:* those who elicit, analyze, specify, validate, and manage the requirements

Though the roles contained in these categories could be considered to belong to multiple groups, each is discussed in terms of its primary work product. Each of these groups may have subgroups that are used to help clarify the responsibilities. Depending on the size of the company and the size of the program, many roles may be combined.

Requirement Suppliers

These individuals hold roles that are responsible for defining the needs to be satisfied by the Internet product. This includes supplying all the detail from the initial idea through each incremental iteration of the Internet product. Requirement suppliers fall under two categories:

1. *Product direction:* those people responsible for the strategy and direction of the Internet product
2. *Requirement detail:* those people responsible for providing the details that define all the Internet product needs

These subroles do not necessarily imply that two individuals must be involved. The same individual who sets the direction may also supply some (but rarely all) of the detail. Other individuals from the different business communities (for example, legal, marketing) may also contribute to the strategy as well as provide detail.

Product Direction Roles

The success of the Internet product depends on the management team setting the strategy and direction for all team members to understand and follow. An unclear strategy opens up the possibility of having a product that does not produce the highest return on investment, which could expose the corporation to great risk.

It is the responsibility of the members of the executive management committee[1] to define the product strategy in a form that is correct, clear, concise, and complete. They must ensure that all project team members adhere to the strategy and that it correlates to the philosophy and direction of the corporation as a whole. The individuals assigned to these product direction roles support the requirement effort in the capacity of managing, controlling, or sponsoring the Internet development and implementation.

These individuals are usually management personnel. Together, they comprise the executive management committee. They are responsible for resolving any conflicts in requirements, deliverables, resources, and budgetary issues between the different Internet project teams that the business sponsor cannot resolve. They review the status and make decisions as to the continuance or direction of the product at specific checkpoints. The executive management committee at minimum consists of the following roles:

- Business initiator
- Product sponsor
- Product manager
- Key executive participants

Note that this same executive management committee reviews all mission-critical projects. The size of the corporation helps determine the number of these projects and the staff allocated to work on them. In many cases, the same individual participates to some degree on multiple mission-critical projects. It is the responsibility of the executive committee to prioritize these projects. Every team member must understand his or her priorities when time conflicts occur (and they will occur often) as to what the corporation wants to be done first and foremost.[2]

---

1. In smaller organizations, the executive management committee may consist of one person, who may be the president of the company. Larger organizations could have as many as twelve to fifteen individuals clarifying the strategy.

2. As a warning, it is not wise to be put in a position of conflict of interest by being the lead of multiple projects competing for the same resource pool, whether the projects are mission-critical or not!

Business Initiator

The idea to build an Internet-based product must be initiated through the business community, although the idea (that is, the initiating requirement) may have been identified by someone outside the corporation (for example, customer, government, or competitor) or within another area of the corporation. In any case, a specific group or individual, the business initiator, champions the idea. The business initiator defines the concept for the product. He is responsible for developing the material to present to the corporation's executive committee for approval to move forward on the concept.

To prepare for executive approval, the business initiator develops the business case along with a presentation and/or summary.[3] After approval, the executive committee, which will now consist of an executive representing the business initiator group, allocates the funds to begin the process of developing the Internet product.[4]

Product Sponsor

The executive committee assigns a business product sponsor to the project. This role is ultimately responsible for the project's success or failure. This person has the authority to allocate budgeted funds and resources to the project and, if need be, to cancel the project. The product sponsor also has an understanding of the company's strategic direction. If conflicts arise between needs (requirements) among the different communities, it is the responsibility of the product sponsor to make decisions that resolve any conflicts. If need be, conflicts can be defined as issues and brought to the attention of the executive management committee for resolution. In light of these responsibilities, there should be only one person assigned to this role.

The product sponsor deliverables include for each iteration:

- Product status
- Issues affecting budget, resources, and deliverable time frames
- Business case adjustments (specifically, changes in the projected return on investment)

---

3. A requirements engineer may be elected to assist in the deliverable. The requirements engineer is skilled in asking questions that will help define the scope and costs section of the business case.

4. In small companies, where the product sponsor is the executive committee, the approval may come from a bank or venture capital firm. In this scenario, the executive committee provides an outside source of money.

Once the first iteration of the Internet application has been implemented, the product sponsor delivers, in addition to the preceding items, the following:

- Report of revenues generated
- Business trend analysis
- Feedback summary from clients
- Issues affecting future iterations and corporate strategy
- Recommended direction for the Internet product

Product Manager

Product managers are responsible for the day-to-day planning, management, and control of the entire Internet program. These activities include the successful completion of the stage products, on time, within budget, and to the specified quality standards. People in this role lead the different project teams and report project progress and issues to the executive management committee.

For Internet applications, it is important to have at least one product manager for each community. Information technology needs a product manager as well as marketing and human resources managers, each of whom manages his community's deliverables and prepares a status report on its piece of the Internet development.

Some corporations have created the role of lead product manager, to whom all product managers report status and budgetary requests. In most corporations, all product managers report directly to the product sponsor.

The product manager's deliverables to the product sponsor include the following for each iteration representing his community:

- Product status
- Issues affecting budget, resources, and deliverable time frames
- Any issues that could be potential showstoppers or may affect other communities

Key Executive Participants

It is important to note that the executive committee consists of other key executives who have minimal involvement in producing product deliverables but have an impact on the program. These individuals are involved in the budgetary process for all projects, including the review and approval of funding. For example, the risk management officer may identify major financial risk to the corporation when he reviews the concept and direction of the Internet product. The chief financial officer, for example, may know of other financial commitments forcing the Internet product to be postponed. These individuals may supply financial, delivery, or scope constraints on the program.

Regardless of how critical to the success of a company, Internet programs must still go through the proper budgetary channels. True, it may be streamlined or rushed through the budgetary process, but the same individuals who approve any other project need to approve the Internet program too. These individuals are part of the executive committee and must be continually kept informed about the program and its effect on the company budget. These members either control the purse strings or protect the corporation from financial or political exposure that could put the company out of business. Internet programs are too risky, even after these past ten years of Internet growth, to skip steps in the budgetary process. All parties must be involved and informed to ensure that the corporation is protected.

Requirement Detail Roles

The second requirement supplier subgroup consists of those individuals (internal or external to the company) who define the need for their community. They are the requirements engineer's customers, and they supply the needs that must be satisfied by the end product. They are the main source of information upon which all the models, programs, and databases are built. These individuals are responsible for validating the requirements produced by the requirements engineer. These detail suppliers review requirements from other communities as to their possible impact on their own community. They are also called upon to review specific work products produced throughout the development of each product iteration.

These detail suppliers include the following roles:

- Business coordinator
  Business team member
- Knowledge expert
- Customer representative
- E-mail suppliers

Business Coordinator

These individuals ensure that the operational interests of the business are being fully represented in the day-to-day operations of the project. This role also helps identify who from the business areas can add value to the project team. A business coordinator must be identified to represent each community. A business coordinator serves as the point of contact for the community regarding the needs that must be satisfied by the final solution. Individuals from the legal, customer service, inventory control, risk management, and receiving departments (as well as others) can be business coordinators.

Although the business coordinator may also be identified as the community's product manager, the responsibilities of the two roles are different. The community product manager manages the development of the specific Internet product deliverable. The business coordinator does not necessarily present a deliverable to the product sponsor. The business coordinator is responsible for supplying the needs for the business community to the requirements engineer for analysis, documentation, and approval.

In order to provide the community's requirements, the persons[5] assigned this role need to have

- Reasonably detailed knowledge of the business requirement and expectations of the project for its community
- Contacts and influence at the working levels addressed by the program for its community
- The ability to understand the wider business context and any areas affected indirectly by the community's requirements or by requirements of other communities that may affect them
- Knowledge of necessary or desirable operational standards with which the Internet application must comply

Business Team Member

The business coordinator's only responsibility is to supply the requirements or provide access to the individual(s) who has the knowledge. This alternate individual(s) is a business team member who can work with the requirements engineer in defining all requirements for the knowledge base, including all parts of the individual requirements. This includes the:

- Requirement text
- Validation criteria
- Priority
- Associations and links with other requirements (requirement dependencies)

---

5. The number of individuals is tied to the size of the product and company.

Knowledge Expert

No one person knows all the requirements for an Internet product. There are individuals available, either within the corporation or as outside counsel, who have expertise in a particular area to support the Internet product. These individuals are considered members of the product team if only for short periods of time and can be called upon to provide expert knowledge in specific business or technical areas. For example, a project may require someone with expertise in Internet security or international trading laws. Whatever his or her expertise, the knowledge expert is crucial to the success of the Internet product.

The knowledge may be provided verbally or through written documentation. The knowledge expert may contribute to the creation of the specific work products by providing information and may also review products. The key to remember is that the knowledge is valuable and that the knowledge expert's time must be used wisely. These individuals are involved in multiple projects.

Customer Representative

This role represents the customers or users (internal or external to the corporation) most affected by the final results of the Internet product. They may be interviewed through market research campaigns or may be invited to participate in requirements gathering sessions. The latter is common with Internet-based applications where the interface between corporate systems must be clearly defined and agreed upon. Depending upon the type of product being sold, multiple customer representatives may be selected to represent different categories of users (actors). Each kind of user of the Internet product should be represented to supply requirements as well as to validate them.[6]

E-mail Suppliers

Though not really a specific role, e-mail suppliers are a significant source of information for future iterations of the software. It is important to include in the requirements gathering and reviewing process whoever is in charge of reviewing and categorizing all e-mails. The summary information that this person can provide assists in determining requirements, including their priority, which keeps the Internet application customer-focused.

---

6. If the interface is a computer-based system, an IT representative of the company may be assigned to define the exact details for the interface.

Requirement Users

These individuals use the requirements to develop their work products (for example, technical architectures, network plans, application architectures). They assist in the requirements process by validating individual requirements, primarily for feasibility, clarity, and conflicts. They can assist in validating additional quality characteristics.

These individuals supply additional requirements to the Internet requirements set. The additional requirements are usually specific to the perspective, focus, and community these individuals are supporting. The requirements usually pertain to tools to help people develop their work products or to specific equipment, supplies, or resources needed to create the work product.

In larger organizations, many of these individuals are "matrixed" to the Internet program. They report to a manager who may not be the manager for the Internet project or program. In this case, these individuals probably will have additional responsibilities for other projects. The product managers must help manage the requirement users' time by clearly defining the priorities and notifying the executive management committee of time conflicts with other projects. In smaller organizations, requirement users may have responsibility for only one Internet development project and may report directly to the person in charge of the development of the Internet product.

Since the major piece of the Internet product is software, this section concentrates on requirement users for the software deliverables.[7] Each business community has additional staff who develop the final pieces of their contributions to the product. For example, the sales and marketing groups have different individuals who develop the marketing and sales plan versus those who take the plan and create marketing and sales materials.

Software work product users include the following roles:

- Project manager
- Data warehouse specialist
- Database administrator
- Developer
- Usability engineer

---

7. Other non-software-related users of requirements include privacy specialists, marketing/corporate image specialists, customer service specialists (including customer relations management), and so forth.

- Network planner
- Operations analyst
- System designer
- Technical architect
- Test analyst/quality control analyst
- Trainer
- Writer, editor, and user educator

Project Manager

These individuals are responsible for the day-to-day planning, management, and control of their part of the program. This includes the successful completion of all work products, on time, within budget, and to the specified quality standards. People in this role lead the project team (sometimes acting as facilitators) and report project progress and issues to their respective product managers. The individual project managers provide project requirements as to staffing, software, funding, and other items needed to accomplish their work products.

In medium to large companies, there are many project managers, not only for each community but also perhaps for each specific deliverable. For example, a marketing project manager could create the advertising campaign and a software project manager could maintain the billing system to accommodate the Internet project's front-end application. These project managers typically have multiple projects to manage, requiring them to split their time and energy amongst them. Each project manager also could have a group of five or more people to manage, which may take up at least one-third of his or her time. This is important to note; these project managers are usually stretched very thin. Their priorities must be made very clear and their time conflicts removed to avoid a dramatic negative impact on the delivery schedule of the Internet iteration.

Data Warehouse Specialist

A data warehouse is a storage facility of informational data that is integrated, subject-oriented, time-based, and nonvolatile. The warehouse is designed to be easier to access than operational data and to reduce the contention for the data. The data contained in the data warehouse originates elsewhere, either internal or external to the corporation, and are integrated and cleansed from various sources.

Internet applications provide a massive amount of information through the click patterns of users, answers to questionnaires, and questions and comments from e-mails. All this data can be captured, cleansed, and organized in a format that can provide valuable information to corporate members. The information can be reviewed to determine the effectiveness of the Internet product, catalogs or advertising, or sales of specific products. The data can also be sold to outside parties for market research.

Turning this large amount of Internet data into something that can be used by the corporation, other corporations, or clients takes the skills of a data warehouse specialist. This individual (or, more often, a group of individuals) assembles the data to be effectively accessed later. The data can be gathered solely from usage of the Internet product or merged with data captured from other applications (for example, billing, inventory) or outside sources (for example, market research).

Building the data warehouse may be a subset project of the Internet application or a project branched into another already existing division. It may also be the Internet product being sold. The Internet requirements provide valuable information for the development of a productive data warehouse. The sooner the data warehouse specialist understands what is to be built and the information that can be captured, the sooner he will be able to develop the best data warehouse to meet the user's needs.

Initially, the data warehouse specialist looks at the first three software perspective levels of the requirements pattern to help organize the data warehouse. All software focus areas are important. Once the design of the Internet application is complete, the data warehouse specialist looks at the data formats and when they will be available to help complete the process of loading the data into the data warehouse.

Database Administrator

A database administrator is a project team member who is responsible for the operation and administration of the database management system and the creation of physical database designs and performance tuning. More than one person may be assigned this role. Database administrators become involved during the designer perspective as the work of the data analyst is turned over to them. Though their involvement is in all business communities, their main focus is satisfying the "what" requirements in a manner that supports other focus requirements. They identify additional requirements for monitoring tools, database schema creation tools, and storage, for example.

Developer

Developers are responsible for developing code and fixing bugs that are found during testing. They are involved at the subcontractor perspective, satisfying primarily the "how" focus area for a specific business community. The requirements they may submit to the requirements set relate to tools (hardware and software) that help developers develop and test the code. They may be involved sooner in smaller organizations.

Usability Engineer

Never underestimate the power of presentation. Even the smallest of inconveniences can drive potential clients away from using your product. The only exception is if you are the only game in town. With the growth of the Internet, being the only game in town is a very short-lived position. Your competitors will learn from your inconveniences and gain your market share.

Usability engineers do more than just make eye-catching sites. They create the experience shell by examining workflow, streamlining clicks for the user, applying nonintuitive navigation and browse facilities, and using current data (overwriting out-of-date information). They have a marketing eye and keep users in mind (for example, with regard to ergonomics and human factors understanding). They find the best place to require registration (if not payment) for valuable information and help identify what information should be captured for customer analysis.

Their main responsibility is to design a presentation of the site that will make the client comfortable with doing business and will protect the corporation's assets as well. They review "who, what, when, where, why, and how" requirements to understand

- The different types of users
- The information users need to provide and what they want to see
- The workflow that they use
- From what parts of the world users access the Internet application
- What laws must be enforced for each global region

Usability engineers also look at the needs of the corporation. What image does the company want to portray? The Disney site (*www.disney.com*) looks quite different from Sotheby's (*www.sothebys.com*). Both present a corporate image consistent with the kinds of clients they have and their corporate cultures.

Usability engineers begin to review the requirements right at the scoping phase. They begin to develop the Web site concept, adding details to the front-end design as more detailed requirements become available. These individuals should be involved in validating business requirements for feasibility. In addition, they should be involved in reviewing design requirements for technical constraints that may affect the design.

Network Planner

Network planners are responsible for developing the network architecture to support the "where" needs of the product and also support the corporate network infrastructure. They provide requirements related to additional networking equipment or upgrades to existing equipment. Always involve network planners early in the process. Otherwise, network equipment delays could make you miss your first-to-market opportunities. Poor network performance could erode your consumer base. The Internet project is just one of many challenges network planners must plan, develop, implement, and support. They are probably the same group (including requirements engineers and others involved in developing the Internet product) who is responsible for your work environment network.

Operations Analyst

Individuals responsible for the physical operation of the production computing environment fall under the category of operation analysts. They look at the Internet application (primarily data and processing) to determine whether adjustments to the corporate data facilities and equipment are needed. They add to the requirements set any changes to the existing facilities and equipment required to support the Internet application.

System Designer

This is the project team member responsible for translating business systems requirements into a physical system design. The primary involvement is during the builder perspective but may come earlier during the designer perspective. This role focuses primarily on the "how" requirements. System designers develop the application architecture for their piece of the application (for example, billing). At times, this role may be encompassed by the technical architect role, which is discussed next.

Technical Architect

This role helps ensure the technical quality of the architecture and the architecture components. Technical architects design the system infrastructure and work with the system designers to select technical architecture components. They assist with identifying all the technical tasks and standards that need to be followed. The technical architect must have

- Knowledge of all major technical aspects to be covered for the Internet application as well as the other interfaced applications (for example, billing, inventory, and so on)
- Contacts for other technical areas affected (for example, network planning infrastructure)
- Knowledge of the technical methods and standards applicable to Internet applications (for example, Unified Modeling Language)

Test Analyst/Quality Control Analyst

These individuals are responsible for executing product reviews and testing throughout the program. This includes participation in walkthrough and inspection reviews of all work products developed throughout the program (for example, project plans, requirements specifications, marketing material, legal documents, front-end designs), as well as unit, integration, and system testing of the Internet software for each iteration. A thorough tester is worth his weight in gold! He or she reviews the Web site for navigational dead ends, invalid information, and breaks in security.[8]

This is not a task for one individual.[9] The same test analyst will not be assigned the responsibility to review legal documents and to test navigation. Furthermore, one test analyst may plan the testing of the application while a different analyst tests billing integration. The number of test analysts varies depending on the Internet application and iteration. It is important to remind planners not to be stingy on testing resources. Ultimately, there are two truths about testing:

1. You cannot test quality into a product.
2. You must decide how much to spend on testing and then spread this amount across the different types of testing required according to risk analysis.

Quality control analysts provide a valuable service throughout the life of the Internet product. They usually become involved right at the scoping level by reviewing the business case, scope document, or Internet strategy.

---

8. You can hire specialists specifically to test your security.
9. The average tester-to-developer ratio is one tester to one to three developers. I recommends a one-to-two correlation.

The test analyst/quality control analyst is responsible for creating the following documents:

- Test strategy
- Test plan
- Test case
- Test data

Trainer

A trainer is a program team member responsible for the provision and administration of training and education for both technical and user areas. There are two kinds of training required: (1) external (that is, the public view) and (2) internal (that is, the organization's view). The public view, for example, may involve supplying requirements to developers to create a tutorial on how to use the Internet application. Trainers may need to train the B2B companies on how the new process will be executed. It is important to look at the Internet product and identify all areas that could potentially require training and to determine the format for the training.[10]

Writer, Editor, and User Educator

"Woe is I."[11] Although English may be a commonly used language, it is a very difficult language. It is even more difficult for those potential customers whose primary language is not English. In fact, all languages are difficult. When it comes to Internet products, the choice of language depends on the customers you are trying to reach. In many cases, multiple languages are used with a link to display the site in the viewer's preferred language. No matter which languages are used, technical writers either write the information or edit the information you provide. They ensure that you have consistent information from Web page to Web page.

These individuals may also be responsible for some technical writing that creates the "help" subsystem, user documentation, and technical project documentation. They may be responsible for writing promotional materials sent to prospective customers.

---

10. When rolling out the concepts from this book to any company and program, additional training will be required to teach the team members the requirements process. The requirements engineer can do this task or teach a formal trainer to form a reusable course. As a third alternative, several independent consultants and training organizations are available for this purpose.

11. Yes, that is the correct grammar. See O'Conner 1996.

In some organizations, the technical writers and editors take a prominent role in product development. For instance, Microsoft has developed a team model for developing software. The writer and editor roles have expanded to include anything that will enhance the Internet user's performance to ensure that they are as productive as possible using the site.[12] These individuals, in essence, become the customers, standing in their shoes when using the product. They are involved during all perspectives as advocates for the customers. They develop any material available for the customer to use while using the site (reference, help, wizards, and even courses).

Requirement Supporters

These individuals are responsible for supporting the requirement effort. They may be involved in looking at both the completed requirements and the requirements processes that are followed to judge their helpfulness for future projects. These individuals and groups provide support in the capacity of managing, controlling, or sponsoring the effort. They assist the individuals who are responsible for eliciting, analyzing, specifying, validating, or managing the requirements set for the project.

These requirement supporters have the following roles:

- Facilitator
- Process manager
- Quality assurance
- Group manager
- Anthropologist

Facilitator

Facilitators are individuals responsible for organizing, designing, and running workshops for the objective of capturing requirements, running formal inspections, or resolving conflicts and issues with requirements. Facilitators do not determine the objectives, content of the discussion, or resulting products. They should be considered independent entities who express no bias. Their objective is to facilitate the group in achieving its objectives. Because they have no bias toward any conclusion, a facilitator may be used for a politically charged product

---

12. See http://www.microsoft.com/trainingandservices/content/downloads/ MSFTeamModelforAppDev.doc, accessed in August 2001.

that crosses dominant business boundaries (perfect for Internet products!). Different divisions within the organization (or between corporations) will have their own agenda for how the Internet product should look and work. Using an unbiased, skilled leader during requirement elicitation or conflict resolution helps uncover the best resolution for all parties involved.

Process Manager

Process managers are responsible for the development and maintenance of processes (methods and procedures). The process manager is also responsible for ensuring that processes are appropriately selected or rejected for individual projects to ensure the success of a project. This is accomplished by granting or rejecting waivers to project managers requesting the deletion of standard activities from their project plans. For Internet products, the process manager develops the guidelines for the requirements management, project management, and configuration management processes. The process manager works with the product manager and product sponsor to tweak the processes to meet the demands of the Internet product. They may recommend additions that will help ensure quality with the different interactions.

Quality Assurance

The process manager's staff includes quality assurance analysts who act as auditors to ensure that agreed-upon standards and processes are carried out during the program. The quality assurance analyst supports the process manager in defining processes and procedures and assists the project manager in adjusting the process for the specific Internet project without sacrificing the quality of the end product.

The quality assurance analyst then has the added responsibility of conducting process reviews/audits throughout the program life cycle to ensure standard processes and procedures are being followed. This may fall under the quality control responsibilities since it is a postactivity.

Group Manager

This chapter began by talking about leads. These leads are group managers. The lead manages a specific group of individuals to reach the business objective. As stated previously, the success of any project is never due to one exceptional person. A successful project occurs through the efforts of many people extending beyond department boundaries. This project team consists of many individuals with varying levels of skills, talents, work styles, and knowledge.

The project team needs to have a common goal, a common vision, and a clear understanding of what is expected of them. The group of individuals, regardless of the reporting structure, must be an effective, motivated team to achieve the business objectives. The group manager (the individual project manager), as the leader of that team, is responsible for motivating the team members to achieve the objectives in a productive manner.

The Internet program has several distinct teams, each with its own group manager. Each of these teams produces its piece of the Internet solution. The individual managers support the requirements engineering effort by providing staff for the Internet effort. These managers usually manage multiple projects, of which the Internet project is only one of their many deliverables. They manage individual workloads to ensure that their staff have all that is needed to produce high-quality deliverables.

Anthropologist

Exposing what used to be internal applications to the global world of Internet users requires some additional skills not usually associated with the process. "Dot-com" companies have found a need to add a human touch to their products. Providing applications for the public requires that the designs be more usable, resulting in more compelling products and services. In the department of human behavior and culture, the expertise of anthropologists and other social scientists can add a great deal. Webster's online dictionary (*www.dictionary.com*) defines anthropology as, "The scientific study of the origin, the behavior, and the physical, social, and cultural development of human beings." Anthropologists can answer important Internet design questions such as:

- How do humans use online shopping?
- What are users' fears (security)?
- How many clicks will users tolerate to achieve the objective?
- What triggers and associations will humans supply to achieve the answers they want from search engines?
- What words are most commonly misspelled and should be accepted for searches?
- How long will a consumer wait for a response to a question?

In most cases, usability engineers have anthropology skills. It is mentioned here just to point out the importance of human dynamics in Internet design. Minimizing the human dynamics could result initially in ineffective use of the product and ultimately in loss of customer base. If the Internet product does not work easily for your clients, it will not matter whether you provide what they need; another Internet product probably can provide it as well. For example, eToys.com and ToysRUs.com provide the same products. Many individuals found one site much easier to use (for example, fewer clicks, easier search criteria), and that site did far better in sales during the 1999 holiday season.

Requirement Producers

In short, these individuals are responsible for capturing the requirements. In more explicit terms, these individuals hold roles that are responsible for eliciting, analyzing, specifying, and coordinating the validation and approval of all the requirements required to satisfy the business solution. They are also responsible for managing the requirements to ensure compliance and integration throughout the life of the product.

Common Deliverables

Requirement producers create all requirements specifications based on interviews, documentation, and observations of the process in action. For software requirements, the most common deliverables[13] that requirements engineers are responsible for producing are

- Requirements specification
  - Text to support requirements
  - Specification across communities
  - Specification across perspectives
  - Specification across focus areas
  - Category cell interfaces
- Information technology diagrams/models
  - Activity
  - Component package
  - Data/class
  - Deployment
  - Interaction/sequence/collaboration

---

13. This is *not* a complete list and will vary by method of requirement analysis and specification.

- Process/object
- State transition
- Use case

- Validation documentation for reviews
  - Validation that all requirements have been managed through the approval state
  - Validation that all requirements were managed throughout the evolution of the requirement
  - Validation that all future work products incorporate all approved requirements for the specific iteration

Each requirements engineer may be responsible for a subset of the above deliverables and only for specific communities, perspectives, and focus areas. If this is the case, the requirements engineers must work together to ensure that they note and account for all associative requirements that affect each category cell.

Meeting Minutes

Another less common deliverable that is extremely valuable in requirement clarification is meeting minutes. Meeting minutes help with the process of requirement clarification, an important step between requirement elicitation/analysis and requirements specification. It is a tool that requirements engineers rarely use, but when they do, they usually do not take full advantage of its power. For this reason, this requirements engineering deliverable is mentioned here in more detail. It works for all perspectives, focus areas, and communities.

Meeting minutes are a summary of what the requirements engineers[14] heard and illustrate what they interpreted from the information provided. Meeting minutes provide an opportunity to verify that what you heard was what the requirement supplier meant to say. They provide the requirements engineer with an opportunity to "twist" some of the requirements to ensure that his or her under-

---

14. A scribe may actually take notes and produce the meeting minutes while the requirements engineer facilitates the session. The requirements engineer should review the minutes before distribution to ensure controversial points are added to spark additional discussion if necessary.

standing of the requirements is correct or to uncover additional requirements.[15] Minutes also provide another opportunity for requirement suppliers to rethink the information they presented and to correct or clarify what they meant to say.

Meeting minutes should be produced for all meetings within twenty-four hours of the meeting, when the meeting is fresh in both the suppliers' and producers' minds. To save time, some companies develop the minutes during the session and e-mail them to all attendees and distribution lists immediately at the close of the meeting. When requirement suppliers review the meeting minutes, they usually provide additional information that was not previously supplied.

When working with untrusting suppliers, meeting minutes can help quickly build acceptance by the users. Meeting minutes are a way to develop rapport with requirement suppliers by showing that the requirements engineer is

- Listening to them
- Understanding them
- Accepting their input as important
- Illustrating that the requirement suppliers' time was used well, not wasted

Meeting minutes (see Table 8.1) are not a court stenographer's reading of exactly what was said, word for word. Some thought needs to go into how you summarize the information received from the requirement suppliers.

Requirements Engineering Roles

The requirement producers in the area of requirements engineering include the following roles:

- Requirements architect
- Requirements controller
- Requirements engineer

---

15. The twisting of specific requirements should be done *only* in meeting minutes and *never* in requirements specifications. Twisting a correct requirement into an incorrect requirement stimulates discussion that will assist in capturing more requirement details. It is important that the twisting of requirements be done by senior or lead requirements engineers with years of experience in requirements engineering. If twisted requirements are included in meeting minutes, the minutes must be read by all users. Even when these two criteria are met (done by experienced requirements engineers and read by all users), this technique should be used sparingly.

Table 8.1   Meeting Minutes Template

Topic	Project name/topic label
Date	Month, date, year
Time	Start and end times
Place	Physical location (mention locations for videoconferences
Version	Version and revision numbers
Attendees	Names of all attendees and chairperson
Distribution list	Names of all attendees and people receiving the meeting minutes
Meeting minutes finalized	Date and time by which any changes, corrections, or comments must be submitted
Next team meeting	Date, time, place
Purpose	Reason for the meeting
Discussed items	Itemized list of discussion topics
Next steps to be completed by day, date.	Itemized list of tasks, including person(s) responsible and completion date for each
Open issues discussed	Itemized list of issues (if any) with indication of priorities
Referenced documents	List of document names and locations of soft copies

These roles are described briefly below. The natural progression of skill levels within the requirements engineering roles and the alignment of the requirements engineering staff within different organizational styles are discussed in other sections later in this chapter.

Requirements Architect

Requirements architects are responsible for developing the requirements set framework for the product. They have the overall responsibility for the entire product requirements set or a specific requirements subset. This includes managing the allocation of the requirements to the appropriate group as well as reviewing all changes and additional requirements for possible impacts on existing requirements in the requirements set. They are responsible for ensuring that all requirement-related work products are produced in a quality manner. In addition, requirements architects are responsible for assuring that the requirements management and configuration management processes are adhered to as well. They assist the configuration management roles in:

- Defining the requirement-related configuration items
- Validating requirement associations within and between category cells
- Validating requirement linkages to other work products
- Defining and validating requirement notification

Requirements Controller

People in this role are responsible for maintaining the integrity of the requirements within the tool used as the repository for all the product/service requirements. This includes maintaining the software for the repository, executing regular backups, and issuing regular reports to management of the repository contents and usage. They also maintain security identifiers of individuals and control group access. They are the configuration management controllers for the requirements and, as such, are responsible for all configuration management activities for the requirements. This includes

- Baseline management
- Change control
- Version control
- Library control
- Status accounting
- Reviews and audits of the baselines

Requirements Engineer

The requirements engineer does it all. This is a generic role responsible for eliciting, analyzing, and specifying all requirements, as well as coordinating their validation and approval. The role may encompass specialized roles whose responsibilities are tailored toward a specific perspective, focus, or community. For example, the data modeler concentrates on information requirements ("what") for the planner, owner, designer, and possibly builder perspectives. The network analyst, on the other hand, concentrates on location communication ("where") requirements.

In most organizations, the key subcategories that fall within the category of requirements engineer are the following:

- Business analyst
- Data analyst

- Network engineer
- System analyst/engineer
- Software analyst/engineer
- Object-oriented analyst

These individuals may belong to a group that supports multiple projects in the same capacity. They understand the needs of the corporation and work to keep all projects, including the Internet program, in line with the corporate direction. Each of these specialized roles concentrates on one focus area.

Business analyst. Business analysts are project team members responsible for the translation of user needs into detailed specification of requirements for software implementation. They are involved primarily with the "who," "when," "why," and "how" focus areas for all business communities. They may also be responsible for the other focus requirements: "what," "where," product constraints, and project constraints.

The primary perspective levels of involvement are

- Planner (scope requirements)
- Owner (business requirements)
- Designer (essential requirement details)

Business analysts' involvement may continue into the builder perspective as a turnover to the key resources involved in developing the physical design of the software solution. They may still be assigned responsibility to capture builder and subcontractor perspective requirements. For requirements management activities, they are responsible for the following:

- Adhering to the requirement tracing rules
- Developing the requirement associations between category cells
- Validating requirement linkages to other work products
- Establishing the notification parameters for their developed requirement

In addition, business analysts are responsible for notifying the requirements controller when requirements are ready for review.

Data analyst. A data analyst is a requirements engineer who is responsible for the development of information requirements for the product and business. The focus area is the "what" or data requirements for all business communities. This may also include capturing "why" requirements for the information- or relationship-related business rules. The primary perspective levels of involvement are the same as those for the business analyst: planner, owner, and designer. Data analysts' involvement may continue into the builder perspective as a turnover to the key resources involved in developing the physical design of the data requirements. They may be responsible for capturing data requirements through the remainder of the product's life and through the remaining perspectives.

The data analyst has the same responsibilities for requirements management activities as the business analyst (see preceding list). They too are responsible for notifying the requirements controller when requirements are ready for review.

Network engineer. A network engineer is a requirements engineer who is responsible for the development of the "where" requirements. This pertains to locations from which the actors (businesses, customer base, other applications, and staff) access the Internet application and also the type of access device (Internet, wireless) supported. Network engineers tend to work through all perspectives. They must also work with network planners to ensure that the requirements conform to the enterprise standards and plans.

The network engineer has the same responsibilities for requirements management activities as the business analyst and data analyst (see preceding list). They are also responsible for notifying the requirements controller when requirements are ready for review.

System analyst/engineer. *System analyst* is a generic term used by some corporations to categorize persons responsible for designing any technology product. System analysts lead the effort in assisting to define the scope through the implementation of the product. They are responsible for defining the technology concept and then allocating the requirements between the different communities (usually between hardware and software). For Internet products, they are responsible for all focus areas and perspectives for the information technology community.

Software analyst/engineer. This is also a generic term used by some corporations for people responsible for designing any software product. They, like systems analysts, lead the effort in assisting to define the scope through the implementation of the product. If a software analyst is involved, he is allocated the software requirements. He is then responsible for clarifying the software requirements and then allocating them among the application architecture communities. For Internet products, a software analyst is responsible for all focus areas and perspectives for the software community.

Object-oriented analyst. Object-oriented analysts have introduced techniques for capturing requirements as well as analyzing them. Their titles vary between many of those previously discussed (for example, business analyst). They are responsible for capturing "who," "what," "where," "when," and "why" requirements. Most commonly following the Unified Modeling Language (UML) approach, they lead the effort in assisting to define the scope through the implementation of the product. Many times, they are responsible for developing the requirements as well as the physical design. Though UML is an excellent approach, it must be noted that the approach does not, nor does it intend to, capture all the requirements. The most commonly produced analysis documents (see Figure 8.1) that depict the UML requirements set require that additional requirements (see Figure 8.2) must be captured, if not by the UML requirements engineer then by another role.

Requirements engineer wrap-up. Which role (see Table 8.2) is responsible for capturing requirements varies from organization to organization, depend-

DIAGRAM	PURPOSE	FOCUS	PERSPECTIVE
ACTIVITY (AC)	Workflow of specific scenarios of events	What, When, How	Designer
CLASS (CL)	Things important to the business and the relationship between the things and the activities performed on the things	What, Why, How	Owner, Designer, Builder
COMPONENT PACKAGE (CP)	Dependencies between objects	Who, What, Where, How	Builder
DEPLOYMENT (DE)	Physical layout of components	Who, What, How, Where, When	Builder
INTERACTION (SEQUENCE/COLLABORATION [SC])	Behavior between objects for specific scenarios	What, How,	Owner, Designer, Builder
OBJECT (OB)	Relationship between instances of classes	What, Why, How	Owner, Designer, Builder
STATE (ST)	Object transition between states	What, When, How	Owner, Designer, Builder
USE CASE (UC)	Role responsibility scenarios	Who, When, How	Owner, Designer

Figure 8.1   Common UML Deliverables

Focus	Who	What	Where	When	Why	How	Product Constraints	Project Constraints
Planner								
Owner	UC	CL / SC OB / ST UC		SC ST UC	CL OB UC	SC ST UC		
Designer	UC	AC CL / SC OB / ST UC		AC / SC ST UC	CL OB UC	AC CL / SC OB / ST UC		
Builder	CP DE UC	CP CL / SC DE / ST OB	CP DE	CP DE / SC ST UC	CL OB	CP CL / SC DE / ST OB UC		
Subcontractor								

(Perspective — vertical axis label)

Figure 8.2   UML Requirements Pattern Coverage. (For definitions of abbreviations, see Figure 8.1.)

ing on the size of the organization and the division of responsibility. The typical role assigned for each perspective and focus for capturing software requirements (see Figure 8.3) is many times a subset of the coverage by the requirements engineering role.

Table 8.2   Requirements Engineering Subrole Abbreviations

Requirements Engineering Subrole	Abbreviation
Business analyst	BA
Data analyst	DA
Network engineer	NE
Object-oriented analyst	OA
System analyst	SyA
Software analyst	SA
Project manager	PM

				Focus				
		Who	What	Where	When	Why	How	Product Constraints	Project Constraints
Perspective	Planner	BA SyA	DA BA SyA	NE SyA	BA SyA	BA DA SyA	BA SyA	BA SyA	BA SyA
	Owner	BA SyA	DA BA SyA	NE SyA	BA SyA	BA DA SyA	BA SyA	BA SyA	BA SyA
	Designer	SA	DA SA	NE SA	SA	DA SA	SA	SA	PM
	Builder	SA	SA	NE	SA	SA	SA	SA	PM
	Subcontractor	SA	SA	NE	SA	SA	SA	SA	PM

Figure 8.3   The Common Requirements Roles. (For definitions of abbreviations, see Table 8.2.)

Necessary Skills for Requirements Engineers

It is important to realize that every project needs qualified people, although it is not always possible to find them. It is the responsibility of an organization to *develop* its people, sponsoring everyone from the trainee to the top-level requirements engineer through continuing education and opportunities to use what they learn.

The common mistake that many corporations make when staffing an Internet project is to hire individuals with programming skills in the latest software language. Though that helps with software development, it is important to hire the right *team*—project managers, testers, requirements engineers, and all those roles previously mentioned in this chapter. These "tool-independent" people are needed on the project!

Due to the mission-critical nature of Internet applications, some organizations hire individuals who have the most experience for each role. This is a short-term view into the life of the Internet product. It is also important to staff the project with junior employees or trainees who can grow with the Internet product through its continual evolution.

It is important to view the different levels of qualifications for requirements engineers alongside the tasks related to the requirements process. Yes, be sure to assign a senior requirements lead. In fact, assign multiple individuals at that level. However, also include some junior individuals so they can learn from the masters. The positive payback to the corporation will be immeasurable. It is recommended to keep the ratio of two experienced (master or expert level) requirements engineers to one trainee. This allows for trainees to learn from individuals with different filters and points of view, which permits the trainees to develop their own styles.

Meilir Page-Jones[16] wrote an article segregating levels of competency. Though the article uses terms that are out of date, the concept of segregating the different levels is still important (see Table 8.3). Individuals with expertise levels 3 through 6 (trainee through architect) should be used to staff the Internet program.

For the purposes of this discussion, let's look at these four levels. Years of experience (over different type of projects) separates requirements engineering skill levels; the level of expertise is tied to experience.

Table 8.3   The Seven Levels of Expertise

	Level Name	Level Description	Requirements Engineer Level
1	Innocent	Has never heard of requirements engineering	Not applicable
2	Aware	Has read an article on requirements engineering	Not applicable
3	Apprentice	**Has attended a three-day seminar on requirements engineering**	**Trainee**
4	Practitioner	**Is ready to use requirements engineering on a real project**	**Junior**
5	Journeyman	**Uses requirements engineering naturally and automatically in his job**	**Full, senior**
6	Master	**Has internalized requirements engineering; knows when to break the rules**	**Lead, architect**
7	Expert	Writes books, gives lectures, looks for ways to extend requirements engineering	Advisor, author, teacher

16. See Page-Jones 1998.

The required skill set (see Table 8.4) documents the minimum knowledge needed in six broad categories:

1. Practical experience (related accomplishments)
2. Engineering (knowledge in system/software engineering)
3. Project management (knowledge in managing the requirements engineering effort)
4. Techniques and tools (knowledge in analyzing and specifying; requirements set coverage)
5. Quality (knowledge in building a quality product)
6. Personality (people skills)

Notice that the Internet is not a topic under any of the categories. Though the Internet has its own particularities, it is more important that the Internet team select a skilled requirements engineer than an individual with minimal requirements engineering knowledge but extensive Internet knowledge. This list of categories and topics applies to any IT project, *including* Internet-based ones.

Practical Experience

Practical experience defines the minimum experience the person has had working on real projects in the area of requirements engineering. The person may have extensive knowledge in one focus area for a single business community. If so, this would be considered a junior-level position when taking into account all the perspectives, focus areas, and communities that a requirements engineer may be asked to assist with when capturing requirements. A key difference between the full (level 5) and lead (level 6) positions is the understanding that the requirements engineer must leave his business community knowledge in the background and concentrate on the requirements engineering community. This may be difficult for the full (level 5) requirements engineer.

Engineering Knowledge

The engineering knowledge category represents an overall familiarity with the software engineering disciplines. This includes understanding the differences between process, method, policy, and procedure. It also means having an understanding of requirements management, project management, project oversight and tracking, configuration management, and so forth. The more advanced requirements engineer's skill set includes knowledge of how to implement processes

Table 8.4 Skill Levels for Requirements Engineers

Skill Category	Topic	Junior	Full	Lead
Practical experience	• Focus • Perspective • Communities • Large-scale projects	• One focus • Two perspectives • One business community • Zero large-scale requirement efforts	• Four focuses • Three perspectives • Multiple business communities • Four large-scale requirement efforts	• All focuses • All perspectives • Can separate business community knowledge from requirements engineering knowledge • Six large-scale requirement efforts
Engineering	• Process understanding • Methods • Standards • Training	• Junior	• Senior	• Architect
Project management	• Estimating • Project planning, tracking, and control • Writing and presenting • PMBOK	• Trainee	• Full	• Lead
Techniques and tools	• Focus • Perspective • Metric • Testing	• Junior	• Full	• Architect
Quality	• QA versus QC • IEEE and ISO/IEC • CMM and SPICE • Demings	• Trainee	• Senior	• Lead
Personality	• Mentor • Teacher • Sales • Diplomacy	• Trainee	• Full	• Lead

Abbreviations: CMM, Capability Maturity Model; IEC, International Electrotechnical Commission; IEEE, Institute of Electrical and Electronics Engineers; ISO, International Standards Organization; PMBOK, project management body of knowledge; QA, quality assurance; QC, quality control; SPICE, Software Process Improvement and Capability Determination.

at the project, division, and corporate levels. Someone at the master level promotes the use of software engineering processes on a continual basis.

Project Management Skills

Knowledge about managing the requirement effort is an important part of the requirements process. In a nutshell, project management is the repeated execution of such activities as estimating, planning, reorganizing, integrating, measuring, and revising until the project's business objectives are achieved. This is accomplished through people management, user involvement, and issue resolution. A skilled requirements engineer has managed multiple projects and understands the need the management committee has for status reports, accurate estimating, proper use of resources, and prompt issues identification and resolution. All requirements, functional as well as nonfunctional, feed the project plan to determine accurate scheduling and resources. As the requirement evolves through each perspective, the plan is adjusted with information to accurately depict the status of the final delivery. It is important for the experienced requirements engineer to have knowledge in project planning techniques in order to be able to support the project manager.[17]

The other necessary project management skill is risk management. At no other phase of the project is the product more at risk of failure than during the requirements process. The more experienced requirements engineer has risk management knowledge and experience with spotting risks and alerting the executive committee with suggested countermeasures.

Understanding of Techniques and Tools

The area of techniques and tools is the most common starting point for requirements engineers. Every requirements engineer learns at least one method for capturing requirements (for example, data modeling, object modeling, structured analysis). However, as the requirements pattern has illustrated, knowing one, two, or all three previously mentioned methods does not lead to capturing all the requirements. Some methods do well for data focus, others for network focus. It helps to know and have experience with the different techniques (for example, data modeling, object-oriented analysis, use cases, event partitioning)

---

17. Refer to the Project Managers Institute for best practice information on project management: www.pmi.org.

since they are proven methods for capturing at least a subset of the requirements set. The more tools a requirements engineer knows that span the different focus areas, the more he has an awareness of what information needs to be captured to accurately define the different requirements.

Knowledge of other techniques and tools not particularly geared for capturing and specifying requirements (specifically, tools and techniques associated with testing) is also important for the requirements engineer. With this knowledge the requirements engineer can give quality control analysts the requirements information needed to build appropriate test strategies, plans, cases, and data.

Knowledge about Quality Issues

Knowing how to build a quality product is unfortunately the area where many requirements engineers are weakest. They may understand the characteristics of good requirements but lack the fundamental understanding of quality initiatives in the quality movement. Under this category are topics that expand beyond the requirement characteristics, including standard resources that can be used to improve the requirements process, techniques, and the quality of the requirements set.

Personality and People Skills

Personality is the key to success for the project. Requirements come from people. Even if the requirements engineer is capturing some requirements from existing documentation, these requirements must still be validated by people. This involves communication with others in multiple formats (for example, e-mail, one-on-one contact, and group sessions). A requirements engineer will not succeed if he remains in his cubicle without contact with business users during the requirements process.

Personality in this context does not mean being happy, a good joke teller, or a good conversationalist (though that will help you on difficult days). It means that the requirement elicitor can communicate with all kinds of individuals in multiple formats. The requirements engineer must feel comfortable talking with all levels in the organization and in front of all group sizes. He must have an understanding of different work styles and be able to quickly determine an individual's strengths (every person adds value to the requirements set).

The Internet is a global product. It is not uncommon to work with team members in countries where English is not the primary language. Therefore, the personality category must include an ability to work with people from different cultures. Also included in this skill category is the need to be a skilled diplomat and to be able to work with all different personality types.[18]

As stated earlier, the requirements engineer's skill set is valid for every type of software application. This includes Internet products as well as other applications. The next section reviews how the requirement producers, including all requirements engineer skill levels, fit in with the emerging Internet organization.

The Requirements Engineering Organization

Corporations have multiple options for implementing an organization that supports requirements engineering and meets the demands of fast-paced Internet development. These options include the organizational style of the group itself and the definitions of the specific responsibilities assigned to the role of requirements engineer. Thus it is important to understand the different organizational styles that may exist in a corporation.

Organizational Styles

Organizational style refers to how the requirements engineers are organized within the corporation. There are four different styles:

1. Central or divisional matrix
2. Focused matrix
3. Project aligned
4. Combination

Central or Divisional Matrix Style

Central or *divisional matrix* refers to organizations in which the requirements engineers are pooled together in a central group, reporting directly to either the business or information technology community. If each division within the corporation has its own information technology development staff (for example, banking can have both a retail and a wholesale side) with a pooled group of requirements engineers, then the corporation has a divisional matrix style. The point is that the requirements engineers are not scattered among the different project teams but report to a single group (see Figure 8.4). They are then assigned

---

18. Some situations involve potentially hostile employees who may have reduced commissions or responsibilities because of the new product.

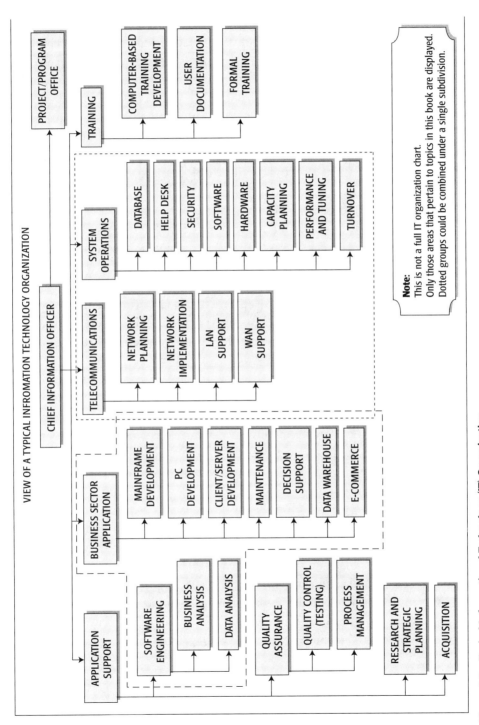

Figure 8.4   Typical Informational Technology (IT) Organization

to different projects as needed, creating a matrix-style management structure. For each project (or iteration of a product), the requirements engineer reports to both the project manager for the project and his own requirements engineering manager. Having all requirements engineers grouped together allows for continual sharing of ideas, techniques, and, of course, assistance. Better communication exists when each requirements engineer is able to discuss each group project, hoping to stimulate conversation on how one project's requirements may impact those of another project. This creates a requirements center of excellence!

Though rare, some central or divisional-matrix organizations do report directly into the business unit. The benefit of this alignment is that the requirements engineer can be alerted of new projects or changes in direction immediately and help the business unit by capturing nontechnology requirements. The risk of this organizational style is the possibility of not having access to technologists or technology information—such as data structures, program listings, and other valuable information—to uncover additional requirement-essential details. Having the requirements engineering manager (for the entire requirements engineering centralized group) report to the chief information officer and allowing him to participate on the executive board countermeasures this risk.

Focused Matrix Style

Focused matrix is similar to the central or divisional matrix style in that requirements engineers are assigned to different projects as needed, creating a matrix management style of reporting. The requirements engineer, for each project, reports to both the project manager for the project and his own requirement-focused manager. The difference is that the type of requirements they capture may separate them. For example, the data analyst (capturing "what" requirements) may be separated from the business analyst (capturing "how" requirements), who may be separated from the network engineers (capturing "where" requirements). Under the requirements engineering group (see Figure 8.4), business analysts and data analysts are broken out. These focus area groups probably do not report to the same manager. In this scenario, it is the responsibility of the program manager to coordinate the efforts of each focused requirements engineer. The program manager must ensure that all the requirements are complete and consistent and that no conflicts exist among the different requirements.

Project Aligned Style

Project aligned is a decentralized approach to organizational style. Requirements engineers report directly to one manager. This manager is responsible for a specific project (in this case, the Internet product). This style does not facilitate the continual growth of requirements engineers. It does not allow for moral support if the project manager does not believe in the requirements engineering process. Each project team may follow a different requirements engineering process to capture requirements, creating an eclectic set of requirements that may or may not be reusable. For example, the dashed line on Figure 8.4 combines the requirements engineering group with the business sector application group. In such a situation, the requirements engineering group reports directly to the business sector application group; the billing group has its own requirements engineers and so does the inventory application group. Most start-up companies use this type of organization. Larger companies may do so as well if the Internet product was outsourced for development.

Combination Style

What is seen most often in corporations is a *combination* of the matrix and aligned organizational styles. Some focus areas are separated (usually the network engineers and possibly the data analysts). Those responsible for the other types of requirements are usually aligned with the project manager. Those matrixed are usually aligned with the physical implementers for the focus area. The data analysts are grouped with the database administrators. This allows for key corporate infrastructures (data and network, in this example) to be corporate-focused. The other types of requirements are left to the ability of the requirements engineer and project manager to be coordinated with other projects and written in a reusable manner. Notice that the requirements engineering group in Figure 8.4 that contains the business and data analysts is separated from the network engineers, who are part of the telecommunications group.

When a decentralized organizational style (focused matrix, project aligned, or combination) is used, it is strongly recommended that at minimum a monthly joint meeting occur with all categories of requirements engineers to share their experiences and knowledge. Requirements engineering as a discipline is in its adolescent stage of development. Sharing and helping others is key to achieving maximum return on the corporation's investment.

Support for Responsibilities in All Organizational Styles

No matter which of the organizational styles is used, it is important that the responsibilities associated with requirements engineering be covered in some fashion. Within the corporation and program, someone must be responsible for the activities that are described next. For simplicity, the organization used in this discussion exemplifies a central/divisional organizational style.

Basically, the requirements engineering organization can be segmented into three categories of responsibilities:

1. The process-oriented group
2. The project-oriented group
3. The requirements management–oriented group

The requirements engineering organization would have a manager who should report directly to the head of the specific business unit, either the chief executive officer or the chief information officer (which is the norm). Reporting to anyone lower in the organization will minimize the organizational focus and will increase the risk of "the right hand not knowing what the left hand is doing." This manager will potentially be a member of the planning or executive board (recommended). This will enable him to be the first to hear of corporate direction and new initiatives and to align the requirements engineering organization to assist from the beginning, therefore building quality requirements at the proper speed.

Each of the three groups would report to the requirements engineering manager (see Figure 8.5). Each would have a divisional or department charter that defines its roles and responsibilities in a manner that describes the benefits provided toward achieving corporate goals. The requirements engineering manager must ensure that the three departments work together produce quality requirements. This same individual will be required to "sell" the benefits of following a high-quality requirements engineering process and using skilled requirements engineers on all types of projects (including mission-critical, maintenance, Internet, and non-technology-oriented programs).

Process-Oriented Group

The process-oriented group defines quality assurance (proactive) activities as they relate to requirements engineering, all of which would assist and not impede the development of quality requirements. One special responsibility is the evaluation and recommendation of tools and techniques. The process-oriented group should supply options to the different projects. Each project will be different and has special needs. The requirements engineering process-oriented group should not dictate tools and techniques but should continually research new tools and techniques and build selection criteria. They can then assist the

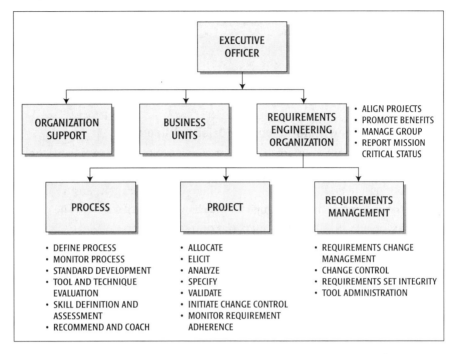

EXECUTIVE OFFICER

ORGANIZATION SUPPORT

BUSINESS UNITS

REQUIREMENTS ENGINEERING ORGANIZATION

- ALIGN PROJECTS
- PROMOTE BENEFITS
- MANAGE GROUP
- REPORT MISSION CRITICAL STATUS

PROCESS

- DEFINE PROCESS
- MONITOR PROCESS
- STANDARD DEVELOPMENT
- TOOL AND TECHNIQUE EVALUATION
- SKILL DEFINITION AND ASSESSMENT
- RECOMMEND AND COACH

PROJECT

- ALLOCATE
- ELICIT
- ANALYZE
- SPECIFY
- VALIDATE
- INITIATE CHANGE CONTROL
- MONITOR REQUIREMENT ADHERENCE

REQUIREMENTS MANAGEMENT

- REQUIREMENTS CHANGE MANAGEMENT
- CHANGE CONTROL
- REQUIREMENTS SET INTEGRITY
- TOOL ADMINISTRATION

Figure 8.5   The Requirements Engineering Central/Divisional Style Organization

project manager in choosing what would be best for the specific project. The major categories of responsibility include

- Process definition
- Standard development and recommendations
- Technique evaluation and coaching
- Tool evaluation and coaching
- Definition of roles and responsibilities, including skill assessment

Project-Oriented Group

The project-oriented group consists of the requirements engineers who allocate, elicit, analyze, specify, and validate the requirements. Group members use the techniques and tools recommended by the process-oriented group. They document the requirements using the approved standards and process defined by the process group. The project-oriented group is matrixed (or aligned) to the project manager. Its members supply input to the process-oriented group about improvements to the process, standards, techniques, and tools. The major categories, by skill level, include

- Architect
- Engineer (all skill levels)
- Facilitators (requirement supporters)

Requirements Management–Oriented Group

The requirements management–oriented group is responsible for the configuration management activities as they relate to requirements. This means coordinating the change-control process and all activities that ensure the integrity of the requirements set through all the change-control states.[19] The group is subdivided into the following categories of responsibility:

- Configuration control
- Requirement-related tool administration

As stated earlier, it is important that the responsibilities associated with requirements engineering be covered in some fashion. How this works for Internet-based projects is discussed next.

The Internet Organization

Most of the roles discussed in this chapter are generic to all kinds of software development. The peculiarities of the Internet (such as continual incremental or component release, global risk, velocity of change) require tailoring the role explanations to clearly define the specific Internet-related responsibilities and their impacts on the final product. Let's first look at the way many corporations are establishing Internet organizations.

Determining which organizational style to use depends on:

- The size of the corporation
- The number of projects
- The kinds of projects
- The number of skilled requirements engineers
- The skill sets of the requirements engineers

---

19. For more information on requirement configuration management, refer to Chapter Seven.

Due to the high demand and exposure of Internet businesses, large companies are forming new divisions to concentrate on developing Internet solutions. As a result, these new groups are obtaining carte blanche to build the solution quickly. They have board approval to ignore the old and to start from scratch to build a flexible infrastructure. The project team is primarily assembled with new talent that has experience in Internet tools. These new members often lack knowledge of the existing application architecture, business workflow, and information architecture.

Unfortunately, the core of a successful Internet-based product is information. The information is contained in existing databases and business applications. If the Internet group members build without any concern for what already exists, they will require significant overhead (usually resulting in delayed delivery) to integrate with the core applications already in place. It is imperative that these new divisions keep in mind the need to integrate with existing systems. It is the responsibility of the executive committee to be committed to building an Internet team that consists of new and old guard in order to fill all the roles described in this chapter.

For some start-up companies, the Internet is the only program. By default, they form a centralized requirements engineering group. This may become fragmented if a separate requirements engineer is assigned to different pieces of the solution or by iterative release. The risk can be minimized by employing a central requirements architect whose responsibility is to coordinate the requirement effort. The requirements architect is then supported by the requirements controller, who ensures the integrity of the requirements set.

The most commonly used organizational style for Internet environments has been the project-aligned approach, in which a dedicated requirements engineer or group of requirements engineers report only to the Internet information technology manager. Keep in mind that one of the most difficult tasks for Internet-based applications is integrating them with the Internet product. This type of organizational style increases the risk of integration by minimizing the lack of information that may be readily available to the requirements engineer with regard to existing infrastructure issues (data, process, and connectivity).

For larger companies that are adding an Internet division, a centralized requirements engineering group or at least a focused group may already be in place. In this scenario (see Figure 8.6), it is best that the Internet program manager obtain commitment from the manager(s) for the dedicated requirements engineer(s) to support all focus areas as well as all configuration management support. *Dedicated* means that the requirements engineers work on *only* the

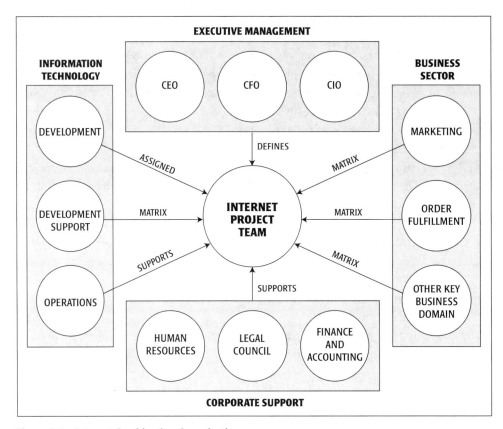

Figure 8.6   Internet Combination Organization

Internet program during the three perspective levels—planner (scope requirements), owner (business requirements), and designer (essential requirement details)—for as many iterations as the Internet program manager sees fit.

Conclusion

One of the most difficult challenges in the new paradigm is retaining employees. Which employees to keep depends on each person's skills and work style. Retaining employees includes providing good training, creating opportunities for them to grow and use what they have learned, and seeing the benefits of their work (understanding the contributions to the corporation's bottom line).

Typically, technical architects and those with specific technical knowledge are paid the most. This chapter illustrated that additional roles are necessary for the successful implementation of an Internet-based product, requirements gathering being the first step in the process. If you get the requirements wrong, it doesn't matter whether the technical architects build the best infrastructure. The Internet product will fail to deliver key consumer and supplier needs. In the end, it is critical to build a qualified Internet team that includes a qualified requirements engineer.

CHAPTER NINE

Parting Thoughts

Chapter Key Topics
- How long will this take?
- How to get started
- Key points to remember

The Internet Impact

The Internet has changed the business model to be customer focused. Customers, suppliers, and especially those persons building and maintaining the Internet solution have felt the impact. To facilitate the seed of change and the need for continual improvement requires capturing requirements that are beyond the boundaries of software.

When I began writing this book, I selected several "dot-coms" as examples because they would be well known to the general reading public. The selected companies provided specific examples of a customer-centric focus and an end-to-end workflow that expanded beyond corporate boundaries. Some of them were start-ups; others were brick-and-mortar companies that had expanded their business to the Internet (due to coi8mpetition from the start-ups). Some of the sites—such as Amazon.com, Yahoo.com, LandsEnd.com, eCost.com, mySimon.com, and eBay.com—illustrated that the companies had a good understanding of the four key concepts behind the Internet:

1. Continual iterative release
2. Velocity of development

3. A full requirements set

4. A commitment to put the customers' experience first

However, some of the companies were good examples of what *not* to do. In fact, by the time I handed the manuscript for this book to the publisher, those companies had gone out of business. Two examples (Pets.com and eToys.com) had a good customer focus. The failures of these companies illustrate that in order to succeed in the Internet world, the Internet-based application is not the only piece that must be done well. They both had good customer experience shells. Neither of the requirements sets, however, was complete! They had not fully integrated the non-IT requirements. They did not identify the cost of doing the workflows across corporate boundaries, forming profitable business partnerships, and interfacing the back-office support systems.

One brick-and-mortar company, ToysRUs, realized that it did not have the best Internet approach but had the infrastructure to support the full end-to-end workflow (that is, order fulfillment). So ToysRUs.com agreed to form a business partnership with amazon.com, which had the brand acceptance for a customer-centric approach.

The world of commerce on the Internet is settling down. The pattern of seeing dramatic increases in stock value without showing a profit is slowing down. Brick-and-mortar companies are now entering the field that was knocked open by start-ups.[1] These "pre-Internet" companies had additional challenges to face. They had to interface the new front-end with existing back-end processing. They had to change the focus from a cost-cutting mentality to a customer-centric strategy.

All corporations must face these challenges. According to Elif Kaban, in an article that appeared on Yahoo.com on February 19, 2001:[2]

> U.S. Forrester Research said keeping up with the Web was the single biggest challenge for 68 percent of executives it surveyed at 50 private banks and asset management groups in the United States, Canada, Europe, South Africa, Japan and Australia. Only 16 percent felt they were ahead of the game.

---

1. One of the key points in Clayton Christensen's book, *The Innovator's Dilemma*, is that big businesses find it difficult to implement truly new ideas. Christensen believed that truly disruptive innovations almost always occur first from a small business. I believe this is especially true with the Internet explosion.

2. See Kaban 2001.

In the old days, private bankers used to have more information than their clients. But now they risk losing that competitive advantage to the wired affluent as technology forces a change in the balance of that relationship, the survey said. . . .

"Our clients want access to their accounts, want to transact online and want our research online. And after we offer that, they want features like wireless access and collaborative browsing," the survey quoted him as saying.

The private bankers surveyed said technology was now high on the checklist clients used to select a bank.

"We have to figure out what the next major development will be," added a British private banker. "Should we deliver account information via WAP phones or is there something beyond that?"

Do not forget the flood of new businesses that were possible because of the technology. A good example of this new type of business is the need for automatic response (Swiftresponse.com) of e-mails from customers. Other examples include being the front end (for example, amazon.com for ToysRUs) or the back end (for example, Cardstore.com for Kodak) for larger existing companies.

As these innovative examples illustrate, the Internet is here to stay for the long haul. Companies simply must understand *all* the needs that have to be satisfied in order to be successful. If the Internet product provides value (for example, quick and easy access) for the clients, the business will grow for years to come. On the other hand, say you build an Internet solution that doesn't fully take the customer into account. Some customers come. . . . then they leave. The key is whether you built a product that provides the information they need in a manner that is easy to find and use. If not, customers won't return. You may have a first month flooded with activity that dwindles over time. The result is a negative return on investment that could result in the failure of the business.

Many companies, consultants, developers, business representatives, executives, and managers can look back on at least one failed Internet-based project. Failure can be defined as cost overrun, a delay in product launch, missing features, or defects. Of all the causes for these kinds of failures, absent, poor-quality, or mismanaged requirements tend to top the list. Given the risk associated with the Internet and the newness of this business medium, it is important to identify a tool that helps capture, develop, and manage the requirements.

An Internet requirements pattern was presented in this book to help identify *all* the requirements necessary for building a high-quality Internet product. The pattern does not dictate the use of a specific tool or method for capturing these requirements, but it does suggest using a formal requirements process, specifying requirements in a quality format, and managing the requirements to facilitate the sheer number of changes that occur during a product's evolution.

How Long Will This Take?

The first question any requirement supplier from the business practice or the executive committee asks is, "How long will this take?" The answer requires having a crystal ball.

Estimating the time it takes for the requirements effort is more of an art than a science. Each business and IT community will have its own process for creating work products. Some guidelines exist that typify a common software development effort.[3] Unfortunately, there is minimal statistical information on planning just the requirements effort, and no statistics exist for Internet-type applications.

For larger corporations, statistics from other large-scale development efforts (that is, ones that had multiple projects that needed to be coordinated) may be available to help in estimating time tables for future projects. The actual work effort statistics captured can be applied as a guideline for planning the Internet requirements effort.

If you are planning a specific iteration after the first implementation of a product, the amount of time spent on requirements can be estimated as a portion of what was spent on the first iteration. The planning for each subsequent iteration can be based on the iterations that came before it.

There are no industry-standard statistics available for calculating the work effort (in time) involved when using the requirements pattern. Unfortunately, it is extremely difficult to say how long it will take at project kickoff if you do not yet know the scope of the project! Many times, all you have is a business statement of an idea. With this minimal information, all you can estimate is the definition of scope. Remember, there are no silver bullets (at least none found by the software community). Whatever estimate you define, even for just the scoping

---

3. Some rules state that the requirements effort is 20 percent of the entire effort to build a technology solution. However, how does one determine 20 percent of that?

phase, will probably be incorrect by as much as 35 percent at least 75 percent of the time. This preliminary estimate is simply a means for management to budget and allocate staff.

Planner Perspective Estimation

The following six guidelines are intended to help requirements engineers plan the amount of time required for their activities.

1. Three days to set up and organize for the project and obtain any material about the business community.
2. Five days to review any existing material about the business community. If none exists, still add the five days since the next step will increase.
3. Two days for each person who will be interviewed to define the scope. This encompasses scheduling the meetings, holding the meetings (one to two hours each), analyzing the information gathered, writing and issuing meeting minutes, addressing any follow-up questions, and resolving any conflicting research. Interview at least one individual from each business area that may potentially be involved with or affected by the project. If there are more than six individuals, the use of a facilitator is recommended to organize a facilitation session to clearly define the scope. Each facilitation session would be counted as three days (preparation, session, postanalysis).
4. Five days to produce a scope definition report, covering all types of requirements and expectations.
5. Two days to schedule and hold a final meeting with the executive sponsor and to make any final adjustments to the scope.
6. Two days to initiate change control of the approved requirements.

It is important to jot down thoughts as they arise. Remember to put them *in writing* during all phases of the project and plan. Include notes on the following types of issues:

- Altered estimates based on similar projects with similar corporate styles (never underestimate your intuition).
- Altered estimates based on the project type (new, maintenance, enhancement).
- Politically charged environments that will prolong the effort as well as users new to the business community.
- Projects without business executive sponsorship, which will add time.

- The requirements engineer's skill set, which will either increase or decrease the estimate.
- The addition of new tools, techniques, or processes that will increase time.
- Allowance for at least 33 percent more time for interviewing. Expect people to interview to come out of the woodwork, especially if the project has high visibility.
- Any vacations or holidays that will occur during the scoping phase; adjust the schedule accordingly. Plan for a percentage of unexpected absences.
- Realistic expectations of a "full" day of work. IBM used to (and may still) estimate that employees would have only four hours in a day to accomplish planned work. The rest of the time is spent on telephone calls, e-mails, unexpected meetings or ad hoc discussions, interim reports to executives, and so forth.

It is important to set the expectation level of those who will be involved in the requirements process. Remind them that in the early stages this is *only* a definition of project scope; detailed business requirements will not be produced until later. You are just refining the area of investigation by clearly defining the concept. Make sure that the executives have the proper expectation at this stage. True estimating methods are complex and require the integration of many kinds of information that are not available so early in the project.

Owner Perspective Estimation

Once the scope has been defined, the projected work effort can be calculated using the following fifteen guidelines.

1. Start with three days to set up and organize for the owner perspective phase of the project.
2. For each "who" scope-level requirement, estimate two days to talk to people in each area to identify the details of their responsibilities and the means of interaction with the scope.
3. For each "what" scope-level requirement, estimate three days to refine the entity class or entity and its relationships.
4. For each "where" scope-level requirement, estimate a day to refine your understanding.
5. For each "when" scope-level requirement, estimate two days to define the event and the high-level use case.

6. For each "why" scope-level requirement, estimate two days to define the business rules.

7. For each "how" scope-level requirement, estimate three days to define the product functions and features needed by the users.

8. For each product constraint and quality of service scope-level requirement, estimate one day to clarify product expectations.

9. For each project constraint scope-level requirement, estimate two days to clarify constraints concerning project management.

10. Allow two days for each intersecting requirement cell to uncover additional derived requirements.

11. Allow ten days to produce a business requirements specification covering all types of requirements and expectations. This includes the time spent cleaning up any diagrams so they are readable for all reviewers.

12. Allow five days to validate the requirements specification.

13. Allow two days to schedule and hold final meetings with the executive sponsor and to make any final adjustments to the requirement definitions (logical/business perspective).

14. Allow four days for requirements configuration management support.

15. Allow two days for process-improvement adjustments.

Scope creep, discussed in detail in Chapter Five, begins to appear even at this early stage. If this happens, use the following three guidelines to adjust the estimate from the above recommendations.

1. Add 7 percent for small projects or when skilled requirements engineers are involved.

2. Add 15 percent for medium-sized projects or when varying skill sets are involved.

3. Add 22 percent for large projects with many risks or when the skill set is unknown or multiple trainees are involved.

At the owner perspective point in the project, you may be increasing the number of requirements engineers working on the project. Once you have more than one involved, a requirements architect is needed to coordinate the efforts, to ensure that all requirements are captured (including any associative requirements between requirement cells), and to resolve any conflicts between requirements. Depending on the size of the program, a requirements engineer is assigned to represent each business community in the product scope. Weekly meetings occur to review findings and discuss potential requirement conflicts.

Designer Perspective Estimation

Now the requirements have evolved to the designer perspective level. At this stage, a tool such as KnowledgePLAN by Software Productivity Research (*www.spr.com*) can be used to assist in determining the duration and cost of the project. The results are based on actual metrics from over 8,000 projects. The product is extremely easy to use and can be calibrated with experience from your company's past projects. Your own process can be incorporated and cross-referenced to the knowledge project template.

At this point in the project, the scoping requirements have already evolved into business requirements. Now the business requirements evolve into a designer's view or designer-level requirements. The third perspective, designer, is the most detailed and takes the most amount of time to define the requirements. Remember that when the essential details of the requirements are defined, they must be technology independent.

Even with the use of a tool like KnowledgePLAN to estimate the whole program effort, it is important to also use your own experience to estimate this phase of requirement evolution. During this phase, take into account the same adjustment variables that were described for the scoping phase. Also add the scope creep estimates described in the section on the owner perspective. Both of those adjustments are made to initial manual estimate based on the following thirteen guidelines.

1. Start with three days to set up and organize for this phase of the project.
2. For each "who" business requirement, estimate two days to talk to people in each area, identifying the details of their responsibilities and means of interaction with the scope.
3. For each "what" business requirement, estimate four days to refine the object or entity and its relationships.
4. For each "where" business requirement, estimate two days to refine your understanding.
5. For each "when" business requirement, estimate two days to define the event and use case.
6. For each "why" business requirement, estimate three days to define the business rules.
7. For each "how" business requirement, estimate three days to define the product functions and features needed by the users.

8. For each product constraint and quality of service business requirement, estimate two days.

9. For each project constraint business requirement, estimate three days. Assembling a project plan that includes a full schedule takes time.

10. Estimate three days for each intersecting requirement cell to uncover additional derived requirements.

11. Estimate fifteen days to assemble a detailed requirements specification, covering all types of requirements and expectations. This includes the time spent cleaning up all models produced during this phase.

12. Estimate ten days to validate the requirements specification, which will take multiple individual reviews.

13. Estimate two days to schedule and hold a final meeting with the executive sponsor and to make any final adjustments to the detailed requirement definitions.

This is a manual estimate that is much less reliable than the experience of Software Productivity Research. This proposed method of estimating requirement development would be considered by most of the software community as an art rather than a science. However, it serves as a beginning to coach everyone who uses the Internet requirements pattern to begin capturing actuals. This information can be fed into a product like KnowledgePLAN to begin adjustments based on years of experience.

By this point approximately 20 to 30 percent of the entire project has been completed. This includes the first three perspectives (planner, owner, and designer) for each community and focus area. This is by no means the end of the requirements evolution. Derived requirements and scope creep will continue as the development process continues. The remaining perspectives will not be as time consuming. In fact, the requirements engineers will need to begin capturing scope-level requirements for the next Internet iteration. For the remaining perspectives, allocate approximately 5 percent of the program's phase/stage time to requirements. This includes modifications to existing requirements, validation of other work products adhering to the requirements set, and developing new initial (due to scope creep) and derived (for specific perspectives) requirements.

This approach for estimating work effort does not take into account the use of development outsourcing or commercial off-the-shelf software for portions of the Internet solution. Both of these will have an impact on the estimate. The quality of the management team running the different Internet projects will also affect the estimates.

How to Get Started

If the company is not used to using a requirements engineer for capturing anything other than software requirements, you will need to do some backtracking. So, going back, the business case has probably already been written and has been approved to move forward. The requirements engineer, being a skilled diplomat, will find a way to obtain a copy of this document and any supporting material.

It is important that the requirements engineer ensure that all the other business communities are involved; in other words, that the idea has been allocated to the other groups for development. The requirement sponsor needs to have the time to coordinate all the different projects that make an Internet program. If not, you may want to recommend that a program coordinator be assigned.

If you are lucky to start from the beginning, provide an overview to the program team about the complexity of the Internet. Explain the need for participation from all business communities and briefly explain the requirement allocation process.[4] You will provide the program team information that illustrates that you understand what it takes to build a high-quality Internet product in the shortest amount of time. You will illustrate that the Internet is not just software but also involves work products from different business communities. Presenting this information will begin to build respect for requirements engineering and yourself (if you are new and have not already illustrated your skills). It will promote an environment that will allow you to carry out your responsibilities in the most efficient manner.

The next step is to begin to set up meetings. Read the business case and use the company organizational chart to determine who needs to be interviewed. Begin with the business practice initiating the program; this group will probably be the largest supplier of requirements.

Smaller start-ups probably do not have an extensive organizational chart. However, the functions and responsibilities that are typically performed by each of the business communities (business practice, business organization, business support, and information technology) must be performed by someone. That someone may be internal or external to the company. These functions and responsibilities must be added into the workflow scenario to identify the business community requirements subset.

After this, follow the Internet requirement work breakdown structure (see Appendix C). Start each meeting with an explanation of the business objectives

---

4. Requirement allocation is defined in detail in Chapter Two.

for the program. Explain your role and the type and level of detail of the requirements you want to begin to capture. Bring your Internet requirements pattern (as described in Appendix B or customized for your Internet program) with you to *all* meetings. It will provide support for your first Internet product and for the many iterations that come thereafter.

Applying the Requirements Pattern to Other Application Types

Every project, whether or not it is related to information technology, has the dimensions described by the requirements meta pattern. Every project has community, perspective, and focus and requires cell-associative requirements. The community structure correlates to the corporate structure. The requirements evolve from the owner through the subcontractor perspectives. And each perspective for each community has focuses that pertain to functional ("who, what, where, when, why, and how") or nonfunctional (product and project constraints) requirements. Therefore, the requirements meta pattern can be applied to any type of project or program.

The specific product-type requirements pattern varies from others in its area of concentration. As we saw with the Internet requirements pattern, the bulk of the questions pertain to workflow. Data, though very important, are secondary. With the Internet pattern, the focus is split between data and workflow, depending on the type of customer application. For instance, buying-type systems need a robust search engine and a well-designed database for clients; ordering the product is secondary. For either kind of electronic application (data-oriented versus transaction-oriented), the product constraints are of utmost importance. The requirements that pertain to security, performance, and scalability carry weight equal to that of the data and processing.

The Internet product differs from other kinds of applications in terms of the breadth of who must be involved and the coordination of parallel efforts for different product iterations. However, the infrastructure for requirements that has been proposed in this book can be tailored to any kind of product development. To start to develop your own product-specific requirements pattern, follow these ten steps.

1. Begin with the requirements meta pattern matrix of community, perspective, and focus.
2. Identify all communities that must be involved.

3. Decompose the communities or arrange the communities into allocation levels.

4. Use the requirements meta pattern concepts and objectives to begin to develop product-specific questions.

5. Apply the product-specific requirements pattern to any previous similar projects.

6. Note any cells that have potential weaknesses or gaps as seen from previous projects of this product type.

7. Tweak the question list by adding, changing, and clarifying any questions cell by cell and with all interfaces.

8. Develop anti-patterns for each weakness if necessary.

9. Use the product-specific requirements pattern for one project.

10. Tweak the product-specific requirements pattern based on the postanalysis of the success of each product that uses it.

Key Points to Remember

In order to implement the pattern, there must be agreement to the following ten key points.

1. Requirements are any needs to be satisfied by the delivered product.

2. Requirements evolve throughout the process.

3. A single requirement will impact multiple communities. As a result, every requirement must be documented in a format that everyone in all the different groups will be able to interpret, validate, and approve.

4. Requirements must be written so all reviewers can understand them and agree on the same understanding.

5. Requirements must be managed individually, in groups (models and cells), and in subsets (allocation levels and communities), as well as by Internet iteration.

6. Every cell will have questions to be answered.

7. Every cell should have at least one requirement.

8. It is more important for the requirements engineer to be experienced in the requirements engineering community than in the product's community (for example, banking, product delivery, Java).

9. Quality control occurs at each development phase. All requirement documents must be reviewed to identify any gaps in knowledge of what needs to be built.

10. Following one method and/or technique will *not* capture all the requirements.

Conclusion

A mistake that many large corporations make is to place an Internet front end on an existing application. Though this may seem to be the quickest and easiest approach to getting into the Internet game, this traditional approach to business puts at risk the corporation's potential profits. When launching an Internet product, it is important to elicit requirements as if it were an entirely new business venture. The requirements engineer may need to elicit requirements from vendors and customers to force the paradigm shift.

The Internet has not gone out of style nor will it in the near future. The number of customers who are finding this medium to be easy and time-saving is increasing daily. The number of users is increasing yearly. According to an article by Andy Sullivan posted on Yahoo.com in February 2001:[5]

> The study, which has a margin of error of 3 percentage points, also found that more Internet users, 56 percent, were going online every day, compared with 52 percent in the first half of 2000. E-mail remained the primary use for most surfers. . . . E-commerce gained ground as well, with 52 percent of Internet users surveyed saying they had made a purchase online, an increase of 6 percentage points.

It is precisely here that the requirements engineer becomes of value to a corporation. Requirements engineers can assist a company of any size in developing an Internet-based business. They can facilitate the definition of a business strategy that involves forming partnerships to outsource specific business functions. Requirements engineers understand the process of eliciting, analyzing, specifying, validating, approving, and managing requirements. These skills are independent of community, making requirements engineers experts in the requirements *process* rather than in a specific kind of business. For this reason, they provide a valuable asset to a business beginning to build an Internet product. They can work within and outside corporate boundaries. They work from the business concept, evolving the information into detailed requirements. Knowing the type of requirements that need to be captured, they can assist in allocating the responsibility of evolving the requirements into all the different work products.

As new requirement-related techniques and tools are promoted, the requirements engineer still has the basis to select the tool set that is best. The basis, in

---

5. See Sullivan 2001.

this case, is the understanding of the different types of requirements that need to be captured and the best time to ask for details. The requirements engineer has the luxury of selecting the different tools and techniques he wants to use as long as the requirements set is fulfilled in a quality manner. The Internet requirements set framework presented here provides the infrastructure against which all new tools and techniques can be evaluated and selected based on their merits.

These are exciting times for requirements engineers. With every business paradigm shift comes an opportunity to enhance businesses by using requirement skills—obtaining a full requirements set, managing requirements through their initial evolution and several incremental implementations, and ultimately creating a high-quality Internet application. All will have positive impacts on corporations for years to come.

Internet Requirements Pattern Specification Format

This appendix contains a suggested requirements specification format, which complements the Internet requirements pattern.[1] The format can be entered into a word processor or requirements management tool as the specification standard for a project or organization. This suggested format encompasses four IEEE standards:

1. Std 830: Software Requirements Specification
2. Std 1233: System Requirements Specification
3. Std 1362: IT System Concepts of Operations (System Definition)
4. Std 1058: Software Project Management Plans

It is strongly recommended that all people involved in developing requirements for an Internet solution purchase a copy of the *IEEE Software Engineering Standards Collection* from the IEEE (*www.computer.org*) as a first point of reference. The four standards (listed above) are just a few of the many standards available to assist the requirements engineer.

---

1. The Internet requirements pattern is described in Chapter Four. The actual pattern is contained in Appendix B.

The format proposed in the standards is optional, but it is recommended as a checklist to ensure that all requirement information is contained in the specification.

How to Use This Format

The IEEE standards as well as this format communicate the requirements of the customer to the technical community. It is the "contract" between the customer and the technical community and serves as a commitment of what is to be delivered. This specification has two audiences: the customer (for validation: requirement providers/supporters) and the technical community (for understanding: requirement users).[2] Others (requirement suppliers) will review the document with other pairs of eyes during the review/validation process.

The format described here will work with any perspective. Each perspective will have additional details needed to convey the requirements for that perspective and focus. As requirements evolve, so can this document.[3] Much of the information can also be stored in various CASE and requirements management tools.

Remember that requirements evolve. The requirements approved in one perspective should be included in the next perspective (and in all further perspectives). A separate document should be produced for each perspective for auditing purposes and for future reference.[4] Each requirement specification will vary in size due to the detailed requirements captured during that perspective (see Figure A.1). During the builder perspective, for example, the requirements are transformed into implementable work products (for example, code, databases, router configurations). Though typically not called a requirements specification, each of these separate documents will have a section dedicated to requirements since requirements will be captured at *every* perspective. The compilation of all volumes, regardless of perspective and community, comprises the requirements set.

---

2. For more information on roles and responsibilities, refer to Chapter Eight.
3. For quality purposes, it is recommended that a separate specification be issued for each perspective.
4. Internal web sites can be created to store approved requirement specifications for read only access.

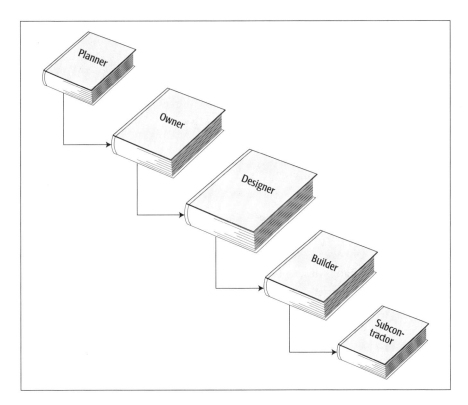

Figure A.1   Requirements Specification Evolution

Sample Table of Contents for the Information Technology Community and Owner Perpsective Level (Covering All Focus Areas)

1. Table of contents

2. Introduction

    2.1. Purpose of document

    2.2. Contact information

    2.3. Scope of document

        2.3.1. Community

        2.3.2. Perspective

        2.3.3. Focus

    2.4. Definitions, acronyms, and abbreviations

        2.4.1. Business-related

        2.4.2. Information technology–related

2.5. References

    2.5.1. Business-related

    2.5.2. Information technology–related

2.6. Overview of the business need *(restate or summarize the idea, business concept, and business objective)*

3. Approval

3.1. Signatures

3.2. Conditions

3.3. Assumptions

3.4. Next steps

4. Documentation change history

4.1. Date of change

4.2. Change name

4.3. Change description

4.4. Requester

4.5. Responsible party

4.6. Change status

4.7. Status date

5. Requirements

5.1. Functional focus requirements

    5.1.1. "Who" (actors/users/external interfaces)

        5.1.1.1. "Who" introduction

            5.1.1.1.1. Explanation of "who" requirements

            5.1.1.1.2. Reference

                5.1.1.1.2.1. Patterns

                5.1.1.1.2.2. Anti-patterns

                5.1.1.1.2.3. Role and responsibility descriptions

            5.1.1.1.3. What to validate

        5.1.1.2. Diagrams

            5.1.1.2.1. Notation legend/how to read the diagram

            5.1.1.2.2. What to validate on the diagram

            5.1.1.2.3. Diagrams

        5.1.1.3. Actors

            5.1.1.3.1. Label

            5.1.1.3.2. Name

            5.1.1.3.3. Priority

            5.1.1.3.4. Status

5.1.1.3.5. Description (include responsibilities)

5.1.1.3.6. Subtype (person, organization, system)

5.1.1.3.7. Validation criteria

5.1.1.3.8. Relationships (within cell)

> 5.1.1.3.8.1. Description between actors
>
> 5.1.1.3.8.2. Type of relationships
>
> 5.1.1.3.8.3. Qualification relationships
>
> 5.1.1.3.8.4. Validation criteria

5.1.1.4. Association information (outside cell)

> 5.1.1.4.1. Community/perspective/focus
>
> > 5.1.1.4.1.1. Label
> >
> > 5.1.1.4.1.2. Name
> >
> > 5.1.1.4.1.3. Priority
> >
> > 5.1.1.4.1.4. Status
> >
> > 5.1.1.4.1.5. Description
> >
> > 5.1.1.4.1.6. Validation criteria
> >
> > 5.1.1.4.1.7. Matrices

5.1.1.5. "Who"-related questions/issues

5.1.2. "What" (data/information)

5.1.2.1. "What" introduction

> 5.1.2.1.1. Explanation of "what" requirements
>
> 5.1.2.1.2. Reference
>
> > 5.1.2.1.2.1. Patterns
> >
> > 5.1.2.1.2.2. Anti-patterns
> >
> > 5.1.2.1.2.3. Role and responsibility descriptions
>
> 5.1.2.1.3. What to validate

5.1.2.2. Diagrams

> 5.1.2.2.1. Notation legend/how to read the diagram
>
> 5.1.2.2.2. What to validate on the diagram
>
> 5.1.2.2.3. Diagrams

5.1.2.3. Entity class/entities

> 5.1.2.3.1. Label
>
> 5.1.2.3.2. Name
>
> 5.1.2.3.3. Priority
>
> 5.1.2.3.4. Status
>
> 5.1.2.3.5. Description (include responsibilities)
>
> 5.1.2.3.6. Subtype (associative, subtype, and so on)

5.1.2.3.7. Validation criteria

5.1.2.3.8. Relationships (within cell)

    5.1.2.3.8.1. Description between entities/entity classes

    5.1.2.3.8.2. Type of relationships

    5.1.2.3.8.3. Qualification relationships

    5.1.2.3.8.4. Validation criteria

5.1.2.4. Association information (outside cell)

    5.1.2.4.1. Community/perspective/focus

        5.1.2.4.1.1. Label

        5.1.2.4.1.2. Name

        5.1.2.4.1.3. Priority

        5.1.2.4.1.4. Status

        5.1.2.4.1.5. Description

        5.1.2.4.1.6. Validation criteria

        5.1.2.4.1.7. Matrices

5.1.2.5. "What"-related questions/issues

5.1.3. "Where" (network locations)

5.1.3.1. "Where" introduction

    5.1.3.1.1. Explanation of "where" requirements

    5.1.3.1.2. Reference

        5.1.3.1.2.1. Patterns

        5.1.3.1.2.2. Anti-patterns

        5.1.3.1.2.3. Role and responsibility descriptions

    5.1.3.1.3. What to validate

5.1.3.2. Diagrams

    5.1.3.2.1. Notation legend/how to read the diagram

    5.1.3.2.2. What to validate on the diagram

    5.1.3.2.3. Diagrams

5.1.3.3. Nodes

    5.1.3.3.1. Label

    5.1.3.3.2. Name

    5.1.3.3.3. Priority

    5.1.3.3.4. Status

    5.1.3.3.5. Description (include responsibilities)

    5.1.3.3.6. Subtype (building, wireless, Internet, and so on)

    5.1.3.3.7. Validation criteria

5.1.5.3.8. Relationships (within cell)

5.1.5.3.8.1. Description between business rules

5.1.5.3.8.2. Type of relationships

5.1.5.3.8.3. Qualification relationships

5.1.5.3.8.4. Validation criteria

5.1.5.4. Association information (outside cell)

5.1.5.4.1. Community/perspective/focus

5.1.5.4.1.1. Label

5.1.5.4.1.2. Name

5.1.5.4.1.3. Priority

5.1.5.4.1.4. Status

5.1.5.4.1.5. Description

5.1.5.4.1.6. Validation criteria

5.1.5.4.1.7. Matrices

5.1.5.5. "Why"-related questions/issues

5.1.6. "How" (procedures, functionality)

5.1.6.1. "How" introduction

5.1.6.1.1. Explanation of "how" requirements

5.1.6.1.2. Reference

5.1.6.1.2.1. Patterns

5.1.6.1.2.2. Anti-patterns

5.1.6.1.2.3. Role and responsibility descriptions

5.1.6.1.3. What to validate

5.1.6.2. Diagrams

5.1.6.2.1. Notation legend/how to read the diagram

5.1.6.2.2. What to validate on the diagram

5.1.6.2.3. Diagrams

5.1.6.3. Functionality/methods

5.1.6.3.1. Label

5.1.6.3.2. Name

5.1.6.3.3. Priority

5.1.6.3.4. Status

5.1.6.3.5. Description (include responsibilities)

5.1.6.3.6. Subtype (function, transaction, and so on)

5.1.6.3.7. Validation criteria

5.1.6.3.8. Relationships (within cell)

    5.1.6.3.8.1. Description between functions

    5.1.6.3.8.2. Type of relationships

    5.1.6.3.8.3. Qualification relationships

    5.1.6.3.8.4. Validation criteria

5.1.6.4. Association information (outside cell)

    5.1.6.4.1. Community/perspective/focus

        5.1.6.4.1.1. Label

        5.1.6.4.1.2. Name

        5.1.6.4.1.3. Priority

        5.1.6.4.1.4. Status

        5.1.6.4.1.5. Description

        5.1.6.4.1.6. Validation criteria

        5.1.6.4.1.7. Matrices

5.1.6.5. "How"-related questions/issues

5.2. Nonfunctional requirements

    5.2.1. Product constraints and quality of service (QoS) questions/issues

        5.2.1.1. Product constraints introduction

            5.2.1.1.1. Explanation of QoS requirements

            5.2.1.1.2. Reference

                5.2.1.1.2.1. Patterns

                5.2.1.1.2.2. Anti-patterns

                5.2.1.1.2.3. Role and responsibility descriptions

            5.2.1.1.3. What to validate

        5.2.1.2. Product constraints

            5.2.1.2.1. Label

            5.2.1.2.2. Name

            5.2.1.2.3. Priority

            5.2.1.2.4. Status

            5.2.1.2.5. Description (include responsibilities)

            5.2.1.2.6. Subtype (security, performance, and so on)

            5.2.1.2.7. Validation criteria

            5.2.1.2.8. Relationships (within cell)

                5.2.1.2.8.1. Description between QoS requirements

                5.2.1.2.8.2. Type of relationships

5.2.1.2.8.3. Qualification relationships

5.2.1.2.8.4. Validation criteria

5.2.1.3. Association information (outside cell) *(note reference to any other requirement the product constraint directly impacts; qualify the impact)*

5.2.1.3.1. Community/perspective/focus

5.2.1.3.1.1. Label

5.2.1.3.1.2. Name

5.2.1.3.1.3. Priority

5.2.1.3.1.4. Status

5.2.1.3.1.5. Description

5.2.1.3.1.6. Validation criteria

5.2.1.3.1.7. Matrices

5.2.1.4. Product constraint–related questions/issues

5.2.2. Project constraints

5.2.2.1. Project plan introduction

5.2.2.1.1. Explanation of project constraints requirements

5.2.2.1.2. Reference

5.2.2.1.2.1. Patterns

5.2.2.1.2.2. Anti-patterns

5.2.2.1.2.3. Role and responsibility descriptions

5.2.2.1.3. What to validate

5.2.2.2. Project-constraining requirements

5.2.2.2.1. Label

5.2.2.2.2. Name

5.2.2.2.3. Priority

5.2.2.2.4. Status

5.2.2.2.5. Description

5.2.2.2.6. Subtype (budget, staff, time, and so on)

5.2.2.2.7. Validation criteria

5.2.2.3. Association information (outside cell) *(note reference to any other requirement the project constraint directly impacts; qualify the impact)*

5.2.2.3.1. Community/perspective/focus

5.2.2.3.1.1. Label

5.2.2.3.1.2. Name

5.2.2.3.1.3. Priority

5.2.2.3.1.4. Status

5.2.2.3.1.5. Description

5.2.2.3.1.6. Validation criteria

5.2.2.3.1.7. Matrices

5.2.2.4. Project constraint–related questions/issues

Internet Requirements Pattern for the Information Technology Community

This appendix describes the Internet requirements pattern for the information technology community only. The pattern can be easily modified to cover other key communities for the Internet product (see Figure B.1). This community subset conforms to the description of the requirements meta pattern defined in Appendix D.

The Internet requirements pattern provided here is a summary of the type of requirements and requirement details to be captured as they evolve from concept through implementation. Requirements are categorized by perspective and focus area to assist in capturing a complete set of requirements for the Internet product. The contents of each requirement cell can be applied to Internet-based applications of any size.

The Internet requirements pattern subset for the IT community is both method- and notation-independent. All diagrams and models that are potential representations of requirements will vary by the methods and notations used by your organization. No matter which approach is used, all graphic representations of requirements *must* include textual components.

In the requirements pattern that follows, each row of the requirements set framework (see Chapter Three) represents a unique perspective. The composite of all cell models in a row represents a complete description of the solution from the perspective of that row. Many iterations of a row may occur

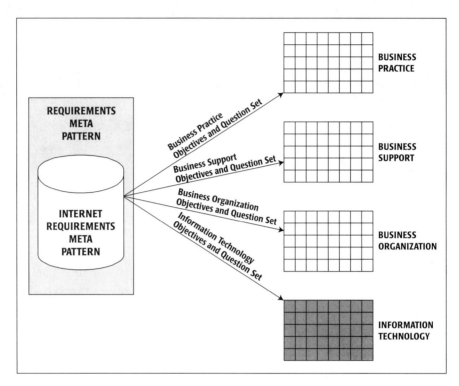

Figure B.1   The Information Technology Community

to satisfy a portion of what is to be implemented. Each allocation to another row or execution of a row requires a quality check.

There is no specific order required for the columns (which represent focus areas), although in this appendix they are presented in the order used in Chapter Three. Each is relevant to some type of requirement description, and it is up to the requirements engineer to determine which should be included or emphasized in any given situation (analytical versus transaction-stressed application). The columns are nonredundant, but there is an extractive relationship (that is, complementary extractions at similar levels of detail for that perspective may be represented by different illustrations or notations). Different focuses may move faster through a particular perspective than do other focuses (or communities). However, care must be taken to ensure that the advancement of one focus does not risk the integrity of another.

Some of the requirement cells have a built-in cross-check for other specific focus/perspective requirements. This facilitates the capture of association-type requirements.

The potential elicitation questions are for the purpose of initiating discussion. Answering all these questions will not guarantee that you have a complete requirements set. Further analysis of the information captured, along with gap analysis, assists in identifying additional questions to ask the requirement suppliers. *Keep in mind that an Internet product is a cross-enterprise product.* Therefore, the same questions may need to be asked of each business community and of each corporation (across business partners)—all those impacted by the Internet product. All of their requirements need to be satisfied by this single Internet solution, though they may be satisfied in different iterations. All questions need to be viewed from three points of view: first, the customers; second, the business partners; and third the corporate communities. This promotes a customer-centric business model while still protecting the interests of the company.

The requirements engineer working on a small or large project for a small, medium, or large company should ask specific questions (see the following list). The difference between these types of projects and companies will be the number of people involved as requirement suppliers. No matter what the size of the company, outside sources (for example, venture capitalists, business experts, e-mail) will provide some answers to these questions.

Before the Internet requirements pattern can work, it is important to understand some basic information. The following sample questions should be asked when evolving the idea to the concept. Answering these questions assists in developing the business case. Defining a high-quality business case facilitates the allocation process and the delegation of responsibility by the community categories. The question set should include the following:

1. *What is the business problem?* This begins to identify what is to be investigated.
2. *What is the business trying to do?* This identifies purpose.
3. *Where is the corporation going?* This identifies future growth in scope.[1]

---

1. Increase in scope (data, process, or network) before the implementation of a project is referred to as "scope creep." These additional requirements carry a higher price tag the later they are uncovered in the software development process.

4. *Is this product another means of reaching a customer?* This identifies whether nonelectronic means to accomplish the business case exists in theory (for "dot-com" start-ups) or within the corporation (for brick-and-mortar companies).

5. *How will an Internet solution help the corporation reach its business objectives?* This ties the Internet to the corporate strategy.

6. *What are the benefits to the business if it proceeds with the Internet product?* This identifies tangible and intangible benefits for proceeding. This is for cost justification and for setting the program priority.

7. *What will the effects be on the business if we do not proceed with the Internet product?* This identifies the business impact if the program does not proceed. This assists in setting the program priority.

8. *Who will be the business sponsor for this program initiation or iteration?* This defines the program organization.

9. *Who will be the key sponsor for each business community?* This identifies the executive steering committee for the program.

10. *Are there any time or budget constraints associated with this program?* This identifies any solution restrictions.

11. *What similar Internet products are available?* This provides an additional source of information that can be used to identify potential requirements.

12. *What makes this site competitive with the other Internet products?* Copycat models rarely work unless you have identified key competitive advantage differences.

13. *What things do you see as critical success factors for your job at this time?* This identifies the high-priority items requiring extensive testing.

14. *What things do you see as critical success factors for the Internet product at this time?* This identifies the high-priority items for the Internet product.

15. *What things do you see as critical success factors for the business partners?* This identifies the needs of each business partner.

16. *What things do you see as critical success factors for the customer base?* This identifies the needs of the customer.

The remainder of this appendix provides specific information on the objectives, possible specification formats, and possible elicitation questions for each requirement cell in the requirements pattern for the IT community. The Cell Template section briefly explains how the subsequent information is organized. The Introduction sections describe the perspectives, and the Cell sections provide information for specific cells.

Cell Template: Information Technology/Perspective/Focus

Objective

Defines the requirement-capturing objective of the requirement cell.

Priorities for This Perspective

Describes the main areas of activity to undertake for the perspective.

Delivered Work Products

Itemizes potential document names used by different organizations to issue specifications at the end of each perspective. Each focus area may have a specific model or document. These documents would be listed under the representative notation and would be considered part of the specification listed in the introductory section.

IEEE References

Itemizes IEEE standards from the *IEEE Software Engineering Standards Collection* that can be used as references for building the above perspective-level work products. The list provided is an initial set and not a comprehensive list. Many other standards[2] exist (including IEEE standards). As a generic reference, see Std 610, the *IEEE Standard Glossary of Software Engineering Terminology*.

Individual Requirement Contents

Provides a generic list of what is needed to describe the textual requirements. The information will become available as the requirement evolves through the perspectives. The generic list includes

- Identifier
- Name
- Description

---

2. Efforts are under way to coordinate the ISO/IEC 12207 standard as the umbrella standard for software life-cycle processes. For quality management, the ISO 9001 and ISO 9000-3 standards were selected. For project management, the chosen standard is the Project Management Institute's *Guide to the Project Management Body of Knowledge* (2000). All of this is explained in *Software Engineering Standards: A User's Road Map* (Moore 1998), published by the IEEE.

- Volumetrics (number of each item over what time period)
- Volumetric breakdown for periods of minimum, maximum (peak), and average usage (if available)
- Point A (master) name
- Point B (detail) name (if needed)
- Initiating or derived requirement identifier (association/relationship indicator)
- Qualifier (if applicable)
- Priority
- Cost
- Optionality
- Status
- Audit trail

Possible Specification Formats

Textual description: Describes the type of information to be captured to meet the requirement objective for the cell. All requirements should be documented in textual format.

Representative notation: Identifies popular representative models/diagrams used to illustrate the textual descriptions above. *No requirement should be illustrated in diagram form alone!*

Possible Elicitation Questions

Target: Summarizes the concept of the question set.

Samples: Provides examples of the kinds of questions that could be asked. This is not an exhaustive list. Add questions appropriate for the cell based on missed requirements identified during the quality gate reviews, defects found in previous iterations, or feedback from users of the Internet application.

Cell: Introduction—Information Technology/Planner

Objective

To define the scope of the investigation. This includes what is both in and out of scope clearly identifies the boundaries between divisions and organizations. Because of business partnerships, boundaries may cross corporate lines when business partners are involved in the end-to-end workflow. Questions that arise during this perspective of development are attempting to determine the initiating requirements set.

The generic work product from the planner perspective consists of a list of items for each of the focus areas. Each item has a description, volumetric information, and a priority. Each item is an initiating requirement that must have an audit trail.

It is the responsibility of the executive committee to validate the initiating requirements and the priorities set by the requirement suppliers. The executive committee needs to resolve any conflicts in definition of terms and priorities. The executive committee should include representatives of any business partners for requirements that affect those companies.

Priorities for This Perspective

- Concentrate on obtaining requirements within the cell. Relationships and details can come later.
- Concentrate on obtaining a single, clear, and concise definition for each list item. Details about each item can come later.
- Concentrate on getting consensus on priority by determining the tangible impact on the e-business. Volumetrics will help determine the tangible benefit.
- Leverage the use of a requirements management tool at this early stage.

Delivered Work Products

- Project charter
- Business case scope

IEEE References

- Std 1058: Software Project Management Plans
- Std 1490: Adoption of PMI Standard

Individual Requirement Contents

- Identifier
- Name
- Description
- Volumetrics (number of each item over what time period)
- Volumetric breakdown for periods of minimum, maximum (peak), and average usage (if available)
- Priority
- Status
- Audit trail

Cell: Information Technology/Planner/Who

Objective

To understand the categories of who will and should not interface with the Internet product.

Possible Specification Formats

Textual description for (permission = allowed or denied):

- Actors
- External entities
- Sources
- Recipients
- Organizational units
- Role lists
- Customers
- Applications

Supporting representative notation:

- Lists
- Scope diagram
- Context diagram

Possible Elicitation Questions

Target: Questions related to "who" (person, organization, or system) that will and will *not* require access to the solution.

Samples:

1. *What kind of clients will want to use this Internet product?* To identify the different client base.

2. *What systems (internal and external) will be interfacing with the Internet product?* To identify all integration points between systems.

3. *What departments (internal and external) will need to interface with the product?* To define potential users other than the client base.

4. *Who should not be using this product?* To help clarify the client base.[3]

5. *Does each "who" receive and/or provide information?* To define the purpose of the access.

6. *How would you describe the role and responsibility of each item on the list?* To clarify the responsibilities of each "who" on the list.

7. *Why is it needed?* To identify the business purpose.

8. *How important is each "who" to the success of the Internet product (or iteration)?* To clarify the requirement priority.

9. *What new role needs to be developed to support the e-business?* To determine the need for new Internet monitoring roles such as privacy and usage.

10. *How does one user type differ from another?* To identify any overlap in user definition.

11. *What role will the business partners play in the Internet product?* To define the gray area interfaces.

12. *Why?* To clarify the reasons why each "who" requirement is on the list.

13. *Approximately how many of each type of users are expected during the first month of operation through the first year?* To begin to estimate the size of the user base.

14. *Will there be a peak time for any of the customers when they will use the product?* To clarify the usage patterns.

15. *What else should I be asking about the "who" requirements?* To capture any additional, useful information.

---

3. Included in this list should be the actor "predator" to assist in anticipating any security requirements (as well as the level of security). Refer to Chapter Five.

Cell: Information Technology/Planner/What

Objective

To understand the scope of the information to investigate.

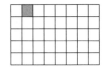

Possible Specification Formats

Textual description for:

- Things important to the business (for example, product and customer)
- Entity
- Entity class

Supporting representative notation:

- Lists

Possible Elicitation Questions

Target: Questions related to what "things" or "business objects" are important to the business.

Samples:

1. *What business objects are important to the business?* To identify what is within the scope of investigation.
2. *How would you describe the purpose of each business object?* To define each business object in business terms.
3. *How would other departments, people, and systems define the business object?* To obtain agreement on terminology from all business units.
4. *Why are these business objects important to the e-business?* To clarify the need for this information.
5. *What business objects are important to the business partners?* To identify additional business objects.
6. *What information is the client interested in finding on the site?* To identify additional business objects.
7. *What kind of customizable information will be provided to clients?* To identify customer information needs.
8. *What is missing from reports you are currently reviewing?* To identify any missing information.
9. *What personalization information will be provided to clients?* To identify enticing information to instigate further purchases (for example, buyer search and purchase analysis to suggest similar books available on *www.amazon.com*).

10. *How important is each "what" to the success of the Internet product (or itera-tion)?* To identify the requirement priority.

11. *How many of each item are expected the first month through first year of oper-ation?* To begin to capture volume information.

12. *Is there a time when this information will be accessed more than others?* To clarify the usage pattern of the information.

13. *What else should I be asking about the "what" requirements?* To capture any additional, useful information.

Cell: Information Technology/Planner/Where

Objective

To understand the scope of the connectivity to the business product.

Possible Specification Formats

Textual description for:
- Locations where the business operates
- List of customer locations where they may require access
- List of concentration areas for the business

Supporting representative notation:
- Lists
- Geographical map

Possible Elicitation Questions

Target: Questions related to "locations" in which the business operates.

Samples:

1. *Where does the business operate?* To identify the central point of operation for the business product.

2. *Where do the business partners operate?* To identify the locations of all busi-ness partners.

3. *Is there a geographic concentration of the client base?* To identify key geo-graphic areas.

4. *What forms of access will the client base be using?* To identify the different types of access that must be considered (for example, wireless).

5. *What forms of access will the business partners require?* To identify the different types of access that must be considered (for example, extranet).

6. *How important is each "where" to the success of the Internet product (or iteration)?* To identify the requirement priority.

7. *Where will the e-product work products be developed?* To determine the locations of all business communities that will be developing the work products.

8. *What number of hits is the site currently getting?* To determine the current traffic. This number can also be used to estimate the number of potential e-mails that will need to be addressed automatically or specifically (roughly 3 percent of the current traffic).

9. *What else should I be asking about the "where" requirements?* To capture any additional, useful information.

Cell: Information Technology/Planner/When

Objective

To understand the scope of the triggering events that initiate action by the business.

Possible Specification Formats

Textual description for:

- Events
- Triggers

Supporting representative notation:

- Lists
- Stimulus response table

Possible Elicitation Questions

Target: Questions related to triggers and responses to the triggers.

Samples:

1. *What conditions would cause a triggered action within the Internet product?* To define the reaction-type triggers.

2. *What events must the business support?* To identify all the processing essential to the business.

3. *How can the Internet product be purchased?* To begin to identify the standard triggers for the product.

4. *Can the product ordered be altered?* To begin to identify the standard triggers for the product.

5. *Can the product be cancelled?* To begin to identify the standard triggers for the product.

6. *What happens at the start of the day?* To begin to identify time-triggered events.

7. *What happens at the end of the day?* To identify time-triggered events.

8. *Any daily, weekly, monthly, quarterly, or yearly standard activities?* To identify time-triggered events.

9. *When is there a peak time when these events occur?* To identify seasonal trends (close of market, open of market, holidays).

10. *How important is each "when" to the success of the Internet product (or iteration)?* To identify the requirement priority.

11. *How often does this event occur?* To obtain volumetrics such as number, time period for minimum, average, and maximum volume.

12. *What would be the impact to the business if this event were not available in the e-business product?* To identify any backup procedures if this event were not available.

13. *How often does each business event occur (low, medium, high)?* To give the information technician an idea of transaction volume.

14. *Is the business event cyclical?* To identify whether the event is time dependent.

15. *What else should I be asking about the "when" requirements?* To capture any additional, useful information.

Cell: Information Technology/Planner/Why

Objective

To understand the scope of the business rules and policies that define the business strategy and culture.

Possible Specification Formats

Textual description:

- Business policies
- Business practices
- Regulatory restrictions (for example, state, national, and international tax laws)

Supporting representative notation:

• Lists

Possible Elicitation Questions

Target: Questions related to constraints that must be enforced to protect the integrity of the corporation.

Samples:

1. *What state, national, and international laws affect buying and selling the product?* To begin to identify the different rules that may constrain the processing of product.
2. *What corporate policies will the Internet product affect?* To identify the internal business rules that may be affected with the potential change in culture.
3. *What corporate policies of business partners potentially conflict with ours?* To identify potential risks with the business partnership.
4. *What constraints must stay in effect?* This identifies any restrictions in business organization, procedure, or policy that must remain in effect.
5. *How important is each "why" to the success of the Internet product (or iteration)?* To identify the requirement priority.
6. *Do you want to impose any limits on the customer or business partner in using the Internet product?* To identify new rules that must be developed in order to protect the liability of the business. (For example, transferring only a specific amount of money between accounts without further authorization.)
7. *What would be the effect on the customer or business partner if one of these rules were broken?* To identify the potential risk to the company from outside the corporate boundaries.
8. *What would be the effect if the business policy were broken?* To identify the repercussions (if any) of the lack of adherence to the business policy.
9. *Who else should be involved in supplying requirements about business rules, policies, and procedures?* To uncover knowledge experts such as legal and marketing.
10. *What rules need to be enforced to maintain profitability?* To identify policies that will limit options for users or trigger other events when marketing conditions occur.
11. *What legal rules need to be enforced to protect the corporation?* To identify legal policies that need to be enforced.

12. *What policies need to be changed to meet the Internet objectives?* To identify any potential outdated business rules.

13. *What would be the effect on the business if one of these rules were broken?* To clarify the risk of not satisfying the requirement.

14. *What else should I be asking about the "why" requirements?* To capture any additional, useful information.

Cell: Information Technology/Planner /How

Objective

To understand the scope of the business functionality to investigate.

Possible Specification Formats

Textual description for:

- Processes the business performs (for example, billing and inventory management)

Supporting representative notation:

- Lists
- Subject-level diagram

Possible Elicitation Questions

Target: Questions related to the business processes that are important to the business.

Samples:

1. *What business functions need to be performed to enable the Internet product?* To identify key business functions.

2. *What is the purpose of each of these functions?* To describe each function.

3. *What does the client want to do with the site?* To identify specific functions that customers will look for at the site.

4. *What functions do competitors have that must also be included?* To identify additional functions.

5. *What functions will be performed by the business partners?* To identify additional functions even if they will be developed by the business partners.

6. *How will clients find the information they are looking for?* To clarify the need for types of search (within the site, spiders, ferrets, collaborative searches).

7. *Which functions currently exist in the corporation?* To identify current versus new business functions, especially functions or systems that need to be integrated into the Internet system.

8. *How must these functions change to meet the Internet objectives?* To begin to understand what needs to be changed.

9. *How important is each "how" to the success of the Internet product (or iteration)?* To identify the requirement priority.

10. *What problem does the function not tackle?* To identify new processes.

11. *What key questions would you like the Internet-based application to answer?* To define key functionality requirements.

12. *What else should I be asking about the "how" requirements?* To capture any additional, useful information.

Cell: Information Technology/Planner/Product Constraints

Objective

To understand the perceived expectations of the Internet product capabilities.

Possible Specification Formats

Textual description for:

- Product restrictions (for example, performance, security, maintainability, reliability)
- Operation scenarios (for example, batch processing windows)

Supporting representative notation:

- Lists

Possible Elicitation Questions

Target: Questions related to product expectations that will constrain design decisions.

Samples:

1. *What expectations does management have concerning the Internet product?* To identify market opportunity limitations.

2. *What expectations will users of the Internet product have?* To identify a list of quality of service requirements.
3. *What expectations will the business partners have for the Internet relationship?* To define the expectations of processing between business partners.
4. *What constraints do the business partners apply to the design of this product?* To identify any restrictions that affect design choices.
5. *What is the maximum number of clicks for accomplishing a task that the client will accept before becoming annoyed?* To define usability requirements.
6. *How quickly do the business partners need to respond to a request?* To define performance expectations.
7. *What level of privacy is needed by the corporation, business partners, and customers?* To identify security issues related to user confidence.
8. *How can I clarify each expectation?* To describe each product constraint.
9. *How important is each "product constraint" to the success of the Internet product (or iteration)?* To identify the requirement priority.
10. *What else should I be asking about the "product constraints" requirements?* To capture any additional, useful information.

Cell: Information Technology/Planner/Project Constraints

Objective

To understand the restrictions associated with developing the solution.

Possible Specification Formats

Textual description for:
- Constraints applied to the project (staff, cost, working location)
- Assumptions
- Critical success factors
- Potential risks
- Dependencies (on other projects)

Supporting representative notation:
- Lists

Possible Elicitation Questions

Target: Questions related to limits applied to the program execution.

Samples:

1. *Who will be the business sponsor for this project iteration?* To define the project organization.

2. *How should status be reported?* To define the process for keeping management informed.

3. *At what points should management be alerted to changes in scope, resources, budget, and schedule?* To define the conditions that warrant immediate notification.

4. *Are there any budgetary constraints that need to be applied to the development of the Internet product/iteration?* To identify key project constraints.

5. *Are there any staffing limitations?* To identify resource constraints.

6. *Who will develop the Internet product?* To define the responsibilities of developing the Internet solution (could be outsourced, divided among business partners, or a combination).

7. *Where will the development occur?* To determine the development location to begin setting up the development environment.

8. *What is the delivery expectation of management for this iteration?* To define delivery dates.

9. *Why are these constraints applied to the project?* To clarify the need for each constraint.

10. *What would be the risk if each constraint were not upheld?* To begin developing the critical success factors and dependencies for the project.

11. *How can these risks be avoided?* To begin the development of the countermeasures for each potential risk.

12. *How important is each project constraint to the success of the Internet product (or iteration)?* To identify the requirement priority.

13. *Who are the knowledge experts for each community (subcommunity)?* To identify key resources to assist with supplying or clarifying requirements.

14. *What is the availability of these knowledge experts?* To plan around the knowledge experts' availability and to determine the level of management support for the project.

15. *What else should I be asking about the project constraints requirements?* To capture any additional, useful information.

Cell: Introduction: Information Technology/Owner

Objective

To define how all the business communities view the scope and to identify the relationship between the things in and out of scope defined in the previous perspective. The view and questions are independent of any technological bias.

Questions are attempting to understand what currently exists,[4] the perception of the current workflow, and the new requirements. In doing so, the relationships between the items on the lists from the previous perspective are documented. Some of the questions across focus areas will seem to be identical. The purpose is to ask the same question with a different focus to see whether one receives a consistent answer. In most cases, additional requirements will be captured.

The generic work product from the owner perspective consists of matrices that tie together items within the focus area and items in other areas. Each relationship has a description, volumetric information, and a priority. Each relationship is a derived requirement based on the initiating requirement. These derived requirements must have an audit trail.

It is the responsibility of the executive committee to validate these relationship requirements and priorities set by the requirement suppliers. The executive committee needs to resolve any conflicts in definition of relationship terms and priorities. The executive committee should include representatives of any business partners for requirements that affect those companies.

Priorities for This Perspective

- Concentrate on determining the relationships within the cell first.
- Concentrate on determining the relationships with other focus areas within the community second.
- Concentrate on determining the relationships across communities last.

---

4. Project after project I have seen the same mistake made by business representatives. Whether in writing, e-mail, or verbal conversation, the business representative always begins with "This is what I want." This is very important information; however, it should come after a brief explanation of what, how, when, and where it works today. It is very important to begin with what is known. This refers to understanding the current workflow and manipulation of information. It is impossible for information technologists to build a new system until they have an understanding of what currently exists. This includes interfaces outside the scope of investigation. Therefore, refrain from addressing what is wanted until information technology understands what already exists.

- Label and describe the dependencies between requirements. Worry about the details of the relationship later.
- Which cell the cross-cell relationship is stored in is not as important as capturing the relationship.
- Use the requirements management or case tool to associate the relationship to the initiating requirements.

Delivered Work Products

- Project plan
- High-level requirements specification
- Business model
- Test strategy

IEEE References

- Std 730: Software Quality Assurance Plans/Planning
- Std 828: Software Configuration Management Plans
- Std 830: Software Requirement Specification
- Std 1042: Guide to Software Configuration Plans
- Std 1058: Software Project Management Plans
- Std 1059: Software Verification and Validation Plans
- Std 1233: Developing System Requirements
- Std 1320: Conceptual Modeling Language (IDEFIX)
- Std 1362: System Definition—Concept of Operation

Individual Requirement Contents

- Identifier
- Relationship name
- Description of the relationship
- Volumetrics (number of each item over what time period)
- Volumetric breakdown for periods of minimum, maximum (peak), and average usage (if available)
- Point A (master) name
- Point B (detail) name (if needed)
- Qualifier
- Priority
- Status
- Audit trail

Cell: Information Technology/Owner/Who

Objective
To understand the relationship between the interfaces.

Possible Specification Formats
Textual description for:
- Role responsibilities
- User characteristics
- User class
- High-level use case

Supporting representative notation:
- High-level use case diagram
- Context diagram
- Organization chart
- Role responsibility matrix

Possible Elicitation Questions
Target: Questions related to the relationship between each actor and interface other initiating requirements.

Samples:
1. *What is needed to do each user's job?* To remind designers of the need for back-office access.
2. *What does each internal user type need to do his or her job?* To identify any needs as far as information and functionality.
3. *Which users initiate which events?* To identify the correlation between events and user type.
4. *What information is each user looking for?* To identify the correlation between information and users.
5. *What functions should each user be allowed to perform?* To correlate users and processing.
6. *What restrictions need to be applied to each user type?* To correlate users and business policies.
7. *What are the risks if the user type does not have access to the functionality or information requested?* To identify potential points of risk.
8. *What would happen if the user type does not have connectivity to the e-business for one to two days, one to two weeks?* To identify the potential impacts of network outages.

Cell: Information Technology/Owner/What

Objective

To understand the cardinality between the business objects
and other requirements.

Possible Specification Formats

Textual description for:

- Relationship
- Cardinality
- Object instances

Supporting representative notation:

- Entity relationship diagram
- Conceptual class diagram

Possible Elicitation Questions

Target: Questions relating to the relationship between business objects.

Samples:

1. *What is the relationship of each business object to other business objects?* To define the impact of one business object on another.
2. *What is the cardinality between the relationships?* To define the type of the relationship (optionality and number).
3. *How would you define the relationship between the entities?* To define the business rule that ties the entities together.
4. *Is there different processing between a delete and a cancel of a business object?* To clarify different states and conditions.
5. *What other status changes of the business object do you need to know about?* To identify any changes in the state of the business object.
6. *What conditions change the state of the business object?* To identify the processing or triggers that affect the change in status of the object.
7. *What expectations do the users, by user types, have as far as performance, security, or usability?* To identify the correlation of user and quality of service requirements.
8. *Does one user type need input from another user type at any point?* To clarify the interaction between user types.

9. *If so, why?* To identify the reason and the impact on other requirements (especially those not captured).

10. *What information already exists within other corporate applications?* To identify whether anything needs to be changed.

11. *What is the condition of this existing information?* To identify any data that needs to be cleansed.

12. *Who owns this data?* To identify whom else to consult about the availability and quality of the data.

13. *Does the information need to change to support the e-business?* To identify the impact on existing data.

14. *What causes the business object to be created, updated, or deleted?* To define the correlation between events and information.

15. *What cascading effect does a change to one object's state have on other objects?* To define the referential integrity guidelines.

16. *What information must be protected from which user types at all costs?* To identify any security issues.

17. *Which information can be transmitted through wireless means?* To identify any security issues.

Cell: Information Technology/Owner/Where

Objective

To understand the relationships between the locations and what can be done from each location.

Possible Specification Formats

Textual description for:

- Nodes

Supporting representative notation:

- Logistics network

Possible Elicitation Questions

Target: Questions related to the connections between nodes and with other requirements.

Samples:

1. *Who needs access to the information and functionality?* To identify communication locations.

2. *How many users need access at each location?* To identify all possible users of the software system.

3. *What type of equipment is currently available?* To define what is currently available that would affect a local area network.

4. *What type of communication is currently available?* To identify any usable communication vehicle and any required enhancements to the telecommunication environment.

5. *How long is the current response time?* To identify any need to increase network communication line speed.

6. *Who should be prevented access through each connection type?* To begin to develop security requirements.

7. *What functions can each access type perform?* To clarify what can be done via the Internet and wireless versus only through internal networks.

8. *What is the number of concurrent users?* To build into the network and database design capacity requirements.

9. *What information can each access type access?* To clarify what can be transmitted (particularly wireless).

Cell: Information Technology/Owner/When

Objective

To understand the order and impact of each event.

Possible Specification Formats

Textual description for:
- Preconditions
- Postconditions
- Flow of events
- Dependencies
- Inference

Supporting representative notation:
- Event-response list
- Stimulus/response sequence

- Activity sequence
- Event-correspondence diagram
- Activity diagram
- Collaboration diagram
- State transition diagram
- Entity life history

Possible Elicitation Questions

Target: Questions related to the relationships between triggering events and other requirements.

Samples:

1. *Is there any order to the list of events?* To uncover the dependencies of events.
2. *Who triggers each event?* To uncover the relationships between "who" and "when" requirements.
3. *How does the event get triggered?* To determine what information is received to initiate the event.
4. *Who gets the response from the event?* To determine the relationships between "who" and "when" requirements.
5. *What is the response from the event?* To determine the information output from the event.
6. *Are there any geographic dependencies to the events?* To identify any regional focus to the events.
7. *Why would each "who" interact with the Internet product?* To begin to identify the standard triggers for the product.
8. *Does this event conflict with any business policies?* To identify the relationships between "when" and "why" requirements.
9. *Does this event occur because of any business policies?* To identify the relationships between "when" and "why" requirements.
10. *What is the performance expectation for this event?* To identify the relationships between "when" and quality of service requirements.
11. *Who should not be triggering this event?* To identify the security relationships.
12. *What would be the risk to the business if such a user triggered this event?* To identify countermeasure points to protect the corporation.
13. *What stimulates the business event?* To identify the triggers for the event.
14. *What is the reaction to each business event?* To identify the action to take place for each event.

15. *What is the response to each business event?* To identify the output information or function from each event.

16. *Who triggers the business event?* To identify the source department, system, or person.

17. *Who is the recipient of the business event?* To identify the receiver of the event (department, system, or person).

18. *Is there a relationship between business events?* To identify the workflow dependencies.

Cell: Information Technology/Owner/Why

Objective

To understand the impact of the policies.

Possible Specification Formats

Textual description for:

• Rule-impacted items

Supporting representative notation:

• Rule dependency matrix
• Rule impact analysis matrix

Possible Elicitation Questions

Target: Questions related to the impact a rule has on other scope items.

Samples:

1. *How does each business policy affect each user type?* To identify the relationship between each "who" and "why" requirement.

2. *How does each business policy affect each business object?* To identify the relationship between each "what" and "why" requirement.

3. *How does each business policy affect each business object relationship?* To identify the relationship between "why" requirements and "what" relationship requirements.

4. *How does each business policy affect each business event?* To identify the relationship between each "when" and "why" requirement.

5. *How does each business policy affect each business function?* To identify the relationship between each "why" and "how" requirement.

6. *What information is needed to enforce the business rule?* To identify the correlation between information and the rule.

7. *What functions need to be performed to enforce the adherence to the business rule?* To identify the correlation between the rule and function.

8. *Is the rule geographically dependent?* To identify the extent or regionality of the rule.

9. *Is the rule dependent on any other rule?* To identify the relationship between rules.

10. *Does the satisfaction of this rule affect any other rule?* To identify the relationship between rules.

Cell: Information Technology/Owner/How

Objective

To understand the business and to understand the impact it has on the scope.

Possible Specification Formats

Textual description for:
- Product functions
- Product features
- Collaboration

Supporting representative notation:
- Subject-level diagram (DFD)
- Functional decomposition
- Functional-entity matrix
- Functional-responsibility matrix

Possible Elicitation Questions

Target: Questions related to how the function currently works, any business policies that cause constraints between the processes, and the input-output of each process.

Samples:

1. *In what one, two, or three areas would failure to perform hurt the e-product or the corporation the most?* To identify the high-priority items requiring extensive testing.

2. *Whom would you notify if a failure occurs?* To identify possible recipients of information.

3. *Where would you hate to see something go wrong?* To identify the high-priority items requiring extensive testing.

4. *If you were isolated from the business for two weeks, with no communication at all, what would you most want to know about the e-business when you return?* To identify the high-priority items requiring extensive testing.

5. *What information will provide you with the knowledge to answer those questions?* To define processes to calculate key information.

6. *Are there any current bottlenecks and issues?* To identify possible process improvement requirements.

7. *What are your current responsibilities?* To identify the knowledge base and possible missing functionality.

8. *How would you like it to work?* To identify possible process improvements.

9. *What information is needed for that process?* To define the required input.

10. *What is the output of that process?* To define the required output information.

11. *Where does the output go and what is done with it?* To follow the data path and identify output. To identify new processes or whether the process is no longer required.

12. *What order must the processes follow?* To identify process dependencies.

13. *Are there any support-type processes that enable the business to run?* To identify any missed housekeeping processes like adding, deleting, or updating a client.

14. *Who has authority to trigger the process?* To identify security access privileges.

15. *Who can best describe the process?* To identify the business knowledge expert.

16. *Does the process differ by geographic area?* To identify the restrictions by location.

17. *Does the process differ by user type?* To identify the restrictions by user.

18. *Are there any legal issues in performing this process or not performing this process?* To define the link to legal business rules.

Cell: Information Technology/Owner/Product Constraints

Objective

To determine the impact any restrictions may have on other scope items.

Possible Specification Formats

Textual description for:

- A list of other requirements this requirement impacts

Supporting representative notation:

- Impact analysis matrix

Possible Elicitation Questions

Target: Questions related to specifics of the restriction on the scope items.

Samples:

1. *What is the impact to existing applications?* To clarify the need for integrating with existing applications.
2. *What are the performance expectations by user type for each event?* To clarify performance requirements.
3. *What level of security does each user type need for each event?* To clarify security needs.
4. *What information needs to be provided on the different devices that can be used?* To define the priority of information that has to be displayed on handheld devices or larger monitors.
5. *If all the information is displayed, will a requirement to keep the number of clicks below the maximum tolerated by users still be met?* To identify the user click tolerance.
6. *What would the risk be if the number of clicks needed for each event increased?* To clarify the impact of usability and events.

Cell: Information Technology/Owner/Project Constraints

Objective

To understand the impact the constraint will have on other focus areas and their requirements.

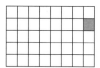

Possible Specification Formats

Textual description for:

- Quantity and qualification of impact

Supporting representative notation:

- Resource allocation matrix
- Budgetary allocation matrix
- Risk impact matrix

Possible Elicitation Questions

Target: Questions referring to the allocation of resources and impacts on other requirements.

Samples:

1. *What would be the cost to implement each requirement?* To determine any conflict between costs and requirement priority.
2. *How does the cost to implement the requirement affect the software return on investment?* To determine whether the requirement is worth implementing in this iteration.
3. *How would delays in development affect other community work products?* To determine implementation impacts on the entire requirements set.
4. *How would the nonsatisfaction of each requirement impact other community work products?* To determine the relationship between work products.
5. *What would be the impact to the corporation if the development could not be staffed?* To determine the impact of software delay.
6. *What flexibility in hiring is available to meet the market delivery date?* To identify the possibility for outsourcing some of the work in order to meet the delivery date and to determine how hard and fast the delivery date is when cost is applied to the equation.

Cell: Introduction: Information Technology/Designer

Objective

To define the essential details of the requirements to run the business. This includes the definitions of the individual requirements and the details that enable the relationships between the requirements. This is still technology independent.

The generic work product from the designer perspective consists of details that enable the successful completion of the requirement description. All the details are additional derived requirements that must also be satisfied. Each of these requirement details has its own priority. Each of these details must be associated to a requirement defined at the owner level. These derived requirements must have an audit trail.

Each requirement may have multiple requirement details. Each requirement detail is still managed as a separate requirement and not managed within the associated requirement.

A requirement detail may be associated with multiple requirements. The requirement detail should be associated with an identifier link and *not* repeated. If the qualification differs between the multiple requirements, that should be noted with the association identifier.

In both of the above scenarios, the requirement is handled as a relationship requirement described in the owner perspective. The association (and the qualifier, if required) is managed as a separate supporting-type requirement.

It is the responsibility of the executive committee to validate these relationship requirements defined by the requirement suppliers. The executive committee needs to resolve any conflicts in the detail and the priorities. The executive committee should include representatives of any business partners for requirements that affect those companies. Requirement users must validate the requirements for feasibility and understanding of the requirements set.

Priorities for This Perspective

- Complete each requirement (initial and derived) with details.
- Define the means of validating each requirement (including relationships).
- Ensure that each cell and each relationship between cells have been discussed.
- Evaluate dependencies and priorities to segment requirements into iterations.
- Clarify the feasibility (and the cost) of satisfying each requirement.

Delivered Work Products

- Test plan
- Business model
- Logical architecture

IEEE References

- Std 829: Software Test Documentation
- Std 1012: Software Verification and Validation
- Std 1420: Software Reuse (Data)
- Std 1430: Software Reuse (Libraries)

Individual Requirement Contents

- Identifier
- Detail name
- Description of the detail
- Volumetrics (number of each item over what time period) *if different from initiating requirement*
- Volumetric breakdown for periods of minimum, maximum (peak), and average usage *if different from initiating requirement*
- Initiating or derived requirement identifier
- Qualifier (if applicable)
- Priority
- Optionality
- Status
- Audit trail

Cell: Information Technology/Designer/Who

Objective

To understand the specific needs of each interface.

Possible Specification Formats

Textual description for:

- Responsibility procedures

Supporting representative notation:

- Responsibility-data matrix
- Responsibility-process matrix
- User-location matrix

Possible Elicitation Questions

Target: Questions related to the interface specifics of each external user, organization, and system.

Samples:

1. *How will the e-business know that the user is who he says he is?* To identify additional security information at the user level.

2. *What information does the user need to provide to perform a function?* To identify the input from the user.

3. *At what point in the process is the information needed?* To minimize the need to carry information throughout the process.

4. *What other processing requests the same information from the user?* To minimize the need to enter the same information multiple times.

5. *What do you want to know about the user for marketing purposes?* To identify the information to request from the user.

6. *What information about the user do you need to personalize the user's experience?* To identify the information to facilitate client customization.

7. *What specific limits do you need to apply to each user?* To identify the type of restrictions that will require storage and processing checks. These may include maximum orders, maximum order amount, the type of access, and the type of functions.

8. *How do you add, alter, change, review, and monitor the user?* To identify the specific housekeeping for each user.

9. *What will be the acceptance test criteria?* To identify how to adequately test the software.

Cell: Information Technology/Designer/What

Objective

To determine the details of each item of interest to the business.

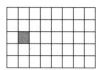

Possible Specification Formats

Textual description for:

- Data item details
- Attributes details
- Instance details

Supporting representative notation:

- Logical data model
- Logical class diagram
- Logical object diagram
- CRUDL matrix

Possible Elicitation Questions

Target: Questions relating to the details of each entity/class/object.

Samples:

1. *Where does it come from?* To identify the source of the information.
2. *Where does it go?* To identify the receiver (process) of the information.
3. *How is this information used?* To identify how the information is manipulated.
4. *Who views this information?* To identify the receiver (department and/or person) of the information.
5. *What information requires quick access and manipulation?* To identify key information and processing requiring quick response times.
6. *What is the range of possible values for a specific field?* To identify all the editing criteria.
7. *What information is needed about each business object?* To identify all the attributes that define the business object.
8. *What other information would be nice to know about each business object?* To identify optional information.
9. *How is the housekeeping on each business object performed?* To identify the different means of maintaining the business object.

10. *In what format should each object detail be displayed?* To identify data attribute formats.

11. *How long should this information be kept?* To determine the amount of history needed.

12. *In what level of detail is this history needed?* To determine whether summarization is required.

13. *How soon is the history needed for analysis?* To determine the archival method options.

14. *When is this information needed?* To determine the supply strategy of the information.

15. *Who determines the amount of history kept?* To determine whether this is customizable by users.

16. *What actions can be performed on each class detail?* To identify the methods associated at the data attribute level.

17. *If the information contents change on this data attribute, what else should be triggered?* To identify the method details associated with the data attribute.

18. *Who can see, change, add, or delete the contents of the data attribute?* To identify the security level of the data attribute.

19. *Are there instances when this information should not be transferred?* To identify whether there are geographic or device restrictions to transmitting the data attribute contents.

20. *How many of the data attribute instances can be transmitted at one time?* To identify the maximum of the lists displayed by device type or function.

21. *Can the number of instances vary by the specific user?* To determine whether this is a customizable variable.

22. *Is the information heavily accessed?* To build design performance considerations into the database.

23. *Describe in detail the specific information format.* To obtain a clear and full understanding of information needs and views.

24. *How many instances of the business object exist (low, medium, high averages)?* To identify the average number of instances of each business object. This may be divided by time scale. For example, the number of instances may be higher at the end of the month than at the beginning.

25. *What are the average instances between business objects?* To identify the average number of each relationship between business objects.

26. *What do you do with this information?* To identify any calculations that can be stored.

27. *Are there peak times that this information is accessed?* To identify patterns in retrieving the information.
28. *What will be the acceptance test criteria?* To identify how to adequately test the software.
29. *How often is it or should it be refreshed?* To identify how often the information must be updated.
30. *How would you want to see or view it?* To identify the format in which the information should be displayed and printed.
31. *How long must this information be available?* To identify history requirements.
32. *Must history information be immediately accessed?* To identify retrieval options.
33. *Are there levels of restricted access to any information?* To identify security levels.
34. *Who can validate the information during a test?* To identify the business knowledge expert.

Cell: Information Technology/Designer/Where

Objective
To determine capacity needs.

Possible Specification Formats
Textual description for:
- Network configuration
- Topology

Supporting representative notation:
- Process-location association matrix
- Data-location association matrix
- User-location association matrix

Possible Elicitation Questions
Target: Questions related to volumetric information (amounts and time periods).

Samples:
1. *How much information would be retrieved by each location for each business event?* To identify the amount of data transferred on the communication link.
2. *How much information is uploaded by each location for each business event?* To identify the amount of data transferred on the communication link.

3. *What type of information is transferred?* To identify graphical or textual information transmitted on the communication link.

4. *How often does this happen (low, medium, high estimates)?* To determine traffic loads.

5. *Is there a peak time this event occurs?* To determine traffic patterns on the network.

6. *By what time must the download information be available?* To determine traffic patterns.

7. *How often must the information be uploaded?* To identify traffic patterns on the network.

8. *Does any of this information vary by device type?* To prepare for different devices. Wireless may be handled differently than direct connection.

9. *Does any of this information vary by user and device type?* To determine whether this is a user-specific, customizable variable.

10. *What is the rule when a customized variable conflicts based on user, function, location, and device?* To determine how to resolve any conflicts in customizable information.

11. *What is the availability time frame at each location?* To determine when backups can be initiated.

12. *When is the expected peak for each user type, event, and location?* To determine capacity requirements.

13. *What would be the expected performance for those peak periods?* To determine the flexibility of performance parameters.

14. *What would be the priority by geographic location and processing?* To determine the priority between customer and internal and business partner requests when conflicts or overloads occur.

15. *What will be the acceptance test criteria?* To identify how to adequately test the software.

Cell: Information Technology/Designer/When

Objective

To understand the details of the action for the event.

Possible Specification Formats

Textual description for:

- Event details

Supporting representative notation:

- Logical activity diagram
- Logical sequence diagram
- Event correspondence diagram
- Logical state-transition diagram

Possible Elicitation Questions

Target: Questions related to volumetrics and processing.

Samples:

1. *What conditions must be satisfied in order for this event to occur?* To define the dependencies for the event execution.
2. *What happens if one of these conditions is not met?* To define any alternate means of executing the event.
3. *What actions take place when the event is triggered?* To define the process associated with the event.
4. *Are there any exceptions to the actions?* To define alternate processing if an exception occurs.
5. *What is done when an exception occurs?* To define the process for an alternate action.
6. *What is the response from the event?* To clarify the processing.
7. *What information is passed with the response?* To clarify the information needs.
8. *Does the activity the event initiates differ by specific users?* To identify customization of the event by users?
9. *What information is updated based on the event?* To identify the information detail of the processing.
10. *What are the interdependencies, if any, with parallel events?* To define the triggering sequence and information sharing between events.
11. *What will be the acceptance test criteria?* To identify how to adequately test the software.

Cell: Information Technology/Designer/Why

Objective:

To understand the specific changes in policy and procedures.

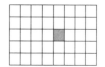

Possible Specification Formats

Textual description for:
- Policy impact
- Procedure impact

Supporting representative notation:
- Policy manual
- Procedure manual

Possible Elicitation Questions

Target: Questions related to the modification of business policies.

Samples:

1. *How will you monitor adherence to the business policy?* To define monitoring facilities.
2. *What should occur if the policy is broken?* To define a process associated with the business rule.
3. *What information is needed to monitor the business policy execution?* To define the data attributes to monitor.
4. *Does adherence to the business policy vary by customer?* To identify whether this is a customizable rule.
5. *Who enforces adherence to the rule?* To define responsibility between business partners.
6. *Are there times when the business rule can be broken with no action required?* To define alternate satisfaction of the rule.
7. *Are there degrees to which the rule can be broken?* To define variables to the rule.
8. *What is the range of that degree?* To determine how to validate (yellow flag or red flag an issue).
9. *When do you want to be notified that the rule may potentially be broken?* To determine the process for warning signs.
10. *What will be the acceptance test criteria?* To identify how to adequately test the software.

Cell: Information Technology/Designer/How

Objective

To understand the detailed workflow.

Possible Specification Formats

Textual description for:

- Process details
- Function details
- Method details
- Operation details

Supporting representative notation:

- Data flow diagram
- Collaboration diagram
- Quality function deployment (QFD)
- Decomposition diagram

Possible Elicitation Questions

Target: Questions related to the desired workflow (look, feel, and action).

Samples:

1. *Describe the current workflow.* To determine how the current process works.
2. *What would you like changed in the current workflow?* To identify the new requirements.
3. *What is impeding that change?* To determine any technological, business organization, policy, and procedure issues that are preventing the change.
4. *How is a specific formula calculated?* To document the inner workings of each calculation.
5. *Describe in detail how a specific process works.* To obtain a clear and full understanding of functionality.
6. *What conditions would alter the work process?* To obtain the details of an alternate process.
7. *What information needs to be viewed together?* To define the window or screen design.
8. *What combination of information and processing requires special access privileges?* To identify special access requirements.

9. *During what processes is this information reusable?* To identify any reusable components (specifically windows and screens) of the workflow.

10. *How would you like to access the information and function?* To identify how to display the information (report, screen, window design).

11. *Any exceptions to the normal workflow?* To identify any additional processing to support overrides to the existing functionality.

12. *How does the process work today?* To document the current workflow.

13. *Why does it work that way?* To identify any processing constraints.

14. *When is this process reusable?* To define reusable components to the system.

15. *Can the process vary by user?* To define customization.

16. *Is this process always performed?* To define optionality of the process.

17. *What information is captured or changed from this process?* To clarify, from a data attribute point of view, what information is manipulated.

18. *Are all users involved in this process?* To define customization or specialty of the process.

19. *How often is the calculated result needed?* To identify the need to store derived information.

20. *How often can a calculated result change?* To identify the need to recalculate any information.

21. *Provide details of existing hardware and system software.* To obtain a clear and full understanding of system interfaces.

22. *What error, informational, and help messages would you like to see?* To document any messages that the end user must be made aware of.

23. *Who can validate that the process works correctly?* To identify the business knowledge expert.

24. *How would you like messages worded?* To clarify any error, information, and help message wording.

25. *What will be the acceptance test criteria?* To identify how to adequately test the software.

Cell: Information Technology/Designer/Product Constraints

Objective

To understand the application impact.

Possible Specification Formats

Textual description for:

- Current system environment limitations
- Available bandwidth, storage, memory, and so on

Supporting representative notation:

- Matrices

Possible Elicitation Questions

Target: Questions related to the application architecture.

Samples:

1. *What kinds of system access do end users currently have?* To identify how end users will get to the software system. This is especially important for end users outside of the company. They may require special Internet access.

2. *What system software and hardware configurations will end users be using?* To identify all hardware and system software that must be supported by the new software system.

3. *Is the transferred information downloaded into a personal computer software package?* To identify any special requirements to download directly into existing software (for example, Microsoft Excel).

4. *What personal computer software must the software system interface with?* To identify any special requirements to interface with existing software (for example, Microsoft Excel).

5. *How will users access the system?* To identify any new restrictions on how end users will get to the software system.

6. *What users will require access?* To set up all user access privileges to the systems.

7. *Does one user type have priority over another?* To determine load balancing.

8. *Does one function have priority over another?* To determine load balancing.

9. *What variables can change priority in processing?* To determine conditions that could change a priority of one transaction over another.

10. *What degree of security is required for each user—from what device, from which location, for what processing, and of what information?* To clarify security details.

11. *What would be the restore sequence in case of a system error?* To understand the details of recovery procedures.

12. *What will be the acceptance test criteria?* To identify how to adequately test the software.

Cell: Information Technology/Designer/Project Constraints

Objective

To understand the impact of issues, risks, and changes to the plan.

Possible Specification Formats

Textual description for:

- Project status (time, cost)
- Issue-tracking log
- Impact analysis
- Plan adjustment
- Next phase detail schedule

Supporting representative notation:

- Gantt chart

Possible Elicitation Questions

Target: Questions related to the progress of the project.

Samples:

1. *What issues are preventing the progress of the project?* To identify roadblocks.

2. *How does each issue affect the work products?* To identify the degree of impact.

3. *How can the issue be resolved?* To define multiple means of resolving the issue.

4. *Does the effect on the work products trigger any project tolerance criteria?* To determine whether alternate action is required, including escalation to higher management.

5. *Is the scope of the project affected?* To determine the degree of impact.

6. *What is the status of all work products?* To determine whether the plan is on target.

7. *Does the status impact any other work products?* To determine the impact of the status on the final delivery.

8. *Is any other requirement at risk if the particular requirement being discussed is not satisfied?* To determine the cascading effect on the requirements set.

9. *What adjustments need to be made to the project plan and the program plan?* To identify any modifications to the plan of action (including resources, schedule, or cost).

10. *Are all project/program risks being avoided?* To determine whether the countermeasures are active.

11. *What can be done to facilitate the velocity of development of the work products?* To identify any time-saving modifications to the plan.

Cell: Introduction: Information Technology/Builder

Objective

To define the technological solution to the business problem/ opportunity. This is the transition between the logical business point of view and the physical implementation. Therefore, requirements that enable the building of the solution are captured.

Requirements captured from this perspective pertain to providing the tools to build the product. The requirements are contained in the specific work products as a lead into the definition of the different architectures. The number of questions decreases. However, additional requirements that should have been captured during previous perspectives will emerge. These requirements need to be captured in the same detail as all other requirements in order to determine the impact the newly uncovered requirements have on other requirements (including project schedule).

The generic work product from the builder perspective consists of details to build the product based on the requirements approved in the designer perspective. All requirements are derived requirements that must be satisfied in order to build the product. Each of these requirements has its own priority, is defined to satisfy the quality characteristics, and has an audit trail. Each is associated to a designer-level requirement. These requirements are also dependent on nonfunctional requirements (product and project constraints) and require association requirements to be approved.

It is the responsibility of the executive committee to validate the relationship requirements defined by the requirement suppliers (usually the requirement users). The executive committee needs to resolve any conflicts in the detail and the priorities (usually related to cost, delivery schedule, or priority). The executive committee should include representatives of business partners for requirements that affect those companies.

Priorities for This Perspective

Identify any supporting requirements, in detail, that enable the building of the e-business product.

Delivered Work Products

These refer to work products that have a textual description of the supporting requirements.

- Design specification
- Technical architecture
- Application architecture
- Network architecture
- Distribution architecture
- Test script

IEEE References

- Std 1016: Software Design Description
- Std 1062: Practices for Software Acquisition

Individual Requirement Contents

- Identifier
- Name
- Description
- Cost
- Priority
- Status
- Audit trail

Cell: Information Technology/Builder/Who

Objective

To understand who gets what in order to build and implement the solution.

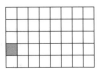

Possible Specification Formats

Textual description for:

- User functions
- User views

Supporting representative notation:

- User function matrix

Possible Elicitation Questions

Target: Questions about who gets what.

Samples:

1. *Who gets what hardware/software?* To determine the distribution of tools to build the product.
2. *What access is required at start-up?* To determine who needs access to the implemented solution without going through the regular channels.
3. *What test data is needed to simulate all actors?* To assemble test information to validate access (and nonaccess) by all potential users of the product.

Cell: Information Technology/Builder/What

Objective

To determine what is needed to assist in testing the product.

Possible Specification Formats

Textual description for:

- Data distribution
- Data keys
- Software packages

Supporting representative notation:

- Physical data model
- Physical class model
- Deployment diagram
- Physical object diagram

Possible Elicitation Questions

Target: Questions relating to information access by the builders.

Samples:

1. *What information does each team participant need to build and test the product?* To define a potential test bed of information.
2. *What needs to be populated at start-up?* To define what information has to be in the database at rollout.
3. *What COTS products can be purchased to start the population of information?* To determine any possible software acquisition of subject knowledge/databases.

Cell: Information Technology/Builder/Where

Objective

To determine the access requirements needed to build the product and implement the product in production.

Possible Specification Formats

Textual description for:

- Site configuration

Supporting representative notation:

- Deployment diagram
- Site map
- Network schema

Possible Elicitation Questions

Target: Questions related to the development and production environments.

Samples:

1. *Who needs access to what and when?* To obtain a clear and full understanding of network requirements of builders.

2. *What equipment needs to be purchased for product rollout and when is it needed?* To determine the production requirements.

3. *Can anything from the development and testing environment be used for the production system?* To leverage existing network components.

4. *Can any COTS products be purchased to monitor traffic?* To determine software package acquisition.

Cell: Information Technology/Builder/When

Objective

To determine the timing requirements to build the product and implement the product in production.

Possible Specification Formats

Textual description for:

- Concurrent process
- Dependency process
- Module interface
- Software package

Supporting representative notation:

- Physical sequence diagram
- Physical state transition diagram
- Physical activity diagram

Possible Elicitation Questions

Target: Questions related to the development and production environments.

Samples:

1. *When will builders begin?* To obtain a clear and full understanding of timing for what needs to be delivered and implemented for the development environment.

2. *Can any COTS products be purchased to perform specific events?* To determine software package acquisition, such as shopping baskets and credit card processing.

3. *Do any simulators need to be developed for testing?* To determine specialized programming to simulate portions of functionality or events (including volume load balancing).

Cell: Information Technology/Builder/Why

Objective

To determine the policy requirements related to building the product.

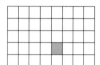

Possible Specification Formats

Textual description for:
- Proposed changed set of policies
- Proposed changed set of procedures
- Legal disclaimers

Supporting representative notation:
- Policy impact matrix

Possible Elicitation Questions

Target: Questions related to development of the product.

Samples:

1. *What policies and procedures apply to the builders of the product?* To obtain a clear and full understanding of standards that need to be adhered to by the developers and testers of the product. This is crucial if the product is being developed outside immediate control of the organization (outsourcing or developed by other business partners).

2. *What is the impact to the corporation with the purchase and use of COTS products?* To determine any licensing issues.

3. *What are the procedures if any policies are ignored?* To define procedures when business rules for developers or product suppliers are broken.

Cell: Information Technology/Builder/How

Objective

To determine the requirements for building the functionality for the product.

Possible Specification Formats

Textual description for:
- Module distribution
- Software packages

Supporting representative notation:
- Physical object diagram
- Physical data flow model
- Structure charts
- Application schema
- Backup restore procedures

Possible Elicitation Questions

Target: Questions related to development and production environment.

Samples:
1. *How will the Internet product be rolled out?* To understand what features will be made available.
2. *Can any COTS products be purchased to perform specific functions?* To determine software package acquisition, such as invoicing and help desk monitoring.
3. *Can any portion of high-risk functionality be tested separately?* To identify the components that are considered high-risk or sensitive (volume, financial formulas).
4. *Is there any specialized code requirement to facilitate this test?* To identify additional functionality that needs to be developed.

Cell: Information Technology/Builder/Product Constraints

Objective

To determine the requirements needed to build the production environment.

Possible Specification Formats

Textual description for:

- Equipment list

Supporting representative notation:

- Technical architecture
- Application architecture

Possible Elicitation Questions

Target: Questions related to the development and production environments.

Samples:

1. *How do you report equipment problems?* To define problem-reporting procedures.
2. *Who will follow up on issues reported to vendors?* To define the internal procedures for any vendor-related issues.
3. *Are any special simulators required to test quality of service requirements?* To identify potential new software or programming to validate that the quality of service requirements have been satisfied.

Cell: Information Technology/Builder/Project Constraints

Objective

To understand the impacts of issues, risks, and changes to the plan. Note that this cell is identical to the previous perspective's cell except for verification that all the preparations are set for implementation.

Possible Specification Formats

Textual description for:
- Project status (time, cost)
- Issue tracking log
- Impact analysis
- Plan adjustment
- Next phase detail schedule

Supporting representative notation:
- Gantt chart

Possible Elicitation Questions

Target: Questions related to the progress of the project.

Samples:
1. *What issues are preventing the progress of the project?* To identify roadblocks.
2. *How does each issue affect the work products?* To identify the degree of impact.
3. *How can the issue be resolved?* To define multiple means of resolving the issue.
4. *Does the effect on the work products trigger any project tolerance criteria?* To determine whether alternate action is required, including escalation to higher management.
5. *Is the scope of the project affected?* To determine the degree of impact.
6. *What is the status of all work products?* To determine whether the plan is on target.
7. *Does the status impact any other work products?* To determine the impact of the status on the final delivery.
8. *Is any other requirement at risk if the particular requirement being discussed is not satisfied?* To determine the cascading effect on the requirements set.

9. *What adjustments need to be made to the project plan and the program plan?* To identify any modifications to the plan of action (including resources, schedule, or cost).

10. *Are all project/program risks being avoided?* To determine whether the countermeasures are active.

11. *What can be done to facilitate the velocity of development of the work products?* To identify any time-saving modifications to the plan.

12. *Detailed questions on process, data, and network.* To help finish developing the code for software.

Cell: Introduction: Information Technology/Subcontractor

Objective

To define the details to build the physical (technological for IT community) solution and the successful operation of the product. After this perspective the product is a functioning Internet system.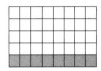

Requirements captured from this perspective pertain to three subjects:

1. Running the product (building the physical production environment)
2. Monitoring the success of the product and program
3. Facilitating the capture of requirements for future iterations

The Internet exposes the corporation to a wide range of potential customers. Therefore, it is important to capture click-stream data to analyze whether what was the perceived customer is the actual customer, whether what was thought to be the needs of the customer actually were. Capturing client responses and using the information in a productive analytical manner enables quick response and satisfaction in the earliest iteration of the Internet product.

The generic requirement work product from the subcontractor perspective consists of details that enable successful monitoring of the success of the project. All the details are additional derived requirements that must also be satisfied. Each of these requirement details has its own priority. Each of these details must be associated to the business objective or the initiating requirements. These derived requirements must have an audit trail.

It is the responsibility of the executive committee to validate the relationship requirements defined by the requirement suppliers. The executive committee needs to resolve any conflicts in the detail and the priorities. The executive committee should include representatives of any business partners for requirements that affect those companies.

Priorities for This Perspective
- Complete each requirement (initial and derived) with details.
- Define the means of validating each requirement (including relationships).

Delivered Work Products
- Code specifications
- Data specifications
- Test cases
- Operations specifications (including start of day, end of day, backup restoration, problem reports)
- Help documentation
- Feedback procedures

IEEE References
- Std 982: Dictionary of Measures to Produce Reliable Software
- Std 1008: Software Unit Testing
- Std 1028: Standard for Software Reviews
- Std 1044: Classification for Software Anomalies
- Std 1045: Software Productivity Metrics
- Std 1063: Software User Documentation
- Std 1219: Software Maintenance

Individual Requirement Contents
- Identifier
- Name
- Description
- Priority
- Status
- Audit trail

Cell: Information Technology/Subcontractor/Who

Objective

To determine preparedness for implementing "who" requirements.

Possible Specification Formats

Textual description for:

- Monitoring checklist
- Feedback procedures

Supporting representative notation:

- Scenario diagrams

Possible Elicitation Questions

Target: Questions pertaining to preparedness for implementation and monitoring requirements usage.

Samples:

1. *How will users be trained?* To plan for the rollout or distribution of the software.
2. *Is the help information acceptable?*[5] To finalize the textual help documentation in hard-copy and online formats.
3. *Are user manuals (online and hard-copy) complete and distributed?* To ensure that all documentation is available for end users prior to or jointly with the implementation of the software.
4. *Has all the necessary training occurred?* To verify that everyone has been trained to use the new software system.
5. *Whom will users call for support?* To ensure that the proper level of support is available for new users of the software.
6. *Does the software work at an acceptable level to be implemented?* To fulfill the final checkpoint for implementation.

---

5. Technical writers sometimes write help information. However, on smaller projects and in smaller companies, this information is compiled first by the information technologist and corrected by the business representative. Information technologists are notoriously bad writers. Therefore, let the owner beware!

Cell: Information Technology/Subcontractor/What

Objective

To determine preparedness for implementing "what" requirements.

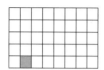

Possible Specification Formats

Textual description for:

- User views by access type

Supporting representative notation:

- Data map

Possible Elicitation Questions

Target: Questions pertaining to preparedness for implementation and monitoring requirements usage.

Samples:

1. *What are the backup and restore procedures for the data?* To finalize recovery operations.
2. *What are you looking for to determine user patterns of data usage?* To itemize specifics on how to monitor user activity.
3. *Does the test data cover all the actions that could occur for every attribute?* To review that the test cases are complete.

Cell: Information Technology/Subcontractor/Where

Objective

To determine preparedness for implementing "where" requirements.

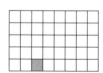

Possible Specification Formats

Textual description for:

- Equipment configuration

Supporting representative notation:

- Network diagram

Possible Elicitation Questions

Target: Questions pertaining to preparedness for implementation and monitoring requirements usage.

Samples:

1. *Is all the information available to configure the routers?* To determine whether all the plans are in place to set up the network.
2. *When is the cutover to the network?* To finalize the implementation of the network portion of the configuration.
3. *Are any spare network cards available in case of failure?* To determine whether additional equipment needs to be ordered.

Cell: Information Technology/Subcontractor/When

Objective

To determine the preparedness for implementing "when" requirements.

Possible Specification Formats

Textual description for:

- Backup procedures

Supporting representative notation:

- Technical architecture

Possible Elicitation Questions

Target: Questions pertaining to preparedness for implementation and monitoring requirements usage.

Samples:

1. *How will you identify spurts in usage of peak events?* To define a contingency plan if volume is exceeded.
2. *Do you have enough storage to support unexpected spurts?* To identify the need for additional hardware.
3. *Have you performed a sufficient volume and performance test for these spurts?* To identify the need for additional testing.

Cell: Information Technology/Subcontractor/Why

Objective

To determine preparedness for implementing "why" requirements.

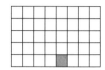

Possible Specification Formats

Textual description:

- Policies
- Procedures

Supporting representative notation:

- Organizational structure

Possible Elicitation Questions

Target: Questions pertaining to preparedness for implementation and monitoring requirements usage.

Samples:

1. *How are these new procedures distributed?* To identify who will roll out the updated policies and procedures and how that will occur.
2. *Was the distribution tested?* To identify the need for additional testing.
3. *Did the right procedures go to the right actors?* To validate the distribution process.

Cell: Information Technology/Subcontractor/How

Objective

To determine preparedness for implementing "how" requirements.

Possible Specification Formats

Textual description for:

- Problem-reporting procedures

Supporting representative notation:

- State chart

Possible Elicitation Questions

Target: Questions pertaining to preparedness for implementation and monitoring requirements usage.

Samples:

1. *How should defects and suggestions of functionality changes be handled?* To identify a means of classifying and acting upon functionality defects and enhancements.

2. *Are you monitoring the right usage of functionality?* To identify any changes to monitoring procedures, including a reevaluation of tolerance parameters.

3. *Are the scenarios or workflows being used as anticipated?* To identify any changes in functionality.

Cell: Information Technology/Subcontractor/Product Constraints

Objective

To determine preparedness for implementing product constraint requirements.

Possible Specification Formats

Textual description for:

- Contingency plan

Supporting representative notation:

- Technical architecture

Possible Elicitation Questions

Target: Questions pertaining to preparedness for implementation and monitoring requirements usage.

Samples:

1. *What should be done in cases of equipment failure?* To identify contingency plans.

2. *At what point should additional equipment be ordered?* To determine capacity-planning requirements.

3. *What information would you look for from user comments?* To identify action or notification if a user comment affects any of these requirements.

Cell: Information Technology/Subcontractor/Project Constraints

Objective

To understand what needs to be captured to determine the program metrics that will help with planning for future iterations. All questions will be defined for each iteration to follow.

Possible Specification Formats

Textual description for:

- Things to measure (for example, resources, cost)
- How to measure (for example, by feature complexity)
- Source of measures (for example, charge-back information)

Supporting representative notation:

- Resource work actual graphs
- Actual cost graphs
- Cost by feature
- Resource usage by feature
- Planned versus actual graphs

Possible Elicitation Questions

Target: Questions related to improving the next iteration of the Internet product.

Samples:

1. *What were some bottlenecks in the process of developing this iteration?* To identify potential areas for improving the process for velocity and quality.
2. *What worked right in the development of this iteration?* To identify areas that worked well in achieving the development of the work products.
3. *What was missed during the requirements gathering that caused problems later in the development process?* To identify gaps in the requirements process that may result in the development of anti-patterns to be used in future iterations.
4. *Were all the targeted requirements satisfactorily implemented in the final solution?* To determine any gaps in the transition of requirements to physical design.
5. *How will this change impact the business?* To identify the priority of the request. Those changes that have the most dramatic impact on the business will obtain the highest priority.

6. *What is the impact if you do not make the change?* To identify the priority of the request. Those changes that have the most dramatic impact on the business will obtain the highest priority.

7. *What is the priority of the change?* To prioritize changes related to defects uncovered in existing systems. Those defects that cause abnormal termination require immediate attention from IT. Changing the wording on an information message would probably have a low priority and would be combined with other items in a later release of the software.

Requirements Pattern Work Breakdown Structure

The following list of tasks is organized to facilitate the development of a full requirements set. It incorporates the use of the requirements specification (Appendix A) and the Internet requirements pattern (Appendix B). It is generic enough to be followed for any requirements effort using the requirements set framework described in Chapter Three.

This is a work breakdown structure and *not* a process! It is essentially a checklist of things to do. A process would include the following:

- A description of each line item
- The predecessor and successor
- The inputs/outputs for each line item
- The participating roles for each line item
- Each role's responsibility for each line item
- Descriptions of the work product deliverables
- A description of how to determine that the task was completed
- Samples of the work product deliverables
- Suggested technique and tool set
- Estimating formulas

How to Use This Requirements Pattern Work Breakdown Structure

Every project has its own peculiarities. Therefore, before using this work breakdown structure, review the tasks to see if they apply to your project. Before removing, adding, or changing any task, ask yourself two questions:

1. Will this compromise the filling of the requirements set framework?
2. Will the quality of the requirements set be put at risk?

When the work breakdown structure is the way you like it, feed it into your preferred scheduling product. Most of the low-level tasks depend on completion of the previous task. Exceptions are focus-level tasks that can be accomplished in parallel. Add resources and work effort to every low-level task. At this point, you have the beginnings of a project schedule that should be fine-tuned based on past experience.

How to Incorporate the Tasks into Existing Development Processes

Only requirement-related tasks are included in the task list. It addresses the sub-processes (elicit, analyze, specify, validate, approve, and manage) as well as the higher process that supports the different allocation levels (corporate, division, architecture, and product). All items should be incorporated into an existing program schedule or development process that is targeted to building an Internet product.

Work Breakdown Structure Summary List

1. **Need statement**
    1.1. Interpret need
        1.1.1. Review need
        1.1.2. Define current situation
        1.1.3. Evaluate impact
    1.2. Document need
        1.2.1. Define proposed adjustment
        1.2.2. Identify potential tangible benefit
        1.2.3. Identify potential intangible benefit
        1.2.4. Define priority

1.3. Act on need

    1.3.1. Document proposed next step

    1.3.2. Obtain approval to continue

    1.3.3. Issue acknowledgment to customer

1.4. Plan next phase

    1.4.1. Identify needs for next phase

    1.4.2. Schedule next phase

    1.4.3. Close file

2. Idea

2.1. Phase preparation

    2.1.1. Confirm budget commitment for phase

    2.1.2. Elicit requirements engineer's assistance

    2.1.3. Identify phase participants

    2.1.4. Schedule requirement definition meetings

    2.1.5. Gather existing documentation

    2.1.6. Issue copies of need statement

    2.1.7. Organize documentation library

2.2. Scope requirements definition

    2.2.1. Elicit high-level business requirements

        2.2.1.1. Identify potential interfaces

        2.2.1.2. Identify potential information ("what" requirements, including data, voice, image, video)

        2.2.1.3. Identify potential key functions

        2.2.1.4. Identify potential business events

        2.2.1.5. Identify potential locations

        2.2.1.6. Identify potential business rules/policies

        2.2.1.7. Identify potential solution constraints

        2.2.1.8. Identify potential project constraints

    2.2.2. High-level impact analysis

        2.2.2.1. Identify changes to existing interfaces

        2.2.2.2. Identify changes to existing information

        2.2.2.3. Identify changes to existing key functions

        2.2.2.4. Identify changes to existing business events

        2.2.2.5. Identify changes to existing locations

        2.2.2.6. Identify changes to existing business rules/policies

2.2.3. Specify requirement scope model

2.2.3.1. Define individual priority

2.2.3.2. Perform critical requirements analysis

2.2.3.3. Define requirement interrelationships

2.2.3.4. Define potential risks associated with the proposal

2.2.3.5. Define potential risks if the project does not get approved

2.2.3.6. Define countermeasures to the potential risks

2.2.3.7. Assemble requirement scope model

2.2.4. Validate requirement scope model

2.2.4.1. Schedule review meeting

2.2.4.2. Review high-level requirements

2.2.4.3. Document changes

2.3. Assemble business case

2.3.1. Estimate the project costs

2.3.2. Quantify benefits

2.3.3. Analyze risk

2.3.4. Define business success criteria

2.3.5. Document business case

2.4. End-phase assessment

2.4.1. Schedule business case review

2.4.2. Review business case

2.4.3. Obtain approval for next phase

2.4.4. Set up requirements management tool for product

2.4.5. Insert high-level requirements into requirements management tool

2.4.6. Baseline requirement scope model

3. Business requirements

3.1. Phase preparation

3.1.1. Identify staffing requirements

3.1.2. Develop phase plan

3.2. Detail business requirements definition

3.2.1. Elicit requirements clarification

3.2.1.1. Functional decomposition from high-level requirements

3.2.1.1.1. Elicit list of potential "who"

3.2.1.1.2. Elicit list of potential "what"

        3.2.1.1.3. Elicit list of potential "where"

        3.2.1.1.4. Elicit list of potential "when"

        3.2.1.1.5. Elicit list of potential "why"

        3.2.1.1.6. Elicit list of potential "how"

    3.2.1.2. Nonfunctional decomposition from high-level requirements

        3.2.1.2.1. Elicit list of potential product constraints

        3.2.1.2.2. Elicit list of potential project constraints

3.2.2. Requirements analysis

    3.2.2.1. Identify conflicts within focus area

    3.2.2.2. Identify conflicts between focus areas

    3.2.2.3. Determine scope requirements coverage

    3.2.2.4. Identify additional requirements to resolve conflicts

3.2.3. Specify requirements clarification

    3.2.3.1. Identify documentation standard

    3.2.3.2. Develop product overview section

    3.2.3.3. Specify general product description

    3.2.3.4. Specify product functional requirements

3.2.4. Validation activity

    3.2.4.1. Validation preparation

        3.2.4.1.1. Identify reviewer

        3.2.4.1.2. Arrange review session

        3.2.4.1.3. Deliver specification

    3.2.4.2. Validation

        3.2.4.2.1. Desk-check requirements

        3.2.4.2.2. Draft review with requirement suppliers

        3.2.4.2.3. Internal requirements engineering review

        3.2.4.2.4. Formal specification review

    3.2.4.3. Postvalidation

        3.2.4.3.1. Assemble comments

        3.2.4.3.2. Document issues

        3.2.4.3.3. Determine degree of change

        3.2.4.3.4. Determine configuration state

        3.2.4.3.5. Initiate baseline of approved requirements

        3.2.4.3.6. Initiate change process for requirements

3.2.5. Approval activity

    3.2.5.1. Approval preparation

        3.2.5.1.1. Format requirement overview

        3.2.5.1.2. Arrange executive approval meeting

        3.2.5.1.3. Review project tolerance indicators

    3.2.5.2. Approval

        3.2.5.2.1. Hold executive approval meeting

        3.2.5.2.2. Discuss and resolve issues

        3.2.5.2.3. Discuss project status

        3.2.5.2.4. Plan next perspective steps

    3.2.5.3. Postapproval

        3.2.5.3.1. Issue summary of resolved issues

        3.2.5.3.2. Develop a plan of action based on resolution

        3.2.5.3.3. Prepare a final report of phase activities

3.3. End-phase assessment

    3.3.1. Reevaluate return on investment

    3.3.2. Obtain approval for product continuance

    3.3.3. Determine product tolerance levels

    3.3.4. Develop product status–reporting procedures

    3.3.5. Develop master product project plan

4. Corporate allocation

4.1. Allocation preparation

    4.1.1. Obtain organizational structure

    4.1.2. Identify key community sponsors

    4.1.3. Develop allocation agenda

    4.1.4. Schedule allocation meeting

    4.1.5. Identify resources for allocation responsibilities

    4.1.6. Develop allocation presentation material

    4.1.7. Issue allocation preparation packet to attendees

4.2. Allocation

    4.2.1. Confirm attendance

    4.2.2. Hold allocation meeting

    4.2.3. Document issues

    4.2.4. Allocate requirements

    4.2.5. Develop meeting minutes

    4.2.6. Issue meeting minutes

4.2.7. Review comments on meeting minutes

4.2.8. Update meeting minutes

4.3. Postallocation

    4.3.1. Update scope requirements in requirements management tool

    4.3.2. Define allocation traceability

    4.3.3. Schedule requirements management tool training

    4.3.4. Follow up on issue resolution

    4.3.5. Update master project plan

5. Community execution (information technology)

5.1. Project management

    5.1.1. Community project initiation

        5.1.1.1. Project kickoff

            5.1.1.1.1. Establish initial project sponsor

            5.1.1.1.2. Complete start-up activities

            5.1.1.1.3. Establish business objectives

            5.1.1.1.4. Establish scope of investigation

            5.1.1.1.5. Outline solution

            5.1.1.1.6. Review and compile products

        5.1.1.2. Scheduling and budgeting

            5.1.1.2.1. Define project approach and schedule

            5.1.1.2.2. Prepare project budget

            5.1.1.2.3. Define next-stage activities and schedule

            5.1.1.2.4. Review and compile products

        5.1.1.3. Project organization

            5.1.1.3.1. Define the project organization

            5.1.1.3.2. Determine training requirements

            5.1.1.3.3. Review and compile products

        5.1.1.4. Project-control procedures

            5.1.1.4.1. Customize quality plan

            5.1.1.4.2. Define test strategy

            5.1.1.4.3. Customize problem-reporting procedures

            5.1.1.4.4. Establish additional control procedures

            5.1.1.4.5. Review and compile products

        5.1.1.5 Product management procedures

            5.1.1.5.1. Customize configuration management plan

            5.1.1.5.2. Define product review strategy

            5.1.1.5.3. Define product baselining methods

5.1.1.5.4. Define relationships between configuration items

5.1.1.5.5. Define reuse strategy and methods

5.1.1.5.6. Review and compile products

5.1.1.6. Project initiation phase assessment

5.1.1.6.1. Define business case

5.1.1.6.2. Finalize project initiation report

5.1.1.6.3. Review/baseline project deliverables

5.1.1.6.4. Prepare end-phase assessment

5.1.1.6.5. Conduct end-phase assessment

5.1.1.6.6. Complete process review

5.2. Community project tracking and oversight

5.2.1. Project control

5.2.1.1. Phase management

5.2.1.1.1. Kick off the phase

5.2.1.1.2. Monitor project progress

5.2.1.1.3. Identify and resolve issues

5.2.1.1.4. Manage exception situations

5.2.1.2. End-phase assessment

5.2.1.2.1. Develop requirements traceability matrix

5.2.1.2.2. Review and baseline project/deliverables

5.2.1.2.3. Complete software configuration management audit

5.2.1.2.4. Develop schedule for next phase

5.2.1.2.5. Review project plan

5.2.1.2.6. Create phase report

5.2.1.2.7. Conduct end-phase assessment

5.2.1.3. Project Closure

5.2.1.3.1. Final product evaluation

5.2.1.3.1.1. Prepare product evaluation

5.2.1.3.1.2. Conduct product evaluation

5.2.1.3.1.3. Initiate maintenance process

5.2.1.3.2. Project completion

5.2.1.3.2.1. Close outstanding project work

5.2.1.3.2.2. Prepare for project closure meeting

5.2.1.3.2.3. Conduct project closure meeting

5.2.1.3.2.4. Follow up on project closure meeting

5.2.1.3.3. Product and process improvement

    5.2.1.3.3.1. Review and baseline project deliverables

    5.2.1.3.3.2. Collect project feedback and metrics

    5.2.1.3.3.3. Collate and analyze metrics

    5.2.1.3.3.4. Analyze product quality

    5.2.1.3.3.5. Complete process review

5.2.2. Product tracking and oversight coordination

    5.2.2.1. Supply project status to master product plan

    5.2.2.2. Incorporate impacted changes from other communities

    5.2.2.3. Determine impact of changes

    5.2.2.4. Analyze tolerance parameters

5.3. Planner perspective

5.3.1. Elicitation activity

    5.3.1.1. Elicitation preparation

        5.3.1.1.1. Obtain list of allocated requirements

        5.3.1.1.2. Review supporting reference documentation

        5.3.1.1.3. Obtain dictionary of terms for business community

        5.3.1.1.4. Develop a list of questions

    5.3.1.2. Elicitation

        5.3.1.2.1. Clarify the community specifics against allocated requirements

        5.3.1.2.2. Identify community-specific list of "who"

        5.3.1.2.3. Identify community-specific list of "what"

        5.3.1.2.4. Identify community-specific list of "where"

        5.3.1.2.5. Identify community-specific list of "when"

        5.3.1.2.6. Identify community-specific list of "why"

        5.3.1.2.7. Identify community-specific list of "how"

        5.3.1.2.8. Identify community-specific list of product constraints

        5.3.1.2.9. Identify community-specific list of project constraints

        5.3.1.2.10. Elicit description for community-specific requirement

5.3.1.2.11. Determine priority of each community requirement

5.3.1.2.12. Elicit a sense of stability for each requirement

5.3.1.2.13. Research volume estimates for each community requirement

5.3.1.3. Postelicitation

    5.3.1.3.1. Develop meeting minutes

    5.3.1.3.2. Issue meeting minutes

    5.3.1.3.3. Review comments on meeting minutes

    5.3.1.3.4. Update meeting minutes

5.3.2. Analysis activity

  5.3.2.1. Analysis preparation

    5.3.2.1.1. Assemble meeting minutes

    5.3.2.1.2. Obtain perspective pattern cells

  5.3.2.2. Analysis

    5.3.2.2.1. Enter information into CASE tool

    5.3.2.2.2. Determine requirements completion

    5.3.2.2.3. Determine requirements coverage

    5.3.2.2.4. Identify conflicts within focus area

    5.3.2.2.5. Identify conflicts with other perspective cells

    5.3.2.2.6. Identify additional requirements to resolve conflicts

  5.3.2.3. Postanalysis

    5.3.2.3.1. Obtain access to requirements management tool

    5.3.2.3.2. Link requirements to original allocated requirements

5.3.3. Specification activity

  5.3.3.1. Specification preparation

    5.3.3.1.1. Develop introduction

    5.3.3.1.2. Develop notation explanation

    5.3.3.1.3. Assemble list of reference material

    5.3.3.1.4. Develop glossary

  5.3.3.2. Specification

    5.3.3.2.1. Label all requirements

    5.3.3.2.2. Name all requirements

    5.3.3.2.3. Assemble requirements

    5.3.3.2.4. Format requirements in an organized fashion

5.3.3.2.5. Enter all requirements into the requirements management tool

5.3.3.2.6. Set status as "ready for review"

5.3.3.3. Postspecification

5.3.3.3.1. Assemble specification

5.3.3.3.2. Produce delivery format

5.3.4. Validation activity

5.3.4.1. Validation preparation

5.3.4.1.1. Identify reviewer

5.3.4.1.2. Arrange review session

5.3.4.1.3. Deliver specification

5.3.4.2. Validation

5.3.4.2.1. Desk-check requirements

5.3.4.2.2. Draft review with requirement suppliers

5.3.4.2.3. Internal requirements engineering review

5.3.4.2.4. Formal specification review

5.3.4.3. Postvalidation

5.3.4.3.1. Assemble comments

5.3.4.3.2. Document issues

5.3.4.3.3. Determine degree of change

5.3.4.3.4. Determine configuration state

5.3.4.3.5. Initiate baseline of approved requirements

5.3.4.3.6. Initiate change process for requirements

5.3.5. Approval activity

5.3.5.1. Approval preparation

5.3.5.1.1. Format requirement overview

5.3.5.1.2. Arrange executive approval meeting

5.3.5.1.3. Review project tolerance indicators

5.3.5.2. Approval

5.3.5.2.1. Hold executive approval meeting

5.3.5.2.2. Discuss and resolve issues

5.3.5.2.3. Discuss project status

5.3.5.2.4. Plan next perspective steps

5.3.5.3. Postapproval

5.3.5.3.1. Issue summary of resolved issues

5.3.5.3.2. Develop a plan of action based on resolutions

5.3.5.3.3. Prepare a final report of perspective activities

5.4. Owner perspective
 5.4.1. Elicitation activity
  5.4.1.1. Elicitation preparation
   5.4.1.1.1. Obtain list of planner requirements
   5.4.1.1.2. Review supporting reference documentation
   5.4.1.1.3. Obtain dictionary of terms for business community
   5.4.1.1.4. Develop a list of questions
  5.4.1.2. Elicitation
   5.4.1.2.1. Clarify the community specifics against allocated requirements
   5.4.1.2.2. Identify relationships between cell requirements
   5.4.1.2.3. Identify relationships outside cell requirements
   5.4.1.2.4. Define qualification for relationships
   5.4.1.2.5. Elicit description for relationship-specific requirements
   5.4.1.2.6. Determine priority of each community requirement
   5.4.1.2.7. Elicit a sense of stability for each requirement
   5.4.1.2.8. Research volume estimates for each community requirement
  5.4.1.3. Postelicitation
   5.4.1.3.1. Develop meeting minutes
   5.4.1.3.2. Issue meeting minutes
   5.4.1.3.3. Review comments on meeting minutes
   5.4.1.3.4. Update meeting minutes
 5.4.2. Analysis activity
  5.4.2.1. Analysis preparation
   5.4.2.1.1. Assemble meeting minutes
   5.4.2.1.2. Obtain perspective pattern cells
  5.4.2.2. Analysis
   5.4.2.2.1. Enter information into CASE tool
   5.4.2.2.2. Determine requirements completion
   5.4.2.2.3. Determine requirements coverage
   5.4.2.2.4. Identify conflicts within focus area

5.4.2.2.5. Identify conflicts with other perspective cells

5.4.2.2.6. Identify additional requirements to resolve conflicts

5.4.2.3. Postanalysis

5.4.2.3.1. Obtain access to requirements management tool

5.4.2.3.2. Link requirements to original allocated requirements

5.4.3. Specification activity

5.4.3.1. Specification preparation

5.4.3.1.1. Develop introduction

5.4.3.1.2. Develop notation explanation

5.4.3.1.3. Assemble list of reference material

5.4.3.1.4. Develop glossary

5.4.3.2. Specification

5.4.3.2.1. Label all requirements

5.4.3.2.2. Name all requirements

5.4.3.2.3. Assemble requirements

5.4.3.2.4. Format requirements in an organized fashion

5.4.3.2.5. Enter all requirements into the requirements management tool

5.4.3.2.6. Set status as "ready for review"

5.4.3.3. Postspecification

5.4.3.3.1. Assemble specification

5.4.3.3.2. Produce delivery format

5.4.4. Validation activity

5.4.4.1. Validation preparation

5.4.4.1.1. Identify reviewer

5.4.4.1.2. Arrange review session

5.4.4.1.3. Deliver specification

5.4.4.2. Validation

5.4.4.2.1. Desk-check requirements

5.4.4.2.2. Draft review with requirement suppliers

5.4.4.2.3. Internal requirements engineering review

5.4.4.2.4. Formal specification review

5.4.4.3. Postvalidation

    5.4.4.3.1. Assemble comments

    5.4.4.3.2. Document issues

    5.4.4.3.3. Determine degree of change

    5.4.4.3.4. Determine configuration state

    5.4.4.3.5. Initiate baseline of approved requirements

    5.4.4.3.6. Initiate change process for requirements

5.4.5. Approval activity

  5.4.5.1. Approval preparation

    5.4.5.1.1. Format requirement overview

    5.4.5.1.2. Arrange executive approval meeting

    5.4.5.1.3. Review project tolerance indicators

  5.4.5.2. Approval

    5.4.5.2.1. Hold executive approval meeting

    5.4.5.2.2. Discuss and resolve issues

    5.4.5.2.3. Discuss project status

    5.4.5.2.4. Plan next perspective steps

  5.4.5.3. Postapproval

    5.4.5.3.1. Issue summary of resolved issues

    5.4.5.3.2. Develop a plan of action based on resolutions

    5.4.5.3.3. Prepare a final report of perspective activities

5.5. Designer perspective

  5.5.1. Elicitation activity

    5.5.1.1. Elicitation preparation

      5.5.1.1.1. Obtain list of owner requirements

      5.5.1.1.2. Review supporting reference documentation

      5.5.1.1.3. Obtain dictionary of terms for business community

      5.5.1.1.4. Develop a list of questions

    5.5.1.2. Elicitation

      5.5.1.2.1. Clarify the community specifics against allocated requirements

      5.5.1.2.2. Complete each requirement (initial and derived) with details

      5.5.1.2.3. Define the means of validating each requirement (including relationships)

      5.5.1.2.4. Review that each cell and relationship between each cell has been discussed

5.5.1.2.5. Evaluate dependencies and priorities to segment requirements into iterations

5.5.1.2.6. Clarify the feasibility (and the cost) of satisfying the requirement

5.5.1.2.7. Elicit description for community-specific requirements

5.5.1.2.8. Determine priority of each community requirement

5.5.1.2.9. Elicit a sense of stability for each requirement

5.5.1.2.10. Research volume estimates for each community requirement

5.5.1.3. Postelicitation

5.5.1.3.1. Develop meeting minutes

5.5.1.3.2. Issue meeting minutes

5.5.1.3.3. Review comments on meeting minutes

5.5.1.3.4. Update meeting minutes

5.5.2. Analysis activity

5.5.2.1. Analysis preparation

5.5.2.1.1. Assemble meeting minutes

5.5.2.1.2. Obtain perspective pattern cells

5.5.2.2. Analysis

5.5.2.2.1. Enter information into CASE tool

5.5.2.2.2. Determine requirements completion

5.5.2.2.3. Determine requirements coverage

5.5.2.2.4. Identify conflicts within focus area

5.5.2.2.5. Identify conflicts with other perspective cells

5.5.2.2.6. Identify additional requirements to resolve conflicts

5.5.2.3. Postanalysis

5.5.2.3.1. Obtain access to requirements management tool

5.5.2.3.2. Link requirements to original allocated requirements

5.5.3. Specification activity

5.5.3.1. Specification preparation

5.5.3.1.1. Develop introduction

5.5.3.1.2. Develop notation explanation

5.5.3.1.3. Assemble list of reference material

5.5.3.1.4. Develop glossary

5.5.3.2. Specification

5.5.3.2.1. Label all requirements

5.5.3.2.2. Name all requirements

5.5.3.2.3. Assemble requirements

5.5.3.2.4. Format requirements in an organized fashion

5.5.3.2.5. Enter all requirements into the requirements management tool

5.5.3.2.6. Set status as "ready for review"

5.5.3.3. Postspecification

5.5.3.3.1. Assemble specification

5.5.3.3.2. Produce delivery format

5.5.4. Validation activity

5.5.4.1. Validation preparation

5.5.4.1.1. Identify reviewer

5.5.4.1.2. Arrange review session

5.5.4.1.3. Deliver specification

5.5.4.2. Validation

5.5.4.2.1. Desk-check requirements

5.5.4.2.2. Draft review with requirement suppliers

5.5.4.2.3. Internal requirements engineering review

5.5.4.2.4. Formal specification review

5.5.4.3. Postvalidation

5.5.4.3.1. Assemble comments

5.5.4.3.2. Document issues

5.5.4.3.3. Determine degree of change

5.5.4.3.4. Determine configuration state

5.5.4.3.5. Initiate baseline of approved requirements

5.5.4.3.6. Initiate change process for requirements

5.5.5. Approval activity

5.5.5.1. Approval preparation

5.5.5.1.1. Format requirement overview

5.5.5.1.2. Arrange executive approval meeting

5.5.5.1.3. Review project tolerance indicators

5.5.5.2. Approval

5.5.5.2.1. Hold executive approval meeting

5.5.5.2.2. Discuss and resolve issues

5.5.5.2.3. Discuss project status

5.5.5.2.4. Plan next perspective steps

5.5.5.3. Postapproval

5.5.5.3.1. Issue summary of resolved issues

5.5.5.3.2. Develop a plan of action based on resolutions

5.5.5.3.3. Prepare a final report of perspective activities

5.6. Builder perspective

5.6.1. Elicitation activity

5.6.1.1. Elicitation preparation

5.6.1.1.1. Obtain list of allocated requirements

5.6.1.1.2. Review supporting reference documentation

5.6.1.1.3. Obtain dictionary of terms for business community

5.6.1.1.4. Develop a list of questions

5.6.1.2. Elicitation

5.6.1.2.1. Elicit builder's needs

5.6.1.2.2. Elicit description for each requirement

5.6.1.2.3. Determine priority of each requirement

5.6.1.2.4. Determine cost of need

5.6.1.2.5. Research volume estimates for requirements

5.6.1.3. Postelicitation

5.6.1.3.1. Develop meeting minutes

5.6.1.3.2. Issue meeting minutes

5.6.1.3.3. Review comments on meeting minutes

5.6.1.3.4. Update meeting minutes

5.6.2. Analysis activity

5.6.2.1. Analysis preparation

5.6.2.1.1. Assemble meeting minutes

5.6.2.1.2. Obtain perspective pattern cells

5.6.2.2. Analysis

5.6.2.2.1. Enter information into CASE tool

5.6.2.2.2. Determine requirements completion

5.6.2.2.3. Determine requirements coverage

5.6.2.2.4. Identify conflicts within focus area

5.6.2.2.5. Identify conflicts with other perspective cells

5.6.2.2.6. Identify additional requirements to resolve conflicts

5.6.2.3. Postanalysis

5.6.2.3.1. Obtain access to requirements management tool

5.6.2.3.2. Link requirements to original allocated requirements

5.6.3. Specification activity

5.6.3.1. Specification preparation

5.6.3.1.1. Develop introduction

5.6.3.1.2. Develop notation explanation

5.6.3.1.3. Assemble list of reference material

5.6.3.1.4. Develop glossary

5.6.3.2. Specification

5.6.3.2.1. Label all requirements

5.6.3.2.2. Name all requirements

5.6.3.2.3. Assemble requirements

5.6.3.2.4. Format requirements in an organized fashion

5.6.3.2.5. Enter all requirements into the requirements management tool

5.6.3.2.6. Set status as "ready for review"

5.6.3.3. Postspecification

5.6.3.3.1. Assemble specification

5.6.3.3.2. Produce delivery format

5.6.4. Validation activity

5.6.4.1. Validation preparation

5.6.4.1.1. Identify reviewer

5.6.4.1.2. Arrange review session

5.6.4.1.3. Deliver specification

5.6.4.2. Validation

5.6.4.2.1. Desk-check requirements

5.6.4.2.2. Draft review with requirement suppliers

5.6.4.2.3. Internal requirements engineering review

5.6.4.2.4. Formal specification review

5.6.4.3. Postvalidation

5.6.4.3.1. Assemble comments

5.6.4.3.2. Document issues

5.6.4.3.3. Determine degree of change

5.6.4.3.4. Determine configuration state

5.6.4.3.5. Initiate baseline of approved requirements

5.6.4.3.6. Initiate change process for requirements

5.6.5. Approval activity

    5.6.5.1. Approval preparation

        5.6.5.1.1. Format requirement overview

        5.6.5.1.2. Arrange executive approval meeting

        5.6.5.1.3. Review project tolerance indicators

    5.6.5.2. Approval

        5.6.5.2.1. Hold executive approval meeting

        5.6.5.2.2. Discuss and resolve issues

        5.6.5.2.3. Discuss project status

        5.6.5.2.4. Plan next perspective steps

    5.6.5.3. Postapproval

        5.6.5.3.1. Issue summary of resolved issues

        5.6.5.3.2. Develop a plan of action based on resolution

        5.6.5.3.3. Prepare a final report of perspective activities

5.7. Subcontractor perspective

    5.7.1. Elicitation activity

        5.7.1.1. Elicitation preparation

            5.7.1.1.1. Obtain list of allocated requirements

            5.7.1.1.2. Review supporting reference documentation

            5.7.1.1.3. Obtain dictionary of terms for business community

            5.3.1.1.4. Develop a list of questions

        5.7.1.2. Elicitation

            5.7.1.2.1. Elicit monitoring needs

            5.7.1.2.2   Elicit disaster recovery needs

            5.7.1.2.3. Elicit description for each requirement

            5.7.1.2.4. Determine priority of each requirement

            5.7.1.2.5. Determine cost of need

            5.7.1.2.6. Research volume estimates for requirements

            5.7.1.2.7. Elicit description for community-specific requirements

            5.7.1.2.8. Determine priority of each community requirement

            5.7.1.2.9. Elicit a sense of stability for each requirement

            5.7.1.2.10. Research volume estimates for each community requirement

5.7.1.3. Postelicitation

    5.7.1.3.1. Develop meeting minutes

    5.7.1.3.2. Issue meeting minutes

    5.7.1.3.3. Review comments on meeting minutes

    5.7.1.3.4. Update meeting minutes

5.7.2. Analysis activity

  5.7.2.1. Analysis preparation

    5.7.2.1.1. Assemble meeting minutes

    5.7.2.1.2. Obtain perspective pattern cells

  5.7.2.2. Analysis

    5.7.2.2.1. Enter information into CASE tool

    5.7.2.2.2. Determine requirements completion

    5.7.2.2.3. Determine requirements coverage

    5.7.2.2.4. Identify conflicts within focus area

    5.7.2.2.5. Identify conflicts with other perspective cells

    5.7.2.2.6. Identify additional requirements to resolve conflicts

  5.7.2.3. Postanalysis

    5.7.2.3.1. Obtain access to requirements management tool

    5.7.2.3.2. Link requirements to original allocated requirements

5.7.3. Specification activity

  5.7.3.1. Specification preparation

    5.7.3.1.1. Develop introduction

    5.7.3.1.2. Develop notation explanation

    5.7.3.1.3. Assemble list of reference material

    5.7.3.1.4. Develop glossary

  5.7.3.2. Specification

    5.7.3.2.1. Label all requirements

    5.7.3.2.2. Name all requirements

    5.7.3.2.3. Assemble requirements

    5.7.3.2.4. Format requirements in an organized fashion

    5.7.3.2.5. Enter all requirements into the requirements management tool

    5.7.3.2.6. Set status as "ready for review"

5.7.3.3. Postspecification

    5.7.3.3.1. Assemble specification

    5.7.3.3.2. Produce delivery format

5.7.4. Validation activity

  5.7.4.1. Validation preparation

    5.7.4.1.1. Identify reviewer

    5.7.4.1.2. Arrange review session

    5.7.4.1.3. Deliver specification

  5.7.4.2. Validation

    5.7.4.2.1. Desk-check requirements

    5.7.4.2.2. Draft review with requirement suppliers

    5.7.4.2.3. Internal requirements engineering review

    5.7.4.2.4. Formal specification review

  5.7.4.3. Postvalidation

    5.7.4.3.1. Assemble comments

    5.7.4.3.2. Document issues

    5.7.4.3.3. Determine degree of change

    5.7.4.3.4. Determine configuration state

    5.7.4.3.5. Initiate baseline of approved requirements

    5.7.4.3.6. Initiate change process for requirements

5.7.5. Approval activity

  5.7.5.1. Approval preparation

    5.7.5.1.1. Format requirement overview

    5.7.5.1.2. Arrange executive approval meeting

    5.7.5.1.3. Review project tolerance indicators

  5.7.5.2. Approval

    5.7.5.2.1. Hold executive approval meeting

    5.7.5.2.2. Discuss and resolve issues

    5.7.5.2.3. Discuss project status

    5.7.5.2.4. Plan next iteration steps

  5.7.5.3. Postapproval

    5.7.5.3.1. Issue summary of resolved issues

    5.7.5.3.2. Develop a plan of action based on resolutions

    5.7.5.3.3. Prepare a final report of perspective activities

5.8. Refactoring

    5.8.1. Elicitation

        5.8.1.1. Review requirements for next iteration

        5.8.1.2. Review whether quality of service parameters are being met

    5.8.2. Analysis

        5.8.2.1. Identify any tweaking needed to improve quality of service

        5.8.2.2. Determine impact on application architecture

        5.8.2.3. Determine impact on technical architecture

        5.8.2.4. Determine impact on existing approved requirements set

        5.8.2.5. Calculate cost of impact (cost, schedule, resources)

    5.8.3. Specification

        5.8.3.1. Document impact analysis

        5.8.3.2. Document risk of changes

        5.8.3.3. Document risk of not doing changes

        5.8.3.4. Document recommendation

    5.8.4. Validation

        5.8.4.1 Review impact with technical team

        5.8.4.2 Review impact with requirements team

        5.8.4.3 Review impact with business community

        5.8.4.4 Review impact with executive committee

    5.8.5. Approval

        5.8.5.1 Obtain executive approval to alter application architecture

        5.8.5.2 Obtain executive approval to alter technical architecture

        5.8.5.3 Submit changes to requirements

        5.8.5.4 Develop recommendation into new requirements

        5.8.5.5 Submit requirements into the requirements management tool

        5.8.5.6 Initiate requirement change-control process

6. Evaluation of return on investment

    6.1. Evaluation preparation

        6.1.1. Determine the requirements implemented in the release

        6.1.2. Determine the cost to implement requirements

        6.1.3. Obtain revenue generated from product

6.2. Evaluation

    6.2.1. Calculate return on investment for product

    6.2.2. Match actuals to projections in business case

    6.2.3. Develop a report for executive management

6.3. Postevaluation

    6.3.1. Identify corrections to existing iteration

    6.3.2. Identify corrections to iterations under development

    6.3.3. Evaluate impact of change

    6.3.4. Initiate requirement idea phase

Requirements Pattern Language

Introduction

A pattern is any reusable framework or architecture that has been shown through experience to solve a common problem in a specific content. The common problem with requirements is an incomplete requirements set brought about by gaps in knowledge, participation, or process. The purpose for using a formal pattern language for an incomplete requirements set is the same as for any design component. A pattern language provides a common standard between all patterns (requirements-related or not) for easier understanding and usage.

Contained in this appendix are different requirements patterns with differing degrees of specifics. Each pattern defines the problem the pattern is meant to assist in avoiding. All are based on the requirements set framework (community, perspective, focus, and association) outlined in this book. A requirements pattern[1] provides thought provoking questions for each requirement cell to assist in stimulating the capture of all requirements. A requirements anti-pattern discusses specific situations and specific cells in the requirements set framework and requirements pattern.

---

1. For the purposes of this book, the differentiation between requirements patterns and requirements anti-patterns is by the framework coverage. Requirements patterns include question sets for *every* cell. The question set assists in minimizing gaps in knowledge, participation, or process. Requirements anti-patterns provide a technique or guide to handle specific cells or specific requirement-related situations.

The first pattern in this appendix is the requirements meta pattern (identifier 000001). The individual cell question set is not provided. However, the language is important to read for an understanding of the syntax for all other requirements-related patterns and anti-patterns.

This book discusses the nuances of requirements related activities for Internet-based applications. This type of application creates unique challenges that need to be highlighted early in the requirements process. The second pattern (identifier 000002) discusses these problems. As the rules of requirements meta pattern usage dictate, the Internet requirements pattern question set (refer to Appendix B) is organized by the requirements set framework.

All requirement-related patterns are based on the same premises:

- A requirement is any need that must be satisfied in order to meet the business objective.
- A requirement evolves in detail through a process and into work products that support the business objective.
- Each requirement is allocated to the appropriate group for development into the work products that assist in meeting the business objective.

The common thread in the previous points is that the pattern must assist in meeting the business objective. All requirements-related patterns (see Figure D.1)

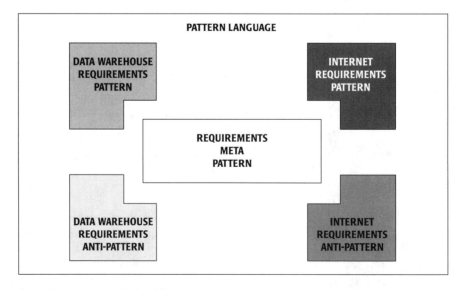

Figure D.1   Pattern relationships

Table D.1   Pattern Checklist

✔ Describes a single kind of problem
✔ Describes the context in which the problem occurs
✔ Describes the solution to the problem as a constructible requirement
✔ Describes requirement activities, steps, or rules for constructing the solution
✔ Describes the forces leading to the solution
✔ Describes evidence that the solution optimally resolves forces
✔ Describes details that are allowed to vary and those that are not
✔ Describes at least one actual instance of use
✔ Describes evidence of generality across different instances
✔ Describes or refers to variants and subpatterns
✔ Describes or refers to other patterns that rely on this pattern
✔ Relates to other patterns with similar contexts, problems, or solutions

must work together to achieve this one goal—*to build a quality product that supports the business objective.*

This appendix is not a complete list of patterns and anti-patterns available to either requirements engineers or Internet application developers. Additional patterns and anti-patterns can be developed as long as the format correlates with the pattern language used here and the patterns adhere to basic rules (see Table D.1):[2]

To implement any of these patterns or anti-patterns, you must have support from the project team, including requirement suppliers, requirement users, requirements engineers, and requirement support personnel. Each must understand what needs to be done as well as the potential impacts on other work products (including the schedule). Acceptance depends on the anticipated level of risk if the pattern or anti-pattern is not implemented.

Patterns

Name: Identify All Types (Requirements Meta Pattern)

Identifier: 000001

Mnemonic: RMP

---

2. Adapted from Doug Lea's checklist at http://hillside.net/patterns/checklist.htm, accessed in September 2001 by Doug Lea.

Also known as: Requirements meta pattern, requirements pattern

Based on: Not applicable

Cell applicability: All

Refactored solution type: Not applicable

Problem: Requirement errors account for one-third of the reasons for project failure. One of the problems is attributed to an incomplete set of requirements. How do you know if you have identified all the requirements needed to meet the business objective? This pattern categorizes requirements and provides a question set for each requirement cell to facilitate the capture of all requirements and their associations between communities, perspectives, and focus areas. Some requirements are identified too late or not at all. *Identify All Types* provides the requirements engineer with a list of tailored questions and a way to spot weaknesses in the requirements set, thus preventing project failure. The pattern is based on the corporate structure to facilitate the allocation of responsibility to the correct organizational community.

Context: The breadth of requirements may not be captured if:

- Only one or two modeling techniques are used to capture requirements.
- The process omits the delegation of requirements development.
- Not all business communities are involved from the start.
- The process omits the associations between requirements.

A solution to a business objective requires multiple divisions of an organization working together. Each works at its own velocity developing its work products but is dependent on information gathered by other organizational communities.

Forces: You want to identify as many of the requirements as possible as soon as possible. This allows multiple concurrent efforts to evolve the requirements into pieces of the solution or product. You want to be able to involve the right individuals as soon as possible to remedy project delays, cost overruns, and missed market opportunities due to an incomplete set of requirements. Missing requirements will minimize the return on investment for the product! Missing requirements may potentially impact the final design, forcing rework and retrofitting[3] of needs in future product releases.

---

3. Rework and retrofitting are not to be confused with Refactoring. Refactoring refers to tweaking the design based upon actual information. Rework and retrofitting occur because a quality requirements process was not followed, which would have facilitated the allocation, elicitation, analysis, specification, validation, and approval of the requirements set.

Solution: A combination of a process that properly allocates responsibility to evolve requirements along with a framework that categorizes the requirements provides concurrent work efforts and a facility to quickly identify gaps in the requirements set. *Identify All Types* uses a list of questions tailored by perspective, focus, and community to guide the requirements engineer. Additional questions are supplied to support associations between cell boundaries.

Resulting context: A question set is provided to ensure that each cell has at least one requirement. The question set offers a skeleton springboard to ensure that the basic information is captured. From this basic question set, additional questions will arise, and community, perspective, and focus or association requirements can be categorized by the requirements set framework. Any gaps in the requirements set can be identified early in the process. Other work products are developed from a more complete set of requirements, minimizing the need for rework prior to product release. Future iterations can concentrate on new enhancements rather than bug-related maintenance.

Rationale: As suggested by the Zachman framework (see Chapter Three), a complete requirements set encompasses the different perspectives and focuses. The requirements set framework expands Zachman's work by viewing each focus and perspective in terms of the type of requirements needed to build the specific work product. *Identify All Types* also identifies the need for collaboration among other organizational units (communities) that produce nontechnical work products.

Syntax: The pattern must adhere to the same dimensions as described by the requirements meta pattern, *Identify All Types*. Every cell (perspective, focus, community) in the requirements pattern must be fulfilled. The pattern must include the need for specific association requirements to allow for collaboration between cells. Each cell must document the overall objective of the questions and the roles and responsibilities for the cell. The objective must be a specific "qualifier" representation of the objective stated in the requirements meta pattern. The cell may recommend specific deliverables and techniques that represent the specific questions. Each question within the cell must be geared to derive a specific requirement tailored by the qualifier and be within the scope of the cell. The allocation process of moving from one perspective to the other must be documented. Each answer to a question (the specific requirement) must satisfy the eight criteria for quality requirements specification as defined in the IEEE Std 830: Software Requirements Specification. To prevent requirement gaps, the qualifier pattern must institute a validation checklist for each perspective that is based on the *Identify All Types* validation checklist.

Suggested requirements patterns: A collection of requirements patterns may be customized by business community (marketing, accounting, medical, and so on) but must include collaborating communities (human resources, legal, customer service, and so on) that need to be involved to reach the business objective. A collection of requirements patterns may be customized by technology focus (for example, data warehouse, Internet) but must include nontechnical community involvement (human resources, legal, billing, and so on). A collection of requirements patterns may be tailored by IT impact (new development, enhancement, or maintenance) but must include reference to other communities that may have different IT impacts (such as maintaining the contents of a file/table/object).

Suggested anti-patterns: A collection of anti-patterns may be customized to represent conditions when one or more of the cells are omitted for a specific pattern. Example qualifiers could be customized to support the use of one or two specific methods or the use of specific tools that would not capture all cell requirements.

Name: Identify All (Internet) Types

Identifier: 000002

Mnemonic: I-RP

Also known as: Internet requirements pattern, requirements pattern for Internet-based products

Based on: *Identify All Types* (the requirements meta pattern)

Cell applicability: All

Refactored solution type: Not applicable

Problem: Building an Internet-based product requires the identification of all requirements. All organizational units must be involved and must work at their own velocity even though they are dependent on information gathered by other organizational communities. The purpose of this pattern is to provide a question set to facilitate capturing a complete and quality requirements set for Internet-based applications.

Context: The Internet requires continual releases of components that require parallel work efforts. Given the speed at which each component is developed, there is a risk that not all the requirements will be captured, and they may not be managed through a formal process to ensure a quality Internet product. Requirements should be captured that define important quality of service issues (security, performance) and their impacts on functional requirements (data processing, network). Requirements are easily missed, provided in poor format, or captured late, thus affecting the quality of the iteration and reducing the product's return on investment.

Forces: Internet products are globally visible and expose the corporation to great risk. This risk could result in losing the consumer base, opening up legal exposures, or minimizing the opportunity to meet any of the stated business objectives. A poor-quality Internet product (or any of its iterations) could have a direct negative impact on the corporation's success in the Internet market. Internet applications fail due to identified scenarios, performance issues, or hacker problems, all of which can be addressed in requirements.

Solution: The requirements set framework is used since the breadth of requirements that need to be captured is similar to that of any product. Tailored questions are included that pay particular attention to community involvement, quality of service, and the associations and impacts between requirements. Requirement allocation is key to concurrent efforts for Internet applications. Specific allocation questions are included to identify each organizational unit's level of involvement. The requirements engineer is guided by the use of the tailored question set for each requirements set framework cell to build the Internet product. (See Appendix B for Internet requirements pattern details).

Resulting context: *Identify All Internet Types* provides the requirements engineer with a list of tailored questions and a way to spot weaknesses in the requirements set, thus preventing project failure. The pattern is based on the corporate structure and Internet specifics to facilitate the allocation of responsibility to the correct organizational unit.

Rationale: As illustrated by the evolution of Web-based applications, Internet applications entail different risks than do other software products. The material and process must be smooth for a wider variety of actors. Additional attention must be given to eliminate the possibility of hackers. *Identify All Internet Types* identifies the need for collaboration between the multiple applications (search, order entry, invoicing, and security at multiple levels) and other communities that produce nontechnical work products.

Syntax: The Internet pattern must adhere to the syntax rules of the requirements meta pattern (*Identify All Types*). Additionally, *Identify All Internet Types* must be specific to Internet applications, with a high priority applied to performance, security, usability, and business risk.

Suggested Internet requirements patterns: Internet applications consist of both analysis and transactional types. *Identify All Internet Types* may be further refined to support one or both types of applications. Specific patterns may be developed for business-to-business uses, business-to-customer sites, click-stream data analysis, informational Web sites, or any combination of these.

Suggested anti-patterns: A collection of anti-patterns may be tailored to represent conditions that occur when one of the cells is omitted and the global impact it has on the business. Examples could be tailored to support the minimization of the need for performance, security, usability, and business risk requirements.

Name: Predator

Identifier: 000003

Mnemonic: P-RAP

Also known as: Hacker anti-pattern, capturing security-level requirements

Based on: *Identify All Internet Types*

Cell applicability: Security product constraints and their impacts on all cells

Refactored solution type: Gap in knowledge

Problem: Security is one of the areas of concern for corporations, business partners, and clients. Security precautions can be costly. The objective of this anti-pattern is to capture the level of security as it applies to all focus-delineated requirements.

Context: The Internet has opened the doors for intruders who mean to do harm to corporate assets, whether they be data, processes, customers, policies, or procedures. They intrude by using Trojan horses, piggybacking on other users, dialing analog modems, and so on. During the haste to develop the product, security is second to the common functionality of the product. Security requirements can be either missed or misrepresented in terms of the level of security really needed in different scenarios. The impact of associating requirements could prevent overspending, underprotecting, or missing important security gates that need to be defined.

Forces: Corporate assets are at risk if an unauthorized person, organization, or system infiltrates the corporation's information resources via the Internet. Similarly, applying the highest level of security at every potential point of entry is costly and could degrade performance, thus resulting in conflicts with other requirements.

Solution: Assuming that the requirements set framework is used:

1. *Include a predator in requirements:* Add an actor or user called "predator" to your list of "who" requirements.

2. *Develop scenarios:* Add predator scenarios to every use case and workflow where other users are listed.

3. *Create predator association and priority matrices:* Develop an association between the predator and each class/subclass (entity/subtype), network node, event, business policy/rule, and function. This can be accomplished by developing matrices for each type of association.

4. *Prepare for the inevitable:* Document a process and procedure to follow if a predator slips through the tracks and infiltrates.

(See Chapter Five for solution details.)

Resulting context: The needs as they relate to security are identified and documented. The level of security for each point is identified to alert the designers and builders of the degree of security. Also, procedures are documented for handling infiltrations in case they occur.

Rationale: This anti-pattern forces the requirements engineer and the requirement supplier to think ahead when it comes to security needs.

Syntax: Requirements must be categorized as defined by the requirements set framework. Security-related questions must be part of the question set for the Internet requirements pattern. The matrices developed as part of the supporting documentation for the requirements specification should be similar to those defined by this anti-pattern (see Chapter Five). The key to success of the use of this anti-pattern is the capturing of the associations between security requirements and other requirements. The associations must be qualified to reflect the level of security. All requirements and their levels of security must be approved before being acted upon. Executive management must understand the impacts on project constraints (budget, staff, and other resources). The design of the product must incorporate these requirements.

Suggested similar requirements anti-patterns[4]:   Similar anti-patterns can be developed to use similar matrices for other actors that require special attention.

Name: Quality of Service

Identifier: 000004

Mnemonic: QoS-RAP

Also known as: Product constraints pattern

Based on: *Identify All Internet Types*

Cell applicability: Product constraints and their impacts on all cells

Refactored solution type: Gap in knowledge

Problem: Quality of service (QoS) requirements (such as performance, usability, reliability, and privacy) are part of the customer-centric approach to the Internet. By not defining them along with the impact on functional and product constraint requirements, designers and builders develop their work products based on an incomplete set of requirements.

Context: Capturing only what a modeling tool or a technique requires to develop intricate models represents just a portion of the requirements that need to be satisfied in order to meet the business objective. Most tools omit the need to document nonfunctional requirements that will have a direct impact on the final design.

Forces: Omitting any of the QoS requirements can dramatically affect design decisions and the quality of the Internet product.

Solution: The requirements engineer should take the following steps.

1. Define the QoS topics to be addressed.
2. Define each topic and obtain approval of each definition.
3. For each QoS topic, qualify the association to each owner-level requirement as a separate derived requirement. This can be accomplished with the use of tables or matrices.

---

4. Anti-patterns should be written in a format that does not require additional anti-patterns. This section is provided for the first three anti-patterns only to suggest similar anti-patterns that can be developed by the reader.

4. Rewrite each derived requirement to meet the quality characteristics of a good requirement.

5. Review and approve all impacts prior to implementation.

(See Chapter Five for solution details.)

Resulting context: The impact of each QoS requirement on other requirements is documented in a format that can be traced through designer and builder work products. Defining them as separate requirements enables test engineers to quantify that these requirements were satisfied along with other previously defined requirements.

Rationale: By using this anti-pattern, the requirements engineer can identify QoS requirements and their specific impacts on other requirements. This can be done in addition to and in association with using a preferred CASE modeling tool or modeling language.

Syntax: Requirements must be categorized as defined by the requirements set framework. QoS-related questions must be part of the question set for the Internet requirement pattern. The matrices developed as part of the supporting documentation for the requirements specification should be similar to those defined by this anti-pattern (see Chapter Five). The key to success of the use of this anti-pattern is the capturing of the associations between security requirements and other requirements. The associations must be qualified to reflect the level of impact (for example, performance requirements may vary by actor or device). All requirements and their levels of impact must be approved before being acted upon. Executive management must understand the impacts on project constraints (budget, staff, and other resources). The design of the product must incorporate these requirements.

Suggested similar requirements anti-patterns: All associations between requirements can be handled with a similar approach if defined as separate anti-patterns.

Name: CRUDL

Identifier: 000005

Mnemonic: E-RAP

Also known as: Capturing all entity class events

Based on: *Identify All Internet Types*

Cell applicability: "What", "How", and "When" focus areas

Refactored solution type: Gap in knowledge

Problem: Important events that affect the creation, reading, updating, deleting, or listing of entity class details are missed.

Context: In many instances separate individuals or groups develop data and process requirements. As a result, not all actions on entity classes may be identified. For example, a user may be able to create an order but not be able to delete or change it.

Forces: Missing any requirements may prevent the proper manipulation of information, resulting in missed functionality. Missed functionality (such as the omission of allowing a user to delete an order) reduces customer confidence in the Internet product.

Solution: The requirements engineer must ensure that an event exists for each of the five entity class events (CRUDL) for each entity class. This can be documented through matrices. The next step is to create a similar matrix that documents the associations between the five event types for each entity class and the "how" requirements.

(See Chapter Five for solution details.)

Resulting context: Every event that affects every entity class is identified. Every entity class has its life defined by having an event that can create, update, and delete it. In most cases, each entity class has an event that reads and lists its contents.

Rationale: By using this anti-pattern, the requirements engineer can identify all manipulations against each entity class and ensure that a process is associated to perform each manipulation.

Syntax: Requirements must be categorized as defined by the requirements set framework. CRUDL-related questions must be part of the question set for the Internet requirements pattern. The matrices developed as part of the supporting documentation for the requirements specification should be similar to those defined by this anti-pattern (see Chapter Five). The key to success of the use of this anti-pattern is the capturing of the associations between entity class requirements and other requirements. The associations must be qualified to reflect what in the entity class is changed. All derived requirements must be approved before being acted upon. The design of the product must incorporate these requirements.

Suggested similar requirements anti-patterns: All associations between focus area requirements can be handled with a similar approach if defined as separate anti-patterns.

Name: Business Model Tolerance Parameters

Identifier: 000006

Mnemonic: BMTP-RAP

Also known as: Business triggers

Based on: *Identify All Internet Types*

Cell applicability: "When" focus area

Refactored solution type: Gap in participation

Problem: "When" requirements that are triggered when a condition is reached are many times forgotten. Instead, they are left to be produced in standard reporting. Tolerance parameters should be identified to initiate notification or a countermeasure procedure as soon as the tolerance is reached.

Context: Ad hoc queries and review of standard reports usually determine the success of the Internet product. Given the speed at which the Internet moves, these reports may arrive too late to initiate a countermeasure to correct negative conditions.

Forces: As an example, a flood of e-mails are received based on a new release of the Internet product. Reading the e-mails illustrates that the public is reacting negatively to the new iteration. If no one is capturing the fact that the number of e-mails increased dramatically, the company cannot react to the public reaction. Other examples include sales figures, number of searches without orders, and so on.

Solution: The requirements engineer must elicit from management what the committee members would like to track as a measure of success. The next step is to identify the point at which to trigger action when the measure meets or exceeds the specified tolerance parameters. As part of these measures, a "when" event needs to be defined that triggers reporting, notification, or any other processing that needs to take place. Each allocation level and community may have its own tolerance level that can be documented in a table. How the notification or even the countermeasure will be performed can also be specified in a table. (See Chapter Five for solution details.)

Resulting context: All the conditionally triggered events for which managers requested notification that a condition has been reached or occurred are considered and events created to trigger reports and/or e-mail to the person requesting notification.

Rationale: By using this anti-pattern, the requirements engineer can begin eliciting factors that may affect the projected business model. The requirements engineer is asking questions that will ensure that the management committee identifies when corrective action needs to take place and what that action should be.

Syntax: Requirements must be categorized as defined by the requirements set framework. Business tolerance–related questions must be part of the question set for the Internet requirements pattern. The matrices developed as part of the supporting documentation for the requirements specification should be similar to those defined by this anti-pattern (see Chapter Five). The key to success of the use of this anti-pattern is to capture what needs to be monitored and what should be done when the tolerance level is reached.

Name: Network Engineer Involvement

Identifier: 000007

Mnemonic: NE-RAP

Also known as: Network-related requirements, network engineer requirements subset

Based on: *Identify All Internet Types*

Cell applicability: Relationships between all focus areas based on location points

Refactored solution type: Gap in participation

Problem: Network engineers are often brought into the requirements process too late, in many cases after the design of the Internet application is complete. Network engineers must then work in reaction mode. This can delay the implementation of the product or its iteration due to their late involvement.

Context: Cabling, telephone circuits, and other networking equipment items need to be designed, ordered, configured, and tested before production. Telephone companies may apply additional restrictions that will delay implementation. Network engineers are also pulled in multiple directions to support the organization's projects (internal and external) beyond the Internet product.

Forces: Internet projects are time sensitive. This requires that all communities develop their pieces of the product's solution in parallel. The network is the backbone of the Internet product. Bringing network engineers late into the process guarantees delayed delivery and potentially poor performance.

Solution: The requirements engineer must ensure that requirements are allocated to the network group for early notification of needs. Network engineers must be part of the review process since many other requirements will impact their decisions. Particularly, they need to understand *who needs what when* and *how they will initiate transmission from and to where.* They also need to know product (performance, reliability, security) and project (budget) constraints that will impact their design decisions. Much of this information can be specified in a network location impact matrix. (See Chapter Five for solution details.)

Resulting context: All the information that the network engineers need to design the network is assembled in a format that is easy for them to use and read.

Rationale: By using this anti-pattern, the requirements engineer can verify that all the information needed for the network engineers is available. The network engineers can review the simple tables quickly.

Syntax: Requirements must be categorized as defined by the requirements set framework. Network-related questions must be part of the question set (Appendix B) for the Internet requirements pattern. The matrices developed as part of the supporting documentation for the requirements specification should be similar to those defined by this anti-pattern (see Chapter Five). The key to success of the use of this anti-pattern is to capture the associations between "where" (location) and other focus requirements. The association must be qualified to reflect *who needs what when* and *how they will initiate transmission from and to where.* All derived requirements must be approved before being acted upon. The design of the network must incorporate these requirements.

Name: Click-Stream Data

    Identifier: 000008

    Mnemonic: AP-RAP

    Also known as: Analytical processing, data mining

    Based on: *Identify All Internet Types*

    Cell applicability: "What" and "How" focus areas

Refactored solution type: Gap in participation

Problem: Sales, marketing, executive, and other groups of internal employees need to mine click-stream information to understand or forecast the success of the product being sold. The requirements to perform such actions are sometimes pushed off to another release or forgotten until the last minute. The problem with this is that the information may not be available for these personnel to perform their analyses.

Context: Seldom are databases organized to support both transaction and analytical processing simultaneously. If they are designed for analytical processing, it is because that information is the product being sold. Information may need to be offloaded and reorganized to provide access for internal analytical purposes.

Forces: The internal analysts may require information to be captured from customers or business partners using the Internet product. Not capturing the information or capturing only a subset of the information may provide inaccurate results for the analysts. This may lead to incorrect business decisions that could negatively impact the next evolution of the product.

Solution: The requirements engineer must ensure that analytical needs are captured, even if as a separate project in the program. The needs must be coordinated with transaction processing (or Internet product processing) to ensure that all the information is captured at the point that is relevant to the analysts. The requirements engineer must define the different analysts as separate actors and clarify the kind of analysis they will be performing. The process of populating and maintaining the analytical database needs to be defined as "when" and "what" requirements. Confirmation needs to be made with the executive committee about whether this is a separate project or must be contained with the previously defined budgetary restrictions. (See Chapter Five for solution details.)

Resulting context: The potential need for analytical analysis is identified, with a potential data warehouse project initiated, and all the information to perform the analysis is captured.

Rationale: By using this anti-pattern, the requirements engineer can identify the analysts' needs.

Syntax: Requirements must be categorized as defined by the requirements set framework even if it is considered a separate project. Analytical processing–related questions must be part of the question set for the Internet requirements pattern. The matrices developed as part of the supporting documentation for the requirements specification should be similar to those defined by this anti-pattern (see Chapter Five). The key to success of the use of this anti-pattern is to capture the associations between analytical processing and transaction processing requirements. The associations must be qualified to reflect what information is needed and at what point the information is valuable. The design of the product must incorporate these requirements.

Name: Scope Creep

Identifier: 000009

Mnemonic: SC-RAP

Also known as: Volatile requirements set

Based on: *Identifying All Internet Types*

Cell applicability: All

Refactored solution type: Gap in process

Problem: New requirements are added to the requirements set without a full understanding of their impacts on *all* other requirements (including project constraints) or work products (design, code, legal agreements) already developed.

Context: Requirements have been approved, and the design has already been started if not finished. The program is on schedule and within budget when new requirements are identified and the requirement supplier insists that they be incorporated in the forthcoming iteration of the Internet product. The impact is not assessed and other requirements are not adjusted based on the new requirements. Specifically, project constraints (budgets, time, resources) are not adjusted to reflect the inclusion of the new or dramatically altered requirements. Management is unaware of the addition and assumes all is well until the request is made for more money, time, and resources.

Forces: The addition of new requirements could dramatically increase costs, delay implementation, or change the design, making the product more difficult to enhance as it matures. This needs to be reviewed with the executive management committee to determine the impact on the return on investment; committee members must decide whether to incorporate the request.

Solution: Scope creep becomes a problem if a process is not defined to evaluate and approve the impacts the new or volatile requirements will have on the Internet program or a specific iteration. The requirements engineer must document the new requirement in its entirety (including priority) and assess the impacts of the new requirement (or any change to a requirement) on the approved requirements set. The impact must be reviewed and approved as a whole. This means that the new or changed requirement will probably create a change to project constraints such as budget, time, and resources. (See Chapter Five for solution details.)

Resulting context: Requirements added to the requirements set follow the approval path, impacts on other requirements and work products are documented, and the project constraints of budget, resources, and schedule are adjusted to reflect changes in the requirements set.

Rationale: By using this anti-pattern, the requirements engineer can follow a process that captures requirements, assesses impacts, and obtains approval to incorporate the changes to the requirements set for the next release. Feasibility is reviewed to ensure that the change does not prevent other previously approved requirements from being satisfied.

Syntax: A matrix should be developed that works with a defined process to address the impact of the new or changing requirements. The matrix should be organized as defined by the requirements set framework. Impact-related questions must be part of the question set for the Internet requirements pattern. The matrices developed as part of the supporting documentation for the requirements specification should be similar to those defined by this anti-pattern (see Chapter Five). The key to success of the use of this anti-pattern is obtaining executive approval to follow and enforce this process.

Name: Designer Takeover

Identifier: 000010

Mnemonic: Phy-RAP

Also known as: Technology for the sake of technology, physical design transformation, resume-ready decisions, single vendor solution

Based on: *Identify All Internet Types*

Cell applicability: All

Refactored solution type: Gap in process

Problem: Products are selected because of their features and not because they satisfy all the needs (for example, functionality, QoS, and budgetary requirements).

Context: Requirements are written in a fashion that implies a technology or product. A product on the market is selected due to features that represent the latest and greatest technology. The product features far exceed the needs of the Internet product for the current implementation or a year's worth of requirements for future iterations. The other extreme is that products are selected because they are from the same vendor as other products, creating a single-vendor solution.[5]

Forces: Four forces may be in play to create this situation:

1. Requirements are not written in a design-independent manner.
2. The approved requirements are not given the highest priority when determining solutions.
3. Reviews may be inadvertently converting the requirement to be design-dependent.
4. Budgetary requirements are not associated to the product constraints.

Solution: The requirements engineer must ensure that all requirements are written in a format that meets the quality characteristics. After every review, changes to requirements must be rechecked to ensure that they still meet the quality characteristics. A requirement checklist that incorporates the requirement should be created to assist in evaluating vendor products. This includes tolerance parameters of how well they should satisfy the requirement (for example, performance or storage features of the product do not have to exceed the need by 100 percent if the projected growth of the product is only 25 percent for the next five years). Design decisions that specify products must be associated to the requirements that are satisfied. (See Chapter Five for solution details.)

Resulting context: (1) Requirements do not imply a technical solution and (2) the hardware/software purchase requirements (builder requirements) support the business requirements (planner through designer perspectives) and neither conflict with the product and project constraints defined by the business sponsor.

---

5. This may be a product constraint defined by the organization's product standards group. If so, that requirement does need to be satisfied. This example is provided as a case when that constraint is not in place. In such a scenario, the products may not work together (even if they are part of a suite) and they may not satisfy approved business requirements.

Rationale: By using this anti-pattern, the requirements engineer can control the selection of vendor products or other design decisions to ensure that they accurately satisfy the current and future needs of the product. This ensures that the requirements are the highest priority for design decisions and technical architecture decisions.

Syntax: Requirements must be categorized as defined by the requirements set framework. Review-related questions that ensure requirement compliance by the technologist must be part of the question set for the Internet requirements pattern. The process for evaluating the technical and physical architecture against the requirements set should be clearly defined.

Name: Imposed Deadline

Identifier: 000011

Mnemonic: DL-RAP

Also known as: Deliverable feasibility, project constraint identification and association

Based on: *Identifying All Internet Types*

Cell applicability: Project constraint impacts on the rest of the requirements set

Refactored solution type: Gap in process

Problem: A deadline is accepted with the highest priority without assessing the feasibility of what can be delivered in the time frame allotted.

Context: The schedule, which may or may not have been validated, is accepted verbally and not defined as a requirement. The need automatically carries a high priority even though it does not follow the requirements development process. Staff works at high speed to fulfill this requirement along with all others in attempts to meet the deadline.

Forces: Either quality or cost (or both) are sacrificed in attempts to meet the deadline.

Solution: The requirements engineer must ensure that project constraints (especially schedule) are defined as requirements adhering to the quality characteristics. The project constraints must follow the same process as other requirements. The impact or feasibility must be evaluated and approved by the executive committee. (See Chapter Five for solution details.)

Resulting context: The project deadline is not approved without the identification of what can feasibly be accomplished by that date. The deadline requirement is defined clearly as to the business reason for that date.

Rationale: By using this anti-pattern, the requirements engineer can identify and assess the feasibility of schedule-related requirements. The process includes approval of these requirements against the quality characteristics (especially feasibility). The requirements engineer can facilitate the negotiation that keeps quality, time, and cost in concert.

Syntax: Project constraint requirements as well as all other requirements must be categorized as defined by the requirements set framework. Scheduling questions concerning the clarification of the need and its impact on or association to the other requirements must be part of the question set for the Internet requirements pattern. The schedule requirements and the associations must be reviewed for impact and feasibility. The matrices developed as part of the supporting documentation for the requirements specification should be similar to those defined by this anti-pattern (see Chapter Five). The key to success is to include project constraints in the requirements specification and process. This ensures that they are validated for feasibility during reviews and approved by executive management. By using this anti-pattern, the requirements engineer can verify that all the information needed by the network engineers is available in a format that they can readily use.

The Pattern at Work

Introduction

The requirements pattern and anti-patterns have been used on several projects. They include projects ranging from new applications to enhancements of existing Internet products. The four examples discussed in this appendix were selected to illustrate the following key points from this book:

- *Requirement coverage:* using the pattern to capture the breadth of requirements
- *Requirement allocation:* distributing the requirements to initiate and ensure proper participation
- *Requirements process:* coordinating the efforts to effectively manage change

To protect the confidentiality of these initiatives, names, product functionality, and such details were changed or omitted.

Focus Coverage: Commodities Clearing

Background

Three existing companies joined forces to develop an Internet service for clearing trades for the U.S. energy market (for example, electricity, gas, coal, water, crude oil, and petroleum products). Two of the companies offered experience in the energy market, the other in clearing government securities.

All three companies provided knowledge experts[1] who were geographically dispersed. The business case was already developed and approved by all three companies' executive managers.

Four requirements engineers were assigned to this effort. One was the lead and architect of the requirements set, another a trainee, and the remaining two were fully trained in requirements engineering best practices but not in the specific tool, technique, or pattern usage. None of the requirements engineers had experience in either the clearing of any financial instruments or the energy market.

Their assignment was to develop a software requirements specification that could be submitted to eight internal and external organizations to obtain an accurate development and implementation estimate. In the minds of the knowledge experts and the members of the management committee, the business case was complete and only the software requirements needed to be documented.

The Requirements Process

The first meeting between the knowledge experts and the requirements engineers was held in one location for an afternoon. The agenda called for the knowledge experts to express their expectations for the requirements phase and to walk through portions of the business case that pertained to the product concept. By the end of the meeting, the knowledge experts felt overwhelmed by the amount of information that was missing and needed to be defined to clarify the product concept. They agreed in their original estimate that it would take two weeks to complete the requirements phase was not feasible.

The business case defined the product concept but omitted the following information:

- *Who:* Only the primary users of the product were defined. They did not include a risk manager, regulatory agencies, or accounting systems that would produce invoices.
- *What:* The only information that was identified to be captured was product information, customer information, and trade information. By the end of the meeting the list had expanded to support 22 additional key pieces of information[2] that were needed.

---

1. Only one of the knowledge experts had previous experience in working with information technology to develop a software application. Over time, it was discovered that the previous experience was less than pleasant. This hostile requirement supplier was dealt with using extreme diplomacy!
2. Through analysis, this list of 25 grew to 65!

- *Where:* The primary concentration of traders was located in Texas. The operations for the clearing facility were to be in New York. Other than that, the only location information contained in the business case was the need to use the Internet for all transactions. [3]
- •*When:* The only responsibility, at first glance, was to support the front-end submission and matching (buyers with sellers) of trades. If questions were not asked about other events, billing the traders (and many others) would have been omitted.
- *Why:* The business rules were defined in legal documents that were separate from the business case. They defined the business partnership between the three companies and the responsibilities of all potential customers.
- *How:* These same legal documents provided information that led to more than just business rules. Through reading these documents, the requirements engineers identified additional data, actors, and processes that needed to be performed to complete the workflow.
- *Product constraints:* No product constraints were identified in the business case. The discussion on software expectations identified 15 items that were important to them, which covered security, performance, and usability issues.
- *Project constraints:* The business community set no limits that would constrain either the design or the project until asked how they determined the potential return on investment! It was at that point that the knowledge experts realized how much they had underestimated the cost of developing a software solution.

After this session, more questions were raised and unanswered than these knowledge experts could have imagined. The knowledge experts spent the next hour issuing e-mails to other knowledge experts to obtain additional scoping requirements. At the end of this session, flight arrangements were changed to accommodate continuing the requirements evolution through to the next perspective.

The next day was extremely productive. The knowledge experts had arranged for additional support by having additional requirement suppliers teleconference into portions of the meeting.

---

3. The requirements engineers categorized this specific need as a product constraint that would be associated to the appropriate actors, data, events, and processes that specifically used the Internet.

Describing the requirements set framework kicked off the first half hour of the session. This provided everyone with an understanding of perspective and focus. The team also discussed the need for additional work products that were separate from the software requirements specification. Though this was outside the responsibilities of the requirements engineers, the knowledge experts alerted the other business communities (primarily human resources and accounting) because of the discussion of business communities.

Meetings with everyone in the same room were rare. Therefore, the elicitation and validation phases were conducted primarily via e-mails or conference calls at least three times a week lasting anywhere from one to three hours. Each requirements pattern cell was submitted individually and provided an agenda for the meeting. Each cell was updated with additional requirements that the requirements engineers and requirement suppliers asked to keep as a history (and to be used for other projects).

Meeting minutes were developed at the end of every meeting. The requirements were analyzed and any conflicts or issues were documented as part of the meeting minutes. The requirement suppliers read and commented on all the minutes. They thought the minutes provided an excellent communication vehicle as well as an audit trail of business decisions that set the direction for the product.

Postanalysis of Pattern Usage

The entire requirements effort took six months. The resulting 500-page requirements specification was defined through the designer level. The requirement suppliers read and validated every requirement, including associative requirements.

The previously hostile requirement supplier admitted that many requirements would have been overlooked or misrepresented if the group had not used the requirements pattern and anti-patterns. He is now one of the biggest proponents of the pattern within the three companies and carries the specification to every meeting in which work products based on the requirements are discussed.

The requirements specification was packaged and submitted for bids to eight companies. Each one of them commented on how well the specification was organized. They also noted that the specification was in enough detail that they felt comfortable with their fixed price estimates![4]

---

4. The better the requirements are specified, the more accurate the project schedule and cost will be.

The requirements engineers were not part of this phase. They did, however, leave behind the rest of the Internet requirements pattern complete with question lists and anti-patterns for the technical architects. Through research and a full understanding of the requirements, the technical architect found a product that would support most of the requirements. The vendor, after reading the requirements specification, agreed to enhance the product to incorporate the remaining requirements.

Participation Coverage: Online Catalog

Background

An existing catalog company had a successful mail-order business complete with a team of order-entry individuals. The marketing department wanted to join other companies and "be on the web" before the upcoming holiday rush. To meet the time-to-market pressure (two months), the first iteration of the site simply opened the already existing order-entry system to the Web. This task was allocated directly to the builders of the order-entry system. For this first iteration, no requirements engineers or technical architects were involved.

The next printed catalog was mailed with the Web address and a discount coupon for using the new medium for orders. The developers knew nothing about the discount coupon. The site went live just as the potential customers received their mailings. Orders started trickling into the site at the same rate that the order-entry people were receiving mail and phone calls. The problem was that the order-entry individuals were not receiving orders but questions on how to use the site! The Web masters were receiving questions at an alarming rate— questions on how to order products with the discount and complaints about the site's performance.

A network engineer was assigned to address the performance issue. First he asked to see the network requirements that included the data and transaction volume by activity. Since this along with other important information was not available, the network engineer recommended that the company assign a requirements engineer to do a gap analysis and elicit any missing requirement-related information.

The Requirements Process

It was apparent to the hired requirements architect that network-related requirements were not the only requirements missing. By skipping perspectives, the developers had failed to understand the business flow. The only existing written documentation was for the order-entry personnel, complete with sticky notes that explained how to work around the existing system. When reviewing the database contents, it was discovered that order-entry personnel also knew that the system never calculated or captured discounts. They used a manual override facility to supply the correct discounted price for the customer.

The requirements architect met with representatives from the developers of the Internet-based application, the order-entry personnel, and the marketing department. The meeting began with a storyboard of a customer browsing and ordering a product. Database queries were used to identify the number of orders, products, and other key information. Market projections were used to document potential growth and peak season volumes.

The requirements architect developed a requirements specification using the Internet requirements set framework. Where requirement gaps existed, the question list for the requirement cell was inserted (in red) into the specification. The largest gaps included the following:

- No initiating requirements were documented.
- The verbal requirements were not allocated to all the communities (including inventory systems, accounting systems, and advertising).
- No scope-level requirements were documented or reviewed for potential impact within the systems area or across business communities.
- The requirements set captured (and implemented) included only the workflow for documenting an order and the data for a full-price order.
- No one knew the business policies for discounting (apparently, the discount applied only to orders of $150 or more shipped within the United States).

Comparisons were then made between the current system, the Internet-based system, customer e-mails from the first iteration, and the requirements captured during the storyboard session. A summary report included these requirement-related gaps:

- The order-entry facility was not intuitively understood by the average Internet user. Order-entry personnel were a close-knit group where workarounds were verbally discussed but rarely documented. *(Missed business flow— "how" and "what" requirements; lack of participation of a usability engineer.)*

- Neither the internal system nor the Internet-based system supported discounting. *(Missed business scenario—"how," "what," and "why" requirements.)*
- The marketing projections were accurate for peak season but not communicated to the network personnel. *(Missed "when" details and associations with location requirements concerning volumetrics and missed allocation process.)*
- A customer did not know whether a product was on backorder until a confirmation message was e-mailed within 48 hours. In a third of the backorder scenarios, the order was canceled. Unfortunately, the Internet product did not offer the cancellation facility to the customer. Only a small number of order-entry personnel (supervisor level) had that authority. This was due to the fact that canceling an order required access to a separate inventory system. *(Missed "who," "what," "when," and association requirements.)*

Postanalysis of Pattern Usage

The Internet requirements pattern proved to be an effective tool even after the requirements were implemented. While reviewing the gaps, it was determined that the site would be pulled and a new iteration developed from scratch. The site was so poorly designed due to an incomplete requirements set and poor requirements process that the executives felt the exposure would do more damage to potential sales and cost more to support the flood of questions than if they pulled the site.

The process used by the requirements architect was to be implemented immediately after initial training of business and system personnel. A new process included the following key points:

- A businessperson was put in charge of coordinating all the work products, ensuring that they all complied with the same set of initiating requirements *(program management)*.
- Work products were to be reviewed at specific stages of development *(perspective evolution)*.
- Requirements were allocated and managed using a requirements management tool *(allocation activity)*. Allocation was based on the corporate structure including all business communities *(community dimension)*.
- No change was to be accepted without global approval from a representative from each business community and a system representative *(requirements management)*.

- Each requirement specification was to include a section for each focus area (*who, what, where, when, why, how, product constraints, project constraints* and associations).
- The Internet requirements pattern question set was to be used (and improved) during every review session.

Each iteration of an Internet-based application requires that the requirements be allocated, elicited, analyzed, specified, validated, approved, and managed through each perspective to all business and system communities. This enables

- All work products to be based on the same set of initiating requirements
- Everyone within and across business communities who should be involved to be notified of their involvement as soon as possible
- The ability to identify the impact of a change before acting on it
- The changes to be reflected in all work products

The Internet product continues to evolve with a new release every other month. The small development staff now includes a requirements team of three individuals. Their role is to allocate, coordinate, and manage the requirements set across the company. They work closely with the program manager educating new members of the team about the kinds of questions to ask. They developed a specific Internet requirements anti-pattern for the program manager to use for each review session to ensure that all the requirements are communicated and coordinated to all communities.

Getting Started: Community Lifestyle

Background

One person wanted a single site for investigating all the neighborhood activities. This included school information, kids' sports information, grocery sales, local weather reports (with school closings and delays) and so forth. He developed a site with portals into local sites that had this information.

Through general chitchat at a parent-teacher association (PTA) meeting, word about this site spread like wildfire. Pressures came to continually add more portals and update (a manual effort) information in databases when online access was not available.

With the increase in site usage, the idea came to turn this evolving home-grown site into a business. Being a technician by trade, the site creator requested assistance from a requirements engineer who had an understanding of what needed to be developed to build a business case for capital.

The Requirements Process

For the most part the solution was well defined. A few issues concerning maintainability and scalability would require more thought as more neighborhoods were established. This led the team to discuss the need to define the potential users for the different neighborhood sites. The creator had built the site to meet his specific needs, and now he had to broaden the requirements to support neighborhoods located anywhere in the United States and potentially anywhere in the world! The business case had to be built based on a wider audience, illustrating a full understanding of the customizability (and maintainability) for the different neighborhoods.

The objective for the first meeting was to outline the scope section of the business case. The scope focused on the different kinds of users of the neighborhood site, which both clarified the target customers (parents of school-age children) and the extended audience (schools, organizations, advertisers). The community allocation schema (business practice, support, organizational, technical) was used to spark discussion of the different user classes to be supported and those that should be denied access. The next step was to use questions for the owner perspective to identify the relationships between the different user classes and other functional focus requirements (what, where, when, why, and how).

A separate discussion was held to define the culture of the neighborhood offerings. Different business rules (such as privacy of children's personal information and what kinds of companies would not be allowed to advertise on the site) were defined that led to defining the mission statement for this company.

These needs, however, vary from neighborhood to neighborhood:

- How would personnel determine what should be part of the site?
- What is available for each neighborhood?
- Is there a common set of standard portals that every neighborhood would want?
- Do the security requirements change for each portal and/or neighborhood?
- Will anyone pay for the neighborhood service or to be part of the neighborhood service?

Postanalysis of Pattern Usage

The Internet requirements pattern was used to identify gaps in knowledge. For the business case, the planner (lists) and owner (relationships) perspectives were used to clarify the scope and potential growth patterns. The concentration on business rules ("why" requirements) clarified the philosophy of the organization and the neighborhood site. Using the association questions, the impacts of each rule on users, data, and processing were clearly defined.

The planner perspective of the Internet requirements pattern was tailored for each user type identified during the requirements session. The questions were organized by focus area complete with matrices to identify focus interdependencies. These user-type specifics were placed in the business case appendix to illustrate to the grant committees:

- An understanding of the different user needs
- What needs to be captured to implement a specific neighborhood site

Since privacy and security were also key concerns to potential users, antipatterns were customized from those described in this book and also supplied as part of the appendix. Reference was made to these under the risks and countermeasures section of the business case.

Process Coverage: Mobility

Background

The stock-trading system required that traders be at their desks or be within view of a large screen that portrayed the fluctuations in market conditions. Everyone on the trading floor saw the same view. With the expanded use of PDAs, pagers, and cell phones, executives wanted to enhance the system to transfer customized information to individual traders.

Two requirements engineers (one junior and one senior) and a systems architect were assigned to assess the impact this requirement would have on the existing system. The systems architect was one of the original designers of the trading application.

The Requirements Process

The Internet requirements pattern was used to reorganize the system documentation by focus. A list was defined to represent the different components of the system. The list was documented as individual owner-level requirements. Relationships (dependencies) were included in the list. The relationship between the nontechnical description of each requirement and the associated system component (table name, method name, window name) was also important. The names and labels were used as row and column headings for the matrices that were developed.

Postanalysis of Pattern Usage

The process that was used for this project was documented and implemented as a way to assess the impact of any system enhancement. This process provided the ability to capture the current functionality (in terms of requirements) from a nontechnical perspective. This provided a document for the different business communities to validate and approve the necessary changes. Using the requirements set framework provided an organization that was logical to both the business and information technology communities. The correlation between the requirements and the existing system components provided a vehicle for fully determining the impact on the existing system (which program, files, and so on needed to be changed and to what degree). The pattern question set provided a checkpoint to elicit additional requirements and information that might have been overlooked (thus misjudging the potential impact).

Conclusion

The concepts portrayed in this book have been used successfully on several products in various forms. The Internet requirements pattern and its associated anti-patterns were used in the previous examples. These examples illustrated that capturing requirements is a necessary activity for any size project. The Internet requirements pattern can be used to assist in developing a new application from a concept, enhancing an existing product, or validating the requirement coverage. Using the pattern and anti-pattern assumes that a requirements process is followed that develops the concept into the final product release. The different activities in the process assist in allocating, capturing, validating, and managing the requirements. The pattern is a tool that can be used to develop requirements or to illustrate an understanding of concepts to venture capitalists or grant providers.

Glossary

The terms in this glossary are commonly used throughout the field of requirements engineering. The definitions are drawn from several sources listed in the bibliography and are tailored to relate directly to the contents of this book. For example, terms that are often used specifically for software requirements and software engineering have been changed to apply to any product that would require the capturing of requirements. The definitions are provided as a reference for this book alone and are by no means to be interpreted as industry standards.

Acceptance criteria. Criteria used to determine that the proposed requirement' has been satisfied in the information technology solution.

Ad hoc development method. A popular method of developing software where success depends on individuals and not on a set of repeatable tasks.

Allocated requirements. Requirements that have been partitioned and allocated (assigned) to the appropriate lower-level suborganization or system based on the scope of responsibilities.

Allocation. The process of determining and assigning the responsibility of a component to the appropriate lower suborganization or system. *Requirement allocation* refers to the determination and assignment of responsibility to the appropriate individual or group to evolve the requirement into work products.

Allocation level. An organizational break within a business community that determines ownership and responsibility to evolve a requirement. The number of allocation levels depends on the size of the project and the organization standards. This book identifies four core allocation levels: corporate, divisional, architectural, and product.

Ambiguity. The specifics of a requirement are open to different interpretations.

Analysis. The process of studying the requirements to identify the details and how they relate to each other to comprise the whole set. The analysis process is aimed at uncovering any gaps in knowledge in the requirements set. The process also uncovers any inconsistencies between requirements within the requirements pattern cell as well as between cells.

Anti-pattern. A textual document that clearly defines a recurring situation that causes frequent mistakes in projects and provides solutions to avoid the mistakes if the situation occurs. *See also* Requirements anti-pattern.

Architecture. The physical properties of the product. For Internet products, several architectures are developed that must support each other, including application, network, and technological.

Artifact. A piece of information that provides knowledge of the business and its operations. Artifacts can take the form of business models or business rules. Artifacts may be requirements to be satisfied by a specific product. However, not all artifacts are requirements.

Association requirements. Requirements that (1) identify all characteristics relevant to the interfacing of two or more requirements provided by one or more organizations and (2) ensure that proposed changes to these characteristics are evaluated and approved prior to implementation.

Baseline. A snapshot of a work product at a specific point in time. Baselines are typically taken after a change is validated and approved.

Baseline management. In configuration management, the application of technical and administrative direction to designate the documents and changes to those documents that formally identify and establish baselines at specific times during the life cycle of a configuration item.

Bug. *See* Defect.

Business community. An area of the business (for example, marketing, accounting) or other form of activity that shares common functions (for example, information technology organization). It is the third dimension of the requirements meta pattern that is derived from the organizational structure of the corporation. *See also* Domain.

Business requirement. A requirement in nontechnical terms and at the perspective levels: planner (boundary setting), owner (relationship and relation definition), and designer (requirement detail).

Business rule. A declaration of what the business operation must enforce. It can take the form of constraints, heuristics, computations, inferences, or timings. A business rule may be a requirement for the product. It may impact information relationships, optionality, event actions, or procedures. All business rules should be maintained in a rule book that can be stored in a requirements management tool. *See also* Artifact.

Business to business (B2B). *See* Internet application integration, e-business.

Business to consumers (B2C). *See* e-Commerce.

Capability Maturity Model (CMM). A model developed and maintained by the Software Engineering Institute of Carnegie Mellon University for assessing the maturity of an organization's development process. Two models currently being integrated affect the requirements process: (1) software engineering (SW-CMM) and (2) higher-level of systems engineering development (SE-CMM). The models define different maturity levels from initial (ad hoc or chaotic development style) to optimized.

Change control. Refers to the management of requirements as they move from one state to another. Change control describes the management of the change process.

Change-control board (CCB). A group matrixed from related areas that is responsible for activities involving access and security related to the use of specific configuration items. The movement and change of each identified and approved requirement, association, and link needs to be captured. Documented procedures for these activities should be simple, clear, and followed.

Choiceboard. An e-business feature that provides the ability for the customer to customize a product before shipment.

Collaboration/responsibility cards (CRC). First introduced at the Object-Oriented Programming, Systems Languages, Applications (OOPSLA) conference in 1989 by Ken Beck and Ward Cunningham, and furthered by Rebecca Wirfs-Brock, this technique is a training mechanism to shift programmers and designers to the object-oriented paradigm. Each index card represents an event and is passed along to project team participants to supply information and/or processing (methods) they must perform to fulfill the event. This technique is most often used to capture requirements but can also be used to prototype and validate requirements for a business workflow.

Completeness. (1) The individual requirement contains all the pieces required to specify the requirement and to manage the requirement throughout its evolution into the implemented product. (2) The requirements set contains all the fully defined requirements that need to be satisfied in order to build a quality end product that meets the business objective.

Computer Aided System Engineering (CASE). Tools that assist with the analysis, specification, and validation of requirements and assist in the transformation from business to physical implementation of work products.

Concurrent engineering. The ability to develop multiple iterations of a product concurrently with other products within the project or program (for example, marketing personnel develop their work products in conjunction with the Internet-based application development). All must meet the same business objective.

Configuration control. An element of configuration management, consisting of the evaluation, coordination, approval or disapproval, and implementation of changes to configuration items after formal establishment of their configuration identification. *See also* Change control.

Configuration control board (CCB). A group of people responsible for evaluating and approving or disapproving proposed changes to configuration items and for ensuring implementation of approved changes. *See also* Change-control board.

Configuration identification. An element of configuration management consisting of selecting the configuration items for a system and recording their functional and physical characteristics in technical documentation; the current approved technical documentation for a configuration item as set forth in specifications, drawings, associated lists, and documents referenced therein.

For requirements, this includes the individual requirements, the pieces of each requirement (for example, validation criteria), the relationship between individual requirements, the representation of the requirements (models), and the requirements set—all at their different configuration stages.

Configuration item (CI). A distinguishable deliverable that can change throughout the development of the product. A configuration item can consist of several configuration items, just as a car motor has several parts within parts. Each part is a configuration item, as well as the parts within the parts, as well as the relationship between the parts.

Configuration item development record. A document used in configuration management describing the development status of a configuration item based on the results of configuration audits and design reviews.

Configuration management (CM). A discipline applying technical and administrative direction and surveillance to identifying and documenting the functional and physical characteristics of a configuration item, controlling changes to those characteristics, recording and reporting change processing and implementation status, and verifying compliance with specified requirements.

Configuration status accounting. An element of configuration management consisting of the recording and reporting of information needed to manage a configuration effectively. This information includes a listing of the approved configuration identification, the status of proposed changes to the configuration, and the implementation status of approved changes.

Constraint. A restriction on either the design or the management of a project.

Context diagram. A diagram that illustrates the scope of investigation. It illustrates the external interfaces of people (roles/actors), systems, or organizations that will interface with the proposed scope, as well as the beginning and end points of the e-business workflow and the actions that will cause reaction within the Internet-based application.

Correctness. The requirement accurately describes the need to be specified.

Countermeasure. The means that will be taken to avoid specific risks.

Critical item. In configuration management, an item within a configuration item that, because of special engineering or logistical considerations, requires an approved specification to establish technical or inventory control at the component level. An e-business example is the legal notice supplied on a Web site (for example, *www.ebay.com*) describing the responsibilities of the buyer and seller as well as intermediary facilitators.

Customer. The desired person, organization, or system that will interface directly with (and use) the product. Hackers and other people, organizations, or systems that should not have access should not be considered customers or clients.

Customized view. An e-business term referring to the user's ability to customize the look of the front end for the user's purpose. Examples of this customization exist on news sites such as *www.yahoo.com* and *www.msnbc.com*, creating "my.xxxxx.com" for the customer, and on *www.amazon.com*, which has taken customization a step further to provide the customer with "like" information based on the previous buying and search patterns of the user.

Data. Components of information available for interpretation.

Data dictionary. A software tool that contains information about the data and their relationships, formats, business meanings, locations, and so forth.

Data mart. A subset of a data warehouse, designed to support the unique business unit requirements of a specific application.

Data warehouse. A storage facility of informational data that are integrated, subject-oriented, time-based, and nonvolatile. It is designed to be easier to access than operational data and to reduce the contention for the data. The data contained in the data warehouse originate elsewhere, either internal or external to the corporation, and are integrated and cleansed from various sources.

Decision maker. A person with the authority to make a decision about (1) the continuance of a project, (2) the contents of an iteration, and (3) the organizational allocation of requirement responsibility.

Defect. Any part of the solution or work product that does not conform to the needs, as specified by the business.

Derived requirement. A need to be satisfied in order to satisfy a primary requirement.

Domain. A category of knowledge.

e-Business (B2B). Conducting business on the Internet between businesses, such as a vendor and a supplier.

e-Commerce (B2C). Conducting business on the Internet directly between a single organization and its consumers.

Ease of use. A key term in describing the need to build an interface that will be easy for the user to navigate in order to quickly find the information needed. Note that stating a requirement as "ease of use" is ambiguous.

Elicitation. The first of the requirement subactivities, whose purpose is to capture the needs as specified by the requirement suppliers. The activity works in a cycle with the next two subactivities (analysis and specification) and occurs at every allocation and perspective level.

Enterprise application integration (EAI). Integration of applications within the boundaries of an organization.

Essential requirement details. Detailed information about each requirement that is necessary to explain the meaning of the requirement.

Event. Timing or "when" requirements. Four types exist: (1) *standard:* the arrival of data from outside the scope of analysis in a predefined manner (initiated by a person, group, or system); (2) *ad hoc:* a request not in a predefined manner (initiated by a person or group); (3) *time-initiated:* a date/time being reached (initiated by: time of day, expiration date, and so on); and (4) *conditional:* a specific condition coming into existence or being detected (initiated by an internal process).

Executive sponsor. The executive responsible for the success of the e-business product. He or she ensures that the program remains focused on the business objective and is responsible for resolving any organizational conflicts (including allocation conflicts between organizational units that try to take on additional responsibilities or those that try to avoid them).

Extranet. A forum for accessing information between corporations or business partners; not open to the general public.

Facilitation. A workshop dedicated to leading the group toward the agreed-upon outcome. For requirements elicitation, a facilitation session is led by a skilled facilitator to identify and document objective (nonpolitical) decisions.

Feasibility. The degree to which the requirements can be implemented under existing constraints (such as current technology and market pressures).

Feature. A distinguishing characteristic specified by the requirements documentation that appears in the implemented solution. A programmer/developer cannot decide to add a feature to a product without validation and approval by the review team.

Flexibility. The ease with which the work product can be modified for use for the next iteration or in applications or environments other than those for which it was specifically designed.

Focus. A tailored point of view of the community and perspective. The focus areas contain functional ("who," "what," "where," "when," "why," and "how") and nonfunctional (product constraints and project constraints) requirements.

Functional configuration audit (FCA). An audit conducted to verify that the development of a configuration item has been completed satisfactorily, that the item has achieved the performance and functional characteristics specified in the functional or allocated configuration identification, and that its operational and supporting documents are complete and satisfactory. This is a post-requirement activity to ensure that the requirements, as specified and validated, are satisfied in other work products (design, prototypes, databases, code, the final e-business product).

Functional configuration identification. In configuration management, the current approved technical documentation for a configuration item. It prescribes all necessary functional characteristics, the tests required to demonstrate achievement of specified functional characteristics, the necessary interface characteristics with associated configuration items, the configuration item's key functional characteristics and its key lower-level configuration items, if any, and design constraints. With respect to requirements, a functional configuration item is the validation criteria that may be managed separately from the requirements but must be associated to the individual requirement.

Functional requirement. A requirement that must be implemented in one of the work products that represent the final solution. They fall within the focus areas of "who," "what," "where," "when," "why," and "how."

IEC. International Electrotechnical Commission.

Information Systems Architecture. Developed by John Zachman to illustrate the different perceptions and focuses required to implement a software system; also known as the *Zachman framework*. It is the basis for the requirements set framework discussed in this book.

Initiating requirement. The product idea that, once approved, sparks the development of the requirements set consisting of primary and derived requirements. Initiating requirements can come from outside corporate boundaries (external) or from within corporate boundaries (internal). The initiating requirements must be organized around the idea to define the business concept.

Institute of Electrical and Electronics Engineers (IEEE). The world's oldest and largest association of professionals within the computer field, which provides standards to be used in developing software and defines its objective to "advance global prosperity by promoting the engineering process of creating, developing, integrating, sharing, and applying knowledge about electrical and information technologies and sciences for the benefit of humanity and the profession." The IEEE provides conferences, technical community and group benefits, and publications, among which is the *IEEE Software Engineering Standards Collection*, a must-have for the requirements engineer.

Internet. An open-access forum for accessing a wide range of information, products, and services. The access is achieved with the open connection of servers across a public network.

Internet application integration (IAI). Integration of applications across multiple corporations.

Internet requirement. A requirement targeted for an Internet solution to be built or changed.

Internet requirements anti-pattern. A requirements anti-pattern tailored to avoid a specific but common obstacle in capturing Internet requirements.

Internet requirements pattern. A framework based on the requirements pattern that is tailored specifically for Internet-based solutions.

Intersecting requirements. *See* Association requirements.

Intranet. A forum for accessing information within corporate boundaries.

ISO. International Standards Organization.

Key process area (KPA). A set of activities and tasks that, when performed, will determine whether a specific software development process was performed in a quality manner. A set of KPAs is defined for each maturity level of the Capability Maturity Model.

Knowledge expert. A person with detailed knowledge of a specific business community who provides the essential details for all or a subset of the requirements. This person may be internal or external to the organization, possibly a business partner involved in the e-business development.

Meta pattern. A pattern that defines the language for expressing a pattern for a specific work product (for example, a requirements meta pattern is the meta pattern for defining any requirements related patterns).

Method. A description of activities to be performed to develop a specific product.

Methodology. A description of activities, or a group of methods, to be performed to develop a product. It may encompass multiple components and work products; each has a specific method for development.

Metric. A quantitative measure of the degree to which a component possesses a given attribute.

Model. A representation of a work product. Contains a visual representation along with supporting textual descriptions. For software requirements, common models are object and data. Both have diagrams to visibly illustrate the requirements and are accompanied by textual information.

Nonfunctional requirements. Requirements that implicitly impact the solution. They consist of those that constrain the design (sometimes referred to as *quality of service requirements*) or constrain the management of the project (such as delivery dates or budget).

Pattern. Any reusable template based on experience that can be used to generate a solution to a problem or need in a specific context.

Perspective. One of the dimensions of the requirements pattern that defines the level of abstraction of the requirement and product components.

Postcondition. The condition that must be in effect after an action or activity takes place; part of an event and use case definition.

Precondition. The condition that must be in effect before an action or activity can take place; part of an event and use case definition.

Primary requirement. A requirement that comes from the source as a need to be satisfied. It is not a requirement that is to support the satisfaction of another requirement.

Priority. The level of importance assigned to an item. In the Internet environment where multiple business communities are involved, a simple requirement may be a high priority to one community and a low priority to another. It is important that the requirements engineer work with the executive committee to define a single priority for every requirement.

Process. Description of the activities to be performed by specific roles. The process defines an evolution of the work product with inputs and outputs for each activity. The process has a single objective that can be correlated with the objective of building a piece of the final product or monitoring the quality of the product's evolution.

Process outsourcing. The business practice of forming a business partnership with another company to perform tasks no longer performed by the initiating company.

Product configuration identification. From the configuration management lexicon; the current approved or conditionally approved technical documentation defining a configuration item during the production, operation, maintenance, and logistic support phases of its life cycle. The documentation prescribes all necessary physical or form, fit, and function characteristics of a configuration item, the selected functional characteristics designated for production acceptance testing, and the production acceptance tests. With respect to requirements, product configuration identification refers to the definition of the requirement work products, the format of the requirement work products, and the process of evolving from one requirement work product to another.

Product risk. Product risk is the potential for defects to occur in the functionality of the Internet product (features that are absent or not working as desired).

Program. In the context of program management, refers to a major project that incorporates multiple projects with the same business objective. Each of the individual projects has its own project manager and project plan that must be coordinated with a master program manager and plan. All the project milestones, deliverables, and issues must be coordinated through the program office. Changes in the specific project requirements must be reviewed for impact across all the projects under the program office.

Program initiative. The development of a product that includes the successful quality completion of parallel projects. Each of the smaller projects has the same business objective. Each of the smaller projects must be coordinated under the direction of a program manager.

Project management. The discipline for organizing, planning, monitoring, and tracking a project.

Project plan. A project document that defines the roles, responsibilities, activities, standards, and schedule for the product development. The program has an overall plan that includes monitoring of several project plans. The individual project plans are developed with the objective to deliver work products to build the final product.

Project risk. The potential for problems to occur regarding the effectiveness of the project, therefore affecting the return on investment: cost overruns, delayed implementation (especially if a problem results in missed market opportunities or allows another "dot-com" to obtain brand acceptance), or resource conflicts (lack of staff, insufficient skills).

Project schedule. The portion of the project plan that describes the timeline of tasks to be completed by specific roles or specific individuals and dependencies.

Project tracking. The activity of monitoring the status of the project. The work products tracked are the project schedule, issues, and defect reports. The project-tracking deliverable can be an updated project schedule with a summary of project status.

Prototype. A requirement technique used to validate an understanding of a subset of requirements.

Quality assurance. The activity of describing, prior to beginning the project, the process and standards by which the work product should be developed.

Quality control. The activity of reviewing the work product for defects after it is completed.

Quality of service requirements. *See* Nonfunctional requirements.

Requirement. A need that must be satisfied by the product solution.

Requirement category. Defines the cell: community, perspective, and focus, for which the requirement is defined.

Requirement checklist. A tool within each requirement cell or for the requirements set that identifies what to look for when evaluating the requirement cell contents.

Requirement cohesion. The measurement that the individual requirements of the entire requirements set (or within requirements subsets) have a commonality of purpose.

Requirement community. A requirement delegated to a specific business unit with the responsibility for final development. The requirement may be an initial, a primary, or a derived (support or association) requirement. One of three cell category assignments. *See* Requirement focus *and* Requirement perspective *for the other two cell category assignments.*

Requirement conflict. When the satisfaction of one requirement will prevent another requirement from being satisfied.

Requirement constraint. A nonfunctional-type requirement that restricts the design of the product or restricts the management of the project.

Requirement flowdown. The systematic decomposition of requirements into allocated and derived requirements, appropriately assigned to low-level functional components.

Requirement focus. A requirement describing a specific representative view. The requirement may be either functional ("who," "what," "where," "when," "why," or "how") or nonfunctional (product constraint, project constraint). One of three cell category assignments. *See* Requirement, community *and* Requirement perspective *for the other two cell category assignments.*

Requirement perspective. A requirement describing an evolutionary stage in the product's development that implies the level of detail or viewpoint. Can be either planner, owner, designer, builder, or subcontractor. One of three cell category assignments. *See* Requirement community *and* Requirement focus *for the other two cell category assignments.*

Requirement shifting. A change to an approved requirement that changes the meaning of the need. This occurs more frequently with requirements that do not satisfy the quality characteristics (more commonly, priority, ambiguity, correctness, and completeness).

Requirement suppliers. Individuals or groups who are sources of requirement information. They can be those that provide the idea (external or internal to the company) or those that supply details necessary for evolving the requirement into what can be implemented in the work product.

Requirement supporter. Those individuals or groups that support the requirement process. These include facilitators, those that define the process, those that evaluate tools and techniques, and those that evaluate the quality of the requirements and the requirements set.

Requirement type. Defines the framework from which a requirement is derived. There are three types: initiating, primary, and derived. There is some disagreement as to whether the initiating requirement is actually a type of requirement.

Requirement user. Individuals who must work from the approved set of requirements to develop work products that lead to the implementation of the product.

Requirement viewpoint. The organizing and structuring of the requirements specification around the different views of the requirement. The views of the requirement correlates with the views of the different participants (users, actors, sources/recipients) of the requirement and the different perspectives (users, analysts, designers, testers, coders, builders). A viewpoint is the view of a requirement for specifics of focus, perspective, and community.

Requirements anti-pattern. A template to assist in avoiding a specific common pitfall in the development of the requirements set.

Requirements architect. The lead role in the requirements engineering effort, responsible for capturing or delegating the capturing of requirements. This person allocates the responsibility to develop the requirements that are needed in order to satisfy the originating scope-level requirements. The requirements architect decomposes each requirement to determine which community, perspective, and focus should be responsible for providing the essential details to the requirement so it can be satisfied by the product solution.

Requirements engineer. The person assigned the responsibility of allocating, eliciting, analyzing, specifying, and coordinating the validation of requirements; also has the responsibility of managing the requirements to ensure proper tracing through the project and throughout the assorted project work products.

Requirements engineering. The science and discipline concerned with eliciting the need, analyzing the need, documenting the need, and validating the need. Includes the process of approving and controlling the changes of requirements.

Requirements management. The process of controlling the identification, allocation, and flowdown of requirements from the need to the implementation.

Requirements management tool. A computer software product that assists with automating some of the requirements management activities.

Requirements meta pattern (RMP). A reusable template, based on experience, that can be used to guide the evolution of requirements toward a solution to a problem or need in a specific context.

Requirements pattern. A framework for the requirements set that supports the product/service needs, minimizing gaps in knowledge that may cause project failure. The requirements pattern helps capture all types of requirements independent of the kind of design, implementation, or method used to capture and specify the requirements.

Requirements pattern cell (RPC). A portion of the requirement set representing one community, perspective, and focus.

Requirements process. The activities that support the continual evolution of requirement details. The activities include allocation, elicitation, analysis, specification, validation, approval, and management.

Requirements set. All the requirements that need to be satisfied to implement a high-quality product or solution.

Requirements specification. A written document in a specific format that itemizes the requirements for a particular subset of the requirements set.

Responsibility. Accountability for the execution of a specific activity or delivery of a specific work product. The person may not be the one carrying out the activity or developing the work product. However, he or she is held responsible for the completion of the work in a high-quality manner.

Risk. *See* Project risk, Product risk.

Risk analysis. The activity of identifying potential areas of risk and defining the probability of their occurrence, the consequences of the occurrence, and tactics that should be in place to avoid the risk.

Role. An entity that performs a specific set of functions and has a purpose.

Scenario. A requirement elicitation technique used to identify requirements and gaps in knowledge by simulating events ("when") from the point of view of the user ("who") to identify the information ("what") and processing ("how"). A skilled requirements engineer also identifies any specific location ("where") issues and challenges policies ("why") and other potentially outdated business rules.

Scope creep. The inevitable changes that occur as requirements evolve, from the time the requirements set is agreed upon to its implementation.

Simple object access protocol (SOAP). A generic protocol for integrating services on the Internet and intranet. Based on extensible markup language (XML) and hypertext transport protocol (HTTP), it allows data exchange between Internet-based applications.

Specification. A document that specifies, in a complete, precise, verifiable manner, the characteristics of the work product to be built.

Standard. A guide (which should be mandatory) that defines disciplined, uniform approach to developing a specific work product.

Support requirement. A requirement that defins a need to be satisfied in order to satisfy other requirements, for example, the need to purchase hardware or software to build the Internet-based solution. These requirements can be satisfied without the initiating requirement. However, the initiating requirement cannot be satisfied without satisfying the support requirements.

Technique. An approach with a specific objective.

Tools. Devices that assist in achieving a specific objective.

Unified Modeling Language (UML). An object-oriented language for software developed to unify the different (and disparate) object-oriented approaches. It is currently the most common representation of following an object-oriented approach to software development.

User. External interface that initiates or receives information from the product whose needs are captured under the "who" requirements.

Validation. A process in the requirements subprocess that reviews individual requirements against quality characteristics as well as the impact on the quality of the requirements set. The reviewers include requirement suppliers, requirement users, requirement supporters, and requirements engineers responsible for other aspects of the requirements set. The output is the approval that the requirements meet the quality standards.

Waiver. A written authorization to accept a configuration item or other designated item that, during production or after having been submitted for inspection, is found to depart from specified requirements but is nevertheless considered suitable for use as is or after rework by an approved method. Before a waiver can be accepted, the impact of the altered configuration item on other configuration items must be identified and agreed upon by the other configuration item producers and the executive committee.

Wireless application protocol (WAP). A proposed standard platform-independent protocol for wireless communication between the Internet and small devices, such as Internet-enabled cellular telephones and personal digital assistants. The protocol is designed to address the small screens, low memory and power, differing platform technologies, and low bandwidth and high latencies that are characteristic of the technical limitations of small devices. The WAP Forum can be found at *www.wapforum.org*.

Wireless markup language (WML). The scalable protocol language evolved from both the XML and HTML Internet languages. The language is specifically designed for the screen-size limitations of mobile commuting devices. Works in conjunction with WMLScript.

Wireless markup language script (WMLScript). A programming language specific for wireless environments.

Wireless session protocol (WSP). Session controller that minimizes the overhead and number of transactions between the application and user.

Wireless transaction protocol (WTP). Manages requests and response transactions between an application server (for example, an e-business transaction) and the user agent (for example, a personal digital assistant).

Wireless transport layer security (WTLS). The security layer of the wireless application protocol that secures, authenticates, and encrypts data transmission between WAP and mobile devices.

Zachman framework. *See* Information Systems Architecture.

Bibliography

Books

- Androile, Stephen J. 1996. *Managing Systems Requirements: Methods, Tools, and Cases.* New York: McGraw-Hill.
- Berlack, Ronald H. 1992. *Software Configuration Management.* New York: John Wiley & Sons.
- Boehm, Barry W. 1981. *Software Engineering Economics.* Englewood Cliffs, NJ: Prentice-Hall.
- Bridges, William. 1992. *The Character of Organizations: Using Jungian Type in Organizational Development.* Palo Alto, CA: CPP Books.
- Briggs Myers, Isabel, and Peter B. Myers. 1991. *Gifts Differing.* Palo Alto, CA: Consulting Psychologists Press.
- Brooks, Frederick P. 1982. *The Mythical Man-Month.* Reading, MA: Addison-Wesley.
- Brown, William H., Raphael C. Malveau, Hays W. "Skip" McCormick III, and Thomas J. Mowbray. 1998. *Anti-Patterns: Refactoring Software, Architectures, and Projects in Crisis.* New York: John Wiley & Sons.
- Christensen, Clayton M. 2000. *The Innovator's Dilemma.* New York: Harperbusiness.
- Cockburn, Alistair. 2000. *Writing Effective Use Cases.* The Crystal Collection for Software Professionals. Upper Saddle River, NJ: Addison-Wesley.

- Coplien, James O., and Douglas C. Schmidt. 1995. *Pattern Languages of Program Design.* Reading, MA: Addison-Wesley.
- Deming, W. Edwards. 1997 (1982). *Out of the Crisis.* Cambridge, MA: Massachusetts Institute of Technology.
- Dyché, Jill. 2000. *e-Data: Turning Data into Information with Data Warehousing.* Boston, MA: Addison-Wesley.
- Dymond, Kenneth M. 1988. *A Guide to the CMM^{SM}: Understanding the Capability Maturity Model^{SM} for Software.* Annapolis, MD: Process Inc. USA.
- Ferdinandi, Patricia. 1998. *Interpreting Technology for Business: Data Warehousing, Advice for Managers.* New York: Amacom.
- Fowler, Martin, and Kendall Scott. 1999. *UML Distilled,* 2nd Edition. Reading, MA: Addison-Wesley.
- Hatley, Derek, Peter Hruschka, and Imtiaz Pirbhai. 2000. *Process for System Architecture and Requirements Engineering.* New York: Dorset House.
- Herbsleb, James, Anita Carleton, James Rozum, Jane Siegel, and David Zubrow. 1994. *Benefits of CMM-Based Software Process Improvement: Initial Results.* Pittsburgh, PA: Software Engineering Institute.
- Hirsh, Sandra, and Jean Kummerow. 1989. *Life Types.* New York: Warner Books.
- Humphrey, Watts S. 1989. *Managing the Software Process.* Boston, MA: Addison-Wesley.
- Isachsen, Olaf, and Linda V. Berens. 1991. *Working Together: A Personality-Centered Approach to Management.* Coronado, CA: New World Management Press.
- Jones, T. Capers. 1998. *Estimating Software Costs.* New York: McGraw-Hill.
- Keirsey, David, and Marilyn Bates. 1984. *Please Understand Me.* Del Mar, CA: Prometheus Nemesis Book Company.
- Kroeger, Otto, and Janet M. Thuesen. 1992. *Type Talk At Work.* New York: Delacorte Press.
- Kulak, Daryl, and Eamonn Guiney. 2000. *Use Cases: Requirements in Context.* Boston, MA: Addison-Wesley.
- Linthicum, David S. 2000. *Enterprise Application Integration.* Boston, MA: Addison-Wesley.
- Lyon, David Douglas. 1996. *Practical Configuration Management: Best Configuration Management Practices for the 21st Century.* Pittsfield, MA: Raven Publishing.
- Marshall, Chris. 1999. *Enterprise Modeling with UML: Designing Successful Software through Business Analysis.* Reading, MA: Addison-Wesley.

- Moore, James W. 1998. *Software Engineering Standards: A User's Road Map.* Piscataway, NJ: IEEE.
- Moschella, David C. 1997. *Waves of Power.* New York: Amacom.
- O'Conner, Patricia T. 1996. *Woe Is I.* New York: G. P. Putnam.
- Paulk, Mark C., Charles V. Weber, Bill Curtis, and Mary Beth Chrissis. 1995. *The Capability Maturity Model: Guidelines for Improving the Software Process.* Reading, MA: Addison-Wesley.
- Project Management Institute. 2000. *Project Management Body of Knowledge Guide.* Newtown Square, PA: Project Management Institute.
- Rothstein, Michael. 1998. *Ace the Technical Interview,* 3rd edition. New York: McGraw-Hill.
- Schneider, Geri, and Jason P. Winters. 1998. *Applying Use Cases: A Practical Guide.* Reading, MA: Addison-Wesley.
- Sommerville, Ian, and Pete Sawyer. 1997. *Requirements Engineering: A Good Practice Guide.* New York: John Wiley & Sons.
- Thomas, Thomas M., II. 1998. *OSPF Network Design Solutions.* Indianapolis, IN: Macmillan Technical Publishing.
- Tieger, Paul D., and Barbara Barron-Tieger. 1992. *Do What You Are: Discover the Perfect Career for You Through the Secrets of Personality Type.* New York: Little, Brown & Company.
- White, Brian Al. 2000. *Software Configuration Management Strategies and Rational ClearCase: A Practical Introduction.* Boston, MA: Addison-Wesley.
- Wiegers, Karl. 1996. *Creating a Software Engineering Culture.* New York: Dorset House.
- Wiley, Bill. 1999. *Essential System Requirements: A Practical Guide to Event-Driven Methods.* Boston, MA: Addison-Wesley.
- Wilkinson, Nancy M. 1995. *Using CRC Cards: An Informal Approach to Object-Oriented Development.* New York: SIGS Books.
- Zachman, John A. 1987. "A Framework for Information Systems Architecture." *IBM Systems Journal,* 26 (3). IBM Publication G321-5298.

Articles

- Andriole, Steve. 1998. "The Politics of Requirements Management." *IEEE Software,* November/December, pp. 82–84.
- Aoyama, Mikio. 1998. "Web-Based Agile Software Development." *IEEE Software,* November/December. pp. 56–65.

- Bassin, Kathryn, Theresa Kratschmer, and P. Santhanam. 1998. "Evaluating Software Development Objectively." *IEEE Software,* November/December, pp. 66–74.
- Berry, Daniel M., and Brian Lawrence. 1998. "Requirements Engineering." *IEEE Software,* March/April, pp. 26–29.
- Burk, Dan L. 2001. "Copyrightable Functions and Patentable Speech." *Communications of the ACM,* 44 (2):69–75.
- Christensen, Clayton M., and Richard S. Tedlow. 2000. "Patterns of Disruption in Retailing." *Harvard Business Review,* January–February, pp. 42–45.
- Croll, Alistair, and Ben Rothke. 2000. "Fast . . . & Secure." *Information Security Magazine,* January, pp. 1–28.
- Cunningham, Ward, and Kent Beck. 1986. "A Diagram for Object-Oriented Programs." *SIGPLAN Notices,* 21 (11):361–367.
- Curtis, Bill. 1998. "Which Comes First, the Organization or Its Processes?" *IEEE Software,* November/December, pp. 10–13.
- Davis, Alan M. 1998a. "The Harmony in Rechoirments." *IEEE Software.* March/April, pp. 6–8.
- Davis, Alan M. 1998. "A Golden Thread in Software's Tapestry." *IEEE Software,* November/December, pp. 18–21.
- Davis, Randall. 2001. "The Digital Dilemma." *Communications of the ACM,* 44 (2):77–83.
- Ferdinandi, Patricia. 1994. "Reengineering with the Right Types." *Software Development,* July, pp. 45–51.
- Ferdinandi, Patricia. 1998. "Facilitating Communication." *IEEE Software,* September/October, pp. 87–92.
- Ferdinandi, Patricia. 2000. "Are Your Requirements Complete?" *Software Testing and Quality Engineering,* September/October, pp. 18–21.
- Goodman, David J. 2000. "The Wireless Internet: Promises and Challenges." *Computer,* July, pp. 36–41.
- Gottesdiener, Ellen. 2000. "Business Rules Rule." *QSS Newsbytes,* 7, August.
- Highsmith, Jim. 2001. "e-Business and e-Commerce as Drivers of Integration Solutions." *Cutter Consortium,* 1 (2):2–6.
- Hildebrand, Carol. 1995. "I'm OK, You're Really Weird." *CIO Magazine,* October, pp. 86–96.
- Hulme, George V. 2000a. "It's Time to Clamp Down." *Information Week,* July 10, pp. 42–56.

- Hulme, George V. 2000b. "A Security Pitfall: The Dial-Up Modem." *Information Week*, July 10, p. 52.
- Kaban, Elif. 2001. "Survey: Wired Rich Turn the Tables on Private Banks." Accessed on February 19, 2001, at *http://www.yahoo.com.*
- Kitchenham, Barbara, and Shari Lawrence Pfleeger. 1996. "Software Quality: The Elusive Target." *IEEE Software*, 13 (1):12–21.
- Lawton, George. 2000. "Distributed Net Applications Create Virtual Supercomputers." *Computer*, June, pp. 16–20.
- Lear, Anne C. 2000. "New Protocol Simplifies B2B Communication." *Computer*, July, p. 24.
- Leavitt, Neal. 2000. "Will WAP Deliver the Wireless Internet?" *Computer*, May, pp. 16–20.
- McConnell, Steve. 1998. "Weighing In on Standards." *IEEE Software*, November/December, pp. 92–102.
- Page-Jones, Meilir. 1998. "The Seven Stages of Expertise in Software Engineering." Accessed in August 2001 at *http://www.waysys.com/ws_content_al_sse.html.*
- Samuelson, Pamela. 2001. "Intellectual Property for an Information Age." *Communications of the ACM*, 44 (2):67–68.
- Slywotzky, Adrian J. 2000. "The Age of the Choiceboard." *Harvard Business Review*, January/February, pp. 40–41.
- Stokes, David Alan. 1991. "Requirements Analysis." *Computer Weekly Software Engineer's Reference Book*, pp. 16/3–16/21.
- Sullivan, Andy. 2001. "More Than Half of Adults in U.S. Online." Accessed on February 18, 2001, at *http://www.yahoo.com.*
- Weidenhaupt, Klaus, Klaus Pohl, Matthias Jarke, and Peter Haumer. 1998. "Scenarios in System Development: Current Practice." *IEEE Software*, March/April, pp. 34–45.
- Wiegers, Karl. 2000. "Ten Requirements Traps to Avoid." *Software Testing and Quality Engineering*, January/February, pp. 34–40.
- Wilder, Clinton. 2000. "The Complete Package." *Information Week*, October 16, pp. RB4–RB14.
- Wilson, William M., Linda H. Rosenberg, and Lawrence E. Hyatt. 1996. "Automated Quality Analysis of Natural Language Requirement Specifications." Accessed in August 2001 at *http://satc.gsfc.nasa.gov/support/PNSQC_OCT96/pnq.html.*

- Yamaura, Tsuneo. 1998. "How to Design Practical Test Cases." *IEEE Software*, November/December, pp. 30–36.
- Zachman, John, A. 1987. "A Framework for Information Systems Architecture." IBM Systems Journal, 26 (3):276–292.
- Zvegintzov, Nicholas. 1998. "Frequently Begged Questions and How to Answer Them." *IEEE Software*. March/April, pp. 93–96.

Forums

- Portland Pattern Repository, *http://c2.com/ppr/*.
- Software Requirement Engineering, sre@jrcase.mq.edu.au.
- Software Testing and Quality Engineering, *http://www.stickyminds.com*.
- Wireless Application Protocol, *http://www.wapforum.org*.

Miscellaneous

- Balicki, Richard. 2000. "Synergizing Zachman's Architecture Framework with Kilov's Information Modeling." Presentation at OOPSLA 2000, October 15–19, Minneapolis, MN.
- 2nd International Conference on Requirements Engineering. April 15–18, 1996, Piscataway, NJ: IEEE. *http://www.computer.org/proceedings/proceed_i.htm i*.
- 3rd International Conference on Requirements Engineering. April 6–10, 1998, Piscataway, NJ: IEEE. *http://www.computer.org/proceedings/proceed_i.htm i*.
- 4th International Conference on Requirements Engineering. June 19–23, 2000, Piscataway, NJ: IEEE. *http://www.computer.org/proceedings/proceed_i.htm i*.
- "Ninth OOPSLA Workshop on Behavioral Semantics." Conference proceeding at ACM Conference on OOPSLA, October 2000, Minneapolis, MN. *http://oopsla.acm.org/oopsla2k/fp/workshops/03.html*.
- Stevens, Richard. 2000. "Requirements Through the e-Business Lifecycle." QSS Webinar. Accessed on February 2000 at *http://www.telelogic.com/webinars* and *http://www.telelogic.com/webinars/overview/what_are_reqs.cfm*.
- Stevens, Richard, Ian Alexander, and Gary Layton. 2000. "Get It Right the First Time: Writing Better Requirements." Telelogic (Quality Systems and Software) handout. *http://www.telelogic.com/webinars* and *http://www.telelogic.com/webinars/overview/what_are_reqs.cfm*.

Additional Resources

The purpose of this book is to introduce readers to the types of requirements that need to be captured in order to develop Internet solutions. No discussion is included on how to develop the Internet application itself. Nor does this book address what to do with the information once it is captured. For this reason, additional sources have been provided in the form of books, periodicals, Web sites, and forums to help you expand your knowledge and use the requirements pattern in the next phase, building the product.

Books

The list below represents a sampling of books that are valuable to the requirements engineer for developing Internet products. This should not be considered a comprehensive list since there are many other useful publications available.

Requirements Engineering

- Gause, Donald, and Gerald Weinberg. 1989. *Exploring Requirements.* New York: Dorset House.
- Gause, Donald, and Gerald Weinberg. 1990. *Are Your Lights On?* New York: Dorset House.

- Leffingwell, Dean, Don Widrig, and Edward Yourdon. 1999. *Managing Software Requirements: A Unified Approach.* New York: Addison-Wesley.
- Robertson, Suzanne, and James Robertson. 1999. *Mastering the Requirements Process.* Boston, MA: Addison-Wesley.
- Thayer, Richard H., and Merlin Dorfman. 1997. *Software Requirements Engineering,* 2nd edition. Los Alamitos, CA: IEEE Computer Society Press.
- Wiegers, Karl. 1999. *Software Requirements.* Redmond, WA: Microsoft Press.
- Young, Ralph. 2001. *Effective Requirements Practices.* Boston, MA: Addison-Wesley.

Software Engineering Books

- Brown, William H., Raphael C. Malveau, Hays W. "Skip" McCormick III, and Thomas J. Mowbray. 1998. *Anti-Patterns: Refactoring Software, Architectures, and Projects in Crisis.* New York: John Wiley & Sons.
- Bruce, Thomas A. 1992. *Designing Quality Databases with IDEF1X Information Models.* New York: Dorset House Publishing.[1]
- Hay, David C. 1995. *Data Model Patterns: Conventions of Thought.* New York: Dorset House.
- Humphrey, Watts S. 1989. *Managing the Software Process.* Boston, MA: Addison-Wesley.
- Humphrey, Watts S. 1995. *A Disciple for Software Engineering (Discipline)... IEEE Standards Collection on Software Engineering.* Boston, MA: Addison-Wesley.
- McConnell, Steve. 1997. *The Software Project Survival Guide.* Redmond, WA: Microsoft Press.
- Ross, Ronald G. 1998. *Business Rule Concepts: The New Mechanics of Business Information Systems.* Gladys S.W. Lam.
- Stevens, Richard, Peter Brook, Ken Jackson, and Stuart Arnold. 1998. *Systems Engineering: Coping with Complexity.* New York: Prentice Hall.

---

1. Remember, these books (and this book in particular) were selected as good sources for information on capturing a specific type of requirement. IDEF1X is a notation for data diagrams that is used by the government and is becoming a standard in the business industry as well. Do not let the name of this specific book intimidate you.

Internet-Related Books

- Dyché, Jill. 2000. *e-Data: Turning Data into Information with Data Warehousing.* Boston, MA: Addison-Wesley.
- Kalakota, Ravi, and Marcia Robinson. 1999. *e-Business: Roadmap for Success.* Reading, MA: Addison-Wesley.
- Moschella, David C. 1997. *Waves of Power.* New York: Amacom.
- Norris, Mark, Steve West, and Kevin Gaughan. 2000. *eBusiness Essentials: Technology and Network Requirements for the Electronic Marketplace.* West Sussex, England: John Wiley & Son.
- Rosen, Anita. 1997. *Looking into Intranets and the Internet: Advice for Managers.* New York: Amacom.
- Zoellick, Bill. 2000. *Web Engagement: Connecting to Customers in e-Business.* Boston, MA: Addison-Wesley.

Periodicals

The magazines and newspapers listed below cover requirements engineering, software engineering, and the Internet. Yearly subscriptions are available.

- *CIO Magazine*
- *Harvard Business Review*
- *IEEE Software*
- *Information Security*
- *Mobile Computing*
- *The Requirement Engineering Journal*
- *Software Development*
- *Software Testing and Quality Engineering*
- *The Wall Street Journal*

Web Sites

The World Wide Web has become a virtual library of information on anything and everything. Below is a sampling of sites that should be bookmarked for repeated use. After all, Internet-based products require continual updates (iterations) and need to be researched time and again.

Some industry analysts are included on this list. These sites provide general access to older articles. However, for more current information, your information technology organization must pay for access rights. If your organization is a member, you can "ask the experts" or read Frequently Asked Questions sections. A few of these sites offer configuration management tools.

- Bot Knowledge: *www.botknowledge.com*
- Caliber by Starbase: *www.tbi.com*
- Construx: *www.construx.com*
- DOORs by Telelogic: *www.telelogic.com*
- Gartner Group: *www.gartner.com*
- GIGA Group: *www.giga.com*
- IBM: *www.ibm.com*
- IEEE Computer Society: *www.computer.org.*
- Meta Group: *www.metagroup.com*
- NASA Software Assurance Technology Center: *http://satc.gsfc.nasa.gov*
- Norton Utilities: *www.norton.com*
- Object-Oriented Programming Systems, Languages and Applications (OOPSLA): *www.oopsla.org*
- Patterns: *http://hillside.net/patterns/patterns.html*
- Project Management Institute: *www.pmi.org*
- Quality Assurance Institute: *www.qaiusa.com.*
- Quality Systems and Software: *www.qssinc.com.*
- Requisite Pro by Rational Software: *www.rational.com*
- Results Planning (Tom Gilb): *www.resultsplanning.com*
- SANS Network Security: *www.sans.org*
- Software Engineering Institute: *www.sei.cmu.edu*
- Software Productivity Research: *www.spr.com*
- Software Quality Institute: *www.utexas.edu*
- Software Testing and Quality Engineering: *www.stqe.com* (now *www.stickminds.com*)
- Standish Group: *www.standishgroup.com*
- Zachman Information Architecture Framework: *www.zifa.com*

Forums

Forums provide an excellent environment for discussing ideas and solving specific issues. Each of the following forums discusses requirements: processes, management, and types:

- Software Requirement Engineering: sre@jrcase.mq.edu.au
- Software Testing and Quality Engineering: *www.stickyminds.com*
- Wireless Application Protocol: *www.wapforum.org*

Training Organizations

Since this is a book on requirements, it is important to add a section on other training and consulting organizations that offer requirement-related training. With regard to training options, do not limit yourself to specialized training organizations. Many universities have departments dedicated to requirements engineering and Internet topics.

- AmiBug.Com (514-685-2284; *www.amibug.com*). Offers a series of workshops and consulting services that help companies implement light effective processes.
- EGB Consulting (317-844-3747; ellen@ebgconsulting.com). Provides courses on modeling techniques for the "who," "what," "when," "why," and "how" focus areas.
- Financial System Architects (646-215-5094; wff@fsarch.com[2]). Provides consultation and training programs using best requirements engineering practices. The employees are prominent participants in Object Management Group and OOPSLA.
- Process Impact (503-698-9620; kwiegers@acm.org). Karl Wieger's company; he offers different courses and consultation and has authored three excellent books.

---

2. William Frank is the chief scientist who has been very supportive of the development of the requirements meta pattern.

- Strategic Business Decisions, Inc. (973-509-9427; info@SBDi-consulting.com). Courses for the business community on the software development process and requirements documentation. Provides consultants to assist the business community in preparing and developing Internet solutions.
- Tryon & Associates (918-455-3300; catryon@aol.com). Courses for the entire Internet program team on the requirements development process and the management of single-time effort programs.
- Weinberg & Weinberg (*www.geraldmweinberg.com*). Offers an excellent series of courses and consulting services on problem solving and the human aspects of implementing technological solutions.

IEEE Standards

For configuration management, it is always recommended to start with the IEEE standards. Some basic standards include:

- IEEE Std 828: IEEE standard for software configuration management plans
- IEEE Std 830: IEEE recommended practice for software requirements specification (SRS)
- IEEE Std 1016: IEEE recommended practice for software design descriptions
- IEEE Std 1042: IEEE guide to planning software configuration management
- IEEE Std 1233: IEEE guide for developing systems requirements specification (SyRS)

More information can be found in the following book.

- Institute of Electrical and Electronics Engineers. *IEEE Software Engineering Standards Collection*. Piscataway, NJ: IEEE.

Index

A

A2A (application-to-application), 27

acceptance criteria, defined, 457

ad hoc development method
  defined, 457
  early days of Internet using, 226

adaptability requirements, 97-98

aka (also known as), Internet anti-patterns, 193

Alexander, Christopher, 159-160

allocated requirements
  business units and, 14
  defined, 457
  defining scope of responsibility for, 55

allocation
  business units and, 13-14
  defined, 457
  perspective and, 58-60
  preparing ideas for, 121-124
  of requirements, 50-52
  requirements subprocess and, 60-64
  tolerance value and, 181
  validation and, 68

allocation levels
  defined, 458
  overview of, 50-52
  perspective and, 59
  using requirements management tools, 56

also known as (aka), Internet anti-patterns, 193

Amazon.com
  clickstream data of, 181-182
  customer-centric focus of, 21
  joining ToysRUs with, 9
  profits and, 177

ambiguity, defined, 458

analog modems, hacker attacks and, 164

analysis. *See also* feasibility
  builder perspective, 415-416
  defined, 458
  designer perspective, 413
  owner perspective, 410-411
  paralysis, 210
  planner perspective, 408
  of requirements, 64-65
  as requirements subprocess role, 63
  subcontractor perspective, 418, 420
  tools for, 232-233

analysis, gap
  overview of, 153-154
  pattern, 214
  quality-checking and, 170-171, 212-213

anthropologists, roles/ responsibilities of, 284-285

anti-patterns. *See also* Internet requirements anti-patterns; requirements anti-pattern
  defined, 32, 458
  overview of, 159-161

anti-patterns, creating, 190-197
  information to be included, 192-196
  overview of, 190-192
  review and use of, 196-197

application-to-application (A2A), 27

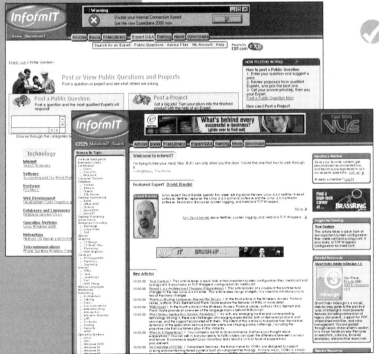